Sinn Féin

'I give you the good old watchword of old Ireland –
Shin Fain – ourselves alone.'
Tim Healy MP, 1892

'You are right – Sinn Féin must be the motto.'
William Rooney in letter to Arthur Griffith, 1899

'To me Sinn Féin is the nation organised.
I never regarded it as a mere political machine.'
Eamon de Valera, 1922

'It would appear that all the required steps were taken to
preserve the continuity of the organisation and that present-day Sinn Féin
is legally the same organisation as that which was born in 1923.'
Justice Kingsmill Moore, 1948

'Who here really believes we can win a war through the ballot box?
But will anyone here object if, with a ballot paper in one hand
and an Armalite in the other, we take power in Ireland?'
Danny Morrison, Sinn Féin *ard fheis*, 1981

'By ignoring reality we remain alone and isolated on the high altar
of abstentionism, divorced from the people of the twenty-six counties
and easily dealt with by those who wish to defeat us.'
Martin McGuinness, 1986

'I would hope that in ten to fifteen years time we would have a sizeable
number of TDs, in double figures. I don't think that's a pipe dream.'
Jim Gibney, 2002

'Hello. Sinn Féin, Westminster.'
Gerry Adams answering his London office phone, 2002

History of Ireland and The Irish Diaspora
James S. Donnelly, Jr.
Thomas Archdeacon
Series Editors

Sinn Féin: A Hundred Turbulent Years
Brian Feeney

The New Irish-American History
Edited by Kevin Kenny

Sinn Féin

A Hundred Turbulent Years

Brian Feeney

THE UNIVERSITY OF WISCONSIN PRESS

The University of Wisconsin Press
1930 Monroe Street
Madison, Wisconsin 53711

www.wisc.edu/wisconsinpress

1 3 5 4 2

A CIP record is available for this title
from the Library of Congress

ISBN 0-299-18670-9 (cloth)
ISBN 0-299-18674-1 (paper)

First published by The O'Brien Press Ltd., Dublin, Ireland

PICTURE CREDITS

The author and publisher thank the following for permission to reproduce visual materials:
courtesy the National Library of Ireland, Picture Section 1, p.1 (ref. KE44), p.2, p.7
(latter from NLI Prints and Drawings); courtesy of Kilmainham Jail and Museum, Picture Section 1,
p.4 (top and bottom), p.5; courtesy of the National Museum of Ireland, Picture Section 1, p.8 (top);
courtesy of Pacemaker Press, Picture Section 2, p.1 (top), p.2 (bottom), p.3, p.4, p.6 and Picture
Section 3, p.1, p.6 (top and bottom), p.7 (top) and front cover (top); images courtesy of *Irish News*,
Picture Section 2, p.1 (bottom), p.2 (top), p.7, p.8 and Picture Section 3, p.1 (bottom), p.2, p.3
(top and bottom), p.4 (top and bottom), p.5 (top and bottom), p.7 (bottom), p.8 (top) and front
cover (bottom) and author photo (back flap); courtesy of *The Irish Times*, Picture Section 2, p.5
(bottom); courtesy of the Press Association, London, Picture Section 3, p.8 (bottom);
courtesy of the author, Picture Section 3, p.3 (two bottom pics).
While every effort has been made to contact the holders of copyrights,
if any omission or oversight has occurred we would request the copyright
holder(s) to inform the publisher.

CONTENTS

DEDICATION

For Patricia, Alistair and Christopher

ACKNOWLEDGEMENTS

I would like to thank everyone who helped me while I was working on this book. Special thanks goes to present and past members of Sinn Féin, Republican Sinn Féin and the Workers' Party who gave lengthy interviews and painstakingly explained the intricacies of republican thinking to me. I hope I have reflected their views accurately though they may disagree with my interpretations.

Kathleen Bell, the super-efficient *Irish News* librarian, has an unrivalled ability to find information, written or photographic, on any topic she is asked about. I am grateful she placed those talents at my disposal. The staff of *An Phoblacht/Republican News* were unfailingly helpful in giving me access to photographs and other Sinn Féin material.

I am specially grateful to Des Fisher who read the book chapter by chapter as it was written, edited the text with an eagle eye and made many helpful, important suggestions. My wife Patricia was ever ready with helpful advice and made it possible for me to have the time and space to write. Whatever mistakes remain are mine alone.

Finally, I must thank Íde ní Laoghaire of The O'Brien Press for keeping my nose firmly pressed to the grindstone, and Michael O'Brien who first suggested to me that I might be able to try to write a book about Sinn Féin.

INTRODUCTION

The most remarkable phenomenon in electoral politics in both parts of Ireland in the final years of the twentieth century was the apparently irresistible growth of the Sinn Féin party, the political wing of the country's republican movement. Now, at the beginning of the twenty-first century, Sinn Féin looks poised to play a pivotal role in the Irish political arena, North and South, well into the future.

The party's electoral strength in the Republic has been transformed since 2001 when it held only one of the 164 seats in the Irish parliament, Dáil Éireann, and sixty-three seats in local councils. The confident predictions of politicians of all parties, opinion pollsters and political commentators that Sinn Féin was set to make substantial electoral gains throughout the Republic proved correct when the party won five seats in the Dáil and narrowly missed two others in the general election of May 2002. Many observers believe Sinn Féin could soon be in a position where it will hold the balance of power and win a place in future coalition governments.

The omens for the party's future are even more convincing in the North of Ireland where the party's success has been spectacular. By the end of 2001, it held eighteen of the 108 seats in the Legislative Assembly, four of Northern Ireland's eighteen Westminster seats and 117 council seats across the North. In Belfast, Sinn Féin was the largest party on the city council and in June 2002 the leader of its councillors became the city's first Sinn Féin mayor. If Sinn Féin's electoral support in the North continues to grow at anything near the rate of the 1990s, then the party could emerge after the next elections as the second largest in the Stormont Assembly and be in line for the position of Deputy First Minister. Sinn Féin's strategists look forward to taking two more Westminster seats in the North in the next British general election due before 2006.

None of this progress happened overnight. Sinn Féin's present phase of political development began during the 1981 H-block hunger strikes in the Maze prison outside Belfast. The sufferings of the republican prisoners and the rigid refusal of the Thatcher government in Westminster to ameliorate their conditions caused widespread revulsion throughout Ireland. In elections North and South, three of the prisoners were elected to national parliaments: Bobby Sands, the first hunger-striker, to Westminster, and two others, Kieran Doherty and Paddy Agnew, to the Dáil. When ten of the prisoners, including the newly elected Sands and Doherty, subsequently died on hunger strike, the shocked reaction throughout all sections of the Irish public convinced leaders of the republican movement that there was scope for further electoral gains.

Immediately after the successes of the hunger-strike elections, Sinn Féin had candidates contesting every subsequent election in the North where the party had previously been strictly abstentionist at all levels. Plans were also made to expand in the South where Sinn Féin had already been contesting local elections and had thirty council seats in 1981. Both North and South the party's electoral successes have been built on 'community politics' and high-profile activism at grassroots level, mainly in impoverished inner-city areas, notably in Dublin and Belfast. Offering a radical political agenda based on energetic and aggressive representational politics, Sinn Féin forged a crucial connection with the electorate that republicans had lacked since the emergence of Fianna Fáil in 1926.

It was this sudden enthusiasm for electoral politics that led inevitably to a split in the movement in 1986 on the issue of taking seats in Dáil Éireann. The split was a defining moment in the history of modern republicanism for two reasons. First, the majority of the movement, following the leadership of Gerry Adams and Martin McGuinness, abandoned what had been one of the fundamental tenets of republicanism since 1922 and agreed to recognise the Dáil, previously dismissed as a 'partition parliament'. Secondly, for the first time in the history of the republican movement, northerners took control of both the military and the political wings of the movement – the IRA and Sinn Féin – thus enabling them to pursue what was famously known as the 'Armalite and ballot box' strategy, in other words, the simultaneous use of armed struggle and electoral politics. Despite being commonly described as a 'split', the events of 1986 were really a splinter as only a tiny group, led by doctrinaires from a previous generation, broke away.

Once Adams and his supporters gained control, they immediately began to place greater emphasis on politics. In 1987, the year after the split, a groundbreaking new policy document appeared, entitled *A Scenario for Peace*. This paper acknowledged, although in carefully guarded language, that there was no real hope for a military victory in the war against Britain and that any hopes of future progress lay in finding agreement with the unionist majority in the North. In 1988 Sinn Féin ventured further into uncharted waters by entering detailed talks on the North's future with the region's main nationalist party, the Social Democratic and Labour Party (SDLP), which lasted nine months.

Although the talks between the two parties had officially concluded in 1988, the two party leaders, John Hume and Gerry Adams, continued to meet in secret. Ultimately these talks led to the public Hume–Adams dialogue of 1993. At the same time, two parallel and secret sets of talks had been taking place between, on the one hand, Irish government officials and Sinn Féin, and, on the other, between British government representatives and the IRA. Out of all these exchanges emerged what became known as the 'peace process'.

Gradually during the 1990s, Sinn Féin successfully distanced itself from the IRA in the eyes of most nationalist voters. Violence was wound down and a ceasefire declared, with the republican movement remaining largely intact under political leaders. The result has been electoral success unprecedented since 1921, which has made Sinn Féin's political leadership of the whole movement impregnable. After the Republic's 1997 general election, Caoimhghín Ó Caoláin became the first Sinn Féin TD since 1922 to take his seat in Dáil Éireann. In the June 1999 local government elections in the Republic, Sinn Féin doubled its vote and increased its number of seats. In the Northern Ireland local and general elections of June 2001, Sinn Féin achieved one of its most cherished long-term goals when it became the largest nationalist party in the North by overtaking the SDLP – for thirty years the main choice of nationalist voters. By early 2002, many observers considered that Sinn Féin had created the most effective political machine on the island of Ireland.

It is more than eighty years since the party occupied such a prominent place in Irish politics and then only for a couple of years. The twenty years of development since the watershed of the H-block hunger strikes constituted the party's most sustained period of success since its foundation at the beginning of the twentieth century as a political pressure group. It was then, and has always been, a mixture of intellectuals, political activists and revolutionaries, though the categories were not, and never have been, mutually exclusive. Throughout its history Sinn Féin has been composed of this type of amalgam, which, of its nature, is prone to fissure. At different times in the last century one or other of the components in that amalgam has come into the ascendant and a split has ensued. Major splits have occurred on four occasions: 1921, 1926, 1969 and 1986, in two cases resulting in internecine violence. Along the way there have been several other minor divisions and defections. All the major splits have taken the same form. A majority in Sinn Féin, sometimes by a perilously close margin, has decided to enter the political arena, slowly, tentatively perhaps, but they have chosen politics as the preferred path to their goal. A minority, sometimes very powerful, sometimes controlling the military capability of the movement, has dissented and often literally stuck to its guns.

The fact that the republican movement has always been simultaneously pulled in two conflicting directions has placed major constraints on Sinn Féin since its inception. Sinn Féin has never been merely a political party. In the beginning Sinn Féin was not actually a political party at all and did not run candidates for office. It has always been only one part of a double-sided movement for Irish self-determination, in which the political and military strands jockeyed for control, and has never been a truly autonomous political party in its own right. Except for the 1930s, the military component of the republican movement has always shared in the leadership of Sinn Féin and vice versa, and for most of its history Sinn Féin has received some funding from the movement's military wing.

As an organisation Sinn Féin sought from the outset to present itself as a national movement, the political expression of Irishness. The party's 1918 election manifesto said: 'Sinn Féin stands less for a political party than for the nation.' The party's first leader, Arthur Griffith, intended Sinn Féin to occupy a total, overarching national position that no mere political party could aspire to, but which members of other parties could support. Since Sinn Féin regarded itself as the embodiment of true Irishness, naturally there could be no compromise with other groups and certainly not with Britain, which had no role to play in Irishness.

Such a movement, with its all-or-nothing stance on Irish self-determination and separateness, has always attracted militarists who, from the beginning, have limited the autonomy of Sinn Féin and constrained its political ambitions. The militarists were attracted to the movement precisely because it was not a political party. A political party by its very nature will make compromises, even on fundamental beliefs. The militarists were prepared to fight and die for their fundamental beliefs.

Sinn Féin, the public face of the republican movement, has therefore always been only one component of a fissiparous movement. In their attempts to keep all the components together, successive leaders have always emphasised the one aspect that was the common attraction for its differing categories of adherents, namely the certainty and constancy of ideology, the unending quest for Irish national sovereignty as defined by republicans.

The downside of such a mindset has meant that the republican movement has traditionally been characterised by dogmatism and rigidity, not only an unwillingness to change but an apparent inability to change. Any prospect of change, always equated by some with a departure from the ideal, has raised the spectre of a split, and a split has almost always resulted in militarists leaving the movement and levelling accusations of betrayal and perfidy at the 'politicians' who remain. Over the century of its existence, the requirement to adhere to historical dogma to appease ideologues and militarists who were prepared to use force against fellow republicans has, until now, prevented Sinn Féin from being able to reach its true political potential.

Paradoxically, despite republican claims to have remained constant and unchanging, in the century since its foundation Sinn Féin has morphed into completely different forms, some unrecognisable from their predecessors. This book sets out to describe the ebb and flow of Sinn Féin's political fortunes since its origins and the various reincarnations the party has gone through. Originating, incredible as it may seem to many supporters today, as a group that advocated the view that Ireland owed allegiance to a British sovereign as one unit of a dual monarchy, Sinn Féin re-emerged after 1916 as the epitome of republicanism, then split on the question of swearing allegiance to the king of England, as required by the 1921 Anglo-Irish Treaty.

In 1926 Eamon de Valera, the former president of Sinn Féin, led the remnants of Sinn Féin and the republican movement into Fianna Fáil, the new party he had founded, a party prepared to enter Dáil Éireann with the commitment to undo the parts of the 1921 Treaty unacceptable to republicans. A small rump of irreconcilables was left behind in Sinn Féin, apparently doomed to extinction as age and infirmity inevitably took their toll. The book will show how, in an image republicans are fond of citing, Sinn Féin, though ostensibly defunct, rose like a phoenix after the Second World War, supported a candidate who got 200,000 votes in the 1945 presidential election, polled 152,000 votes in the North and 65,000 in the South in the 1950s, had two MPs and four TDs, only to disappear from the political scene again soon afterwards. Led by devout, right-wing Catholics in the 1950s, the party swung over in the 1960s to a Marxist-leaning leadership, which was overthrown in the aftermath of the turmoil that erupted in the North in 1969. Those who overthrew them in 1970, calling themselves Provisional Sinn Féin, began the long, painful journey to the party's present prominence.

Sinn Féin and the republican movement have always been able to rely on emotional and sentimental support for their aims from a section of the Irish population. At times of political and economic stress in the country that sentiment has been translated into a protest vote that has often provided republicans with substantial electoral support. Sinn Féin in its different manifestations has been the repository of the votes of the have-nots, whether in the 1930s, the 1950s or the 1990s. In the past, however, the leaders of the republican movement have been wary of electoral success. Usually they claimed, falsely, that the votes were in support of a military campaign for Irish unity because they feared either that the movement would be distracted from its main aim – national self-determination – or worse, would be lured into representational politics, North or South, to the detriment of the military struggle. For the same reason Sinn Féin's social and economic policies were always kept well in the background.

It will be argued here that the present leadership of Sinn Féin is successful because, for the first time since the early 1920s, politicians are in control of the republican movement as a whole – some of whom, like their predecessors in the 1920s, have in the past not been loath to use violence and have gained authority in the movement because of that. Their background and reputations within the military arm of the movement have insulated them from the traditional charge of 'selling out' preferred against anyone advocating electoral politics.

Since the mid-1970s, the party's present leader, Gerry Adams, and his supporters in the movement have argued for political involvement in grassroots issues to maximise the support they knew they enjoyed among the have-nots in nationalist ghettos of the North of Ireland. By gaining support for this view from Derryman Martin McGuinness, one of the most steely militarists in the movement, Adams united the movement for the first time in its modern history behind a political agenda relevant to the here and now, rather than harking back to meaningless shibboleths of 1921.

When the split came in 1986 on the question of recognising the Dáil, it differed from all previous splits in that the new political leadership, which advocated electoral politics in both parts of the island, retained control of the IRA. This command of the military wing by men with IRA backgrounds but committed to political development was the only way the 'Armalite and ballot box' strategy could work. The IRA trusted the Sinn Féin leaders and respected their judgement. But the twin-track strategy was primarily a means to keep the IRA on board while seeking a route into the political mainstream. The movement's leader, Gerry Adams, went to extraordinary lengths to avoid a split in which a significant military group would defect. He believed such a split would mean the emasculation of the republican movement, which would deprive it of all the influence as a political entity and thereby destroy all that he had built up since the 1970s.

Ultimately, the Sinn Féin leadership would have to come to the point where it would be necessary to persuade the militarists to lay down their weapons but, until they judged that the time was right, the IRA would continue its campaign, even broadening it to include devastating attacks on England and assassinations on mainland Europe. At Sinn Féin *ard fheiseanna* both Adams and McGuinness went out of their way to praise the IRA and to assure the military wing of its undiminished importance in the movement. One or other of them, and usually both, attended every IRA funeral and carried the coffin, even though the sight outraged opponents in Britain and Ireland.

At the same time, Adams and McGuinness, along with a few close advisors and confidants, were moving stealthily to devise a political alliance that would bring republicans in from the cold and enable them to run down the military campaign. This book will explain the rationale behind the remarkable political revolution that took place from the late 1980s in which Sinn Féin, the party that has been ostracised and demonised for decades, was taken into the heart of the Irish political process so that the Irish government and the SDLP in the North of Ireland linked up with Sinn Féin's leaders to present a peace initiative to the British government, which in turn led to an IRA ceasefire in 1994 and the Good Friday Agreement of 1998.

This book sets out to show why this process took so long as well as the reasons for its final success. The beginning of the process coincided with the end of Margaret Thatcher's premiership and an intensification of British military action by special forces in the last years of the 1980s. Frustrated and annoyed by the failure of the 1985 Anglo-Irish Agreement to bring the North's troubles to a conclusion, Mrs Thatcher was in no mood to consider any further political initiatives. Instead, her government tried to defeat the IRA with a series of lethal ambushes in which large numbers of activists were shot – the Gibraltar and Loughgall killings being the most contentious. The IRA's response in the early 1990s was to unleash a bombing campaign in cities across the North of Ireland and to have its England Department detonate immense bombs in the financial heart of Britain's capital, which caused, in aggregate, billions of pounds worth of damage.

This renewed bombing campaign continued right up to the 1997 IRA ceasefire. Even after Thatcher's departure it was only with great difficulty that the Irish government managed to persuade the British to pay attention to the shift taking place within republican thinking after the northerners took control. In the opinion of former taoiseach Garret FitzGerald, writing in *The Irish Times* in 2001:

> A major factor in the tragedy of the past three decades was the difficulty successive British governments had in grasping the futility of treating this crisis as one that could be solved by security measures. Such measures gradually drove an ever-growing proportion of the northern nationalist community into the arms of the IRA, and it took two full decades for Irish politicians to convince British governments to review radically that flawed policy.

This book aims to show that by extraordinary bad luck, just as a British government led by John Major began to review 'that flawed policy' and to open contacts with republicans, parliamentary arithmetic at Westminster meant that Ulster Unionists could paralyse Major's government. The opportunity presented by the IRA ceasefire of 1994 was frittered away as internal disputes in Britain's ruling Conservative Party about the European Union were exploited by Ulster Unionists and a tiny coterie of right-wing Conservatives. As a result, most of the 1990s was lost to prevarication, mainly the ploy of demanding that the IRA surrender, or 'decommission', its weapons before entering talks with the British government. Only with the election of Tony Blair in 1997, leading a Labour government with an unprecedented majority, could the procrastination be swept aside and Sinn Féin enter the negotiations which had been promised three years earlier.

In the hundred years or so covered by this book, the last decade of the twentieth century witnessed the most dramatic change in Sinn Féin's fortunes since the years 1917–21. In both instances, from being completely outside the political process and reviled by the established parties and all governments, Sinn Féin found that suddenly, within just a few years, the party's fortunes had been transformed: its leaders were in government and hobnobbing with the great and the good. On the evidence presented in this book, Sinn Féin, in one form or another, seems destined to play a central role in the politics of both parts of Ireland for the first time in eighty years.

1. 'SINN FÉIN MUST BE THE MOTTO'
The Founding Years, 1900–07

Sinn *Féin* translates into English in various ways: 'Ourselves', 'We Ourselves' or 'Ourselves Alone', the last two versions being the most common. The modern Sinn Féin party prefers 'We Ourselves', but each version carries the same clear political message: national self-determination and self-reliance, which requires separation from England and English influence of any description, political or otherwise. This objective consciously harks back to the late eighteenth century and one of the aims of Theobald Wolfe Tone, the founding father of Irish republicanism:

> to break the connection with England, the never-failing source of all our political evils, and to assert the independence of my country.

Arthur Griffith brought the phrase 'Sinn Féin' into the political realm when he labelled the set of theories he published in 1905 *The Sinn Féin Policy*. By identifying his proposals as 'Sinn Féin', Griffith located them firmly within the separatist tradition, while also managing to give the concept of separatism a contemporary resonance. He did this by not simply looking backwards into Ireland's republican past but by slotting his ideas into the mainstream of pre-First World War European nationalist thinking, striking attitudes which were of interest to independence movements across Europe and as far away as India. The ability of Sinn Féin leaders to redefine Irish nationalism to suit the changing mood of the times was to become one of the party's strengths throughout the twentieth century.

The words 'Sinn Féin' had been invoked to express separatist sentiments well before 1905. The earliest printed reference to the words in that context seems to be in a play written in 1882 by Thomas Stanislaus Cleary with the title *Shin Fain* (Ourselves Alone). The play's characters included Erin and the Spirit of Self-Reliance, which fairly well sum up what Sinn Féin is about. The words appear in this chorus:

> No more we bow to kiss the rod,
> But to this health a cup we drain;
> Our native sod, our trust in God,
> And under Him, Shin Fain! Shin Fain!

Ten years later, in the 1892 general election campaign, Tim Healy MP became the first Irish politician on record to use 'Sinn Féin' as a slogan. In a speech given in Letterkenny, County Donegal, in June of that year he said: 'Now they [Parnellites] say against us that we put our hopes in the Liberal Party and that we are bound hand and foot to the Liberal Party. No, I give you the good old watchword of old Ireland – *Shin Fain* – ourselves alone.'

The Gaelic League, founded in 1893 to revive the Irish language and promote Irish culture, chose 'Sinn Féin' as its motto. In March 1898, Douglas Hyde, the League's president, contributed a poem to the magazine *Shan Van Vocht*:

> Waiting for help from France, waiting for help from Spain; the people
> Who waited long ago for that they got shame only.
> Waiting for help again, help from America, the lot who are now waiting

For it, my disgust for ever on them.
It is time for every fool to have knowledge that there is no
Watchcry worth any heed but one – *Sinn Féin amháin* –
Ourselves Alone!

By the end of the nineteenth century the words 'Sinn Féin' had become shorthand for describing a way of thinking, an outlook, a set of ideas, a particular mindset in Ireland. People often used the phrase to describe what was called an 'advanced nationalist' attitude or mentality. They demanded not only political independence, they sought to emphasise and develop Ireland's distinctiveness or separateness from England in all respects – in sport, language, literature, culture and history. They set out to resist Anglicisation, a process they feared was gathering pace in the latter part of the nineteenth century. Advanced nationalists wanted Ireland to be unapologetically, recognisably, even aggressively Irish, and to this end set about purging English influences from the country. As a result of this they were also known as Irish Irelanders. The very fact of being able to express their ideology in a movement with an Irish name was important, symbolically, for those who held such views.

Paradoxically, Irish Ireland ideas were not all home-grown. The concepts did not spring fully formed into people's consciousness at the end of the century. An earlier version had already been developed. Although Ireland had been culturally cut off from mainland Europe for centuries, the leaders of successive rebellions had always sought, and usually found, inspiration, political support and military assistance from Britain's continental rivals. Following in that tradition, Irish nationalists in the early to mid-nineteenth century had looked to European examples they thought would be relevant.

The European romantic nationalists of the 1820s and 1830s attracted the attention of Thomas Davis, Charles Gavan Duffy and John Blake Dillon, leaders of the Young Ireland movement that was founded in 1842. They were drawn to the German concept of *Volksgeist*, the idea that every nationality has a spirit or a 'genius' peculiar to its people. Naturally for the Young Irelanders, there had to be an Irish *Volksgeist*, and the Irish people must be made aware of it. They believed the way to develop the spirit of the Irish people was to follow the example of European nationalists who researched the traditions and culture specific to their own people – myths, legends, folklore, history, religion, language and music – in order to promote their *Volksgeist*.

Young Ireland was modelled on the Young Italy movement that Giuseppe Mazzini had set up in 1831 to agitate for the unification and national independence of Italy. Out of Young Italy grew the *Risorgimento*, the movement for national regeneration which, in 1870, was ultimately successful in creating a united, independent Italy. The slogan of Young Italy in the 1830s, *Italia farà da sé* (Italy will do it alone), struck exactly the same chord as the slogan 'Sinn Féin' would in Ireland sixty years later. Unfortunately for his Irish disciples, Mazzini did not believe Ireland qualified for independence. He did not think it had a culture distinct from England. The Young Irelanders set out to remedy that perception.

The views the Young Irelanders promulgated in their newspaper, *The Nation*, had a profound influence on Irish nationalists at the end of the nineteenth century. The Young Irelanders believed the way to strengthen the sense of nationhood was to educate the people, develop their collective consciousness as Irish men and women and provide a sense of belonging to a singular entity. It was important, therefore, to inculcate national self-respect and 'regenerate the spirit of Ireland'. To this end *The Nation* carried articles which attempted to create a 'heroic' past for Ireland, distinct and disconnected from England's history.

In 1848 the ideas of romantic nationalism were translated into political action across Europe and there were uprisings and *coups d'état*, overthrowing governments from France to Hungary. Unfortunately for the Irish protagonists, the country had been laid waste by the Great Famine (1845–49) and their 'rising' amounted to nothing more than a skirmish in the mud of a cabbage patch in Ballingarry, a few miles outside Kilkenny. The rebels were quickly rounded up and sentenced to life in exile. Those Young Irelanders who were not transported scattered to mainland Europe and America. From then until the 1880s Ireland fell by the wayside in the Europe-wide march to national cultural consciousness.

Nevertheless, the views of the Irish Ireland movement prevailed and the analysis of the Irish Irelanders and Arthur Griffith was to establish the parameters of Irish government policy for more than fifty years following independence. It was not until the 1970s that Irish policy turned away from the concepts of Sinn Féin – Ourselves Alone – as laid out by Griffith, and adopted an outward-looking, European perspective.

The Young Irelanders prefigured the work of people such as Standish O'Grady, who pioneered the copying and translating of Irish texts, and Douglas Hyde, who promoted the Irish language through the Gaelic League. Their influence is also apparent in the Gaelic Athletic Association's (GAA) development of Irish games, the literary revival of the 1890s and, finally, the political manifestation of separatism in Sinn Féin. Young Ireland's cultural nationalism and national self-reliance were Griffith's inspiration, providing exactly the sort of ideologies he would later preach and write about in his own newspapers, the *United Irishman* and its successor, *Sinn Féin*.

The link between the romantic nationalist philosophy of the Young Irelanders of the 1840s and the cultural and political revival of the 1890s was the Young Ireland Society (YIS), a group founded in 1881 to develop Irish culture. Members read papers, held debates and promoted cultural nationalism by erecting memorials to nationalist heroes, staging rallies and marches, selling cultural emblems, like badges, and organising competitions for schoolchildren on the subject of Irish history.

The Dublin Metropolitan Police (DMP) reckoned there were 200 members in the YIS in 1886. The DMP were interested in the YIS because the Dublin Fenians had been in control of the society since 1883.

'The Fenians' was the colloquial name for the Irish Republican Brother-hood (IRB), a secret, oath-bound organisation founded in 1858 with the aim of ending English rule in Ireland. It organised a rising in 1867 and was the first Irish republican organisation to explode bombs in England. Members swore allegiance to an Irish republic and the IRB leadership purported to be the government of Ireland. The 'Organisation', as mem-bers called it, was run by a Supreme Council and the leader of the IRB was known as the Head Centre. There was an elaborate system in place to prevent detection by the police. In reality, the IRB's members were well known to the Royal Irish Constabulary (RIC) who compiled regular, detailed reports of IRB activities for Dublin Castle.

Fred Allen, Head Centre in Ireland, worked at the *Irish Independent* in Dublin where Arthur Griffith was employed in the 1880s. In all probabil-ity Allen introduced Griffith, then a printer's apprentice, to the YIS. He also swore him into the IRB. In February 1885 the fourteen-year-old Griffith, secretary of the Junior YIS, presented a paper on John Mitchel, a Young Irelander who had been transported in 1848 and later became a Fenian. By 1885 the YIS president was John O'Leary, an old Fenian who had been allowed back to Ireland after imprisonment and years of exile. As far as Dublin Castle was concerned, the Young Ireland Society was a Fenian/IRB front.

In the late 1880s, when Griffith joined the 'Organisation', the IRB had been underground for decades. It was good at infiltrating other organisations perceived to be useful for promoting Irish independence. The IRB worked hard to control influential bodies, such as the GAA and later the Gaelic League, and every society – literary, artistic, cultural or political – which looked as though it favoured separatism, even one as insignificant as YIS, would quickly attract onto its committee IRB mem-bers seeking to control and direct it.

The IRB tried to infiltrate the Home Rule Party, led by Charles Stewart Parnell, as it grew in importance in the 1880s. They managed to have some IRB members and fellow travellers elected MPs. IRB leaders were concerned that Parnell's party was prepared to settle for a lot less than independence and were unhappy that so many of its members found Westminster very congenial. At grassroots level the IRB strove to make the Home Rule Party more hard line in its demands and more vociferous in its cultural nationalism. Their efforts had little effect. Repeatedly in elections Irishmen expressed the desire to have Home Rule, which, in practice, would have been self-government of a very limited nature, amounting to not much more than a glorified county council for Ireland.

If achieved, Home Rule would have been delivered through a two-chamber body based in Dublin and administering the whole country, but with few law-making powers. Ireland would have remained part of the United Kingdom, with the British monarch as Head of State. The powers of Westminster to legislate for Ireland would have remained unaffected. Forty-two Irish MPs would have sat at Westminster, which would have retained control over foreign relations, war, defence, treaties, coinage, pensions, national insurance, the postal service, savings banks and a host of other areas. Tax and customs duties would also have been matters for the imperial parliament. Ireland would have had to pay an annual contribution to the imperial exchequer. The so-called Home Rule parliament in Dublin would have had few powers other than allocating monies from its budget to county and borough councils.

Parnell's party of the 1880s was succeeded by the Irish Parliamentary Party (IPP), led by John Redmond, which continued to enjoy the overwhelming allegiance of the Irish electorate until the 1916 Rising. As time went on the IPP became the native Irish establishment. Lack of political competition meant that no one noticed the party was becoming sclerotic. Its MPs were old: many had been in Westminster since 1885, when a substantial extension of the franchise had allowed eighty-six Home Rule MPs to be elected. Some had been MPs prior to 1885. Many seats were not contested at any election since there appeared to be no alternative.

The be-all and end-all of the IPP's existence was to gain Home Rule, yet years after 1885 they were no nearer their goal. In fact, some argued they were actually further from it because the party was completely wedded to the fortunes of the British Liberal Party rather than being independent, as they had been in 1885. Besides, it was quite clear that any Home Rule Bill brought in by a Liberal government would be thrown out by the House of Lords. How, therefore, could Home Rule ever be achieved?

Despite this lack of progress and little hope of any in the foreseeable future, there was no coherent opposition in Ireland to the IPP and its leader, John Redmond. No opposition, that is, within nationalist Ireland; those who held Irish Ireland views were making no impact on the electorate. It goes without saying that amongst Protestants in the northeast of the country opposition to the concept of Home Rule was virtually total. Almost to a man they voted for unionist candidates who kept a watchful eye on any sign of concessions to the IPP.

In these circumstances the prospects of those who advocated something more radical than Home Rule looked bleak indeed. If the mighty IPP, controlling the fate of the Liberal Party, could not wrest Home Rule from the British, how could the small minority who demanded separatism possibly hope to achieve it? Arthur Griffith thought he had the answer.

What was stirring in Ireland in the 1890s fitted perfectly with events and ideas in other small nations across Europe. The Czechs who campaigned for independence from the Austrian Empire with the slogan 'Advance Through Czech' would have understood exactly what the Irish Ireland movement was up to. All nineteenth-century nationalist movements were associated with parallel linguistic movements, which were seen as justifying political demands and providing historical legitimacy. Attempts by Norway to break away from Danish control, by Greece and Romania to gain independence from Turkey, by Hungarians, Czechs and Slovaks to quit the Austrian Empire, by Finns, Latvians and Estonians to throw off Russian domination, all produced native literature and corresponding language movements which demanded the use of 'the native language' in schools and its equal status in official documents. These attempts were not restricted to Europe. The same applied to the Swadeshi movement in India, and to Zionists in Palestine. Today it is true of Wales, Brittany, Quebec and nationalist areas in the North of Ireland.

If Czechs, Hungarians and Poles had stolen a march on the Irish with their emphasis on cultural nationalism based on language, it didn't take long for the Irish to catch up. When Douglas Hyde established the Gaelic League in 1893 there were only six books in Irish in print. Soon the League had its own weekly paper, *An Claidheamh Soluis* (The Sword of Light). Within a few years WB Yeats could claim that the League sold 50,000 Irish textbooks annually. In 1898 there were fifty-eight branches of the Gaelic League; by 1901, 200 branches; and by 1906 there were 900 branches with 100,000 members, mainly in urban areas. The members were literate, educated and had a sense of national pride. They were engaged in a voyage of cultural discovery. They ranged from working men and women to eccentric Anglo-Irish aristocrats, some of whom wore tweed jackets and kilts made of wool woven in Ireland.

Dozens of enthusiasts were engaged in copying, translating and writing Irish books, plays and poetry. It was the done thing to learn Irish, or try to. James Joyce tried. Considering his linguistic abilities it should not have been a problem. It was the ideology poured out by the teacher that he could not put up with. He found that the notion of a pure Irish nation purged of Saxon 'contamination' flew in the face of the linguistic and political realities in Ireland, as well as being largely irrelevant to learning the language; Joyce's teacher was a certain Padraig Pearse.

There was the rub. Despite the naive belief of the founders of the Gaelic League that learning Irish could be a purely intellectual exercise, the evidence from every other European country suggested otherwise. For many people a nation's difference, its uniqueness and the basis for its claim to independence rested in its language. For many Irish nationalists the Irish language, along with sport, literature, culture and religion, became a tool to demonstrate and justify Ireland's claim to political and economic independence.

In the early years of the twentieth century, Griffith's document, *The Sinn Féin Policy,* took the Sinn Féin mentality into the political arena in Ireland where it became a topic of intellectual and political discussion. While only a minority subscribed to the advanced nationalist views Griffith espoused, it was nonetheless an important and influential minority, especially among the Dublin intelligentsia. What Arthur Griffith managed to do in 1904–05 was to provide a new political coherence and structure for disconnected nationalist ideas that had first been mooted sixty years earlier. He succeeded in weaving together various strands of thinking that had been revived and developed in the 1880s and 1890s and he challenged the Irish political establishment to put them into practice.

Griffith was able to disseminate his views through the *United Irishman* newspaper, which he edited, and in the columns of other newspapers and periodicals to which he contributed. These journals had a readership far greater than their sales and helped spread the ideas to cities like Cork, Limerick and Belfast, where there existed pockets of strong nationalist sentiment. Minority views they may have been, but no educated or politically aware person in Ireland at the turn of the century could be ignorant of the ideas, whether they agreed with them or not.

Most intellectuals at the time, including James Joyce, WB Yeats and John Millington Synge, shared the opinion that the nationalism Griffith expounded – that of the Irish Ireland movement – was introspective and culturally impoverished. Tom Kettle, a nationalist MP and academic, summed up that position when he said: 'My only counsel to Ireland is, that in order to become deeply Irish she must become European.' People like Kettle and Joyce feared that the Irish Ireland movement would lead to provincialism if not parochialism.

Griffith, born in 1871, served his time as a printer, but early in life became steeped in nationalist politics. From his teenage years he had been a separatist and before he was twenty was already a member of the Irish Republican Brotherhood. In his early twenties he hung around with the small group of Dublin separatists who sought to influence what became known as the cultural revival. All his spare time was taken up with matters Irish. He attended evening classes in Irish history taught by Kate McBride, the sister of John Devoy, head of Clan na nGael, the American wing of the Fenians that provided finance for the IRB. He was a regular at what could be described as a sort of 'Irish Ireland' café in Henry Street in Dublin, owned by Jennie Wyse-Power, which served only Irish produce, apart, presumably, from the tea and coffee. She was the wife of the ex-Fenian John Power and had been active in politics since the 1880s. The café was a meeting place for republicans.

Membership of the IRB, and association with old Fenians like O'Leary and surviving relatives of Fenians, did not necessarily mean that Griffith, or for that matter any of the others, supported political violence in the circumstances of the time. Neither did it mean they ruled it out in all circumstances. However, in the 1890s no one was seriously proposing a rebellion. Even more than a decade later the British government's assistant under-secretary in Ireland, James Dougherty, would correctly conclude that 'there is no evidence that the IRB is anything but the shadow of a once terrifying name.' It was not until after 1907 that the IRB began to reorganise and set out on the path towards an uprising.

Apart from the commitment of its members, what gave the IRB the edge was cash – regular supplies rolled in from Clan na nGael in the USA. All the newspapers Griffith edited or published received Clan money, which the IRB in Dublin distributed. Access to cash and his journalistic ability were indispensable aids to disseminating his views. The American support provided Irish Ireland views with far greater currency and credibility than they could otherwise have enjoyed.

Although a member of the IRB, Griffith's opinions did not always reflect IRB thinking. Nonetheless his opinions fulfilled the requirements of the IRB in that they promoted Irish independence. His views were clearly laid out in the objectives he had drawn up for Cumann na nGaedheal, the organisation he founded in 1900 after he returned from South Africa where he had sided with the Boers against the British. Those objectives were:

To advance the cause of Ireland's national independence by

1. cultivating a fraternal spirit among Irishmen
2. diffusing knowledge of Ireland's resources and supporting Irish industries
3. the study and teaching of Irish history, literature, language, music and art
4. the assiduous cultivation and encouragement of Irish games, pastimes and characteristics
5. the discountenancing of anything tending towards the Anglicisation of Ireland
6. the physical and intellectual training of the young
7. the development of an Irish foreign policy
8. extending to each other friendly advice and aid, socially and politically
9. the nationalisation of public boards.

Cumann na nGaedheal provided a good example of the elements Griffith believed essential in an organisation. It was loosely organised; it was as broad a front as possible; it was designed to be an umbrella body for political, cultural and social organisations; all kinds of people could join and engage in immediate action, be it in home industries, education or local government; individuals could select one or several aspects without giving up their particular political line as long as they were for an Irish Ireland and national independence, which is, of course, why they would have joined in the first place.

Cumann na nGaedheal incorporated the Celtic Literary Society and

Inghinidhe na hÉireann (Daughters of Ireland), founded at Easter 1900 by Maud Gonne MacBride. That added the attraction of the cause of women's rights to the separatist politics and economics of the Cumann. As with all the tiny separatist organisations, many members of Cumann na nGaedheal were members of all three organisations and others besides, including the IRB. Griffith's new organisation held its first convention on 25 November 1900, the anniversary of the execution of the Manchester Martyrs, Fenians hanged in 1867 for killing a policeman.

Cumann na nGaedheal did not present any clear political policy. Had it done so, its Dublin IRB supporters would have disavowed it. For Griffith the absence of a political policy was an advantage. He did not like political parties. They were the sort of tight organisations he was wary of. He believed organisations 'develop into tyrannies'. He aimed for a popular front, a rallying centre for the nation. PS O'Hegarty, a senior IRB figure, later wrote that Griffith had always tried to create a 'voluntary association rather than a rigid, rule-bound organisation'. Cumann na nGaedheal, with its tiny membership of Dublin intellectuals and hard-line nationalists, may have seemed an unlikely prototype, but Griffith was not deterred.

Alongside Cumann na nGaedheal, Griffith set up, in 1903, the grandly titled National Council. It was intended to be an *ad hoc* pressure group to protest against the first visit of Edward VII to Dublin as king. It comprised the 'usual suspects' who made up the Dublin separatists. The National Council's immediate aim was to prevent Dublin Corporation presenting a loyal address to the king. This time Griffith struck a chord. A group, including National Council members, confronted the lord mayor and John Redmond at a meeting in the Rotunda and demanded to know whether the mayor proposed to present a loyal address. Hand-to-hand fighting broke out in the hall and two MPs were knocked unconscious.

As a result of the publicity surrounding the incident, many people, a number of them influential, joined the National Council to oppose the king's visit. They included WB Yeats, Edward Martyn, a wealthy land-owner and a founder of the Abbey theatre, and Charles Stewart Parnell's sister, Anna. Following a noisy public meeting in the Rotunda the proposal for a loyal address from Dublin Corporation was defeated by three votes. In typically overblown language, Griffith proclaimed in the *United Irishman*: 'For the first time since the Norman invasion the capital has denied before the world the right of the king of England to rule this country.' Ultimately the king was well received in Dublin.

While Griffith was organising Cumann na nGaedheal and the National Council he had also been writing away furiously, mainly in the columns of the *United Irishman*. Here he developed his ideas on how to achieve national independence in the face of total British opposition and the House of Lords' refusal to vote even for a measure as innocuous as he considered the Home Rule Bill proposed by the Liberals. The *United Irishman* had a circulation of 30,000, but because of the tradition of leaving copies in pubs and hotels for customers there could have been as many as 250,000 readers. These readers would have been aware that Griffith's solution to the constitutional problem was a dual monarchy, that is, the same monarch for Britain and Ireland but with two parliaments separate and independent from each other – a good step beyond Home Rule.

Writing in June 1902, Griffith had explained that while he was a separatist (in those days a polite way of saying a republican), he knew most Irish people were not republican and therefore a dual monarchy was a compromise that he believed would satisfy the majority. He also naively regarded it as an outcome that unionists could accept because the monarchy would be retained. He did not seem to realise that if unionists were implacably opposed to Home Rule, limited as it was, they would be horrified by the prospect of legislative independence for Ireland where they would be a permanent minority in elections.

Griffith believed that, under the dual monarchy, Ireland would be governed as it had been from 1782 to the Act of Union in 1801, the system known as Grattan's Parliament. During those years Ireland had enjoyed, for all practical purposes, legislative independence and had passed acts making provision for the development of industry and commerce in the country, which had suffered under Westminster rule. Many, including Griffith, looked back on those years as proof that Ireland would prosper under its own government. Some saw that period as an economic golden age.

Claiming that the Act of Union was null and void because Britain had renounced any right to legislate for Ireland by the Renunciation Act of 1783, Griffith argued that his proposal did not require any new legislation – that way he would get around the House of Lords' veto. Ireland would simply return to the pre-1801 position with its own parliament, governed by the king, lords and commons of Ireland. Britain would be governed by the same king, but by the lords and commons of Great Britain.

Unfortunately it was all constitutional rubbish. Griffith was ignoring the British doctrine of the Supremacy of Parliament and the simple fact that any parliament could amend or repeal any act passed by a previous parliament. The Act of Union (1801) had in fact superseded the 1783 Renunciation Act. For many people, though, Griffith's attachment to a dual monarchy was not as interesting as the method he proposed to achieve it. In answer to the question how he could succeed to move Britain when the Irish Parliamentary Party (IPP), with over seventy MPs, had failed, Griffith referred people to the example of Hungary.

From January to July 1904, in twenty-seven weekly instalments in the *United Irishman*, Griffith outlined his version of the means by which Hungary had managed to extricate itself from Austrian rule if not the Austrian Empire. Hungarian deputies had withdrawn from Vienna as a body and for years had engaged in passive resistance, refusing to accept Austrian authority. As a result, Hungary eventually became one element of the dual monarchy of Austria–Hungary. The Austrian emperor Franz

Josef ruled the empire from Vienna, but he was King Franz Josef in Hungary.

In the final instalment of his series, Griffith presented his programme for Ireland. Irish MPs should withdraw from Westminster and meet in Dublin. The system of local government that had been established under the 1898 Local Government Act could be used to lay the foundation for self-government. Local taxes would be collected and courts established. There would be consuls appointed abroad and campaigns to promote Irish goods and industries. The MPs would simply make the administration of the country their own, boycott the British system of administration and justice and ignore Westminster. It was music to the ears of separatists.

Griffith pulled the *United Irishman* articles together and published them as a booklet in November 1904. He called it *The Resurrection of Hungary: a Parallel for Ireland*. It sold 5,000 copies in twenty-four hours, an Irish publishing record which some believe still stands. By March 1905 the *United Irishman* claimed that more than 20,000 copies had been sold.

The coherence of Griffith's argument and its simplicity captured the imagination of his readers. It attracted many members of the IPP who were dissatisfied with lack of progress at Westminster. It attracted members of the IRB and other 'advanced' nationalists despite their objections to the notion of dual monarchy. For them a convention of Irish MPs and county councillors in Dublin offered a powerful image and suggested embryonic independence. Why should Irish MPs go to Westminster? What was the point in being there when most of the business was taken up by English affairs while the chief secretary ran Ireland from Dublin Castle? This concept of abstention from Westminster would become an article of faith for republicans for the whole of the twentieth century.

Griffith's proposals were in tune with the time. He was building on the actions of Sir Thomas Esmonde, a Wexford MP who, after the 1898 Local Government Act, had proposed having local councils elect a central council of delegates to act as a *de facto* Irish parliament. In 1899 Meath County Council passed a resolution proposed by its vice-chairman, John Sweetman, a former MP, asserting Ireland's right to a parliament. The wealthy Sweetman then financed a general council of three delegates from each county council in Ireland who met regularly for some years, though Ulster Unionists quickly withdrew.

When Griffith's *The Sinn Féin Policy* was published in 1904 a general election was imminent and people were dissatisfied that the principle of Home Rule, which had been conceded by a major British political party twenty years earlier, had still not been enacted nor was likely to be despite its being the wish of the overwhelming majority of the Irish electorate. Nationalists in Ireland felt they were being left behind while places they regarded as 'minor' nations in the Balkans and central Europe asserted their independence from the Ottoman and Austrian empires. The actions of people like Esmonde and Sweetman were demonstrations of the frustration felt in nationalist political circles.

Previous suggestions for withdrawal had been made when there were few MPs of a nationalist disposition. By the end of the nineteenth century, however, there were over eighty.[1] If the eighty-plus MPs withdrew to Dublin, the empty benches at Westminster would be an embarrassment for Britain. Furthermore, the successful Hungarian precedent gave legitimacy to Griffith's proposal. The idea of the majority of Ireland's elected representatives deciding as a body to abstain from Westminster lent a powerful moral strength and authority to the scheme. The beauty of it was that it proposed using British legislation, that is, the Local Government Act, to undermine British rule. The whole idea was peaceful and would have been endorsed by the vast majority of the Irish electorate. Some even believed it was legal. The fact that it was not and that the British government would have strenuously resisted any attempt at unauthorised tax collection did not matter to the scheme's proponents. Abstention from Westminster threw the responsibility on to the British government to explain why they were defying the will of the Irish people as expressed in successive elections.

An added attraction was the impressive-sounding and coherent economic programme that Griffith built on his abstention proposal. The programme drew extensively from the work of Friedrich List, *The National System of Political Economy* (1841), considered very old thinking. List, an economic nationalist like Griffith, had believed nationalism was essential for promoting economic growth. Griffith selected suitable aspects of List's work and ignored others that were distinctly unhelpful.

Griffith argued that Ireland's economic weakness was due to foreign rule, not inadequate resources. Only an Irish parliament could place the country in a position to resist economic exploitation. Ireland could develop its industry and, like Germany, impose tariffs on foreign goods, especially English imports, to give Irish industry and manufacture a chance to grow. This proposal was in tune with Irish Ireland views and chimed with the sentiments of those who disliked free trade and advocated a 'Buy Irish' policy. Griffith's protectionist economic arguments exercised a powerful influence on Irish governments until Sean Lemass's time in the 1960s.

Griffith's economic proposals were based on absurdly optimistic evaluations of the country's industrial potential. Referring to the thinking of the Young Irelanders sixty years earlier, he found support for his arguments in Thomas Davis's writings, which contained even more exaggerated claims than his own. This led him to talk of '400,000,000 tons of coal, the finest stone in Europe and an inexhaustible supply of peat to operate on.' He claimed that these resources could support a huge population and that if it hadn't been for the Act of Union, Ireland's population would have reached twenty million by 1911. Luckily for Griffith, it seemed no one else had read List. Had they done so they would have discovered that List thought the Act of Union was a good idea, that England was right to conquer Ireland and that small nations like Ireland 'only through alliance with some more powerful nations, by partly sacrificing the advantages of nationality ... can maintain with difficulty independence'.

Despite the shortcomings of Griffith's political and economic proposals in *The Sinn Féin Policy*, they were a major talking point in intellectual circles in Ireland. For example, James Joyce thought the Sinn Féin viewpoint was such a familiar and essential aspect of political discussion in the Ireland he left in 1904 that, when writing *Ulysses* more than a decade later, he felt he could not portray Dublin life without devoting a lengthy passage to the ideas of the early Sinn Féin movement.

It was not only the political and economic arguments of Griffith's Sinn Féin which attracted popular support. As with the rest of European nationalism of the time, the Irish version also carried a strong whiff of racial stereotyping and xenophobia. There was always a place in the columns of Griffith's rabidly anti-English newspaper for articles extolling the purity of 'the Irish race'. To the pervasive Anglophobia Griffith added his own anti-Semitism, which regularly seeped through the columns of his paper. For example, in 1904 he penned virulent articles in support of the campaign of the anti-Semitic Limerick Redemptorist, Fr Creagh, and attacked Michael Davitt, the Fenian and former Land League leader, when he sprang to the defence of the Jews of the city. Griffith's anti-Semitism was the reason for Joyce's joke in *Ulysses* when he had Leopold Bloom, a Jew, suggest the idea for the name Sinn Féin, that most exclusively Irish Ireland movement, to its founder.

The fact that Griffith's booklet was such a bestseller in 1905 and that the policies he advocated generated so much discussion raised questions for John Redmond's party, as Griffith had hoped. What would the IPP do after the next election if they found themselves in the same position in Westminster twenty years after Home Rule had first been promised? Griffith did not plan to overthrow the IPP or even set up an alternative party. In any case it would not suit his purpose for the IPP to fragment. He wanted the IPP to commit its members to withdraw from Westminster after the next election. The more numerous and united the body of MPs who acted, the stronger the moral force.

Separatists in general were delighted with the proposals for withdrawal and abstention, but the IRB in particular opposed the dual monarchy idea that most separatists regarded as Griffith's own personal obsession. Anyone joining the IRB, including Griffith, had sworn allegiance to the Irish Republic. The IRB abhorred the concept of monarchy, especially a British monarchy. Griffith seemed to forget or ignore the anti-Catholic bigotry at the heart of the British monarchy, exemplified by the ban on a monarch marrying a Catholic and the exclusion of Catholics from high offices of state. Would that not all apply equally in Ireland?

Republicans did not wish to return to the constitutional status of 1782 and were bewildered by Griffith's starry-eyed view of Grattan's Parliament and the king, lords and commons of Ireland. It all seemed so old-fashioned and backward-looking. Republicans traced their lineage back through the Fenians to the United Irishmen of 1798 and stopped there. For them, separatism meant adherence to the tenets of Wolfe Tone and the United Irishmen, which required the removal of English influence and the monarchy. Griffith's dual monarchy seemed, on the contrary, to copper-fasten and perpetuate the English connection.

For these reasons a dual monarchy, or 'The Hungarian Policy' as it was known in 1904, was not going to have a free ride. Nevertheless, Griffith's ideas had captured the initiative. Gradually during 1905 his Sinn Féin policy, and anything similar, had become known by the generic term Sinn Féin. Griffith had appropriated a phrase that best seemed to sum up the policy he was promoting.

Where did Griffith take it from? His own testimony is that the suggestion came from Mary Butler, a friend and patron, during a discussion in his office at Fownes Street in Dublin one evening in November 1904.[2] Perhaps it was a matter of courtesy to credit her with the inspiration, for there is clear evidence he had thought of it himself years earlier. Griffith's closest friend in his twenties, William Rooney, had written to him in South Africa in 1899 discussing the question of their political position. He wrote: 'You are right – Sinn Féin must be the motto.'

Whatever the inspiration, by spring 1905 'Sinn Féin' had become an all-embracing description for attitudes and behaviour, be they political, social, sporting, educational, cultural or economic, which were separatist or Irish Ireland. It was a movement. It was not yet an organisation. It expressed an attitude of mind and offered an ideology and a political programme to those who wanted to break the connection with England. It incorporated the huge differences among such people as to how that might be achieved. Griffith's newspaper was its voice.

Despite Griffith's wishes, one manifestation was party political. In June 1905 the National Council, the group Griffith had assembled in 1903 to protest against King Edward VII's visit to Dublin, put up twenty candidates for the elections to the Dublin Poor Law Board and got thirteen elected. The National Council had proved unexpectedly popular among the Dublin intelligentsia and had not faded away after the royal visit. Griffith intended to use the National Council as an intellectual ginger group, publishing pamphlets, recruiting members and convincing individual MPs of the error of their ways. Fighting elections ran counter to that plan; confronting IPP candidates at the polls would not convert any of them.

What Griffith would have viewed as the slide towards a political party continued at the National Council's annual convention in the Rotunda on 28 November 1905. Griffith hoped the National Council would remain a Dublin-based coordinating body that people could join on an individual basis. The Dublin members supported him, but provincial members outvoted them and it was agreed to try to set up branches in each electoral district. Despite the internal disagreement on electoral policy, Griffith, as he intended, dominated proceedings at the convention with a three-hour speech in which he laid out his programme. It was this speech that was widely published as *The Sinn Féin Policy*. As far as most people today are concerned, this meeting in November 1905 inaugurated Sinn Féin.

Yet at the time it was not so simple. The Sinn Féin policy agreed in 1905 at the National Council was dual monarchy, but many members remained unhappy with it, concentrating instead on the separatist and abstentionist aspects which appealed to them and which embarrassed the IPP. Nor was the National Council the only separatist body. There still existed Cumann na nGaedheal, the umbrella group Griffith had founded in 1900 and, of course, both it and the National Council had overlapping membership. And in March 1905 a new body, the Dungannon Clubs, had emerged in Belfast led by IRB men Bulmer Hobson, from Holywood, County Down, and Denis McCullough from Belfast. They were both twenty-two years old and impatient for action. By 1906 they had a news-paper with the uncompromising title *The Republic*. They quite simply demanded an Irish Republic.

Bulmer Hobson, the organisation's leading figure, regarded himself and his clubs as belonging to 'the Sinn Féin movement', of which the National Council, Cumann na nGaedheal and a variety of other groups were also part. As well as these, a score of little nationalist clubs in Dublin maintained a separate existence. Perhaps the only unifying force for these clubs, with their overlapping membership, was the voice Griffith's news-paper provided for them. If a good newspaper is a community talking to itself, here was the 'imagined community' nationalists felt part of.

What would the community's political line be? Dual monarchy or republicanism? Control and direction of the movement had become important for a number of reasons. *The Sinn Féin Policy* had been unex-pectedly successful. It was attracting widespread attention and not only in Ireland. The pamphlet was being translated into other languages, includ-ing some Indian languages.[3] But of far greater immediate importance for Sinn Féin's success was the impact of the general election result of January

1906 in Britain. The result was a substantial Liberal victory that seriously weakened the position of Redmond's party at Westminster. The Liberals, with an overall majority, no longer needed Irish support to govern. *The Sinn Féin Policy* had taken on a new significance.

There was another aspect to control of the policy. Behind the scenes the IRB was being reorganised. During 1906 and 1907 new, more extreme men took over. The new wave included Bulmer Hobson and Denis McCullough, who became members of the Supreme Council. They were joined by Dr Patrick McCartan from Tyrone, Sean Mac-Dermott, who had been the paid organiser of the Dungannon Clubs, and PS O'Hegarty, a bookseller from Dawson Street in Dublin, who later swore Michael Collins into the IRB.

These young men were not the only extremists. In 1907 Thomas Clarke returned from America and was co-opted onto the Supreme Council. Clarke had been released from Portland jail in 1898 under an amnesty granted to celebrate the centenary of the United Irishmen's 1798 rising. It may seem amazing, but his release was part of the Conservative government's attempt to undermine the demand for Home Rule by conceding almost every demand of the IPP; the policy was described as trying to 'kill Home Rule with kindness'. Clarke had served fifteen years of a life sentence for a dynamite campaign in England in the 1880s. Prison had made him a skinny, prematurely aged forty-two-year-old when he left for America in 1900. There he immersed himself in the activities of Clan na nGael. When he returned to Ireland in 1907 he was the most experienced 'physical force' man in the country. He ran a tobacconist's shop in Amiens Street, Dublin, which quickly became a meeting place for republicans and a convenient spot for the Irish Special Branch to view their comings and goings.

The reinvigoration of the IRB in 1907 ensured that its leaders would not tolerate control of the most successful element of the separatist movement remaining in the hands of a man who was not promoting republicanism but a link to the British Crown, however he might dress it up. A struggle began for control of 'the Sinn Féin movement', as Bulmer Hobson called it. Arthur Griffith was not going to have it all his own way.

On the face of it there should have been no contest. The IRB controlled the contributions from America, which funded newspapers, pamphlets and posters and enabled a tiny group like the Dungannon Clubs, with at most fifty members, to employ a full-time organiser. How could Griffith continue if the supply of cash were withdrawn? To make matters worse, he was in difficulties because the *United Irishman* had been ruined in a libel action in 1906. But Griffith had wealthy backers in the persons of John Sweetman, businessman and landowner, Edward Martyn, landowner, and Thomas Martin, architect. It was they, not the IRB, who had financed the publication of *The Resurrection of Hungary*.

Edward Martyn became the first president of Sinn Féin in 1905 and John Sweetman joint vice-president with Griffith. Some idea of the money at their disposal can be gauged from the £10,000 Martyn donated to set up the Palestrina choir in Dublin. As for Sweetman, his support for land reform in the 1880s led him to buy 20,000 acres in Minnesota for division into smaller farms. These men were moderates. Martyn had originally been a unionist and had converted to nationalism because of the Boer War. Neither was a republican nor likely to support the kind of separatist policies the IRB men were insisting on.

Throughout 1906 and much of 1907 Griffith fought to keep his movement as broad a church as possible. Were the IRB to succeed in defining the policy exclusively in republican terms, then Sinn Féin would quickly shrink into just another tiny fringe organisation monitored by Dublin Castle detectives and unable to exert any influence on the wider political scene. Some people believe that it was during this time that Griffith left the IRB, though others say it was in 1910.

Events forced the hands of the protagonists. In summer 1907 CJ Dolan, MP for Leitrim North, resigned the whip in exasperation at the IPP's impotence and then agreed to resign his seat and contest it as a Sinn

Féin candidate. Here was the chance for a united front against the IPP. In August 1907 the various components of the separatist movement met to discuss amalgamation. There was a careful fudge in the wording of the aims of the organisation so that both republicans and supporters of 1782 claimed they had carried the day.

The main significance was that Sinn Féin now existed as one united organisation, in tune with Griffith's ideas rather than the IRB's. In view of what happened in 1916, the point needs to be emphasised that the Sinn Féin which emerged between 1905 and 1907 was, and remained, an organisation committed to a dual monarchy, passive resistance, boycotting and non-violent agitation. Its political aim was to convert Redmond's IPP to abstentionism. Other separatists ridiculed them. The most famous phrase is probably that of DP Moran in his newspaper *The Leader*, when he dismissed Sinn Féin as Arthur Griffith's 'Green Hungarian Band'.

Keeping the organisation as broadly based as possible allowed Griffith to have a larger membership, appealing to people who weren't extremists but at the same time having extremists in the movement. Sinn Féin's first executive provides a good example of this. Two wealthy moderates, Edward Martyn and John Sweetman, were respectively president and vice-president. There were three priests: Fr Lorcan Kieran, a parish priest from Monaghan, Fr W Harpur from Wexford and Fr MK O'Connolly from Ballaghadereen. There were IPP councillors and there were, unusually for any organisation in 1907, three women on the executive: Jennie Wyse-Power, Miss Mary Murphy and Miss M Macken. They all sat alongside IRB men, such as Bulmer Hobson, PT Daly and PS O'Hegarty.

Griffith's success at keeping people with such disparate views in the same movement meant that from the outset Sinn Féin carried the seeds of many future battles and many unanswered questions, which remain valid for the republican movement to this day. First of all, the tradition was established of permitting a crossover between the physical force elements of separatism, including the IRB, and those working peacefully for a political aim. Griffith struggled to retain revolutionaries within a movement that was non-violent. It is obvious that the primary loyalty of the IRB men, both on the Sinn Féin executive and at rank-and-file level, lay not with Sinn Féin but with the IRB.

Secondly, the IRB men never accepted the aims of Sinn Féin as stated in *The Sinn Féin Policy*. For them Sinn Féin was an instrument for unblocking the route to an Irish Republic, not for installing any kind of monarchy. In 1907 Sinn Féin was simply the most prominent and successful of a number of other organisations they had infiltrated.

The IRB also used its US money to give it clout in Sinn Féin. Tom Clarke, who after 1907 increasingly dominated the IRB, doled this money out for electioneering, pamphleteering and appointing organisers. What line were his organisers likely to follow? Was Sinn Féin's official position its final one or was dual monarchy merely a step on the road? These were all questions Sinn Féin found it politic to avoid. They sank their differences and refused to be drawn by their opponents on the question of dual monarchy versus republicanism. The official position was that the movement was broad enough to contain both views. This is how Griffith expressed it in *Sinn Féin* in May 1907.

> The Sinn Féin platform is and is intended to be broad enough to hold all Irishmen who believe in Irish independence, whether they be republicans or whether they be not. Republicanism as republicanism has no necessary connection with Irish nationalism; but numbers of Irishmen during the last 116 years have regarded it as the best form for an independent Irish government. What the form of an Irish national government should be is an interesting but not a material question. It is the thing itself, regardless of its form, Ireland wants.

2. ELECTORAL UPS AND DOWNS
Facing the Voters, 1908–17

Sinn Féin has always displayed protean powers that have enabled it to reinvent itself repeatedly during the twentieth century. It has been able to accomplish this feat because it has always been more than a political party. As a movement Sinn Féin has possessed an atavistic, sentimental and emotional appeal that exerts a pull on the psyche of Irish people at home and abroad. Sinn Féin emphasises its continuity with historical Irish resistance to English encroachment but, whether in 1918 or 2002, it presents itself simultaneously as the sole repository of those past values and the radical contemporary exponent of the same values, preserving them unsullied in an ever-changing present. Looking backwards and forwards at the same time – a position not many political parties could be comfortable with – has proven a powerful combination for Sinn Féin down the years. The movement's appeal has frequently produced sudden tidal waves of political passion, which subside just as quickly but leave an indelible watermark on Irish society.

At no time was this type of advance and recession more marked than in the fifteen years after Sinn Féin first emerged in 1905. Its first sudden surge to prominence in a by-election in Leitrim North in 1908 was a ripple rather than a tidal-wave. Within five years Sinn Féin quickly fell back into political impotence, deserted by prominent republicans, its membership drifting away, its leaders unable to fill seats on the party's executive. Yet within another five years, as a very different organisation, Sinn Féin returned as the dominant force in Irish politics, poised to sweep John Redmond's IPP off the national scene forever. How did such transformations come about?

The most obvious explanation, and the one generally accepted, is that Sinn Féin was catapulted to the peaks of Irish politics by a seismic upheaval in public opinion after the Easter Rising of 1916. Aggrieved by the denial of Home Rule, and sickened by the nature and manner of the British response to the Rising, when firing squads executed the leaders one by one, day by day, people expressed their discontent by swinging in behind Sinn Féin. However, the explanation for Sinn Féin's sudden prominence may not be so straightforward.

Obviously there was a swing in the public mood and the reasons given for the change all played a part and cannot be discounted. But it may be that the upheaval in public opinion in the years 1916–17 was not so startling as people assume. It depends how public opinion is defined and it depends on who is voting. The argument of a vast and comprehensive shift from the Irish Parliamentary Party to Sinn Féin assumes that the same people were voting in 1918 as in 1910, but that was obviously not the case. As a result of electoral reform a huge new electorate of women and young men came onto the registers for the 1918 election. Secondly, in a large number of constituencies, the demoralised IPP did not put up candidates in 1918, thereby magnifying the apparent swing to Sinn Féin.

How many of the new voters in 1918, whether women over thirty or men over twenty-one, would always have been Sinn Féin supporters? No one can say. All that is known is that younger voters, then as now, were drawn to Sinn Féin. The events of the years 1916–18 show remarkable similarities with the 1980s in the North and the late 1990s in both parts of the island. Before the H-block hunger strikes of 1981 the extent of support for Sinn Féin was simply unknown because Sinn Féin did not contest elections. The first time it did in the North in 1982 it got 10% of the votes. In both the 1980s in the North of Ireland, and in the 1990s in the Republic and Northern Ireland, Sinn Féin has been able to attract to its colours hordes of young people who canvass indefatigably, march in protest demonstrations, volunteer to hand out leaflets, stick up posters and carry out a thousand thankless tasks. Their great-grandparents were doing exactly the same in 1917 and 1918.

In the first few years after Sinn Féin's foundation, however, all that was in the future. In those early years the level of support for the nationalistic sentiments expressed by Griffith's Sinn Féin is difficult to quantify. Although most people did not have the vote, the cultural and nationalist preferences of the young people for whom Sinn Féin was attractive can be gauged in other ways. There were tens of thousands of young people in the GAA and the Gaelic League. Who would they have supported if they had had a vote? There is no way to tell for sure, but it is a reasonable assumption that John Redmond's IPP would not have set their blood racing.

Advocating a position that recruited art, sport, literature, history, indeed all aspects of Irish life, to the cause of nationalism meant that a movement like Sinn Féin could still be political while not participating in party politics. Griffith's emphasis on Irish industry, Irish language or Irish drama was as political as the GAA's attitude to sport with its ban on 'foreign games', otherwise known as 'garrison games'. Just because that attitude was not represented in electoral politics in the country did not mean it did not exist, although the established channels of public opinion at the time behaved as if it did not. Mainstream newspapers were, on the one hand, pro-union, pro-Empire, or both, and, on the other hand, pro-Home Rule. There was no mainstream paper advocating separatism. Anyone reading the national press, *The Irish Times, Irish Independent, Daily Mail, Daily Express, Cork Examiner* or *Freeman's Journal*, would have had difficulty finding any reference to Irish Ireland attitudes or activities, and if such a reference were found it would be derisory or derogatory.

What is impossible to determine is how far opinion expressed through the national newspapers and major periodicals of the period can be equated with that of the population at large. Since in some areas the majority of young men were involved in the GAA, either as players, club members or supporters, a fact which barely got a mention in newspapers, it can be surmised that the political outlook of a huge slice of the population was not reflected in the national press. By 1906 there were more than 100,000 members in almost 1,000 branches of the Gaelic League, which was in many ways the urban equivalent of the GAA. Again it would be difficult to spot the significance of that organisation in Irish life by reading the national press. Yet we know Dublin was seething with what Professor FSL Lyons called 'a multitude of little clubs'. Their membership comprised the sort of people who supported separatism and revered the idealised national stereotype constructed by Irish Ireland. These were the people who, to the disgust and amazement of the establishment, rioted for a week in 1907 in protest at what they saw as the defamation of that stereotype in JM Synge's play, *The Playboy of the Western World*.

Although Sinn Féin was not a political party in 1905 it did enjoy widespread support for its anti-English sentiments and its political objective of persuading the IPP to withdraw from Westminster and establish a form of self-government in Ireland. Many of the young people who supported Sinn Féin simply wanted to use any means available to undermine and discredit the party their parents supported: the Irish Parliamentary Party. Other people were simply growing impatient with the IPP's lack of progress. For that reason Sinn Féin prospered during times of discomfiture for the IPP.

The years 1905–09 were such times. Many of Redmond's MPs, and probably most Irish voters, assumed naively that when the Liberals returned with an overall majority they would automatically introduce a Home Rule Bill, just as Gladstone had done in 1892 when the Liberals were last in power. In fact, there was every reason to assume this would not happen. Liberals had been disappointingly lukewarm on Home Rule since the 1890s. It was not a vote winner with the strongly imperialist electorate in Britain. It was not going to get past the House of Lords and, if it were to become a manifesto promise that the Lords defeated, it would mean the end of the government. Some Liberals believed it had deprived them of a sustained period in office for twenty years.

One of those who shared that belief was Herbert Henry Asquith, the new chancellor of the exchequer in 1906. He was on record in 1901 as saying that the Liberal Party should never again go into government while depending on Irish MPs. He was vice-president of the Liberal League, a group established to promote anti-Home Rule views in the party. In the run-up to the 1906 election he told Herbert Gladstone, son of the late prime minister, 'If we are to get a majority … it can only be by making it perfectly clear to the electors that … it will be no part of the policy of the new Liberal government to introduce a Home Rule Bill.' The views of Asquith prevailed and became the policy of the new government. There was not going to be a third Home Rule Bill. Instead, the government would move 'step by step'.

The first step was the Irish Council Bill, which would establish a body, partly nominated by the British government, to administer eight of Ireland's forty-five government departments. This body would have no legislative or tax-raising powers. Introducing the bill in May 1907, Augustine Birrell, the chief secretary, commended it to the House of Commons because there was in it no 'touch or a trace, a hint or a suggestion of any new legislative power or authority'.

Redmond and his party leadership hesitated in their response while Griffith fulminated against the British and the IPP in his newspaper, *Sinn Féin* (the successor to the *United Irishman*), and seemed to capture the mood of the whole country, apart from the unionist northeast. It was an insult, he declared. He demanded that the Parliamentary Party withdraw from Westminster. Feelings were running high in the IPP too, with some members supporting Griffith. At a party meeting five of Redmond's MPs actually proposed a resolution backing Griffith's Sinn Féin policy, and at a party convention a proposal using Griffith's description of the bill as an 'insult' was put forward but defeated. The IPP had no alternative but to reject the bill. The British government dropped it in June.

Redmond and his party had misjudged the mood of the country. For Sinn Féin here was evidence that Redmond and his men had been too long at Westminster and were out of touch. They did not appreciate the growth of national consciousness that had developed, particularly among young people. They had underestimated the feeling of outrage that the Irish Council Bill had aroused in many quarters.

In response to this bill and consequent disarray in the Parliamentary Party, John O'Meara MP resigned the whip and CJ Dolan MP offered to resign his seat and fight a by-election in his Leitrim North constituency as a supporter of the Sinn Féin policy. He thus gave Sinn Féin a powerful publicity boost but he also thrust an election upon it. Griffith had never envisaged Sinn Féin as a political party taking on the IPP, but now Sinn Féin would have to fight a by-election in one of the IPP's strongest areas in the full glare of national attention. The precedents were not good. The last time separatists had challenged the Parliamentary Party was when John MacBride stood in the 1900 Mayo South by-election, caused by Michael Davitt's resignation. He was slaughtered six to one in a low poll.

Dolan delayed his resignation and the Leitrim North by-election took place in February 1908. In effect, however, the campaign had lasted eight months from June 1907. Sinn Féin organisers, mainly IRB men led by Bulmer Hobson and Sean MacDermott, had arrived in Leitrim almost immediately Dolan declared his intention to resign. A cheque for £100 duly arrived from John Devoy in America. Griffith used his propaganda skills to the full, pouring out thousands of words in *Sinn Féin* and in Dolan's local paper, the *Leitrim Guardian*, specially funded and published by Sinn Féin in Manorhamilton for the duration of the campaign. They spent £250 on it. Altogether, Sinn Féin spent over £700 on the by-election, a massive sum of money at a time when the average weekly wage for a skilled worker was £1.75.

The IPP took the challenge seriously. The campaign was ferocious. Sinn Féin workers were attacked as anti-clericals and a danger to Catholicism. Special attention was paid to Bulmer Hobson, who had to face accusations, one true, that he was a Quaker from 'the black north', but the rest were inventions: that he was 'a lay preacher down from Belfast to proselytise the people of Leitrim', he was 'from the Salvation Army', he was 'an Orangeman', he was 'against Catholic education'. And that was mild compared to the vituperation heaped on Dolan himself.

Verbal abuse was the least of it. Election meetings, both indoors and outdoors, often became battles royal. Joe Devlin, the MP for the Falls constituency of West Belfast, sent some of his own heavies from Belfast to support the IPP candidate, Patrick Meehan. At Kiltyclogher a band supporting Dolan arrived at a meeting of Meehan's supporters and rendered proceedings inaudible with their music. Meehan's supporters attacked them and damaged their instruments. Sinn Féin had brought Parnell's sister, Anna, to boost its campaign. Along with Dolan and George Gavan Duffy she was pelted with muck and rotten eggs at a meeting in Drumkeerin. Someone threw a bucket of water over Anna Parnell and Gavan Duffy was hit with a stick. His hat was destroyed but it saved his cranium. On the day before polling Dolan himself hit one of the Belfast men in a polling station.

The result was an overwhelming victory for the IPP, which got 73% of the vote. Even so, Sinn Féin was genuinely delighted with its 27% share. Griffith argued strongly that the number of unionists who voted for Meehan to save him from Sinn Féin showed Sinn Féin was the real nationalist party and a bigger threat to the union than Redmond's party. The unionist *Irish Times* agreed with Sinn Féin's conclusion.

The Leitrim North by-election result was the height of Sinn Féin's electoral success before 1917. In other words, at one of the lowest points in the IPP's political fortunes, Sinn Féin had failed to knock a dent in the party, let alone capture a seat, even with a former MP as its candidate. Sinn Féin's delight at garnering just over a quarter of the poll was more a case of relief at avoiding the humiliation it feared. It didn't fight any other by-elections. It stuck to local government in Dublin.

Since 1905 Sinn Féin had been winning seats on Dublin Corporation and Poor Law Boards. By 1906 there were six Sinn Féiners on the Corporation. In 1907 Sinn Féin brought its total of councillors to nine, a significant result because voting in Corporation elections was mainly restricted to ratepayers, a substantial proportion of whom in the capital were Protestants, unlikely Sinn Féin voters.

The following year Sinn Féin won in the working-class wards of Usher's Quay, Merchant's Quay and North Dock, giving it twelve members out of a Corporation of sixty councillors and twenty aldermen. Some of the Sinn Féiners cutting their political teeth in the Dublin tenements would later emerge on the national stage. They included Seán T O'Kelly, the future Irish president, who was elected to the Corporation in 1906, and WT Cosgrave, leader of the Free State government from 1922, elected for Usher's Quay in 1909.

With uncanny similarity to Sinn Féin's campaigns in Dublin in the 1980s, the Sinn Féin council members' approach in 1907 was a mixture of populism, opportunism and their own distinctive brand of Irish Irelandism. They worked hard to improve conditions in the tenements by insisting on repairs; they opposed the power of publicans, the so-called 'whiskey ring', on the Corporation; they publicised the names of councillors who owned tenements; they supported education initiatives and promoted the purchase of Irish goods and services and the use of the Irish language, including having the city's dust carts carry information in Irish on their sides.

While all this work did nothing to promote Sinn Féin's prospects nationally, it did lay the foundation for the party that emerged in the capital in 1917. By 1907 Sinn Féin was a force to be reckoned with in Dublin. People in Dublin knew about the party, had voted for it and had seen it in action at a local level. They knew what it stood for in practical terms. All the activities of its councillors received continuous and exuberant support from Griffith in the columns of *Sinn Féin*, which served to enhance their reputation and keep them in the public eye. The belligerent noises its members made, their unambiguous populism, their virulent Anglophobia, backed up by Griffith's propaganda and the hostility the Dublin Castle authorities exhibited towards Sinn Féiners, led Dublin's citizens to conclude immediately, and wrongly, that Sinn Féin was behind the 1916 Rising.

Outside Dublin the party's fortunes sagged pitifully after 1908 and membership slumped. By 1908 only 581 individual members had paid their shilling and nearly half of them lived in Dublin. Sales of *Sinn Féin* sank back from a high of 65,000 to the 30,000 which had been the normal sales for the organ of advanced nationalism since 1900. The inexorable pattern of the years before 1917 was taking shape. The IPP and Sinn Féin were at opposite ends of a political see-saw. As one rose up, the other plunged down.

In 1909 attention returned to Westminster where the Liberal government was about to take on the House of Lords. Although the issue was the budget, the power of the Lords was a crucial matter for everyone interested in politics in Ireland. If the Lords' power was broken, then there would be nothing to prevent Home Rule being enacted. So people believed. In these circumstances there didn't appear to be much mileage in Griffith's policy of abstention from Westminster. On the contrary, there seemed every reason to have the strongest possible Irish party in there to support the Liberal government in their contest against the peers.

If the British electorate endorsed the Liberals in their confrontation with the Lords then the way was clear to Home Rule, or so it seemed.

Curtailing the Lords' powers was to require two general elections in 1910, the first to obtain a mandate for overruling the Lords on budgets and the second to obtain a mandate to remove the Lords' power to throw out government bills and instead allow them merely to delay them.

All the indications were that the Liberal government was facing a close contest with the Conservatives in the election in January 1910. Irish voters thought Asquith needed all the help he could get. The standing of Redmond's party was transformed. Redmond exercised the constitutional version of 'England's difficulty is Ireland's opportunity'. He threatened to repeat Parnell's ploy of 1885 and advise every Irishman in England not to support the Liberals unless Asquith committed the party to Home Rule. After much soul-searching, Asquith did so. The results of both elections of 1910 left John Redmond holding the balance of power in the House of Commons. Irish MPs would decide who would be British prime minister. There would be a Home Rule act.

Sinn Féin had no role to play in any of this. Home Rule was not its goal. It was the antithesis of everything it stood for. Wisely, Sinn Féin stood aside from the two general elections in January and December 1910. Unfortunately for Griffith's policy, Redmond's close involvement in the British parliament between 1909 and 1911 seemed to demonstrate all the shortcomings of abstention and to prove that Westminster was exactly where Irish MPs should be. Sinn Féin appeared to have got it just plain wrong.

In 1910, as the spotlight focused on Westminster and the role of the Irish MPs there, Sinn Féin rapidly began to fall into its component parts again. Rumours of contacts between Arthur Griffith and William O'Brien, the Cork-based nationalist MP who led the All-for-Ireland League, incensed the IRB men on Sinn Féin's executive. Bulmer Hobson and PS O'Hegarty feared that there might be some kind of electoral pact in the air and a major row broke out.

It is obvious from various accounts that some members of Sinn

Féin's executive were interested in finding a way to influence what were certainly decisive events in Westminster. The alternative appeared to be oblivion for the movement. The outcome of the dispute was a victory for the IRB men: the executive voted against any compromise in their position. It was symptomatic of the movement's serious decline that during the feverish political excitement of 1910's two elections Sinn Féin expended its energy on arguments about who said what at which executive meeting. The Sinn Féin *ard fheis* in the Mansion House in October 1910 was a sad affair. Attendance was small. Finding candidates to go forward for the executive was a problem. IRB members drifted away. It seemed that the party was going nowhere.

It would be possible to show that Sinn Féin activity continued uninterrupted after 1910. Arthur Griffith was as ebullient as ever. His newspaper appeared regularly and his pen never faltered. Yet it was all very much a case of keeping up appearances. The comings and goings of the few activists who continued to support the Sinn Féin policy from 1911 to 1916 were no more than a pale reflection of the movement in the years 1905–8.

The IRB had set up its own newspaper, *Irish Freedom*, which in 1912 claimed that Sinn Féin was temporarily suspended because 'some of its leaders [thought] that they could collar the middle classes and drop the separatists; but when the separatists were dropped there was no movement left.' The RIC agreed. According to police reports, Sinn Féin branches all over the country were dormant. There was no *ard fheis* in 1913.

Griffith and his immediate followers were back to where they had been in 1905: Sinn Féin was a Dublin-based ginger group made up of intellectuals with a few wealthy backers. Instead of Moran's sneer that Sinn Féin was a 'Green Hungarian Band', it was now more like a one-man band. Never was PS O'Hegarty's epigram, 'Arthur Griffith, the man who was Sinn Féin', more true. Yet three years later Sinn Féin was sweeping the country outside the northeast. How did it happen?

As Griffith admitted to Æ[1] in 1912, 'If a good Bill accepted by Ulster had been introduced, I and my party would have disappeared from Ireland. Nobody would have listened to us.' The whole country outside Ulster united in support of the Home Rule Act the British government had at last passed. It was due to come into operation in 1914, when the two-year delay imposed by the House of Lords expired. In reaction, the Ulster Volunteer Force (UVF), a unionist militia, was established by the Ulster Unionist Council in January 1913 to resist Home Rule. In imitation, the Irish National Volunteers (INV), founded by Eoin MacNeill, came into existence in November 1913 to defend Home Rule, though how this would be done in practice was never too clear. Their real aim was to intimidate the British government into forcing Ulster unionists to accept Home Rule just as the Ulster Volunteers set out to intimidate the British into dropping Home Rule. By summer 1914 both sets of Volunteers, north and south, had acquired weapons.

However, for a minority of separatists in the Irish National Volunteers, led by IRB men, Home Rule was not enough. They saw in a substantial body of armed men the opportunity to demand more than Home Rule. They wanted independence, full stop, which was going beyond what Griffith's Sinn Féin advocated.

When the First World War broke out, the separatists in the Irish National Volunteers, led by Eoin MacNeill, whose idea it had been to establish the Volunteers in 1913, resigned at the prospect of supporting Britain in the war, much less fighting for Britain as John Redmond proposed. They called on likeminded Volunteers to join them in a new armed body. Only about 10,000 out of an estimated total of over 180,000 Volunteers seceded. They called themselves the Irish Volunteers as distinct from the larger body, which retained the title Irish National Volunteers, or National Volunteers.

It is at this point, in autumn 1914, that the first germ of evidence emerges to explain how Griffith's moribund Sinn Féin was transformed by 1917. People immediately began to call the breakaway group the 'Sinn

Féin' Volunteers. As early as 5 October 1914, almost as soon as the Irish Volunteers were established, the Redmondite *Freeman's Journal* referred in disparaging terms to the small turnout of 'the Sinn Féin' Volunteers in Limerick.

For some years the description 'Sinn Féin' had been reserved as a term of abuse and derision, a generic term for any person or organisation that espoused extreme nationalist views or expressed anti-English senti-ments. The Redmondites' use of the term 'Sinn Féin Volunteers' refers to the fact that the Volunteers wanted Ireland to refuse to play a role in 'England's war' – indeed, they were 'Sinn Féin' in the sense of demanding Irish self-reliance and separatism in the country's attitude to the conflict. But they were not in any sense organised by the Sinn Féin movement, which, by 1914, was skeletal.

It should also be said that many people, not just Redmondites, would have found it difficult to distinguish the public utterances and actions of prominent Sinn Féiners from those of the leaders of the new Irish Volun-teers. Writing in *Sinn Féin* in 1913, Arthur Griffith had welcomed the formation of MacNeill's Irish National Volunteers. In 1914 he supported the breakaway Irish Volunteers and, along with other Sinn Féin support-ers, he joined them. However strident the nationalist rhetoric of Irish Vol-unteer leaders, they would be unlikely to outdo Griffith. He took part in the Howth gunrunning in 1914 when rifles for the Irish Volunteers were landed and carried into Dublin, causing a confrontation with British troops that resulted in four dead and thirty wounded. Needless to say, the reactions of both Sinn Féin and Irish Volunteers to this incident were identical.

Anyone reading *Sinn Féin* after 1914 could have been forgiven for thinking, despite the wartime censorship, that it was the journal of the Irish Volunteers. There was little to separate the warlike vocabulary in Griffith's columns from the speeches of prominent Volunteers like Padraig Pearse. The identity of outlook was reinforced by the way the Irish Volunteers' membership overlapped with the IRB, Sinn Féin, the

Gaelic League and other Irish Ireland-type clubs. IRB people and Sinn Féin supporters socialised together in Dublin. Why wouldn't they? Many of Dublin's Sinn Féin members were also IRB members.

Since in both popular and official mindsets the Irish Volunteers were 'the Sinn Féin Volunteers', and since there was nothing to distinguish the published positions of the two organisations on the war, the Easter Rising in April 1916 was immediately called the 'Sinn Féin Rising'. *The Irish Times* mentioned 'the "Sinn Féin" insurrection' as early as 28 April, the day before the Volunteers surrendered. Asquith referred to them as 'Sinn Féiners' on 3 May. That can only be because the advisers he was listening to were also describing them in that way.

Kathleen Clarke, the widow of Tom Clarke, writing in 1943 still resented the description 'Sinn Féin Rising':

> This was not correct; the organisation then called Sinn Féin was not a revolutionary one, and had been very nearly defunct. It had very little to do with the Rising. Arthur Griffith, its president, had been one of those who had decided with [Eoin] MacNeill and others, to send out countermanding orders to stop the Rising which had been planned and carried through by the IRB, with the Irish Volunteers, Cumann na mBan and the Citizen Army. I resented it being referred to as a Sinn Féin Rising.

She believed (wrongly) that the Irish Parliamentary Party was responsible for the description, using it to discredit the Rising. Strangely, however, when she was arrested with a group of women after the Rising, they described themselves to their captors as 'Sinn Féiners'.

Once Dublin Castle, officialdom, the RIC and the press had decided it was 'the Sinn Féin Rising', the description stuck. Sinn Féin, with its dozen or so councillors and its newspaper, would have been the only separatist organisation known to the civilian administration in Dublin Castle that had any political presence in Dublin. To the Castle it just was not feasible that a historical relic, the IRB, had organised the Rising. It must have been the 'Sinn Féin Volunteers'. For the first time Sinn Féin had been officially tied to violence; a tie that was to last a long time.

Certainly the 'Sinn Féin Volunteers' were blamed both by the British Army and by a section of the population of Dublin for the Rising and the death and destruction in the city. The conventional view has been as follows: the Volunteers were reviled by the people of Dublin and there was, according to Redmond, a feeling of 'detestation and horror'. This initial feeling was swept away in the great sea change that occurred after the executions of the leaders of the Rising and the arrest and internment of over 3,000 men across Ireland in the summer of 1916. The wave of outrage and sympathy which these arrests produced across the country has been well documented. Sinn Féin became the chief beneficiary of this transformation of public opinion because Sinn Féin was the name everyone associated with the Rising.

Recent research contests this simplistic view. Professor Joe Lee of University College Cork has shown that in working-class areas of Dublin especially there was widespread support for the rebels. Lee quotes AM Bonaparte-Wyse, a pro-Union civil servant, writing on 28 May 1916 of 'a very menacing tone among the lower classes who openly praise Sinn Féiners for their courage and bravery. The sympathies of the ordinary Irish are with Sinn Féin. They want independence ...' There is also evidence from British officers of strong support in working-class areas of Dublin. In January 2001 the British Public Record Office released a War Office report dated June 1916, prepared for the prime minister Herbert Asquith, which showed that the Dublin Metropolitan Police considered North King Street 'a nest of Sinn Féiners'. General Sir John Maxwell, the British commander, told the *Daily Mail* that his men 'tried hard to get the women and children to leave the North King Street area; they would not go; their sympathies were with the rebels ...' It is unlikely that North King Street was the only street in Dublin whose residents felt that way.

Professor Lee has also shown that the route along which the rebels were marched to Dublin port, particularly Northumberland Road, where they were famously reviled and spat upon, was largely inhabited by middle- and upper-class Protestants whose furious reactions would have been predictable. It was probably selected as a safe route for the British soldiers to take their prisoners. Lee has also pointed out that the Catholic servants of those large houses may not have shared the opinion of their employers: there is no way of knowing. Still, it can be said that Northumberland Road was not representative of Dublin.

What is quite certain from the most recent evidence is that, in many parts of the inner city, no startling transformation in public opinion was required for people to become strong adherents of Sinn Féin. People may not have understood the niceties of a dual monarchy versus a republic but they knew that the words 'Sinn Féin' meant independence and they supported it.

No one will ever know the full extent of support for Sinn Féin at the time of the Rising. Military censorship, introduced on the day of the Rising itself, makes the task even more difficult. In any case, few newspapers appeared in the fortnight after the Rising. While it is impossible to quantify the support for the insurrection, what can be said is that the conventional view that opposition to it was total is far from the truth. The sort of insight provided by historians like Professor Lee makes it easier to explain where the open support for the rebels, evident within a month, came from. It was not simply caused by the arrests and executions and the brutality of British troops in some parts of Dublin, though those elements obviously produced a surge of anti-British emotion. It had existed beforehand.

Pretty soon it became fashionable for young men to be 'in Sinn Féin' even if they had never been interned. Better still, of course, to have been interned, though paradoxically most of those interned were not 'in Sinn Féin'. Michael Laffan cites a letter from a University College Dublin student on 8 June 1916 to a prisoner in England: 'You have all become great heroes now. You never saw such wholesale conversion. There are not half a dozen people in the College now who are not Sinn Féiners. You should see us all now sporting republican flags down Grafton Street.' Another student wrote to the same prisoner to assure him the girls in UCD were only interested in men interned after the Rising. 'The very least of us wouldn't be bothered with those that are left. An ordinary "beardless boy" has no attractions for us now.'

With hindsight it is clear that Home Rule was a dead duck by July 1916 despite a last-ditch attempt to secure an agreement on the implementation of the 1914 Home Rule Act, which would involve partition of the six northeastern counties. The political strength of the IPP seeped away as Redmond made concession after concession, only to be abandoned by the southern unionists after he had made the dread decision to accept partition and had tried to inveigle northern nationalists into agreeing to it.

Sinn Féin did not immediately fill the gap left by the collapse of the IPP's policy. It was not possible for Sinn Féin to blossom into a national movement in 1916 for the very good reason that there was no Sinn Féin organisation in existence. The leaders of what did exist were in jail. Although there was still a Sinn Féin executive and a general council based in the movement's offices at 6 Harcourt Street, Dublin, they were of 1905 vintage and as bewildered by the events of Easter 1916 as most people in the country. None of them had any idea how to take advantage of the political capital with which the Rising had endowed the name Sinn Féin. It was the triumphant return of the 'Sinn Féin' prisoners, released for Christmas 1916, which transformed the movement's fortunes.

The returning prisoners found a country waiting for leadership and organisation. The prisoners themselves had been transformed. Internment had produced intense rage and resentment among those affected, prisoners and extended families alike. It had brought together men from all parts of the country and bonded them, even those innocent of any involvement in political conspiracy, into an organic unit. A chain of command had been established. The men had learnt about ideas and policies and techniques which became common to them all, instead of innovations devised and used in one place only. Everyone knew everyone else. If they had been in different jails they had heard on the grapevine about other men from their districts. They emerged from prison as members of an organisation with a sense of belonging and a sense of purpose.

They were still Volunteers, of course, not members of Sinn Féin, many of them despising Sinn Féiners as 'politicians', 'dual monarchists' and '1782ers'. They knew 1916 was not a 'Sinn Féin Rising'. By Christmas 1916 the Irish Volunteers were simply The Volunteers, Redmond's National Volunteers having gone to war or having been dissolved. The Volunteers returning from prison were republican to a man. One of their leaders most hostile to Sinn Féin was Michael Collins, who never lost an opportunity to denigrate '1782ers'. He wrote to Thomas Ashe in Lewes jail about how 'rotten' Arthur Griffith was on some points and told him, 'don't think Master AG [Griffith] is going to turn us all into eighty-two'ites'. Nevertheless, although they adopted a disparaging attitude to Sinn Féin and politics, it was the Volunteers who made Sinn Féin the political wing of separatism and shaped it into a national political party in 1917, but only after they had created it in their own image. They did so in the course of four by-elections that year: Roscommon North on 5 February; Longford South on 9 May; Clare East on 10 July; and Kilkenny City on 10 August.

Despite their electoral success it had been a hesitant start because in early 1917 there was still a general unwillingness on the part of separatists to fight elections. What was the point of it? They were opposed to the British system. They would not be going to Westminster anyway, especially not after what they saw as the perfidy surrounding the Home Rule Act. In any case the Volunteer leadership did not want Home Rule. Furthermore, many Volunteers preferred the prospect of military action to finish the work of Easter 1916 and wanted to concentrate on preparation for that. For them, politics achieved nothing.

What was attractive, though, was the chance to defeat and humiliate the despised Redmondites. Getting them out of the way proved the most important incentive for the young men in the Volunteers. It would clear the decks for the confrontation with the British. The campaigns in 1917 tended to be anti-Redmondite rather than anything else. In all the by-elections it was Volunteers who did the organising and campaigning, often appearing in uniform and armed.

The man who instigated the Roscommon contest was a volatile local curate, Fr Michael O'Flanagan, a political firebrand who had been a member of the Sinn Féin executive since 1910. In 1915, while the body of the old Fenian Jeremiah O'Donovan Rossa lay in state in City Hall in Dublin, O'Flanagan had delivered an impassioned oration that few confused with a sermon. He was regularly in trouble with the clerical authorities, especially after 1921 when he became one of the most outspoken diehards in anti-Treaty Sinn Féin.

O'Flanagan's proposal to fight a by-election in 1917 was itself controversial because of the wartime convention of giving a candidate from the sitting party a free run, which, of course, suited the IPP down to the ground. O'Flanagan, however, would not consider allowing the IPP any leeway. For him a by-election was a golden opportunity to put Sinn Féin's abstention policy into practice. But first he had to find a candidate. As with every other constituency in Ireland, Sinn Féin had no presence in Roscommon: there was a dearth of potential candidates in the county. Drafting in an outsider was a risk; a high-profile Sinn Féin candidate could not afford to lose.

O'Flanagan decided on Count George Noble Plunkett, the father of the executed rebel Joseph Mary Plunkett, a signatory of the 1916 Proclamation. Two other sons had also taken part in the Rising and had been jailed: impeccable credentials. It proved to be an inspired choice. Though the sixty-five-year-old Plunkett was not a member of Sinn Féin, he was respectable. A papal count, he was an art historian and an expert on Botticelli. He had no separatist qualifications at all. In fact, he had spent his whole life trying to find paid employment under the Crown. But the incontrovertible facts about his sons had erased all that. By 1917 Count Plunkett was as anti-British as Fr O'Flanagan could have hoped for.

The campaign itself exhibited all the features which would become commonplace in the other by-elections that year. (There were also striking similarities with Sinn Féin campaigns of the 1980s in the North of Ireland.) There was something new in the air. In those pre-TV days when newspapers were not filled with photos, few electors clapped eyes on the ageing Plunkett. Instead, what they saw was the youth, energy, vigour and commitment of the Volunteers campaigning for Plunkett. In comparison, the IPP's canvassers looked old, tired, disoriented and dispirited. If they did, it is because they were.

In Roscommon, even the elements conspired to accentuate the IPP's handicaps. The worst snowfall anyone could remember made electioneering extremely unpleasant. There was a big freeze; people and animals died. In the midst of all this the young Volunteers, icicles hanging from their hair, struggled along highways and byways, carrying shovels to dig themselves out of snowdrifts. By contrast, Redmond's teams of MPs and paid organisers sat in warm hotels. They were snowed in, unable to canvass, they said.

The result was a huge rebuff for Redmond: Plunkett beat his candidate two to one. Plunkett announced that he was going to abstain from Westminster, though he had been careful to remain ambiguous about that during the campaign.

Each by-election that followed in 1917 was a stepping stone for Sinn Féin. In Longford South the party got its first prisoner elected. It was also the first time the slogan 'Put him in to get him out' appeared on posters in Ireland. Again, the Volunteers had been unsure about fighting the election and whether to nominate a prisoner. Joseph McGuinness, who became the candidate, had not wanted to run. He was unhappy about getting involved in politics. Eamon de Valera, becoming ever more prominent in Volunteer counsels, was also against the move, probably because he thought a prisoner would lose. It was Michael Collins who pressed on with McGuinness's candidature against all opposition, including that of the candidate himself.

Collins was confident of the sympathy an imprisoned Volunteer would attract. He also wanted a Volunteer, not a proxy like Plunkett who immediately after his election had become politically uncontrollable. On the other hand, if Plunkett had lost, it would have been possible to disown him. Not so in McGuinness's case. Therefore, McGuinness had to win or the shiny new Sinn Féin bandwagon would shed a wheel. The campaign was predictably vicious, both verbally and physically. Sinn Féin propaganda threw everything at the Parliamentary Party, including the fact that they had supported the introduction of British Summer Time into Ireland, a measure designed to provide longer daylight working hours for the war effort.[2] Even so, the result was extremely close. Some believed the deciding factor was a statement attacking partition by the Catholic archbishop of Dublin, Dr William Walsh, published in the *Evening Herald* the day before polling. Displaying the sort of opportunism that makes other parties both hate and envy them then as now, Sinn Féin workers had copies of the statement printed on election day and distributed them to the voters, boldly claiming that it meant the Catholic Church supported Joe McGuinness. McGuinness squeaked in by thirty-seven votes on a recount.

But it was to be Sinn Féin's last narrow squeak in by-elections outside northeast Ulster before the 1918 general election. The next in the sequence, Clare East on 10 July 1917, became the most famous of the four, mainly because the Sinn Féin candidate was Eamon de Valera, the last surviving military commander of the 1916 Rising, but also because of the reason for the by-election. It was caused by the death in Belgium, at Messines on the Western Front, of John Redmond's brother, Major Willie

Redmond, and therefore set the two diametrically opposed views of Irish politics before the electorate.

Willie Redmond had obeyed his brother's injunction and had gone wherever the 'firing line extended'. He had subscribed entirely to the idea that absolute loyalty to the British war effort was the only way to persuade British politicians that Ireland could be trusted with Home Rule. It had to be publicly demonstrated that Home Rulers were as loyal and trust-worthy as Ulster unionists. Like thousands of others, he paid with his life.

By the time Willie died, the sacrifice of people like him and the policy of his brother to show Ireland's trustworthiness in time of adversity had been fatally undermined by the actions of men like de Valera, who repudiated the idea that Irishmen should fight 'England's war'. Instead they followed another tradition, which dated back at least to the seventeenth century, that saw England's difficulty as Ireland's opportunity. Now the voters of Clare East were to be given the chance to endorse one or other of the policies.

By the time of the by-election, the third of the year, Sinn Féin had made enormous strides in popularity. It was now 'safe' to support it. Many of the younger clergy had come out openly on its side. There were sixty priests at the Sinn Féin convention that nominated de Valera two days before he was released from jail. Four parish priests and three curates nominated him. Although eight parish priests and one curate were among the nominators of his opponent, Patrick Lynch, this was only to be expected, given the long-established links between the Catholic Church and the IPP. What was new was the enthusiasm of the younger clergy for Sinn Féin, remarkable in this case for a man imprisoned for his part in a violent insurrection.

The timing of de Valera's nomination was opportune because it enabled him to make a triumphant arrival into the constituency sur-rounded by uniformed Volunteers who also acted as marshals to control the crowds. Throughout the campaign the Volunteers played the dominant role. Uniformed Volunteers marched, held band and torchlight parades, organised church-gate meetings after Mass and generally swaggered about the constituency. They ostentatiously took over the role of the RIC. Many of them were armed. They seemed to have access to unlimited resources. The icing on the cake was the support of the county paper, the *Clare Champion*. De Valera won with 71% of the vote, a ringing endorsement not only of him personally, but of Sinn Féin as a movement over the IPP.

When it came to the Kilkenny by-election in August the IPP was thoroughly demoralised. Few of its MPs bothered to turn up to campaign. WT Cosgrave, one of the party's most experienced Dublin councillors, stood for Sinn Féin. He possessed all the proper credentials required by now for successful Sinn Féin candidates. He had fought in the Rising as vice-commandant in the South Dublin Union garrison and had been sentenced to death. With the sentence commuted to life imprisonment, he had been jailed in Frongoch until amnestied in June 1917. As in Clare, the Volunteers did the campaigning, helped now by the new Sinn Féin MPs who came to Kilkenny to make seditious speeches on Cosgrave's behalf. The authorities stood by, powerless, though not powerless enough to give Sinn Féin a boost by the typically silly action of banning the local newspaper, the *Kilkenny People,* for its apparently pro-Sinn Féin coverage. Cosgrave won by a margin of two to one.

Now Sinn Féin had four abstentionist MPs with the prospect of as many more as there were by-elections available. In the meantime, while the attention of the public and the press had been focused on the by-election campaigns in different parts of the country, a grim struggle was taking place behind the scenes for control of the separatist movement. For the most part it was very polite and conducted in a genteel manner, but it was a serious affair.

Count Plunkett's victory in February had quickly gone to his head. He turned out not to be the mere figurehead Fr O'Flanagan had imagined. Naturally he was fêted in many places as the man who had knocked the first dent in the IPP and was generally treated as a person of importance. He got carried away. He saw himself as the leader of separatism. In March 1917 he called representatives of various separatist-leaning groups, including Sinn Féin and the IRB, to a meeting in his house in Kimmage, Dublin, to work out an agreed position.

Plunkett thought he was the obvious candidate for leader. He forgot or ignored Griffith's years at the head of Sinn Féin and clearly had no idea of the extent of the IRB organisation or the political pedigree of the people he was dealing with. For the IRB it was out of the question that Plunkett should lead anything. The IRB, with thousands of Volunteers now at its disposal, was going to lead, and the organisation they had chosen to lead the political charge was Sinn Féin. Sinn Féin was the name with kudos. The only concern the IRB leaders had was to ensure that Sinn Féin adopted a republic as its aim and jettisoned the airy-fairy dual monarchy nonsense. With Griffith still the leader of Sinn Féin, there was some anxiety among senior figures in the Volunteers, like Collins and de Valera, that what they considered to be the politicking, compromising, accommodating Sinn Féin would be in a position to influence Volunteer policy. They set themselves to prevent it.

Over the next six months, as Seán Ó Faoláin put it years later, the IRB captured Sinn Féin. By the end of 1917 the organisation called Sinn Féin bore no resemblance to the one which had emerged in 1905.

Oblivious to the determination of the Volunteers' leaders to run the show, and the fact that they controlled thousands of men, Plunkett continued his efforts to win control of the separatist movement. In April 1917 he called a convention at the Mansion House where he soon found himself overwhelmed. A committee was established to coordinate the efforts both of radical separatists who wanted a republic and the moderate separatists who wanted the Sinn Féin dual monarchy policy to prevail.

The Mansion House coordinating committee was enlarged to

include Michael Collins, Rory O'Connor, Eamon de Valera, WT Cosgrave and Countess Constance Markievicz, who were all hardline republicans at that time. The expanded committee formed a temporary executive of Sinn Féin, operating out of the movement's offices at 6 Harcourt Street until an *ard fheis* in October when a new constitution would be voted on. Given the membership of that executive, there could be little doubt of the outcome: Griffith and the dual monarchists were in a minority on the executive of what had been their own movement. They had no access to the legions of Volunteers controlled by the IRB who would be sending delegates to the convention. While Griffith was to remain president of Sinn Féin, and the movement would retain its dual monarchy policy until the *ard fheis* in October, it was certain that Griffith and his 'Hungarian policy' would be challenged at that *ard fheis* by the newly confident and numerous supporters of a republic. Moderation had gone out the window in the euphoria of 1917.

As it turned out, a challenge to Griffith proved unnecessary. Naturally, Griffith himself could see the writing on the wall but it was also true that he genuinely respected de Valera's abilities. It seems that they agreed between them, at a café in Grafton Street, who would be leader of Sinn Féin – rather in the manner that Tony Blair and Gordon Brown settled the leadership of the British Labour Party after the death of John Smith. Griffith agreed to support de Valera.

The constitution and aims of the movement proved a much more difficult hurdle. Griffith struggled to keep his beloved dual-monarchy plan in the running. He and his 'old Sinn Féiners' believed strongly that making the demand for a republic explicit in the party's documents would alienate unionists in the north forever. They also believed that a more intractable problem would be Britain's total refusal to countenance any such proposition and the inevitable confrontation that would ensue. In the run-up to the convention, arguments on this issue went on for days and nights. For their part, people like Eamon de Valera, Rory O'Connor,

Cathal Brugha, Countess Markievicz and Michael Collins were determined that a republic would be the goal. Volunteers had sworn allegiance to the republic, believed it had been established on 24 April 1916 and were prepared to fight for it. Griffith must have known he would have lost a vote on the issue.

The prospect was that there would be over 1,700 delegates at the *ard fheis* representing clubs from all over Ireland. Overwhelmingly males between the ages of eighteen and forty, they would tend to have been on the receiving end of the Crown forces' attentions in 1916 and 1917. Substantial numbers would have been interned. They were unlikely to have gone along with any proposal to dilute the demands of the 1916 Proclamation. Most believed they owed it to the dead of Easter Week to put their ideals into practice.

Again the issue was settled before the *ard fheis.* A compromise suggested by de Valera had been accepted by the Sinn Féin executive, on which he had a majority. The movement would declare its aim to be a republic and when independence had been achieved the Irish people would be asked in a referendum whether they wanted a dual monarchy or a republic. The convention endorsed the executive's recommendations on this and on the elaborate organisational structure for Sinn Féin, matters that many thought, and Dublin Castle hoped, would split the movement.

A new Sinn Féin emerged at the end of 1917 as a united national political movement with de Valera as president and Arthur Griffith and Fr Michael O'Flanagan as vice-presidents. Its structure set a pattern that the republican movement retained after 1921 and for the rest of the century. The new Sinn Féin was irrevocably tied to a military organisation, the Volunteers, which advocated the use of force to achieve its aims. Sinn Féin's leaders and three of its MPs were also leaders of the Volunteers. They often wore uniform. The dual-monarchy policy was dead. The new Sinn Féin demanded a republic. The ground had been cleared for the final contest with Redmond and his Parliamentary Party.

3. A DIFFERENT TUNE
Northern Nationalism

The north of the country marched to a different tune. Whereas most of Ireland voted repeatedly for Home Rule, northeast Ulster regularly returned around twenty unionist MPs to Westminster. In many parts of the province opposition to even the mildest Home Rule proposal was total. Any suggestion of republicanism could quickly provoke a violent response. The northeast was stony ground for Sinn Féin. The party did not exist there before 1917, and not only because of unionist hostility. The north was a political minefield. Northern nationalists trod warily through it. They faced particular problems in northeast Ulster, including opposition from the Catholic Church. However, after 1912, the main tenet of Arthur Griffith's project – abstentionism – held no attractions for northern nationalists as they grew increasingly concerned about partition. John Redmond's IPP dominated the nationalist political scene in the north and continued to enjoy support even in 1918 as the party collapsed elsewhere in the country.

The special problems caused by their geographical location among powerful opponents meant that Redmond's IPP tried to anticipate potential difficulties for northern nationalists when taking policy decisions. For this purpose Redmond relied on his lieutenant in the north, Joe Devlin, MP for Falls in West Belfast. To all intents and purposes,

northerners in the IPP were a distinct group with Joe Devlin as their recognised leader. Devlin predicted the hazards they might face and interpreted them for Redmond. As Ulster unionist opposition to Home Rule
became ever more strident and their demand for 'exclusion', that is, partition, grew ever more insistent, the problems of the northeast rose to
dominate Redmond's last years. In the end, Redmond's own urgent
political needs in 1916 led to his requesting his northern lieutenant to
consider partition, a request that resulted in the emergence of Sinn Féin as
a political force in Ulster and a split in northern nationalist politics which
remains to this day.

The different social, religious and economic structure of Ulster, and
particularly of its four northeastern counties, was produced by the
seventeenth-century plantation there of thousands of Scots and English
with the injunction to establish new towns defended by earthen fortifica-
tions called bawns. From the very outset, therefore, the planters created circumstances in which they felt surrounded by sullen, dispossessed natives.

Not all the incomers were planters. Before the seventeenth century
many people living in counties Antrim and Down were descendants of
immigrants from Scotland. For centuries there had been commerce,
intermarriage and migration between those counties and southwestern
Scotland, less than thirty miles away by boat, and Antrim and Down
avoided the plantation in the seventeenth century. But the Scots and
English who arrived in Ulster in the seventeenth century by whatever
means – plantation, migration or purchase – were different from their
predecessors in that they were members of a new religion: Presbyterian-
ism or Anglicanism. Unlike previous migrants, they were never to
become assimilated with the native population. Indeed, for the English
government the purpose of the plantation was that they should *not* be
assimilated but provide an English garrison to crush the sort of disloyalty
the Ulster Irish had shown in the last years of the reign of Queen Elizabeth I, from 1594 to 1603.

While there had been other plantations in the sixteenth century in different parts of the country, in the southwest for example, none was so dense or as well organised as that in Ulster; the others all failed. The result in the northeast was that a substantial population of people with a different language, different religion and a different set of loyalties put down roots in Ulster. In the four northeastern counties – Antrim, Down, Armagh and the new county, Londonderry, named to signify that London companies now owned the bulk of the land – planters' descendants eventually came to form the majority of the population, and in Tyrone and Fermanagh a substantial minority.

These circumstances meant that nationalism in Ulster developed into a different kettle of fish from that in the rest of nineteenth-century Ireland. The north of the country was not a homogenous Catholic society, as in the south, but a divided society where two cultures clashed, often violently. Expressing nationalist views was not a practice to be encouraged for people of a nervous disposition. For a start, people who held such views were a minority of a minority. Nationalist views were perceived as a threat to the stability of the land settlement, an attempt to undo the plantations of the seventeenth century.

People with nationalist sympathies watched events in the rest of the country with keen interest but initiated nothing themselves. It was too risky. Political nationalism in the north was an import from the south and was late arriving. When Home Rulers did arrive on the northern political scene they tended to come from southern counties. The first successful candidate, Tim Healy, was from Cork. Northern nationalist caution was evident in the 1885 general election. The Home Rule Party fielded thirteen candidates for Ulster constituencies, only three of whom lived in Ulster.

The arrival of Home Rule candidates produced immediate and predictable violence from Protestants who regarded it as an invasion of 'Protestant territory', a provocation and a threat. The response took the form of an all-class alliance, 'officered by the aristocracy', as Lord Salisbury, leader of Britain's Conservative Party, described it. The 'troops' were the Orange lodges organised in every nook and cranny of urban and rural northeast Ireland.

The instant formation of the all-class alliance came about because the Anglican aristocracy, together with farmers, businessmen and industrial workers of all Protestant denominations, regarded the extension of the vote in the 1884 Franchise Act as an instrument for overturning the privileges which had enabled them to dominate the country. Would Protestants, in a 60% majority in the northeast, agree to live on equal terms with the rest of the people on the island? To do so would automatically mean accepting their minority status on the island and placing their future in the hands of the Catholic majority. The instantaneous, unanimous answer was No.

The majority on the island wanted Home Rule, which the Protestant ascendancy in Ireland and the Protestant majority in the north viewed as a fundamental threat to their way of life. Although Home Rule would give paltry powers to any Irish assembly, the universal belief among Protestants was that it would set them on a slippery slope. As a minority on the island they demanded privileged political status. They believed that only this would enable them to survive as an ethnic group in a homogenous sea of Irish Catholics. The 1884 Franchise Act set the scene for the politics of the northeast of Ireland for the next century. While it gave clout to the Catholic majority in Ireland, it also magnified the power of the Protestant voters where they were concentrated in the northeast, particularly in the Belfast region.

The pro-union aristocracy and big business hurried to organise Protestants as 'unionists'. The means of defending their interests quickly became extreme. Belfast, the major centre of the Protestant population in Ireland, suffered repeated civil disturbances as Protestant mobs attacked the Catholic minority in the city. The unionist historian ATQ Stewart described the violence of 1886 in Belfast as 'so serious as to assume the character of a civil war'. Over thirty people died and many more suffered injury. Scores of homes were destroyed or damaged and twenty-eight Catholic-owned pubs in Protestant areas of west Belfast were attacked and several gutted.

The savagery was probably the result of the huge shocks to the Protestant psyche in the previous two years. In 1885 the first election to be held after the Franchise Act confirmed Protestants' worst fears, for the result left the Home Rule Party controlling the balance of power at Westminster. On top of that, to the horror and consternation of Protestants in Ireland, in December 1885 William Gladstone announced that he had been converted to Home Rule and would introduce a bill to that effect in 1886. For Protestants in Belfast the danger was brought home more immediately by the election of the first nationalist MP for Falls in West Belfast, Thomas Sexton.[1]

The net effect of the shocks of 1884–86 was the complete polarisation of the electorate in the north. The 1885 election destroyed the Liberal Party, which had enjoyed support from well-heeled Catholics and Protestants, particularly better-off Presbyterians. When Gladstone, the Liberal leader, opted for Home Rule, the ethnic imperative of preservation tipped virtually all Protestants into the Conservative camp. On the Catholic side, the emergence of the Home Rule Party committed to advancing Catholic aspirations meant that there was no point in northern Catholics voting Liberal. Catholics now had their 'own' Irish party and voting for it could mean controlling Westminster, which delivered more than Home Rule bills. It produced instant benefits at local level: their 'own' MPs.

There were other ways in which northern nationalists faced different circumstances from their compatriots in the rest of the island. As well as predictable opposition from unionists, nationalists had to face competition for Catholic votes from the Catholic Church. Elsewhere in Ireland the Catholic Church supported Home Rule and the IPP, but in the north the Church feared that confronting the Protestant majority would lead to disaster. Well-off Catholics in Belfast had set out to show the dominant Protestant community that Catholics presented no threat, wished to cooperate and could therefore be trusted. The Catholic Church in Belfast agreed with them. Its clergy believed that nationalism and support for its political manifestations would only provoke a violent reaction. For the successful businessmen and the clergy, nationalism invited exactly the sort of mayhem that had disfigured the city in 1886.

However, there was more to the division within the Catholic community than strategies for dealing with the Protestant community. The extension of the franchise in 1884 had opened up scope for class politics in what was a heavily industrialised city. Both the Catholic Church and Catholic businessmen viewed with dismay candidates who voiced 'socialistic' opinions. It took years of manoeuvring before the nationalist leader, Joe Devlin, who represented the poorest districts of Belfast, was able to wrest political leadership in the city from the Catholic Church and even then at the price of an alliance with the Church. By 1905 this alignment of Devlin and the Catholic Church had helped to widen and solidify the already gaping division between the communities not only in Belfast but in the north as a whole.

Similarly, on the other side of the fence, wealthy unionist factory- and mill-owners had forged unbreakable links with the Protestant working class through the Orange Order. The inflexible maxim was that any gesture towards amelioration in conditions for Catholics meant a corresponding diminution for Protestants and therefore must be resisted. As for constitutional change, such as Home Rule, which might benefit Catholics, Protestants believed it spelled doom for their community.

Against this background it is not difficult to see why republican politics were non-existent in the north. If parliamentary nationalists felt economically and physically vulnerable in Ulster, how much more dangerous must life have been for republicans? If nationalists were being attacked by the Catholic Church and Catholic businessmen and found it difficult to win elections at local level, what point would there be in republicans organising?

Republicans were faced with the fact that northern nationalists saw tangible gains in attaching themselves to the mainstream nationalist movement based in Dublin, which had always been overwhelmingly constitutional. Northern nationalists believed that only as part of a national movement could they exert leverage for their own benefit. Northern nationalist MPs could bring about change at Westminster by using the clout of the eighty or more Home Rule MPs. Ultimately, of course, the great goal was to be carried along in the slipstream of the Home Rule movement and to become part of the governing majority in the country. This is precisely what northern Protestants feared and why they fought so strenuously against it.

The conflict was sharpest in Belfast. In the first place, it was the largest centre of population in the north but, more importantly, it constituted the largest concentration of unionists on the island. For Home Rule to be implemented it would have to be forced through against the ferocious opposition of Belfast's Protestants. Concentration of population is important. Opposition to Home Rule was no less strong in rural areas where men could drill and march around Tyrone or Fermanagh to their hearts' content on the estates of Anglican aristocrats, but the marchers tended to live in isolated farms and small village communities. Communications were poor, making mobilisation slow. Rural unionists were also surrounded by pockets of nationalists and often outnumbered by them. In Belfast, by contrast, tens of thousands of unionist men lived packed into tiny streets. They could, and often did, pour out of these streets at a minute's notice, like an army, ready to engage in pitched battles with Catholics and, if necessary, the RIC or the British Army.

There was another even more important aspect to be considered by republicans. At the mercy of this concentration of Protestant opposition was a hostage community: the Belfast Catholics. For most of the nineteenth century, Belfast was the fastest-growing city in the United Kingdom. Its population grew from 19,000 in 1800 to 378,000 in 1911 when it constituted one-third of the population of the area of the present-day Six Counties. In that year Catholics made up less than a quarter of Belfast's population.

Any British government intent on coercing northern unionists had to face the prospect of hundreds of Catholics being killed in Belfast. The killings and burnings of 1886 were a demonstration of what was likely to happen. If there were such carnage as a result of a failed Home Rule Bill, what would happen if Home Rule were successful or likely to be successful? Anyone who doubts this outcome has only to look at the events of 1920–22 to see grisly evidence of the fate that awaited Belfast's Catholics when the city's Protestants felt threatened by political change. Because of the concentration of numbers, Belfast would always provide the most spectacular figures for death and destruction, but other Catholic 'hostage communities' in the northeast would also suffer in such circumstances: Lisburn, Dromore, Banbridge and, of course, Portadown, scene of the annual Drumcree riots from 1996 to 2000.

The fact that Protestants successfully stemmed the influx of rural Catholics into Belfast in the nineteenth century was the decisive reason Ulster unionists were able to intimidate the British government in the years after 1910. Belfast had become the 'capital' of Protestant territory in Ireland. Catholics were the immigrants, the incomers. As Professor Tony Hepburn of Sunderland University says, Catholics in Belfast after the middle of the nineteenth century were 'the Irish in Belfast' and treated like the Irish in Glasgow, Liverpool or Boston – a minority group in an industrial society in more or less hostile territory.

The reality was that control of Belfast and its surrounding area by armed unionists determined the destiny of the region. Was a British government really going to take on a city of almost 400,000 people, the majority of whom, on past evidence, were prepared to fight and many of whom, also on past evidence, were ready and willing to fall on the 25% minority in the city in the event of British coercion? Added to the horrific consequences of coercion, the British government knew after 1912 that it faced what was, in effect, an armed insurrection, supported for political advantage by senior members of His Majesty's Loyal Opposition.

Faced with the first evidence of Ulster unionists' resolve to resort to armed resistance, Winston Churchill, himself a victim of Belfast mobs for his espousal of Home Rule, wrote to John Redmond on 31 August 1913:

> I have been pondering a great deal over this matter, and my general view is just what I told you earlier in the year – namely, that something should be done to afford the characteristically Protestant and Orange counties the option of a moratorium of several years before acceding to the Irish parliament.

Given the lack of stomach for compulsion among politicians in Britain, which was shared by certain army officers in Ireland, the British government decided tacitly to recognise the Ulster Protestants as an ethnic minority in Ireland and to construct a political niche for them in the shape of the preferred solution at the time all over Europe and further afield: partition. Sinn Féin's answer to the question of Ulster unionism was the opposite of that of the British government: don't recognise the Ulster Protestants as a political minority. As for the question of how recognition could be avoided without bloodshed, Sinn Féin offered no answer. When the British did recognise the Ulster Protestants, Sinn Féin had no fallback position, any more than Redmond's IPP had when partition was first seriously mooted in 1912.

The great majority of Irish nationalists really believed that Ulster Protestants were being duped by their aristocratic landlords and the millionaire factory owners who provided employment in the mills. They believed northern Protestants had been deceived into believing their economic future would be jeopardised if Home Rule were enacted. They could not understand why Ulster unionists rejected, out of hand, the political and economic concessions Home Rulers offered.

Yet even in those concessions the leaders of nationalism, almost exclusively Dublin-based or of southern origin, betrayed their ignorance both of the north and of the mentality of northern unionists. In January 1914 Arthur Griffith laid out a detailed set of proposals to accommodate unionists in the north, including increased representation for Belfast and other urban centres in the north, increased representation for unionists and a guarantee of no tax on the linen trade without the consent of Ulster members.

While it must be pointed out that in 1914 Sinn Féin was in no position to offer anything to anyone on behalf of the Irish people, least of all to Ulster unionists, the details of Griffith's proposals are interesting for the mindset they reveal. If unionists feared for their economic future under Home Rule, then Sinn Féin believed they could demonstrate that there was no intention to discriminate against them. Any safeguards they wanted could be built in. However, the glaring omission in Griffith's proposals was any reference to shipbuilding and engineering.

Linen was still an important constituent of northern prosperity but it had been surpassed by Belfast's role as the biggest shipyard in the world. The city also had the biggest ropeworks in the world. A thousand ancillary metal workshops and foundries banged and clanged away night and day across the city. Engineering firms, like Mackies or the Sirocco works, clattered non-stop to build and export machinery for factories all over the British Empire, the shape and purpose of which machines were beyond the imagination of any of the thinkers and polemicists in Sinn Féin. Yet not a mention of any of this in Griffith's proposals. It was clear evidence that he quite literally had no idea what made the north tick. In this he was no different from any other southern politician.

If Griffith got it completely wrong on the economic front by omitting all reference to the main elements which provided the wealth of the north and made Belfast an integral part of Britain's industrial power, the omission of any reference to religious issues showed the complete lack of understanding among nationalists of the mainsprings of northern Protestant opposition to Home Rule. Here is Captain James Craig, MP, multi-millionaire industrialist, owner of five homes and later Northern Ireland's first prime minister, writing in the *Morning Post* in January 1911:

> Neither Mr Redmond nor the English people has any conception of the deep-rooted determination of the sturdy men and women of Ulster, or of the silent preparations that are being made to meet by armed resistance the encroachment on their civil and religious liberties that would naturally follow the establishment of a parliament in Dublin ... That sentiment has been doubtless strongly augmented by the number of kidnapping cases that have recently come to light consequent upon the Church of Rome decree put into full force with rigour in Ireland. [2]

> There are a very large number of people in other parts of the United Kingdom who are unwilling or unable to believe that Ulster will, if forced, adopt Lord Randolph Churchill's advice: 'Ulster will fight, and Ulster will be right'. Such steps will be taken when the proper moment arises as will convince those unbelievers and the whole of the British public that if the need arises armed resistance of the most determined character will be resorted to sooner than submit to the dominance of the Church of Rome, which any parliament in Dublin would spell to the people of Ulster.

Those sentiments provide some indication of the depth of opposition to Home Rule among wealthy and articulate opponents. Since those attitudes and the steely resolve of leading Ulster unionists to resist Home Rule with armed force were backed up by the Conservative leader Andrew Bonar Law, there was no likelihood whatsoever of Sinn Féin receiving a sympathetic hearing from any unionist. The very name 'Sinn

Féin' struck horror into unionists who, though ostentatiously ignorant of the Irish language, were fully aware of the meaning of the words. A party called 'Ourselves Alone' conjured up for unionists the worst ethnic and racial fears imaginable. For the majority of Ulster unionists, Home Rule, minimal as its provisions were, represented the thin end of the wedge. They believed the majority in Ireland would continue to work to broaden and deepen Home Rule's powers once they were enacted, and that English politicians would not bother to resist such developments.

Their opposition to Home Rule was not tempered in any way by the fact that, under the Home Rule arrangements, Ireland would still be an integral part of the United Kingdom with substantial representation at Westminster. Sinn Féin, which would put an end to that representation, was therefore anathema. In Sinn Féin's plans unionists would have no recourse to Britain, no appeal to the metropolitan centre against the dictates of Dublin. The last thing northern unionists wanted and what they feared most was being left 'alone' in Ireland. Foremost in their minds were the racial and ethnic fears they articulated in almost every speech opposing Home Rule. Some English conservatives shared these views. Lord Willoughby de Broke, an English peer, expressed such sentiments at Dromore, County Down, in September 1912:

> The Unionists of England were going to help Unionists over here, not only by making speeches. Peaceable methods would be tried first, but if the last resort was forced on them by the Radical government, the latter would find that they had not only Orangemen against them, but that every white man in the British Empire would be giving support, either moral or active to one of the most loyal populations that ever fought under the Union Jack.

Walter Long, the leader of Irish Unionism until Sir Edward Carson took over in 1910, provided a good example of unionist attitudes in a speech to the Ulster Unionist Council in January 1910:

> The Unionist Party in Ireland was united, confident and strong ...

> Home Rule for Ireland would mean the loss of individual liberty, the absolute insecurity of property, and the negation of everything they cared for affecting the welfare of the country … They had read in the press recently about the Nationalist conventions to select candidates, and how the police had to be called in to preserve order. Did anyone out of Bedlam suggest that the police should be handed over to the control of Nationalists?

Evidently nationalists would destroy their own country, did not care how it was governed and were incapable of self-control at any level.

Nationalist leaders based in Dublin at best underestimated such feelings, at worst were completely ignorant of them or simply remained in denial. Those who had some awareness of the depth of feeling could not bring themselves to admit that many northern unionists hated and feared them simply because they were Irish. Sinn Féin would point out that there were northern Protestants in Sinn Féin, the Gaelic League and the GAA. Were they not prominent in the IRB too? That failure to appreciate Ulster unionism's visceral antagonism to the concept of Irish self-determination runs through all Sinn Féin literature of the time.

Ignoring the ethnic and racial attitudes in unionism (which, incidentally, were a mirror image of those in Arthur Griffith's newspaper), Sinn Féin members instead concentrated on the economic fears of unionists, which were also very real and genuine. To unionists 'Ourselves Alone' was economic madness. The protectionist policies culled from the work of Friedrich List which Griffith advocated to promote native Irish industries were already out of date when List published them in the early part of the nineteenth century. They would have entailed unionists being cut off from the British Empire and its trade. Such policies must have seemed like lunacy to the wealthy, successful unionist tycoons in the north, experienced in the ways of commerce and industry. They might have seemed suitable for an agricultural society but spelt economic suicide for the industrial complex centred on Belfast. For all these reasons, the Sinn Féin movement conjured up a nightmare for unionists.

However, at the time of the Home Rule crisis in 1912, Griffith's Sinn Féin had no presence in the north. It was not until after a conference of nationalists in Belfast in June 1916 that unionists needed to pay any attention to Sinn Féin. Following the conference, northern nationalism split and support for Sinn Féin began to grow. It was a slow process because, even among the most advanced northern nationalists, there was unhappiness at the prospect of Sinn Féin's abstentionist policy. Only when the spectre of partition loomed did nationalists in the west of Ulster begin to drift to Sinn Féin. Even then it took time. Traditionally northern nationalists stuck together: disunity in the face of the local unionist majority meant a split vote at elections and more unionists elected.

The crisis for northern nationalists started when, at the behest of Lloyd George, John Redmond, frantically trying to salvage something in the aftermath of the Easter Rising, persuaded Joe Devlin to ask northern nationalists to consider temporary partition. Devlin organised a convention. Nationalist-elected representatives and Catholic clergy and notables, 776 of them, met in St Mary's Hall at the city-centre end of Belfast's Falls Road to argue it out. Devlin struggled might and main to have a resolution passed accepting 'exclusion' on a temporary basis. After a five-hour debate the resolution was passed 475–265. For his pains Devlin received a congratulatory telegram from Lloyd George and he split northern nationalists irrevocably.

Devlin faced strong opposition from representatives west of the Bann. They spoke for places with nationalist majorities where people heard with disbelief the suggestion that they might end up, even temporarily, in a unionist-controlled statelet. The leader of the opposition was FJ O'Connor, an Omagh solicitor and president of the Tyrone National Volunteers. He was supported by former MP George Murnaghan, chairman of Armagh District Council Thomas McLaughlin, and clergy from Tyrone, Enniskillen and Derry, including the Catholic bishop of Derry.

This group formed the Anti-Partition League, based in Omagh.

When nationalists in Belfast, Limerick and Dublin joined, the Anti-Partition League became the Irish Nation League. The League was strongly supported by clergy west of the Bann, especially in Tyrone and Derry and that part of Donegal that lay in the Derry diocese. The attempt to show that northern nationalists would accept even temporary partition had failed abysmally and it led to the destruction of the Parliamentary Party as the single united voice of nationalists in the northeast of the country.

Most northern nationalists hadn't paid much attention to the nitty-gritty of partition since 1914. They did not realise that Ulster unionists had rejected all options except one of two alternatives: no Home Rule or, if the British government forced Home Rule through, permanent partition for the six counties of Ulster, where Protestants were concentrated in the biggest numbers. By the end of summer 1916 it was clear there would be no Home Rule for the duration of the war since there were no terms for it that unionists would accept. What would happen after the war? Supporters of the Irish Nation League were not sure what they wanted but, rather like Oliver Cromwell, they knew what they were against, in their case partition, the concept of which Redmond's party had apparently accepted.

For many defecting from the IPP, the Nation League was a staging-post on the way to Sinn Féin. It was respectable. It included among its members elected representatives, professional men and senior clergy, people who had always opposed extremism of any kind, people who in the past had derided 'Sinn Féinism'. One priest put it brilliantly in the *Irish Independent* when he wrote, in an allusion to the Catholic definition of purgatory, that the Nation League was 'a place or state of punishment where some parliamentarians suffered before they joined Sinn Féin'.

Throughout 1917 support for Sinn Féin in the north gradually grew. It followed the lines of the division at the St Mary's Hall conference: west of the Bann, in Tyrone, Fermanagh, Donegal and Derry, the IPP began to disintegrate. In September 1917, emboldened by their by-election victories, de Valera, Griffith, Eoin MacNeill and other senior Sinn Féin figures toured the north, addressing meetings in Omagh, Carrickmore, Belfast, Newry and Armagh.

The younger clergy *en masse* took a strong anti-partitionist line and encouraged support for Sinn Féin. Other not-so-young clerical supporters were more influential. The parish priest of Omagh, Fr Philip O'Doherty, and Canon Patrick Keown, the parish priest of Enniskillen, both attacked 'Redmondism'. Fr O'Doherty became the leading clerical advocate of Sinn Féin in Tyrone. The bishop of Derry, Dr Charles McHugh, was also vehemently anti-partition. Being anti-partition did not make people automatically Sinn Féiners, but it was Redmond's party that was proposing that northern nationalists accept 'exclusion' and Sinn Féin that opposed it.

In September 1917 the Nation League merged with Sinn Féin, its inevitable destination. Those opposed to partition had only one political destination to head for. By the end of 1917 there were thirty-six Sinn Féin clubs in Tyrone, with over 2,000 members. Fermanagh had twenty-two clubs with 1,665 members.

Even so there were reservations. Abstentionism caused northern nationalists great *angst* because they feared it made partition more likely. FJ O'Connor, leading light in the Nation League and the most articulate northern anti-partitionist, had thought Count Plunkett's decision to abstain after winning the Roscommon by-election in 1917 was 'suicidal'. For northerners the primary aim was to avoid partition. By autumn 1917 the primary aim for Sinn Féin and the Volunteers in the rest of the country was an independent Irish republic. Many northern nationalists thought this so terrified unionists and affronted the British that it made partition the probable outcome. Only the apparent compromise on the question of a republic at the Sinn Féin *ard fheis* in October 1917 permitted the northerners to acquiesce in formally merging the Nation League with Sinn Féin. Six northern nationalists were appointed to the Sinn Féin executive.

All the same, many northern nationalists remained unconvinced. The string of by-election victories which set Sinn Féin on a roll in 1917 did not extend to the north, where Sinn Féin's first chance to challenge Redmond's party did not arrive until the Armagh South by-election in January 1918. It was an overwhelmingly nationalist constituency that had always been staunchly IPP – barren land for Sinn Féin.

The IPP were well organised. They decided to go for a quick election even though it meant short campaigning days in the dead of winter. They selected a good candidate, Patrick Donnelly, a well-known solicitor from Newry. The by-election exposed Sinn Féin's weakness in the north. The party could produce no local candidate and had problems finding any prominent northerner. All its senior figures were southern-based, and Sinn Féin had not set down roots east of the Bann. It had to move quickly and settled on Dr Patrick McCartan, a senior IRB man from Carrickmore in Tyrone. At the time he was Sinn Féin's representative in the USA and was practising in a New York hospital. Not only was he therefore completely unknown in the constituency, he was also from a rival Ulster GAA county – always a bad choice for a candidate in Irish politics. Finally, his duties in New York meant that he was unable even to present himself to the voters during the campaign. Perhaps this was just as well because he might have suffered physical injury.

The campaign was the most violent of all the by-elections fought in the years 1917–18. Both the IPP and Sinn Féin threw everything they had into the campaign. Joe Devlin and his supporters knew it was make or break. Sinn Féin had no MPs in Ulster and Devlin was determined to keep it that way. The IPP had lost four by-elections in a row. Armagh South was the place to stop the rot. For Sinn Féin it was an opportunity to break into the north, to demonstrate its national strength and power, win its fifth by-election in a row and perhaps give the Redmondites the *coup de grâce*.

Sinn Féin fought the election like a military operation. Uniformed Volunteer officers directed operations. They sent twenty cars into the constituency driven by Volunteers from as far away as Cork, Kerry and Clare and carrying licences permitting them:

> 'to drive and use a motor car in the performance of the duty assigned to him. In the name of the Irish Republic.'
> Signed Eamon de Valera.

As the Volunteers marched in ranks through the small towns of south Armagh they sang songs like 'Clare's Dragoons', which provoked showers of stones and other missiles from Joe Devlin's heavies sent by train from Belfast. Fist fights broke out in several towns, including Crossmaglen where the president of Sinn Féin, Eamon de Valera, was slightly injured on 30 January. In bigger confrontations the Volunteers preferred hurleys, while the Belfastmen opted for the style of engagement they were used to on their city's streets: eschewing hand-to-hand combat, they relied on a dense hail of bottles, metal and stones hurled from close range.

Neither side seems to have got the better of the other in the fighting. As for the voting, the nationalist candidate easily defeated Sinn Féin's Dr McCartan by two to one. McCartan later claimed it was an excellent result because he had first read of his nomination in a New York newspaper and did not find out the result until he read another New York newspaper report. Arthur Griffith got to work on damage limitation, explaining in numerous articles that the register was a 'stale register', five years old, and that all the unionists in the constituency had voted for Patrick Donnelly, the Newry solicitor, otherwise McCartan would have won.

But party members knew better. The issue in the election had been partition and Sinn Féin had no policy to deal with it. Certainly it had been unable to explain to people in a constituency earmarked for exclusion how abstaining from Westminster would prevent partition. It was a shock to be so heavily defeated after uninterrupted by-election triumphs since spring 1917. The registers in those by-elections had also been 'stale'. The issue in the north was different.

The difference was confirmed in the next Ulster by-election in Tyrone East. It was caused indirectly by the death on 6 March 1918 of John Redmond, the leader of the Irish Parliamentary Party for the past eighteen years. His son, William, a captain in the Irish Guards, decided to fight the by-election in Waterford City caused by his father's death. William had been MP for Tyrone East since 1910 but resigned that seat to fight the Waterford by-election.

In Tyrone East, Sinn Féin was faced again with all the same problems as in Armagh South. A dearth of northern candidates meant it selected one of its senior figures, Sean Milroy. He had been in Sinn Féin since the early days with Arthur Griffith and had fought in 1916, but in the constituency he was to contest he was an unknown outsider. Again, Joe Devlin led the IPP's campaign. Their candidate, TJS Harbison, was a clever choice, a man who had voted against partition at the St Mary's Hall conference. The voters knew he was against partition and also against abstention. The campaign followed much the same lines as in Armagh South and the result was the same. Harbison won by 1,802 votes to 1,222 votes.

In the meantime, Sinn Féin had also lost the Waterford by-election, the writ for which had been hastily moved by the IPP in the wake of their success in Armagh South. De Valera's thugs from Clare renewed their acquaintance with Devlin's Belfast thugs who had been brought in by train. This time the Belfast contingent's violent assaults were augmented by the efforts of Waterford people since the city had an unusually large number of men in the British Army and had a considerable stake in munitions work as well. There was also a substantial number of what were called 'separation women' who were receiving a regular income as a result of their husbands' service in the armed forces. The Claremen got short shrift in Waterford. On one occasion they were besieged inside the Sinn Féin club. On many other occasions Sinn Féiners suffered from the terrible accuracy of the Belfastmen's well-practised throwing arms. Captain Redmond was elected with 1,242 votes to 764. Sinn Féin had now lost three by-elections in a row, albeit for different reasons. The apparently unstoppable momentum built up in 1917 had ground to a halt by spring 1918.

It all left Ulster unionists cold. The internecine dispute between Home Rulers and Sinn Féin was of supreme irrelevance to them. By 1918 it was clear to unionists that the British government had recognised them as an ethnic unit. There was going to be partition of some kind. The area was going to comprise six counties and Lloyd George had intimated to Edward Carson, the unionist leader, that it would be permanent, although he had told John Redmond it would be temporary.

Neither nationalists nor Sinn Féiners had realised just how widespread this determination was in British political circles. Until the 1920 Government of Ireland Act was virtually on the statute book, Irish nationalists of all parties simply did not believe partition was going to happen and made no policy provision to deal with the eventuality. Even after its enactment in 1921 Sinn Féin leaders believed they could still negotiate as if it had not already happened or that its provisions could somehow be reversed after a successful outcome to negotiations between Britain and Ireland. During the whole period from 1916 to 1921 the fate of northern nationalists was literally the last thing the Sinn Féin leadership thought about.

4. A NATION ORGANISED

Sinn Féin takes Power, 1918–21

The years 1918–21 were momentous for Ireland. They were filled with drama and crisis and tragedy and triumph. For the people who lived through them, and for a great many others who did not, the events of those years defined their lives. It was a period that left an indelible mark on Irish politics.

People in Ireland used the 1918 British general election as a plebiscite in which they expressed national self-determination for the first time in history. They voted for independence and in 1919 proceeded to behave as if they had it. They established their own parliament, Dáil Éireann, a court system and an embryonic civil service. All those bodies struggled to operate against the background of guerrilla warfare waged by the Volunteers, soon known as the Irish Republican Army (IRA), and against a military campaign by the British Army, the Irish police and mercenaries known as the Black and Tans, aimed at suppressing the IRA and abolishing the newly established government institutions. Outside the northeast, the whole population was united behind the effort to achieve the independence people had voted for in 1918. They repeated the vote in 1920 and 1921. Then that unity was shattered, the population divided on the terms of the Treaty with Britain and civil war had broken out.

The Sinn Féin party organised in October 1917 under the

leadership of Eamon de Valera was the vehicle and political expression of national self-determination, the political movement that the Irish people chose for articulating their desire for independence. No other political party got a look in. As Professor David Fitzpatrick of Trinity College Dublin has said, 'There was a wonderful oneness about Irish politics.'

Not surprisingly, as the authentic expression of the opinion of the majority of Irish people, Sinn Féin reflected accurately the swings in the public mood. From unprecedented unity in 1918 and from being the single outward and visible manifestation of self-determination, the movement split in 1921 in a way that has affected Irish politics ever since. Other parties, particularly Fianna Fáil, and Sinn Féin in later incarnations, have sought to recapture that all-embracing, transcendent position occupied by the Sinn Féin movement of 1918–21. But it could never be recovered. It was a phenomenon peculiar to the circumstances, not some magical ideology that could be bottled and kept for use in future elections.

Sinn Féin entered 1918 as the fastest-growing political movement in Irish history. In fact, it was the fastest-growing national organisation of any kind there has ever been in Ireland. By the end of the year the party had scored the most tremendous electoral victory any party in Ireland has ever achieved. Three years later, by the summer of 1921, the Sinn Féin organisation had fallen apart, individual membership fees had been abolished and the party had been pushed aside by both Dáil Éireann and the IRA. How and why had this roller-coaster political ride happened?

In the spring of 1918 Sinn Féin membership had reached saturation point in many parts of the country. People flocked to join Sinn Féin and the Volunteers. In some villages almost all young men were either members of one or the other or both and many young women were members of Sinn Féin or Cumann na mBan or both. How many were in the party and who were they?

There were about 1,250 clubs nationwide at the end of 1917. During the spring of 1918 the total climbed to about 1,700. According to the RIC, Sinn Féin's membership went up 29% between March and May 1918. It is unlikely, though, that the total remained so high for long. Taking an average of 100 members per club, Dr Michael Laffan of UCD came to a total of between 120,000 and 130,000 for the party's membership. To give that figure some perspective, Britain's governing Labour Party had a membership of 300,000 in 2001 out of a population of almost sixty million, compared to Ireland's 4.4 million in 1918.

Sinn Féin's membership was not spread evenly across the country. Obviously, in some unionist parts of the northeast membership was zero. Even in Catholic areas of the northeast Sinn Féin was weak. The IPP remained the dominant force. At the end of 1917 there were only eight Sinn Féin clubs in Belfast with 780 members compared to 6,000 in the IPP's organisation, the United Irish League. West of the Bann, however, the trend in other parts of the country applied: Sinn Féin burgeoned.

The pattern in rural Ireland was that agricultural labourers and young men from small farms joined Sinn Féin. In towns, young working-class men joined the party; in both urban and rural areas many also signed up with the Volunteers. Often there was a complete overlap between membership of the two organisations. Volunteer companies marching through the streets during the day turned into Sinn Féin clubs at night. It would not be unusual for the same groups to turn into GAA teams on Sundays. Some football teams set up Sinn Féin clubs or *cumainn*.

There was always a very intense consciousness of community in small Irish towns and villages. For most young people being part of something meant being part of everything. No one wanted to be left out of any current craze. There was no contradiction in being a member of several different clubs and societies. In this spirit very often the officer panel of the Sinn Féin club was replicated in the local Volunteer company, with the Sinn Féin treasurer, for example, doubling as the Volunteer company's quartermaster, and the Sinn Féin president or chairman as company OC.

What was very significant was that by the end of 1917 the *cumann* president was often a local priest.

The by-election victories in 1917 had helped legitimise Sinn Féin, but so had the behaviour of the British forces. The thousands of arrests, often of completely innocent men, the ill treatment of prisoners, especially in Frongoch and in Mountjoy, culminating in Thomas Ashe's death in September 1917 as a result of force-feeding while on hunger strike, swung people behind Sinn Féin. The death of Ashe, a prominent republican who had been elected president of the Supreme Council of the IRB after the Rising, seemed to have a galvanic effect on people. Not only did young people pour into Sinn Féin but many also joined the Volunteers and began to participate in the sort of violent acts which, in 1918, eventually brought large areas of the country into *de facto* rebellion.

Younger clergy quickly followed the sentiment of their flocks. Parish priests tended to remain loyal to the IPP into 1918, but the appearance of priests as presidents of Sinn Féin *cumainn* was ominous. Sinn Féin even began to count bishops among its sympathisers: archbishop Walsh of Dublin, bishops Fogarty of Killaloe and O'Dwyer of Limerick. These bishops were openly critical of the cruelty the British forces showed to the civilian population. Ashe's death seems to have been a turning-point. The *Daily Express* commented: 'The circumstances of his [Ashe's] death and funeral have made 100,000 Sinn Féiners out of 100,000 constitutional nationalists.' The *Daily Mail* claimed that, whereas Sinn Féin had been on the wane a month earlier, 'Sinn Féin today is pretty nearly another name for the vast bulk of the youth of Erin.' The switch in the position of the archbishop of Cashel provides a good illustration of the development of clerical attitudes. In April 1917 the archbishop refused to allow a Mass to celebrate the first anniversary of the Rising, but in September 1917 he himself said Mass for Thomas Ashe and in 1918 he voted Sinn Féin.

Sinn Féin had an added attraction that is often overlooked. It had always been the one political organisation that welcomed women. Indeed that was a feature of all the organisations Arthur Griffith had established. Countess Markievicz stayed in Sinn Féin after 1910 when others left because it was the only organisation that gave women anything like a fair crack of the whip. Jennie Wyse-Power had been on the movement's executive since 1905 and was elected vice-president in 1911. She would later act as treasurer. At the 1917 Sinn Féin *ard fheis*, Arthur Griffith spoke on a motion about female suffrage proposed by Dr Kathleen Lynn. He said:

> I ask delegates to pass this without any further discussion. From the day we founded Sinn Féin we made no discrimination as to sex for any office in the organisation. Mrs Power was one of the first members of the executive of this association. It must be made clear that women are just as eligible for any position in the country.

The Volunteers, however, was an all-male organisation whose members expected Cumann na mBan, the women's branch of the Volunteers, to act as a support group. Many Volunteers also took the same attitude to Sinn Féin, viewing it as an adjunct, but Sinn Féin itself was a mixed organisation which always had women in its highest councils. Dr Lynn later became a vice-president, Áine Ceannt was director of communications and Hanna Sheehy Skeffington director of organisation. Sinn Féin women stood in Dáil and council elections between 1918 and 1921. Usually the only female candidates were those put forward by Sinn Féin.

Nevertheless, despite the unusual number of women in Sinn Féin, the party was overwhelmingly composed of young single men with little or nothing to lose, who got a sense of purpose and importance from signing up. Since emigration had been banned during the First World War there was a surfeit of such men, especially in districts where emigration to the USA would normally have soaked up thousands. That route was no longer available. Travel to Britain for work was also denied to the same young men. After 1916 anyone of military age with an address in Britain was liable to be conscripted. It is no coincidence, therefore, that membership of Sinn Féin was largest in Sligo, Leitrim, Mayo, Clare, Cork and Kerry.

Membership of the Volunteers and Sinn Féin gave unemployed young men something to do both during the day and in the evenings, too. They could drill, go on route marches, attend political meetings and classes for Irish language or military instruction and, above all, behave generally as if they were men with a role in the community. Membership of one or both organisations conferred a status otherwise unavailable to the unemployed and landless.

The form and nature of that membership set the precedent for the rest of the twentieth century for people involved in what later became known as 'the republican movement'. The dual membership of both Sinn Féin and the Volunteers, which was normal at local level, simply reflected what existed throughout the organisation from the top down. Eamon de Valera was elected president of the Irish Volunteers at their convention in October 1917, the day after he was elected president of Sinn Féin. Six of the twenty men elected to the Volunteer executive that day had been elected to the Sinn Féin executive the day before. It was obviously convenient to hold a Volunteer convention at the same time as the Sinn Féin *ard fheis* as so many were members of both. The *ard fheis* also acted as a cover for the Volunteer convention. Thus began a long and hallowed tradition, though when the movement reorganised in 1948 the order of meetings was reversed to reflect the balance of power, so IRA army conventions tended to precede Sinn Féin *ard fheiseanna*.

The new rank and file who poured into Sinn Féin were not converted to the party through a close examination of its ideology. Joining Sinn Féin was simply the done thing. It was the accepted way of expressing anti-British feeling, and wearing Volunteer uniform did not seem in any way incompatible with membership. Being in Sinn Féin was also a way of annoying the British authorities and the RIC, another reason for its attraction for young people. Besides, everyone else was joining. Sinn

Féin became a popular front.

Whatever their reasons for joining, the influx of over 100,000 new members meant the new Sinn Féin was far removed from the intellectual ginger group Arthur Griffith had envisaged a decade earlier. Few of the new members would have had any patience for the intricacies of the dual monarchy Griffith proposed, even if they had understood them. Events had moved too fast since 1916. A republic was a simple slogan even if the consequences of demanding one escaped its supporters. It seemed to mean freedom, Tir na nÓg, a shimmering Shangri-La with 'No polis, no taxes'.

After the by-election defeats early in 1918 in northeast Ulster and Waterford, there was some wishful thinking that Sinn Féin's popularity had been dented, that the heady rush of 1917 was over. It may have been so, but the truth of that speculation will never be known. If Sinn Féin had peaked, the British government was about to come to the party's aid as it has so many times in the movement's history.

Between March and May 1918 Lloyd George in London and his administration in Dublin handed Sinn Féin two custom-built, gold-plated propaganda victories. One, the conscription crisis, allowed Sinn Féin to lead national agitation against the British government and the other, the so-called 'German Plot', gained Sinn Féin national sympathy and the precious commodity called victimhood. The first of these victories was the defeat of Lloyd George's attempt to rush through conscription for Irishmen, a defeat for which Sinn Féin took the credit. The second victory, though it seemed the opposite at the time, was the result of a bizarre and thoroughly dishonest and corrupt effort on the part of Dublin Castle to implicate Sinn Féin in a conspiracy with Germany. The party's leadership was arrested, many of them deported to England, and over 1,000 rank-and-file members were interned. What more could an Irish political movement ask for?

Lloyd George introduced the Military Service Bill to enable conscription of Irishmen on 9 April 1918. Even before he had introduced the

Bill, the hostile reaction in nationalist Ireland was united and overwhelming; in some cases opposition was almost hysterical. By 1918 the population at large was well aware that the Western Front was a meat-grinder. With American troops arriving in Europe in numbers in spring 1918, it was obvious that Irish conscripts were intended for a final push. Given the fate of previous 'final pushes', there was no doubt in the minds of Irish people that men conscripted in 1918 would be slaughtered just as comprehensively as those who had volunteered in 1914 and 1915. The certain death of many who would be conscripted was only one factor in the national opposition. The activities of British forces and the RIC after the 1916 Rising and throughout 1917 had provoked virulent Anglophobia in much of the country. The thought of fighting for England after what its government had done since Easter 1916 made many men's gorges rise.

Sinn Féin had always been consistent in opposing Irish involvement in 'England's war'. The issue was perfect for the party. The party's relentless anti-Britishness entirely suited the mood of the people in 1918. The IPP also opposed conscription, but the government's decision to introduce it and the IPP's humiliating powerlessness to prevent it passing into law at Westminster badly demoralised the party. There was the IPP at Westminster, publicly demonstrating the pointlessness of attending, while Sinn Féin was getting the credit for taking the leading role in Ireland in opposing the measure, even though its new MPs boycotted Westminster. The Bill was rushed rapidly through all its stages and became law on 18 April. That day the IPP withdrew from Westminster forever. By doing so they seemed to admit Sinn Féin's abstentionist stance was correct. The British government had played into the hands of an abstentionist, extra-parliamentary organisation by allowing it to show that it had more clout than a constitutional party with over seventy MPs. Extra-parliamentary agitation carried the day.

The country, with the exception of unionist areas of the northeast, was in uproar. The Catholic hierarchy, the trade unions and political parties were all united. The leaders of the Volunteers began to plan for an uprising in the event of conscription being enforced. This time the Volunteers' leaders were certain that, unlike 1916, there would be widespread popular support for an uprising. Violence had been spreading from the southwest since the autumn of 1917. The RIC had withdrawn from some isolated barracks. The chief secretary of Ireland had West Cork and counties Kerry and Clare declared Special Military Areas. Indeed, even as the Bill was going through Westminster there was an attempted arms raid on Gortatlea RIC barracks in Kerry during which Richard Laide and John Browne were killed, the first Volunteers to die in action since 1916.

Sinn Féin was taking the lead in organising political opposition to conscription. Membership of the party reached its high-water mark in May. On 23 April, five days after the Military Service Act became law, an effective general strike paralysed the country, again with the exception of the unionist northeast. The leaders of Sinn Féin and the Volunteers (the same people) alongside the Labour Party and trade unions were the organisers, but Sinn Féin claimed the credit. Certainly, Dublin Castle laid responsibility at its door. The IPP was trapped into supporting Sinn Féin's initiatives but excluded from planning them. All across the country the two parties were saying the same thing, but people believed the IPP was only running to keep up with Sinn Féin, which the British seemed to regard as their real opponent.

What alternative did the IPP have? Was the whole country not demanding a united campaign? The IPP had a lot of ground to make up. After all, had the party not consistently demanded that people support the war and join the British Army? Had Sinn Féin not consistently opposed the war and urged people not to join the British Army? Why was the IPP now saying that it was wrong for the British government to impose conscription when John Redmond had encouraged men to give their all to the war effort? Even in 1918, MPs from the IPP continued to take their places on recruitment platforms. In the minds of most people Sinn Féin was the only real opponent of the British government.

It quickly became obvious that the attempt to extend conscription to Ireland would fail. It would provoke armed resistance. Thousands of troops would be required to enforce it, which would defeat the whole purpose – the reason for having conscription was to increase the number of men available for the Front. Such coercion would go down extremely badly in the USA, a country the British government could not afford to alienate at that crucial moment. Lloyd George gave up, although he wouldn't admit it, but continued until the autumn to threaten to enforce conscription.

Despite, or perhaps because of this humiliating defeat, the British administration in Ireland decided to deal with the people they regarded as the authors of the defeat: Sinn Féin. Late on 17 May and into the early hours of 18 May, seventy-three Sinn Féiners were arrested on the preposterous pretext of being involved in a so-called 'German Plot'. The trigger was the arrest of one Joseph Dowling, a POW who had been landed in County Clare from a German submarine with instructions to contact the Sinn Féin leadership. No one in the Sinn Féin leadership knew anything about him. Dowling had been arrested almost a week before the Military Service Act became law, but the authorities took no action for over a month. When they did act, on the excuse of the fictitious plot, it was obviously out of simple vindictiveness, not even from a misguided belief that they could finish Sinn Féin by cutting off its head. The widespread arrests of Sinn Féin leaders had profound and long-lasting consequences, not only because of the number of victims created but also because of the men who rose to prominence in the absence of those interned.

Sinn Féin had been expecting some such action against it even before the beginning of the campaign against conscription. The party leaders had taken a decision to allow themselves to be arrested *en bloc* rather than go on the run and be picked up one at a time. Over a month before the arrest operation they had already nominated substitutes to take over their positions in the party. Their belief, correct as it turned out, was that the arrest of the whole Sinn Féin leadership would give them a major propaganda *coup*. Their preparations were aided by detailed information acquired by Michael Collins's spy network, which was developing fast by mid-1918.

Collins managed to alert most of those on the list. They were duly arrested. With the exception of Fr O'Flanagan and Sinn Féin's secretary, Harry Boland, the entire officer board of Sinn Féin was picked up. The detainees included Eamon de Valera, Arthur Griffith, Darrell Figgis, Count Plunkett, WT Cosgrave, Kathleen Clarke, the widow of 1916 leader Thomas Clarke, and Countess Markievicz. In this first sweep seventy-three were transported to England and interned. Eventually the total rose to 115 prominent Sinn Féin people deported to English jails and 1,319 others interned.

The leaders of the Volunteers who were busily preparing for a military campaign to 'finish the business of 1916' did not make themselves available for arrest. Apart from de Valera, they made themselves scarce. The two most important Volunteer figures who escaped arrest were Collins himself and Harry Boland. Other less 'political' leaders, like Cathal Brugha and Richard Mulcahy, also remained free. The net effect of the 'German Plot' arrests was to remove from the scene the moderate leadership of the republican movement. Perhaps it may have seemed to the British administration that the phrase 'moderate Sinn Féin' was a contradiction in terms and that a haul of over seventy prominent Sinn Féiners was a great success. In fact, they had removed any restraining influence on the movement and handed it over to Michael Collins, who advocated what he called a 'forward policy'. He spent the rest of 1918 surrounding himself with likeminded men. If the arrests backfired on the British, they had a similar result in the long term for Collins. His successful efforts to keep out moderates in 1918 meant that in 1921 when he needed the support of people he had disdainfully called 'compromisers', they were not in the Dáil: the Dáil's members were largely made up of those he engineered as candidates in 1918, that is, Volunteers and supporters of a republic.

Regardless of the motives of Westminster politicians or Dublin Castle officials for this arrest operation, the effects were immediately clear to everyone but the British. The IPP had been badly wounded. On 20 April their oldest MP, Samuel Young, who represented Cavan East, had died aged ninety-six. Sinn Féin had immediately nominated Griffith to fight the by-election. Since it was the height of the conscription crisis many, including the Catholic Church, had called on Sinn Féin not to contest the by-election. Most people wanted to avoid a divisive election campaign, preferring to maintain unity in the face of the threat of conscription. Comparisons were made with Offaly where a vacancy in April had been filled by agreement when the IPP withdrew and allowed Sinn Féin's Dr Patrick McCartan to be returned unopposed. After the 'German Plot' arrests that attitude changed. Sinn Féin had been watching the Cavan seat for a long time and was determined to drive home the advantage it had gained from the campaign against conscription.

Whereas in County Offaly John Dillon, Redmond's successor as leader of the IPP, believed his party could not win, he did consider it had a good chance in Cavan. The IPP was strong in the east of the county, there was the chance of help from unionist voters and there was the precedent of other victories against Sinn Féin in Ulster. After the 'German Plot' arrests, however, Sinn Féin saw a chance to win in Cavan East since its candidate, Arthur Griffith, could now be portrayed as a victim of British oppression. Sinn Féin once again took up the slogan it had used in the case of Joe McGuinness in Longford South – 'Put him in to get him out' – and supported it with extensive use of illustrations of Griffith in prison uniform.

The 'German Plot' arrests had allowed Sinn Féin to turn the tables completely on the IPP in Cavan. It now demanded that Dillon give Griffith a free run. It made much of the fact that the IPP was fielding a candidate even though it was now apparently supporting Sinn Féin's policy of abstention after withdrawing from Westminster in protest at the Military Service Act. Sinn Féin speakers had a field day in the campaign. Led by the practically manic Fr O'Flanagan, they were able to claim the IPP had been consistently wrong on all matters national and were to blame for the present problems. They were able to point out that the very fact that JF O'Hanlon, the IPP candidate, was ignored by the authorities and free to campaign showed how effective Sinn Féin was and how the British government perceived Sinn Féin as the real opponent of conscription and the only threat to British rule in Ireland. The result was a foregone conclusion.

Griffith's victory in the Cavan by-election concealed the fact that May 1918 would mark the end of another phase in Sinn Féin's evolution. In the absence of the interned Sinn Féin leadership the Volunteers were to become the real driving-force among separatists in Ireland. From the summer of 1918 Sinn Féin, in practice, played second fiddle to Michael Collins and his immediate entourage. In jail in England, Griffith and the other Sinn Féin leaders had no influence over the party's election manifesto or its choice of candidates to fight the approaching general election.

The effects of the arrests on the leadership of Sinn Féin can be seen in the membership of the party committee that drafted the election manifesto. Instead of the obvious figures, like de Valera and Griffith, there were the ubiquitous Fr O'Flanagan, the director of elections Robert Brennan, and the two party secretaries Seán T O'Kelly and Harry Boland – all hardliners. Adhering faithfully to the position adopted at the *ard fheis* in October 1917, they produced an unequivocally republican manifesto. The strategy after the election would be that the party's elected representatives would abstain from Westminster and form a constituent assembly. They would appeal to the peace conference when it convened after the war and demand independence. When independence was achieved they would hold a referendum on the type of government there should be.

Sinn Féin would advocate a republic.

One other crucial item from the 1917 *ard fheis* was included: the manifesto committed the party to use 'any and every means available to render impotent the power of England to hold Ireland in subjection by military force or otherwise', an exact repetition of the wording voted through at the *ard fheis*. That form of words had caused misgivings at the *ard fheis* when two priests had tabled an amendment objecting to it on the grounds that it could involve anything 'from pitch-and-toss to man-slaughter'. De Valera had headed off their amendment by explaining, with typical casuistry, that 'available means' meant 'justly available in the minds of all Irishmen', though he never explained how this would be ascertained. Arthur Griffith supported de Valera, saying that the party would never break the moral law. In reality, of course, many party members, particularly the young, believed 'in their minds' that force was 'justly available' and many of them had already been actively engaged in such means, with the result that parts of the country were in a state of disorder by autumn 1918.

The use of force was in line with the injunction given by Michael Collins in a letter of 22 May 1917 to the Volunteer executive, which became public in autumn 1918. Collins wrote:

> The principal duty of the executive is to put the Volunteers in a position to complete by force of arms the work begun by the men of Easter Week. The Volunteers are notified that the only orders they are to obey are those of their own executive.

He added that Volunteers should join Sinn Féin only to propagate the principles of their own organisation, which was the only one to which they owed allegiance. By the autumn of 1918 everyone in the country knew that, while a substantial number of Sinn Féin members did not support violence and the party as a whole was not advocating a violent campaign or seeking electoral support for one, nevertheless many members were also Volunteers and were engaged in armed raids for weapons and in other forms of violence.

It was clear that the Volunteers were in the driving seat and that Sinn Féin provided political cover for them. Already Sinn Féin unequivocally supported Volunteer activity despite having no control over it. That being said, Sinn Féin as a party emphatically did not ask people to vote for violence or even suggest there might be a military campaign against the British to secure independence. On the contrary, it presented itself as the peace party that had kept Ireland out of the war and prevented conscription.

What Sinn Féin did ask for was an overwhelming mandate to go to the peace conference, which was to be convened to redraw the map of Europe after the Great War. There they would ask, in the words of de Valera writing in the *Irish Independent* in November 1918, that Ireland might take 'her rightful place in the family of nations'. Bearing in mind that the war had been supposed to have been about the 'rights of small nations', Sinn Féin in its election literature now carefully aligned Ireland alongside the new states of Europe emerging from the wreckage of the collapsed Austro-Hungarian and Ottoman empires, places like Czechoslovakia and Yugoslavia.

Sinn Féin's connections in the USA made it aware of the thinking of the American president – that countries should be established on the basis of self-determination expressed by plebiscites. President Wilson's 'fourteen points', designed to end international conflict, commended themselves to Sinn Féin as eminently suitable for Ireland's case. If the country voted overwhelmingly for independence, how could the peace conference refuse it since the vote would be an act of self-determination in line with Wilson's principles?

The party threw itself into the campaign long before the election was called. Essentially, Sinn Féin was acting as if the election would be a referendum, a plebiscite on Irish independence. Accordingly, it was determined to maximise its vote. Not only would a huge vote for Sinn Féin endorse its demand for independence, but it would also mean it could put into operation its abstentionist policy with the maximum credibility. A comprehensive victory would give Sinn Féin a strong moral claim to speak for the whole country. In many places the Volunteers and Sinn Féin were already acting as if they ran the country. Electoral success would give them the mandate to do so. Fourteen years after he published it, Arthur Griffith's 'Hungarian policy' would be put into practice, minus, of course, any reference to a monarchy.

Sinn Féin's campaign to have what to all intents and purposes would be a national referendum received a major boost on 1 November when the Irish Labour Party yielded to sustained pressure from Sinn Féin and, to some extent, from the Catholic Church and stood down from the election. The leaders of Sinn Féin were jittery about a contest with Labour, especially in Dublin. Since some Sinn Féin estimates had put Labour's chances at as many as twenty seats nationally, Labour's withdrawal gave enormous relief to Sinn Féin in Dublin and some misplaced relief to the party in Belfast. If Labour's decision was a boost for Sinn Féin, it was a serious blow to the IPP. After Labour's withdrawal, the election took on more and more the character of a plebiscite on independence.

During the campaign the Castle enhanced Sinn Féin's election prospects. The RIC broke up election meetings, raided Sinn Féin clubs, repeatedly raided the party headquarters at Harcourt Street, Dublin, and arrested any of the party's election organisers they could. Each time a new director of elections was appointed he was arrested: Sean Milroy, Dan McCarthy and Robert Brennan in turn. Posters were torn down, party literature confiscated and individual members harassed. Censorship bore down particularly hard on Sinn Féin, even to the extent that chunks of its election manifesto were inked out. Of course all this simply confirmed people's belief that Sinn Féin was the only real threat to the British administration in Ireland. The very freedom the IPP enjoyed confirmed in people's minds that the British regarded that party as harmless, a spent force or, worse, supportive of the British position.

Despite all the efforts of the RIC, Sinn Féin was able to canvass almost everywhere and churn out more leaflets and posters than anyone imagined possible, especially given the paper shortage that existed at the end of the war. It even flooded constituencies where there was no contest, where support for Sinn Féin was strongest and its members most numerous, probably because something had to be done to harness the enthusiasm of its youthful supporters.

The party leadership must have known from the vast Sinn Féin membership and almost missionary zeal of its young supporters and Volunteers throughout the country that they were likely to defeat IPP candidates in most places. The signals in the Offaly by-election in April, where John Dillon had difficulty finding a candidate, and in the Cavan by-election in June, where Griffith had a large majority, showed the way the wind was blowing. By the autumn, Dillon's problems in finding candidates had multiplied. About half his sitting MPs decided to retire, a sure sign of the imminent collapse of the party. Dillon had to leave Sinn Féin unopposed in twenty-five constituencies, mostly in the west and southwest, a bonus for Sinn Féin in that they could divert activists to areas where there were contests.

In the north matters were not so simple. There, the strength of the IPP looked as if it would prevent a complete whitewash for Sinn Féin on the nationalist side. In many Ulster constituencies, IPP candidates were well organised, planned to run and stood to benefit from unionists' tactical voting to keep Sinn Féin out. In the well-established Irish tradition, unionists were likely to vote 'agin' Sinn Féin by voting IPP, not because they supported their policies, far from it, but because they knew that a unionist candidate had no chance and the IPP represented the lesser of two evils. The question for Sinn Féin was which Ulster constituencies to contest and how to decide?

Sinn Féin suggested local plebiscites, a sort of preliminary run-off between itself and the IPP to see who should stand in the real election. This happened only in the bitterly contested seat of Fermanagh North where Sinn Féin won easily: 3,737 to 2,026 votes. But because the vote was carried out at Catholic church gates in the constituency, the Sinn Féin candidate, George Irvine, a Protestant who had fought in the Rising, resigned in disgust.

In general, such plebiscites were unacceptable for a number of reasons. How should they be conducted? After Mass on Sundays, thereby reinforcing the sectarianism of the nationalist parties, just as in Fermanagh? Who should supervise the proceedings? The most important objection was that whoever won would not necessarily win the support of the local activists of the losing party. It was one thing to win a local plebiscite. It was an entirely different matter to go out and canvass for your sworn enemy. By autumn 1918 the IPP and Sinn Féin were at daggers drawn in many parts of the north. Furthermore, without central party endorsement of the arrangements, there would be nothing to stop an individual candidate refusing to accept the plebiscite and upsetting all the plans.

The northern Catholic bishops came to the rescue. The spectre of partition hung over the whole election in the northeast. Even cardinal Logue, who harboured misgivings about Sinn Féin and its violent revolutionary tendencies, believed there should be agreed candidates. The clergy feared that split votes would allow unionists to sweep through in the north and that if they were elected across the six northeastern counties they could claim a mandate for partitioning those counties. It was therefore imperative to elect as many anti-partition MPs as possible: that was why agreed candidates were so important to northerners on this occasion. For Sinn Féin the anti-partitionist argument was, of course, important and the prospect of enhancing their referendum-style campaign was equally attractive.

Cardinal Logue suggested that he would allocate the seats between

Sinn Féin and the IPP. This offered Dillon the tempting possibility of four or five seats he was otherwise unlikely to win. His northern lieutenant, Joe Devlin, advised him to accept the proposal since, in his opinion, the party would be lucky to win any seat outside West Belfast. A conference was finally convened on 2 December, very close to the election date – too close to have the names of the unlucky candidates removed from the ballot. It was agreed that there were eight seats at stake. The cardinal decided to divide them four each to Sinn Féin and the IPP. There was not much more nationalists could do to provide conclusive proof for Ulster unionists that Home Rule meant Rome Rule.

While unionists were dismayed at sectarian solidarity depriving them of seven or eight seats, nationalists did not receive the cardinal's decision with universal approval either. There was intense bitterness among some IPP people about Sinn Féin being allocated any seats at all. They saw Sinn Féin as johnny-come-latelies, not even from the north, who until this election had never shown the slightest interest in the northeast. IPP candidates saw seats they had nursed for years being handed to people who had never set foot in the constituency.

In the end, for all the bad blood between the IPP and Sinn Féin, the pact worked. The agreed candidates won in seven of the eight constituencies. In East Down, however, bitterness survived all pleas from clergy and politicians alike and the nationalist vote split, allowing a unionist win the seat. The other Sinn Féin candidates were successful: Arthur Griffith in Northwest Tyrone, Eoin MacNeill in Derry City and Sean O'Mahony, a Dublin hotelier, in Fermanagh South. In nationalist seats where there could be the luxury of a contest, the results confirmed the correctness of Devlin's advice. Without a pact Sinn Féin would have won another two seats. The exception to the rule was the Falls constituency of West Belfast where Joe Devlin had the rare distinction of trouncing Eamon de Valera. It was the single bright spot in an otherwise black vista for the once all-conquering IPP.

In the rest of the country Sinn Féin triumphed. The party fielded seventy-seven candidates, some of them in quixotic contests, because Sinn Féin was determined to squeeze every vote out of the country and also to fight in places the IPP had never appeared. It tried to show that it represented all the people of Ireland. Thus Winifred Carney stood in the unionist hotbed of Victoria in East Belfast. She polled 4%, mainly from the nationalist Short Strand district.

Again, true to the beliefs of Arthur Griffith, the party put forward three female candidates, though not before Cumann na mBan prodded the leaders into nominating women. Apart from Winifred Carney, Countess Markievicz was the only other woman who fought the election. Hanna Sheehy Skeffington turned down the nomination.

The results are well known. Sinn Féin won seventy-three seats, which translated into sixty-eight because five of its candidates won two constituencies. The IPP was reduced to six seats. Unionists won twenty-six seats, twenty-three of them in Ulster. In many parts of the west and southwest there were no contests because the IPP had either withdrawn or could not find a candidate. Accordingly, seventeen of Munster's twenty-four constituencies saw Sinn Féin candidates elected unopposed. Where there were contests, in the midlands and south of the country, Sinn Féin took over two-thirds of the nationalist vote in most places and elsewhere between a half and two-thirds. In the greater Dublin area the party did less well, evidence of the substantial Protestant population living in the area.

Where Sinn Féin went head-to-head against the IPP it defeated the old party comprehensively. It won thirty-five out of thirty-seven contests against the IPP, losing only in Falls in Belfast and in John Redmond's old seat of Waterford City – both special cases. Those overall figures are the most telling results and indicate strongly that the decision of the sitting MPs to leave the field clear for Sinn Féin was soundly based.

A vastly expanded Irish electorate dramatically chose a single party to represent it. In 1918, as a result of electoral reform, all men over twenty-one and women over thirty had the vote. This provision almost trebled the electorate, from 700,000 to just over 1.9 million. About 800,000 of the 1.2 million new voters were women. It was this new electorate that gave Sinn Féin its massive endorsement. It is often overlooked that the IPP's candidates, even in contests in the west and southwest, actually sustained the party's vote quite well. But the old party was simply not attractive to the new young voters, mainly women, and was swamped by them. If the returns for the university seats with their artificial electorate are discounted, the respective figures were: Sinn Féin, 474,859; IPP, 220,226; unionists, 289,025.

Much has been made of these results. For republicans, then as now, the outcome showed the people of Ireland's overwhelming support for independence in the shape of a republic. For them, it was a retrospective endorsement of the 1916 Rising when, in the words of the Proclamation, the Republic had been 'constituted'. That statement, made in 1916 and in republicans' minds reinforced by the countrywide democratic vote in 1918, assumed dogmatic status for republicans and became the Holy Grail of the republican movement throughout the twentieth century. Its denial or frustration was the stated cause of all subsequent campaigns of violence against British governments and unionist administrations in the north of Ireland.

For others, the result signifies nothing of the kind. Revisionist historians and unionists of all stripes have sought to minimise Sinn Féin's achievement in 1918. Such an approach is in line with the official views of Irish and British governments since the outbreak of sustained violence in the North of Ireland in 1969. It certainly accords with the Irish government's position since 1966 when the modern Ulster Volunteer Force (UVF) brought the gun back into Irish politics. At that time the Irish government had organised extensive celebrations for the fiftieth anniversary of the 1916 Rising, including striking a special silver coin with Padraig Pearse's image on one side. But after 1966 the government feared that any suggestion that 1918 bestowed a mandate on Sinn Féin to strive for an all-Ireland republic might be interpreted as lending support to the campaign of 'armed struggle' launched by the Provisional IRA in 1970. They also wanted to avoid lending credence to the claim of Provisional Sinn Féin that it was the legitimate inheritor in lineal political descent from Sinn Féin in 1918. The violence since 1969 might then be construed as an attempt to complete 'unfinished business'.

As part of attempts to minimise the significance of the votes Sinn Féin received in 1918, some detractors point out that the total 'anti-Sinn Féin vote' (minus the university seats) of 509,251 was greater than Sinn Féin's 474,859. This is an absurd argument. Apart from the fact that it is a novel way to analyse a result in the British electoral system, it ignores a number of political realities in the Ireland of the time. First, if there had been contests in the other twenty-five seats Sinn Féin's total vote would have been much bigger. The reason there were no contests in those constituencies is that the IPP knew it would be trounced if it stood. Needless to say, unionists had no chance in the west and southwest of the country.

Secondly, and highlighting perhaps the most unsound aspect of the calculation, it is absurd to lump all non-Sinn Féin votes together. While it is true that all the unionist votes were anti-Sinn Féin, it is ridiculous to suggest that all the IPP votes were. On the contrary, in the northern constituencies with candidates allocated under the Logue pact, votes for the IPP would have been anti-unionist: that's the whole point of agreed candidates. In any case, there is no possible way to join together IPP votes and unionist votes and claim that they add up to an anti-Sinn Féin total. In the absence of IPP candidates, IPP voters chose Sinn Féin rather than support a unionist. That is how Sinn Féin candidates got elected in agreed constituencies. Lumping IPP and unionist votes together as an 'anti-Sinn Fein' vote would also require IPP voters to be in favour of partition – a nonsense.

Thirdly, a common statistical ploy used to minimise Sinn Féin's democratic mandate is to point to all the uncontested constituencies and claim that no one knows the true scale of Sinn Féin support in those areas. In fact, the scale of Sinn Féin's victory was greater than any achieved by any party before or since. The new franchise, with just under two million voters, produced the most democratic vote there had been in the country up to 1918. It is often overlooked that uncontested constituencies were quite normal in Ireland. Incredibly, some constituencies had not been contested since 1892. Compared to the twenty-five left to Sinn Féin in 1918, an amazing sixty-three constituencies had not been contested in 1910, mostly to the benefit of John Redmond's party. Despite that huge number of uncontested seats in 1910 and earlier, no one has ever suggested that John Redmond lacked a mandate to demand Home Rule. The fact is that in December 1918 Sinn Féin received an overwhelming mandate to demand independence for Ireland.

For most of the newly elected TDs[1], as they quickly decided to call themselves, independence meant a republic. Those who were elected and still free (thirty-six were in jail) proceeded to act according to the blueprint laid out by Griffith in 1905. That is to say, they repudiated the Westminster parliament and Britain's right to govern Ireland, declared themselves the government of Ireland and began to act as if they were the official governing body. The TDs met on 21 January 1919 and constituted themselves as the parliament of Ireland – Dáil Éireann.

The massive vote Sinn Féin had received now gave it the moral force it had hitherto lacked, though lack of it had not prevented the party running many parts of the country since late 1917. People talked about 'Sinn Féin courts' and the party did issue instructions, edicts and public statements from its Harcourt Street headquarters in between RIC raids. In practice, however, it was the Volunteers who were the visible sign of the new dispensation. From early 1918 they had kept order in the country as the RIC had gradually withdrawn to barracks and then abandoned remote barracks.

Keeping civil order was an essential and vital requirement for Sinn Féin in 1918. Even before the conscription crisis in April, 'disturbed areas', as the British administration termed them, became widespread. These were designated Special Military Areas, giving the British military in those areas the power to stop, search and arrest, and to introduce curfews. In people's minds, and especially in the minds of the Catholic clergy, Sinn Féin had been and remained associated with violence and revolution. Its leaders had never unequivocally denounced violence and continued to extol the rebels of 1916. On the other hand, those leaders also knew that if they unequivocally supported violence they would not get people to vote for them in the numbers required to give the party the right to speak for the people of Ireland at the peace conference. They would lose moderate support. And Sinn Fein's greatest political fear in 1918 was condemnation by the Catholic Church. To avoid this they did their best throughout that year to behave responsibly in order to gain the confidence, if not the support, of the Church. In this respect the role of the Volunteers as peacekeepers was indispensable.

Fear of anti-State violence was only one concern of the Church and conservative voters. There was also a whiff of revolutionary sulphur about Sinn Féin that caused alarm. Change was in the air but no one knew what form it might take. Sinn Féin and the Volunteers could feel their own strength and showed it by marching along the streets and lanes of Ireland, including districts in Ulster. For unionists it was unsettling and intimidating.

The most disturbing social development had begun to take place in large areas of the west and southwest where the RIC was increasingly unable to maintain order. In Munster in early 1918 local men began driving cattle off pastureland on large estates on the pretext that food shortages caused by the war could lead to famine. In reality, they were after the demesne land of the estates, most of which belonged to Protestant Anglo-Irish landlords. In February 1918 parties of labourers acting in the name of the Irish Republic began ploughing up some of the land they had cleared of cattle with a view to sowing crops.

These cattle drives, often nocturnal, unruly and intimidating, quickly became a source of embarrassment to Sinn Féin, particularly when the first president of the party, Edward Martyn, found himself on the wrong end of such activity at his estate in County Galway. It was just this kind of action that could have pushed the Catholic Church into a position hostile to Sinn Féin. Marching, drilling, raiding for arms and organising cattle-drives, which in Clare and Kerry were unquestionably instigated by members of Sinn Féin, could unleash forces which would not be confined to attacking representatives of the Crown, but would escalate rapidly to widespread attacks on property, to sectarianism and simple revenge. The support of moderates, men of property and the Church – exactly those elements of society needed for legitimacy – was at stake. Cattle-driving and speeches that were revolutionary in word or tone could also produce nervousness among moderates who had recently joined Sinn Féin. Above all, what Sinn Féin had to avoid was any accusation that it was emulating the actions of the Bolsheviks who had just seized power in Russia.

It was vital for the Volunteers to show that they were a force for stability in the country, not social revolution. By March 1918 the leaders of Sinn Féin and the Volunteers, concerned by the fact that agrarian disturbances and violence against Irish people could provide political ammunition for John Dillon's party, had stepped in to call a halt to cattle drives in particular. On 9 March Michael Collins issued a statement from Volunteer headquarters to the effect that raiding for weapons and cattle-driving were expressly prohibited and in direct opposition to orders. The efforts that Sinn Féin and the Volunteers invested in halting such demonstrations of popular emotion largely succeeded in holding zealots in check in 1918. It also helped reassure the hierarchy at a time of high drama, for this was just as the conscription crisis was beginning to break.

That degree of control also helped show that Sinn Féin and the Volunteers really did have unparalleled influence in the most rebellious parts of the country. The conscription crisis, the growing public disorder and the election campaign itself provided not just a demonstration of Sinn Féin's support but of the movement's power. If it was able to convince the Catholic Church and middle-of-the-road people across the country that it was not a collection of red revolutionaries intent on overturning society, it could thereby win the endorsement of members of the hierarchy in the 1918 election. That very same ability to control events terrified unionists.

To unionists the events of 1918, culminating in the overwhelming victory in the general election, proved that Sinn Féin was behind what they saw as anarchy in the countryside and in some towns, and that all too often that anarchy was directed not only against the forces of the Crown, police and military, whom unionists regarded as their defenders, but also against individual Protestant property owners. The role of the Catholic hierarchy in presiding over the selection of agreed candidates in the northeast to minimise the number of MPs unionists could elect was further evidence of the solidarity of nationalists of all hues and their antipathy to unionists. Unionists were staring at a gigantic Gaelic, Catholic, republican juggernaut. Finally, the staggering size of the Sinn Féin vote across the island was the ultimate proof that the only salvation for unionists lay in being able to control their own destiny. Certainly there seemed to be no role for them in the sort of Ireland Sinn Féin envisaged.

In short, the result of the 1918 election made unionists determined to have permanent partition. The depth of their determination, fear and apprehension remained eternally beyond the grasp of the southern-based Sinn Féin leadership. That leadership persisted in its belief, enshrined in the 1916 Proclamation, that any division in the country was artificially created and partitionist feelings deliberately fomented by the British. Somehow, when the British left, unionists would accept the error of their ways and simply swing in behind the rest of the country. While there might have been reason for such a belief in regions where unionists were a tiny minority, most members of the Sinn Féin leadership had no idea of the strength of feeling and solidarity of Ulster unionists where they formed the majority.

This ignorance of Ulster unionism led to a touching naïveté among the Sinn Féin top brass. The movement went out of its way to try to prove to unionists that it wanted them to play a full and necessary part in the independent Ireland it aimed to establish. It fought hardline unionist constituencies, seizing the opportunity to present its case to the people there. Jennie Wyse-Power went to Belfast in November 1918 with over £2,000, a colossal sum, to finance Sinn Féin's Ulster campaign. The party disbursed 38% of its total 1918 election expenditure in Ulster, much of it in unionist areas where it was completely wasted. Sinn Féin leaders could not see that the very aggressive Irishness they espoused was not only anathema to unionists but a threat to their way of life. They did not seem to realise that they were ignoring unionist sensitivities by their emphasis on the Irish language and their virulent anti-British and anti-war propaganda, especially when thousands of unionist men were fighting at the front and Sinn Féin was seen as a supporter of the Germans.

In truth, among Sinn Féin members Ulster unionists were a mystery. Apart from notable exceptions, like Bulmer Hobson and Ernest Blythe, most of the leaders did not know any rank-and-file northern Protestants and tended to assume they had the same attitudes as the southern Anglo-Irish with whom they were more familiar. Should they threaten them or woo them? They did not know. In the end no attempt was made to accommodate them. A classic example of the crassness of Sinn Féin's treatment was the invitation sent to all newly elected representatives to attend the first sitting of Dáil Éireann in January 1919. Naturally, invitations were sent to all unionist MPs. Naturally, the invitations were in Irish. When the roll was called at the first sitting, in Irish, naturally, Carson's name produced guffaws from the assembled members. It was just the sort of scene that helped confirm unionists in their opinion that there was no place for them in Sinn Féin's Ireland, despite Sinn Féin's protestations to the contrary.

On the wider stage, Sinn Féin displayed its ignorance of a much more important set of realities, namely the international climate at the end of the war. How could it know? Sinn Féin was literally composed of innocents abroad when it came to anticipating the outlook of the heads of government meeting at Versailles. In its innocence, faithfully following its election manifesto, which was now endorsed by the vast majority of the Irish people, Sinn Féin plunged ahead and instantly failed.

Those not in jail met as Dáil Éireann in the Mansion House on 21 January 1919 and quickly declared independence, adopted the provisional constitution committing themselves to a republic, issued an address to the free nations of the world and released their Democratic Programme. This was done in a great rush because they had their eye on the Versailles peace conference, which held its inaugural meeting on 18 January 1919. The Democratic Programme, extraordinarily left-wing in its contents for an Irish political party, was designed to appeal to the Socialist International, which was meeting in Berne in Switzerland. The Declaration of Independence was to impress the US government.

The Dáil was urgently putting some flesh on Sinn Féin's international strategy now that the Irish electorate had endorsed it. Yet this feverish activity at the end of January merely served to demonstrate the inexperience and naiveté of the Sinn Féin leadership who remained out of jail. A cursory examination of their peace conference strategy will quickly reveal its futility. How did an organisation that dated its rise to power from the 1916 Rising, a rebellion for which it had sought German arms and *matériel*, propose to present itself with any expectation of a favourable hearing at a conference of leaders determined to render Germany militarily and economically impotent? Sinn Féin revered as a sacramental document the Proclamation read out on the steps of the GPO in

1916, which implied that the Germans were its 'gallant allies' in Europe. How was that supposed to go down with the British and the French who had lost millions of men to those same Germans?

Besides, Sinn Féin had opposed the war, advocated neutrality, resisted conscription with all its might and had stood for election in 1918 as the peace party. How did it expect the British to walk away from the unionists who had enthusiastically endorsed British policy since 1914 and suffered massive casualties as a result? Did Sinn Féin really expect a British government, which had numbered in its Cabinet the leader of the Ulster unionists, to accede to demands which would cast those same unionists out of the British Empire they had fought for? Did Sinn Féin really expect the British government, in its moment of victory, to effectively begin dismantling its empire – as giving independence to Ireland would certainly encourage Indian nationalists who were demanding the same?

Sinn Féin was carried along on a wave of emotion and euphoria, blinded by its electoral success. Many Irish people placed their hopes in the US government and in President Wilson's emphasis on self-determination as a guiding principle for reorganising Europe. The Friends of Irish Freedom struggled manfully in the US and later in Paris to get a hearing for delegates from the Dáil, but in vain.

Sinn Féin failed immediately on all fronts. In its moment of triumph the party went into instant decline as a force within the republican movement. While the Dáil was declaring independence and hastily issuing various documents to catch the eye of people in Geneva, Washington and Versailles, an event was taking place simultaneously that would have a more immediate effect on relations with Britain than all the documents poured out by the fledgling assembly.

At Soloheadbeg in County Tipperary, on the very day the Dáil first met, Dan Breen and Sean Treacy, along with seven other Irish Volunteers, ambushed a cartload of gelignite and shot dead the two RIC men escorting it. This incident is usually taken to be the beginning of the War of

Independence (1919–21). The nature and timing of the attack contained a number of features which illustrate the submissive position Sinn Féin was pushed into in the early months of 1919.

In the first place, the attackers took no cognisance whatsoever of what was happening in Dublin. In his embarrassingly naive autobiography, *My Fight for Irish Freedom* (first published 1924), Dan Breen wrote that the ambush party had lain in wait from before daybreak until two o'clock in the afternoon each day for five days. There was no question of the incident being timed to coincide with the Dáil's inaugural meeting. There is no evidence that the Volunteer squad involved knew or cared about the Dáil meeting. It is clear from his autobiography that Breen had no interest in or knowledge of politics. He and his fellow Volunteers were simply fed up sitting around doing nothing and 'getting imprisoned while we remained inactive'.

The Volunteers had been kept quiet during the election campaign and, apart from the occasional arms raid, confined their activities to electioneering, drilling, torchlight parades, band parades and similar morale-boosting displays with Sinn Féin candidates. It would not have served the purposes of Sinn Féin to initiate fighting during the election campaign. Violence could very quickly get out of control and Sinn Féin would be blamed for starting it. Any deterioration in conditions in the countryside could also have reduced turnout. So the Volunteers literally held their fire. But now that the election was over and the outcome a great success, they wanted to get on with what they had joined up for: fighting 'the Crown forces'.

Breen later claimed, preposterously, that the 'Volunteers were in great danger of becoming merely a political adjunct to the Sinn Féin organisation'. Sean Treacy told Breen, 'We had had enough of being pushed around'. It was the reverse of the truth. Most Volunteers thought Sinn Féin was their adjunct, an organisation made up of people who were either over military age or did not have the stomach to fight. The

Volunteers' overwhelming belief was that the republic would be obtained only by force of arms. They were convinced that they would not have arrived at where they were if it had not been for the Rising. Sinn Féin's massive electoral victory, they believed, had supplied them with the moral right to fight for independence because that demand had been endorsed by the Irish people; Sinn Féin should stand aside and let the Volunteers get on with it.

In his memoirs, Breen accurately reflected the Volunteers' attitude to Sinn Féin, whose members he obviously viewed with contempt and scorn. Most of the leading figures in the Volunteers who subsequently committed their views to print shared his opinions. Breen quotes Sean Treacy's hostility to Sinn Féin's politicians. Ernie O'Malley and CS Andrews also expressed their disdain for 'politicians'. The most senior figure on the military side, Michael Collins, was always particularly scathing about what he called 'the bargaining type' and 'compromisers', that is until December 1921 when he had a sudden need for such people.

After the Soloheadbeg ambush, incidents began to multiply across the south and west. Volunteers followed the example of Treacy and Breen and acted without reference to Dublin. They believed they were fighting for a republic. Soon they began to call themselves the Irish Republican Army. The IRA and its leaders took the initiative. Sinn Féin rapidly lost its grip on the course of events.

The decline of Sinn Féin was partly the fault of the leadership and the view they had of the party's role. Partly it was because a guerrilla war was raging and therefore there was precious little for a political party to do anyway; partly it was because, since the British authorities viewed Sinn Féin as a single movement, they hunted down members of the Dáil and of the party just as zealously as members of the IRA. By the middle of 1919 it became almost impossible for the organs of Sinn Féin to function normally.

The ideal that Sinn Féin leaders, and particularly de Valera, had of the party led them to remove the party from 'politics', which might seem a peculiar idea for a political party to adopt. Not, however, if it is borne in mind that Sinn Féin was supposed to be a national movement. Members of Sinn Féin had to set an example in their community. There had always been a thick vein of Puritanism, if not asceticism, in the movement. In local *cumainn* an emphasis on clean living and wholesomeness prevailed. Involvement in sport and cultural activity was encouraged. Contrary to portrayals on stage and screen, drinking was frowned on in republican circles, especially the drinking of spirits. Republicans were suspicious of any potentially corrupting influence. That extended to politics. Such a suggestion may seem strange, since one might legitimately ask what Sinn Féin members thought they had been 'in' since 1916 if not in politics.

The answer is that they were 'working for Ireland'. For many members of Sinn Féin, Ireland was a concept that existed as something separate from the people who lived on the island of Ireland. Like the idealised German Fatherland or 'Mother Russia', 'Ireland', for many in the republican movement, had an almost spiritual essence. This thinking would have been instantly recognisable to many nationalists on mainland Europe, especially in the new states emerging after the First World War, although by no means confined to them.

Many of the members and certainly the leaders of the republican movement regarded Sinn Féin not as a political party but at one and the same time as the political embodiment of the will of the Irish people and as the vehicle for expressing it. It was above politics and definitely not to become sullied by politics, and it was the desire to preserve this exalted 'uncorrupted' position that led de Valera in April 1919 to separate Sinn Féin, the party, from 'the State' in the shape of Dáil Éireann. He completed this reorganisation in a brief period between the release of the Sinn Féin internees on 10 March 1919 (de Valera had escaped from Lincoln jail on 3 February) and the beginning of the British suppression of Sinn Féin in July 1919. De Valera himself left for the United States on 1 June 1919 and remained there until December 1920.

The changes were voted through at the party's *ard fheis* in April 1919. The issue was how Sinn Féin should relate to the Dáil. The party had been acting as the government in parts of the country in 1917 and 1918. In the eyes of the Sinn Féin leaders there was now an assembly elected to run the country. De Valera was determined that unelected people in Sinn Féin should not control the elected members in the Dáil. Since no other party recognised Dáil Éireann, Sinn Féin's Standing Committee, as a party organisation, could have pushed anything through the Dáil.

There was the corresponding danger that Dáil members who were also senior Sinn Féin figures could abuse the party's organisation as their own political apparatus. De Valera removed this danger by preventing any member of the Cabinet, except the president (himself) and the minister of home affairs, from being elected to Sinn Féin's Standing Committee. He also provided that only one-third of the Standing Committee's members could be members of the Dáil. Similar arrangements came into operation at local level where members of boards or other elected bodies could not be on the local Sinn Féin constituency executive.

While this may have preserved Sinn Féin's 'purity', it caused immediate damage to the party. Which would an activist rather be: a member of Sinn Féin's Standing Committee or a member of Dáil Éireann? Which would a member of Dáil Éireann rather be: a member of Sinn Féin's Standing Committee or a member of the Cabinet? Important figures in the republican movement, most notably Michael Collins, were instantly lost to Sinn Féin and, of course, Sinn Féin was unable to influence them. Since many of the same people were also prominent leaders in the IRA they too disappeared from Sinn Féin's Standing Committee. It was several decades before Sinn Féin never recovered from this loss of status within the republican movement.

By the time of that *ard fheis* in April 1919 it was obvious that, despite Sinn Féin's massive electoral success, its political aims had failed. Its representatives had not been given a hearing at the Versailles peace conference. No one had entertained its claims to speak for Ireland. The only meagre success it had was that the International Labour and Socialist Congress in Berne had admitted an Irish delegation separate from the British one.

Strenuous lobbying of US President Wilson in Paris by the Friends of Irish Freedom to gain a hearing for the Dáil had been to no avail. On 28 June 1919, exactly five years to the day after the assassination in Sarajevo of Archduke Franz Ferdinand of Austria, the Versailles Treaty was signed. There was no reference to Ireland in it. Sinn Féin's mandate and Ireland's claims for independence had been ignored by the victorious allies. Those claims would now be pressed by the IRA in Ireland. What was Sinn Féin to do?

The British government began to turn its attention to Ireland on 4 July 1919 a week after the Versailles Treaty. Sinn Féin, the Irish Volunteers, Cumann na mBan and the Gaelic League were proclaimed illegal in various counties – a combination of organisations that provides an illuminating view of Britain's idea of the republican movement. On 25 November the same organisations were made illegal throughout Ireland. The Dáil had been made illegal on 25 September. Arthur Griffith, acting president of Sinn Féin in de Valera's absence, commented: 'The English government in Ireland has now proclaimed the whole Irish nation, as it formerly proclaimed the Catholic Church, an illegal assembly.'

Griffith managed to hold a rushed Sinn Féin *ard fheis* in October 1919, confusing the British authorities by bringing the date forward two days. Five hundred or so delegates, a fraction of those entitled to attend, managed to meet hurriedly. The Sinn Féin party established in 1917 never succeeded in holding a formal, properly constituted *ard fheis* again. There were extraordinary conventions but no *ard fheiseanna*. Circumstances were so fraught in 1920 that there was not even an attempt to convene one.

Other organs of the party also found it increasingly impossible to function. The Standing Committee, which was supposed to meet weekly, ran into trouble when the party was made illegal in November. It had to reduce its quorum from seven to five persons. It met less and less frequently up to the autumn of 1920 when it fell into abeyance until 1921. At the lowest organisational level, many *cumainn* were wound up as the winter of 1919 approached. Virtually no members had paid their membership fees.

Griffith and Sean Milroy tried to maintain Sinn Féin's role as the civil wing of the republican movement, carrying out the orders of the Dáil. Very quickly, however, the Dáil began to establish its own structures and employ its own functionaries, a bureaucracy even, to implement its instructions. Why have a middle man, especially one who retained pretensions? Sinn Féin's scope for action diminished all the time.

An illegal organisation, its meetings disrupted, its leaders hunted and concentrating on an intensifying guerrilla war, politics pushed to the side, Sinn Féin went underground, then became redundant as an organisation. By August 1921 WT Cosgrave talked of 'the almost complete disappearance of the Sinn Féin Organisation.'

5. NOT MERELY A FORM OF WORDS
Rejecting the Oath, 1923–26

Sinn Féin may have lost more and more functions to the Dáil and the IRA during the years of turmoil between 1918 and 1921 but as a party it still retained the role of providing the political expression of republicanism in Ireland. Its business was to fight elections, but in a special way, a way designed to demonstrate Irish national self-determination. Presenting itself as a popular front, Sinn Féin managed to turn all electoral contests between 1917 and 1921 into a vote endorsing independence for Ireland. Outside the northeast, Sinn Féin was usually the only party standing for election, and in the elections from 1917 to 1921 most voters seemed to agree that the national question was the only issue.

By 1922 the Treaty with Britain was in place and Sinn Féin's electoral work was done in the sense that its *raison d'être* as the all-embracing, unchallenged mouthpiece of the Irish people was gone. That was far from a universal view, however. A significant minority of the republican movement vehemently disagreed that what had been achieved in the Treaty was the independence Sinn Féin had campaigned for or the Irish people had voted for, so the party split. The minority, led by de Valera, who hung on to the name Sinn Féin, insisted that, with its unchanging principles, namely the demand for a sovereign, independent Irish Republic, only the Sinn Féin they belonged to still provided the political expression of republicanism and that its work was not done. They insisted that there was still only one issue – the national question – and that, contrary to what the majority in the country mistakenly believed, this issue had yet to be resolved. For such people, political time stopped in 1921. The united front that had been maintained up to then was replaced in 1922 by civil war. That internecine conflict created the deep division that formed the faultline of Irish politics for generations and created animosities still visible in elections today.

De Valera summed up the way people regarded Sinn Féin before the split when he said: 'To me Sinn Féin is the nation organised. I never regarded it as a mere political machine.' There is no doubt about the accuracy of his description. Until the Anglo-Irish Treaty, Sinn Féin was the political expression of the vast majority the Irish people. That position changed instantly after the Dáil endorsed the Treaty on 7 January 1922 by the narrow margin of sixty-four votes to fifty-seven. Within less than a year Sinn Féin went from being the single, united political voice of the Irish people outside the northeast to political oblivion in 1923.

Over the next twenty-five years an ever-diminishing number of diehards clung to the wreckage of the party and from time to time emerged from obscurity to claim the banner of the all-conquering movement of the years 1917–21. Those who did hold onto the name Sinn Féin and claimed, so to speak, 'apostolic succession' from the men and women of 1921, nurtured a strong sense of grievance and betrayal against their former comrades and Irish governments which persecuted them. How did it come about that the mighty, monolithic, all-conquering Sinn Féin of 1917–21 split? How was it that Sinn Féin shrank from being the biggest political movement in Irish history to become, for fifty years, a marginalised rump?

The very fact that Sinn Féin performed as a popular front between 1917 and 1921 meant, by definition, that it was a movement composed of various sections. On the one hand there were the old Griffithite moderates, a minority by 1917, who had adhered to the original dual monarchy policy published in 1905. On the other hand there were the new members, mostly young and usually Volunteers, who flooded into the party in 1917, demanding a republic. These were the people' who turned Sinn Féin into a republican party in 1917 and who formed the rank and file of the IRA in 1919. Many had no time for political activity, viewing it as a waste of energy. For them the only way to achieve the republic was by force of arms, to 'finish the business of 1916'.

The IRA did not constitute a united body either. Many of their leaders owed allegiance to the secret IRB. The effective leader of the IRA, Michael Collins, was also the head of the IRB's Supreme Council. After the 1918 general election, the Dáil emerged as yet another component of the republican movement. Some men were members of all of the organisations: Sinn Féin, the IRA, the IRB and the Dáil. Separate and overlapping chains of command operated in all four. Even in the best circumstances this chaotic arrangement could not survive. Collins himself realised it when he admitted in a letter to Austin Stack in 1919: 'There is I suppose the tendency of all Revolutionary movements to divide themselves up into their component parts.'

It was more complicated than that in the republican movement. It was not just a matter of moderates and hardliners splitting the movement in two. The disagreement about the Treaty not only caused the movement to disintegrate into its component parts, it also split each component in turn. The central point at issue – the oath of allegiance to King George V, his heirs and successors – divided the IRA, the IRB, the Dáil and, naturally, as the political expression of republicanism, Sinn Féin. Each group split into pro- and anti-Treaty factions. The manner in which the various components split within themselves is vitally important for understanding the 'theology', for want of a better word, of the republican movement for the rest of its existence. That theology was created in the years 1921–22.

The rivalry and tensions among the IRA, the Dáil and Sinn Féin had caused obvious difficulties long before the Treaty. As the people risking their lives in the vanguard of the charge against the British Army and the Black and Tans, the IRA quickly came to dominate the republican movement. It was the IRA, no one else, fighting for the republic. No one was going to tell the GHQ of the IRA how to go about it. The fact that many members of the Dáil and Sinn Féin were also members of the IRA meant that neither of those organisations was going to be critical of the IRA, never mind try to assert authority over it. For its part, the IRA expected Sinn Féin to act as a civilian auxiliary to the IRA – political cheerleaders. In turn the IRA would support Sinn Féin in any election campaign, providing manpower and logistics. It would certainly not have countenanced any Sinn Féin effort to influence it: quite the reverse. The IRA's rapid emergence during the War of Independence as the pre-eminent component in the republican movement and its resistance to any political or democratic authority, whether Sinn Féin or the Dáil, was to have a profound effect on the republican movement until the present day.

As it was they who had fought for the Republic, many members of the IRA considered that the IRA, not the Dáil, was the custodian of the Republic. Republicans saw Sinn Féin merely as their political vehicle. The IRA took the Irish electorate's votes for Sinn Féin in 1920 and 1921 as endorsement of a national insurrection. People had voted for independence in 1918. They had been ignored. The IRA then fought for independence and the Irish people repeated their vote in favour of independence at every opportunity for the next three years. For the IRA, delivering that vote in support of military action was Sinn Féin's function. That attitude left a legacy that still has repercussions within the movement today.

Up until 1923 the name Sinn Féin certainly delivered the electoral goods for republicans. Following the 1918 general election, the first test of public opinion was the local elections which the British administration decided to hold in two separate polls, the first for borough councils in January 1920, county councils would be elected in June. Despite the introduction of proportional representation (PR) and the fact that many of Sinn Féin's working-class voters, not being ratepayers, were ineligible to vote, Sinn Féin emerged as the largest party in most towns and in all the major cities except, not surprisingly, Belfast (though even in Belfast Sinn Féin gained five more seats, thanks to PR). Sinn Féin, along with Labour and, in the North, the remnants of the IPP, known as the Nationalists, controlled 172 out of 206 borough councils. Sinn Féin's performance was all the more striking considering the usual handicaps under which the party laboured: military censorship, remorseless harassment of its candidates and campaigners, destruction of its campaign literature, the IRA's military campaign itself and, not least, the fact that the party was illegal.

One of Sinn Féin's aims in the local government elections was to finish the work of 1918, which almost saw the IPP off the parliamentary scene. Now was the chance to clear them off the political scene completely. There had been no local elections since 1914. Many of the borough councils were still run by IPP mayors and councillors. After January 1920 that was over. Sinn Féin mayors popped up in towns and cities all over the country.

Proportional representation had, however, caused difficulties. Often Sinn Féin emerged as the largest party but did not control the council and had to make deals. It wanted to control as many councils as possible, not simply to oust IPP survivors or to become mayor, important though those goals were. The main reason for striving for an overall majority was to have the party's national policy of recognising the Dáil endorsed. Sinn Féin's policy was for each and every council up and down the country to refuse to deal with Dublin Castle, to refuse to pay taxes or rates to British administrators. Instead they would work with the Dáil's local government department and pay rates and taxes to it, thereby recognising the Dáil as the government of Ireland. It was nothing less than the implementation of

Arthur Griffith's original Sinn Féin policy of 1905.

The outcome of the county council elections in June of that year (1920) was another triumph. In the majority of counties more than half the Sinn Féin candidates were returned unopposed. The party won 258 out of the 263 county council seats in Connacht and Munster. In Leinster, Sinn Féin won 76% of the seats. In Ulster's county councils the party won seventy-nine seats, coming within two of the Ulster unionists' eighty-one seats. All over the country, the county councils joined the Sinn Féin-dominated borough councils in recognising the Dáil.

Sinn Féin had one further major electoral success as a united party. This was in May 1921 when the British decided to hold a general election under the terms of the Government of Ireland Act of 1920. This act had granted Home Rule to Ireland, to be administered through two parliaments, one in Belfast and one in Dublin. Republicans had paid scant attention as the act passed through Westminster, concentrating instead on the intensifying war against the British forces. Some quite senior members of Sinn Féin didn't believe that the British would actually go through with partition. If they thought about the North at all, many appeared to assume the issue would be resolved when the British left or when a settlement was reached after the war.

Suddenly, in early 1921, they were confronted with the prospect of the elections. Northern Sinn Féin asked the party what it should do about the election to the Belfast parliament. Arthur Griffith, the Dáil's minister of Home Affairs, circulated a memo to the Cabinet outlining the problem. The memo produced a series of responses from Collins and de Valera, interesting in themselves because of the combination of ignorance and wishful thinking about the North which the memos reveal.

They agreed on abstention, which was, of course, in line with Sinn Féin policy on all British initiatives. However, Michael Collins completely underestimated the continuing strength of the nationalist party in the North where he believed Sinn Féin could win thirteen or fourteen seats. Collins's memos also went off into fanciful musings about using county councils in Tyrone and Fermanagh and Derry Corporation to reduce the partitioned counties to four in number. The most fatuous suggestion came from de Valera, who believed, on no evidence whatsoever, that abstention by nationalists and Sinn Féin would set 'the Labour and Capitalist sections of the Unionists struggling with each other for control in the Parliament'. The far-seeing de Valera had discerned a powerful labour movement among Ulster unionists not visible to ordinary mortals.

One conclusion evident in the exchange of memos is that Collins, Griffith and de Valera all accepted, despite brave words to the contrary, that there was going to be a parliament sitting in Belfast: there would be partition, perhaps on a temporary basis, but partition nevertheless.

Would they boycott the election and thereby allow the Ulster unionists to claim complete, unchallenged jurisdiction over the north-east? If they could not do anything to stop the election to the northern parliament, they could certainly halt the election to the southern parliament. Sinn Féin's view was that the British had no right to call any election. Fighting it would mean recognising Britain's right to legislate for Ireland. On the other hand, if Sinn Féin fought the election only in the North, even for no other reason than to prevent unionists winning all seats, the conclusion could be drawn that it recognised partition.

Finally and reluctantly, after much soul-searching, Sinn Féin decided to fight the elections on an all-Ireland basis. It was the first time events in the North had driven any policy decision of Sinn Féin. It decided to allocate considerable finance to the North: £6,000 for propaganda, organisation and the election campaign itself. The republican leadership spotted some advantages in the decision to contest the elections: they could reassert Sinn Féin's claim to speak for the people of Ireland; they could gain a retrospective endorsement of the IRA campaign since 1919; they could announce that they regarded the poll not as an election to partition parliaments but to the second all-Ireland Dáil, in short, another expression of self-determination by the people of Ireland. At the same time, a massive vote for Sinn Féin would reinforce what the first Dáil had been doing in denying Britain's right to administer any part of Ireland. It would strengthen its claim that it was acting for the whole country.

Heavily funded from Dublin, northern Sinn Féin launched itself into the election. The line it took was that followed by both Sinn Féin and the northern nationalist party in all Northern Ireland elections until the mid-1960s. It campaigned against partition and denigrated the concept of a northern state with every word it could marshal in the English and Irish languages. Yet partition existed and the form of Sinn Féin's election campaign in 1921, like all subsequent campaigns, served only to solidify partition and confirm the worst suspicions of unionists. Campaigning against partition in elections to northern parliaments could never undo it. It had happened. Just as Sinn Féin had no policy that could prevent it, it had no policy to unravel it.

In terms of purely electoral statistics, however, the elections in both parts of Ireland were a complete vindication of Sinn Féin's tactics. In the twenty-six counties no seats were contested. It was a demonstration of just how hostile people had become to the beleaguered British administration in the country and just how powerful the republican movement had become. Anyone standing for election or expressing any opposition to Sinn Féin could be seen as supporting the British in times when 'authorised reprisals' by Crown forces, which began on 1 January 1921, were being inflicted. These actions were in addition to the death and destruction that unauthorised reprisals had been causing all over the country since 1919. IRA prisoners had been hanged, cities and towns had been burnt and sacked, homes destroyed and livestock killed. Anyone standing against a Sinn Féin candidate would be taking their life in their hands. One hundred and twenty-four Sinn Féin candidates were returned unopposed for the southern parliament.

Unencumbered by contests to the southern parliament, the

republican movement threw everything into the northern elections. They put up twenty Sinn Féin candidates for the fifty-two seats. There were another fifty-seven candidates from different parties, the only occasion in the history of Northern Ireland prior to 1972 when all seats were contested. Unlike 1918, there was no problem about 'split votes' and allocation of seats between IPP and Sinn Féin: split votes do not apply in a PR election. In a 90% turnout, Sinn Féin won six seats, as did Joe Devlin's nationalists. Both parties' candidates had pledged to abstain from the new northern parliament, which was to meet in the Edwardian council chamber of Belfast City Hall. The six elected Sinn Féin candidates declared themselves to be TDs and members of the Second Dáil, which gave the party a total of 130 members in that assembly.

It was Sinn Féin's last hurrah as a popular front. The election results masked the dire mess the organisation had fallen into. There is nothing like an election for invigorating a party. Even the internal contests for nomination energise it. On the face of it, therefore, Sinn Féin should have been a well-oiled machine. In fact, it had not been functioning like a normal political party after 1918 and had not really fought any elections since the local borough council elections in January 1920. The county council elections had been a walkover in most places, and outside the Six Counties there had been no contests in May 1921. Apart from any other reason, of course, the British forces had made it largely impossible for the party to carry on as usual. Given the conditions in the country, most candidates were nominated locally without any central endorsement from Sinn Féin's Harcourt Street HQ. To satisfy requirements for nomination for the 1920 local elections all a candidate had to do was declare support for the republic.

Since the party was illegal and regarded as part of the armed insurrection, the very act of standing could result in severe repercussions from the authorities on a person's family or property. Not surprisingly in these circumstances, most candidates were IRA men on the run or prisoners. In some places, County Clare for example, only IRA Volunteers were allowed to stand, which is a good indication of the secondary role of Sinn Féin within the movement. Of the 125 elected from the twenty-six counties, fifty-two were on the run and forty-seven in jail. In the North, eight of Sinn Féin's twenty candidates were in jail and seven were fugitives.

Once the British government had secured the position of northern unionists and King George V had opened the Belfast parliament in June 1921, the conditions for republicans were transformed. Lloyd George could offer a truce to negotiate a settlement. The truce was duly signed on 9 July and came into effect two days later. Both the Dáil and Sinn Féin could re-emerge into the light after two years underground. In the new peaceful atmosphere, Sinn Féin's organisation enjoyed what appeared to be a revival in the summer and autumn of 1921. Clubs felt that it was again safe to meet and plans were made for the first *ard fheis* since August 1919. It convened in October and it seemed the party had returned to its old numbers again with over 1,300 paid-up branches.

In retrospect, however, it appears that people paid their membership fee to be in the organisation which was involved in negotiations with the British. Their real desire was to align themselves with whatever settlement there was going to be, not to express the kind of fervour for the struggle that being in Sinn Féin had epitomised in 1918. The end was in sight. People wanted to be associated with the successful outcome of the struggle, still by the new year there were over 1,400 Sinn Féin *cumainn*. As Michael Laffan wrote: 'Never had it been more popular or fashionable to be a Sinn Féiner than in the months before the party's disintegration.'

The details of the proximate cause for the party's disintegration have been well rehearsed. As soon as the Anglo-Irish Treaty was signed on 6 December 1921, recriminations which crystallised around the oath of allegiance broke out at all levels in the republican movement. The Treaty's opponents regarded the oath as a betrayal of the Republic established in 1916 that they were sworn to defend, which Sinn Féin had endorsed as its aim in the 1917 *ard fheis* and which the IRA had fought for since 1919. The importance of the oath should be emphasised because as early as spring 1922 many republicans, North and South, took the line that they opposed the Treaty because it partitioned Ireland, and that endorsing any agreement involving partition would be to repeat the 'crime' for which Sinn Féin had castigated Redmond.

Today, a significant proportion of the Irish population believes still that the Civil War was about partition. It was not. It was about swearing allegiance to 'foreign kings' and whether that meant the Treaty had fatally compromised the ideal of the Republic. The fact is that the British government established Northern Ireland as a separate political entity with its own parliament and police force before entering into negotiations with the republican leadership in summer 1921.

Sinn Féin played no role as a party in the dispute about the oath. On the contrary, the party was the victim of the disagreement. Sinn Féin as a party never voted on the Treaty, though there is evidence to indicate extensive support for it. For example, in early January 1922 the *Freeman's Journal* reported over thirty Sinn Féin executives in support and none against. In the middle of the month, Sinn Féin's *ard comhairle*, composed of constituency executives and party officers, elected a new Standing Committee on which pro-Treaty members outnumbered anti-Treaty members by eleven to three.

Did it matter what Sinn Féin's view was? By autumn 1921 Sinn Féin's status and authority in the republican movement lagged far behind that of the IRA and the Dáil. It was the IRA that had brought the British to the negotiating table. It was the Dáil that had sent delegates to London to negotiate with the British. Sinn Féin's central organisation was moribund. Thanks to de Valera's 'purifying' reforms of April 1919, anyone who was anyone in the republican movement was a senior figure in the IRA or a minister in the Dáil or both.

Nevertheless, the view of Sinn Féin did count. The party was still worth capturing, if for no other reason than to possess its name, which still conjured up the magic of 'the nation organised', as de Valera put it. There would have to be elections in 1922 to implement the Treaty. Ownership of the name Sinn Féin would be important in such elections. Whoever owned the name would be able to claim copyright of republicanism and the continuity of the movement that had won the elections of 1918, 1920 and 1921 and expressed the self-determination of the Irish people. It would also be possible to claim that Sinn Féin remained the political embodiment of the self-determination of the Irish people. In spring 1922 there began a tussle for the title deeds to the republican movement. Possession of the name Sinn Féin would be evidence of the ownership of those deeds.

It took the opponents of the Treaty some time to organise. Faced with the overwhelming *ard comhairle* vote in January, which elected eleven pro-Treaty members onto the Standing Committee, de Valera, leading the anti-Treaty group, must have realised that the majority of Sinn Féin did support the Treaty. Even so, at that *ard comhairle* meeting, de Valera had insisted the party was split and should divide in two. Incredibly, he meant that the pro-Treaty people should leave and he would remain as president of the anti-Treaty minority and retain the Sinn Féin organisation. Although he led a minority, de Valera was prepared to face down the majority, a recurring feature in Irish republicanism.

De Valera and his supporters had a number of advantages. There was his personal standing and authority. Though he was no longer president of Dáil Éireann, he was still president of Sinn Féin. Among the Treaty's supporters there was also a deep reluctance to contemplate a split on something so intangible as the wording of an oath; not so among the anti-Treatyites who would have been ready to drive out the majority. The most important advantage de Valera and his supporters possessed was that they were predominantly activists and ideologues, whereas the pro-Treaty Sinn Féin members were rank and file. As far as the latter were concerned, if the British left and the Irish got their own government, sure what did an oath matter?

It mattered to the activists, who were mainly IRA, and to the substantial numbers of Dáil members, many also IRA, who demanded a republic or nothing. As early as 3 January, even before the Dáil had voted for the Treaty, some of the anti-Treaty activists had rented an office in Dublin and set up their own newspaper called *Republic of Ireland*.

The immediate objective in the contest for ownership of Sinn Féin was to overturn the pro-Treaty majority, which had been evident at the January *ard comhairle*. A special *ard fheis* was called for 21 February in the Mansion House, to discuss the Treaty. The anti-Treaty republicans knew they had to control the meeting. If they were outvoted within Sinn Féin, as they had been in the Dáil, they would lose two of the components of the republican movement as well as any claim to the name Sinn Féin. In the process of selecting delegates for the special *ard fheis*, de Valera's people used the strength of their activists, particularly the IRA men, to good effect. What happened in February is a well-known feature of all political parties and many trade unions: most members are moderates, and when faced with zealots the moderates tend to walk away from confrontation and leave the party to the zealots.

Another feature common to most parties is that zealots devote more time to the party than moderate rank-and-file members. The result is the zealots are willing to play representative roles at local and national level, travel to conferences and speak at meetings. In short, activists are likely to form the majority at critical meetings. By the time of the special *ard fheis* in February, this process had taken effect. Although the evidence suggests that a majority of Sinn Féin members in the country supported the Treaty, when the *ard fheis* was held the delegates rejected an attempt to have decisions taken by secret ballot. Pro-Treaty delegates were intimidated by the prospect of voting by a show of hands.

Collins and Griffith made strenuous efforts before and during the meeting to avoid a split. De Valera, not certain of the outcome and still hoping to capture Sinn Féin and its funds, repeatedly argued openly and privately for the need to split – a remarkable line for the president of an organisation to take. After speeches to the delegates and private meetings between de Valera, Collins and Austin Stack, it was agreed to adjourn the *ard fheis* for three months. The decision of Sinn Féin on the Treaty was therefore to take no decision. De Valera remained as president of Sinn Féin but not in control of it because the pro-Treaty membership was too numerous. Nor did he gain access to the party's funds.

The outcome meant that Sinn Féin as a party was left in limbo. What line would it take in the forthcoming election for a Dáil based on the Treaty? People were already organising. Anti-Treaty IRA men and Cumann na mBan, which had formally rejected the Treaty on 5 February, packed *cumainn*. Moderates began to drift away. Since neither faction could control Sinn Féin, two new parties began to emerge, one without a proper name and known only as the treaty election committee, and the anti-Treaty party, Cumann na Poblachta, with de Valera as its president.

Since violence by anti-Treaty IRA men was increasing markedly from April, there is no doubt that they could have prevented an election taking place or rendered it nugatory. In a desperate attempt to avoid the inevitable split within Sinn Féin and to enable the election required by the Treaty to take place, but also as a gesture of solidarity to the beleaguered nationalists in the North (whose plight will be considered below), Collins made a deal with de Valera in May. There would be a national panel of candidates, pro- and anti-Treaty, who would all be described as Sinn Féin candidates.

The number of pro- and anti-Treaty candidates on the panel would be in proportion to their strength in the existing Dáil. Sinn Féin would ratify the panel candidates. That was Sinn Féin's only involvement in the election. Even if it had possessed an electoral organisation, what else could the party do? It could not campaign for or against the major issue of the day, an absurd position for a political party. If a political party cannot agree a united position, it has no function in a campaign.

On 26 July, a month into the Civil War, Jennie Wyse-Power, one of Sinn Féin's treasurers, closed the party HQ in Harcourt Street. Páidín O'Keeffe, its secretary, removed its records. The Standing Committee, elected in January 1922, called it a day on 26 October 1922, and, finally, in February 1924, the two party treasurers lodged Sinn Féin's remaining monies, £8,610, with the chancery division of the High Court.

These actions infuriated de Valera who saw his chance to retain continuity of ownership and leadership of Sinn Féin being taken from under his nose. Equally important was the right to control the money, not just the £8,610 in Ireland, but the millions of dollars he had raised as president of Sinn Féin during his eighteen months in the USA. All attempts at his behest by republican officers of Sinn Féin to reconvene and undo Jennie Wyse-Power's actions came to naught.

The second Sinn Féin was formally dead. Or so it appeared to outsiders. De Valera and his supporters refused to accept the fact and continued to try to breathe life into the corpse.

The War of Independence was waged outside Ulster, mainly in Dublin and the south and west of the country. The four northeastern counties with their large 'hostage' nationalist communities played no significant part. The first IRA division in the Belfast area, the Third Northern, headed by Joe McKelvey, was not even established until spring 1921. Nevertheless, almost everything that happened in the rest of the island had repercussions in Northern Ireland. In most cases the consequences for northern nationalists were horrendous.

What Sinn Féin would have regarded as major IRA successes brought immediate and terrible retribution on nationalist communities in the North. Two examples will suffice. In July 1920 the IRA shot dead Lieutenant-Colonel GBF Smyth, the RIC's divisional commander in

Munster. He came from near Banbridge, County Down, where his remains were taken for burial. Following his funeral in the town, scores of Catholics were expelled from Banbridge and also from the nearby town of Dromore. There were no deaths but there was great loss and destruction of property.

The following month the IRA assassinated RIC District Inspector OR Swanzy, the man reputedly responsible for the murder, on 20 March that year, of the lord mayor of Cork Tomás MacCurtáin. They murdered Swanzy in his home town of Lisburn, County Antrim, with the result that most Catholics and all Sinn Féiners and their families were expelled from the town. Here is an account of the destruction from the diary of the former UVF gunrunner, Fred Crawford.

> It reminded me of a French town after it had been bombarded by the Germans as I saw in France in 1916. We visited the ruins of the Priest's house on Chapel Hill. It was burnt or gutted and the furniture all destroyed. We called at Mr Stephenson's and had tea there. Mrs Thompson and his sister was also with him. They told me of some very hard cases of where Unionists had lost practically all they had by the fire of the house of a Catholic spreading to theirs … It has been stated that there are only four or five RC families left in Lisburn. Be that as it may there certainly are practically no shops or places of business left to the RCs.

The only unusual aspect of these examples is that there were no deaths other than the initial IRA killings.

Retribution came not only after IRA attacks. Communal violence left eighteen dead in Derry in June 1920 and thirty dead in Belfast in August. Attacks on Catholics in the Belfast shipyards and engineering plants in July 1920 resulted in over a dozen deaths. The figures were far worse in 1921 and 1922.

Political developments also fuelled unionist paranoia. It was difficult enough to be a member of the nationalist party, but to be a member of

Sinn Féin was a life-threatening position. Unionists in the northeast regarded Sinn Féin, and indeed any manifestation of republicanism, as a threat to their very existence as a community. Every success for Sinn Féin was a reinforcement of that threat. The aim of unionists was, quite simply, the destruction of Sinn Féin. For their part, Sinn Féin supporters in the North saw the party as the only means to avoid partition, something that by 1919 had become the unionists' only political aim. It would hardly be possible to find two more diametrically opposed groups.

Tragically, neither group had any control over its destiny. The unionists depended completely on the goodwill of the Conservatives at Westminster who dominated Lloyd George's coalition government after the 1918 election. Members of Sinn Féin in the North were also helpless onlookers as the republican movement in the rest of Ireland took on the British Army, the RIC and the Black and Tans. The driving force of republicanism was located in the South, so problems there took precedence over those in the northeast.

In vain did northern republicans plead with their southern comrades to glance North. In an almost shamefaced plea, Louis J Walsh, a solicitor from Ballycastle, County Antrim, speaking as a delegate to Sinn Féin's April 1919 *ard fheis*, asked 'that attention be given to Ulster'. He believed 'the organisation [Sinn Féin] had not sufficiently grappled with that question.' It was a statement that could have been made at any time between 1920 and 1923. Sinn Féin continued to neglect the North. Whenever its leaders did respond it was always too little, too late.

The hard truth, of course, was that there was nothing the republican leadership in Dublin could do to prevent partition, more especially partition along the six-county border, which became the British government's plan in 1920. The failure of Sinn Féin's peace conference strategy in 1919 left the party without a policy not just on the North but for achieving independence for all Ireland. The IRA did have a policy: to fight for a republic. It was a hazardous enough policy, even if the majority of the population supported the fighters. It was impossibly dangerous when the majority was vehemently opposed, as in the northeast. IRA actions in Ulster, which began to increase in frequency in 1920, were therefore a positive invitation to a paroxysm of retaliation.

Sinn Féin in the North followed the party line and demanded a republic, somehow assuming that this would ward off partition. Republicans in the North oscillated between not believing partition would happen and not knowing how to stop it. They had completely unrealistic expectations about what the movement's leadership in Dublin could or should do about it – a syndrome common not only to Sinn Féin supporters but to all northern nationalists, and not only in the years of the War of Independence but right up to the present day.

Throughout 1920, legislation to partition the country worked its way inexorably through Westminster. Both nationalists and republicans appeared not to notice. They behaved as if they believed it would go away if they covered their eyes. Nationalist newspapers barely covered the progress of the partition bill. The *Irish News* pronounced partition 'a vanishing scheme'. Other papers did not even mention it. Of course, the truth was that it was all nationalists thought about. They took every opportunity to demonstrate the injustice, the illogicality and the unworkability of partition whilst ignoring it as it crept relentlessly towards them. Whenever they had an electoral success, as in the 1920 local government elections, nationalists, republicans and their newspapers in the North suddenly came alive to the issue and trumpeted another piece of evidence to support their claim that partition was impossible. After June 1920, when Sinn Féin and the nationalists together controlled Tyrone and Fermanagh county councils, the *Irish News* asked: 'What is "Ulster" now?' When the final results of the elections left unionists with a majority in only four of the country's thirty-three county councils, predictably those in the northeast, republicans and nationalists alike proclaimed the impossibility of the six-county area being a viable entity.

However cogent the nationalists' arguments may have been, they were all to no avail. By late 1920 republicans North and South realised, years late, that the British had decided to treat Ulster unionists separately and to guarantee their position before turning to the rest of Ireland. The Conservatives in Westminster drove events. When it became clear that partition would be on the statute book by Christmas 1920, northern Sinn Féiners started to become edgy, then agitated. They passed ever more urgent resolutions and appealed to their fellow countrymen in the rest of Ireland and to the Irish diaspora in America and Australia. Slowly it dawned on them that the republican leadership had no idea how to deal with the imminent enactment of the bill. By trusting the Dublin-based leaders, northern republicans had developed the Micawberish attitude that something would turn up in an overall settlement to resolve the Ulster question.

Northern nationalists who had switched allegiance to Sinn Féin in 1916 did so in the belief that only Sinn Féin could prevent partition. Yet moving to support Sinn Féin simply meant exchanging one Dublin-led party for another. Sinn Féin's priority after 1918 was a republic. Its leaders took for granted there would be no partition. They were hopelessly wrong. However, in 1921 members of Sinn Féin in the North saw themselves as very much part of a national project, a national organisation that would not leave them abandoned. They regarded the election as yet another opportunity to participate in expressing national self-determination and to send representatives from the North to the Second Dáil, thereby denying the existence of partition and its institutions.

The rump of the IPP, led by Joe Devlin, threatened a dilution of that project. The republican leadership, particularly Collins, hoped in vain that there would be only Sinn Féin candidates in the North, as in the rest of the country, thereby presenting Sinn Féin once again as the single political voice of Irish self-determination. Devlin would have none of it. To Sinn Féin's exasperation he was determined to contest the elections. How many candidates would northern Nationalists field? What would be their attitude to the Dáil? Would the Nationalists sit in the northern parliament? After all, Devlin was still participating at Westminster and thereby recognising Britain's right to govern in Ireland. If the Nationalists did well, would unionists be able to claim that northern Nationalists also acquiesced in partition?

Feelers extended from both sides included a secret meeting in Dublin between Devlin and de Valera. The result was a deal brokered in March 1921 by Sinn Féin's Seán MacEntee, a Belfast native who represented Monaghan South in the Dáil. In effect, Devlin agreed to the Sinn Féin line on self-determination and abstention. IPP candidates would ask voters to give second preferences to the other anti-partitionist party. Devlin had little option. Emotions about the election and partition were running so high among even moderate members of the nationalist community that there was no prospect of adopting a different line from Sinn Féin. Devlin bought his continuing political existence by, to all intents and purposes, adopting Sinn Féin's policy.

So low had the fortunes of the northern IPP remnant sunk that Devlin was unable to field anything like the twenty-one candidates the pact allowed him. In fact, his party had shrunk to be a Greater Belfast organisation, little more than an extension of Devlin's mighty ego. In the end, he managed to scrape up twelve candidates, compared to Sinn Féin's twenty, and insisted on running them, thereby queering Sinn Féin's pitch as the sole voice of nationalist Ireland.

Sinn Féin fielded many prominent southern-based national figures as candidates. Thus de Valera stood in Down, Collins in Armagh, Sean Milroy, Griffith's old crony, in Fermanagh–Tyrone and Eoin MacNeill in Derry. Most candidates had clear and obvious connections with the IRA: de Valera and Collins, Denis McCullough from west Belfast, Frank Aiken from south Armagh and Seán MacEntee, also from Belfast, to name a few. This sort of slate reinforced the impression among unionists that Sinn

Féin was a southern malignant growth spreading poisonous tentacles northwards. To unionists, support for Sinn Féin meant support for the IRA campaign. It was difficult to argue with this view as nine of the candidates from outside the North were in jail and others on the run. This unionist attitude toward Sinn Féin has never changed in the eighty years since 1921.

One of those in jail was the Ballycastle solicitor Louis J Walsh, who was interned in Ballykinlar camp and was the same man who, in 1919, had diffidently raised Sinn Féin's lack of interest in the North. His imprisonment is a reminder of the main reason Sinn Féin nominated prominent southern republicans to contest northern elections. Quite simply, it was extremely dangerous to stand as a Sinn Féin candidate. Members of Sinn Féin were liable to arrest, at the very least. At worst, there was the distinct possibility of being shot by the Ulster Special Constabulary (USC), which had been in operation since 1 November 1920.

In the end, Sinn Féin and Devlin's nationalists won six seats each. Their combined thirty-two candidates won 165,000 votes, a total for nationalist and republican parties in the North not surpassed until 1982. That figure of a dozen seats remained the norm for nationalist representation in Stormont throughout the period 1921–72.

Those elected on the Sinn Féin ticket in May 1921 repaired to the Second Dáil when it convened in August. Interestingly, Joe Devlin and his nationalists did not give their allegiance to the Dáil although they were invited to attend with everyone else elected, including unionists. There was so much rancour about Devlin's continuing attendance at Westminster and his decision to stand for the Belfast parliament that he and his colleagues would have been less welcome in the Second Dáil than the Ulster unionists. Devlin probably reckoned, correctly, that his six members could do less within a completely Sinn Féin Dáil than he and his old colleague, TP O'Connor, the Liverpool MP, could do at Westminster.

In the meantime, the political situation was transformed. At the end of June 1921, Lloyd George invited de Valera to London for talks. The truce that followed the initial talks seemed to sound the death knell of partition. To the joy of nationalists, the 1920 Government of Ireland Act was suspended and the new Northern Ireland government was placed in suspended animation. No more powers were to be transferred to Belfast for the duration of talks. Dublin Castle, still exercising power in the North and blithely ignoring the Belfast parliament, extended the provisions of the truce to the North. To their dismay, British Army and senior RIC officers found themselves sitting across the table from the IRA officers they had been hunting just days before. A senior IRA staff officer from GHQ, Eoin O'Duffy, soon to be IRA chief of staff, arrived in Belfast and opened his office in St Mary's Hall in the city centre. His title was Truce Liaison Officer.

For Sinn Féin in the North, events in July had a similar effect to that in the rest of the country: the truce and the beginning of negotiations legitimised it. It could come out of hiding. People flocked to join the party and the IRA, which was now drilling openly, even in Catholic parts of Belfast where hitherto recruitment had been the weakest in the North. Just as elsewhere in Ireland, people wanted to be on the winning side and in July it looked as though Sinn Féin had won. The IPP vanished outside Belfast, while whole branches in Tyrone and Fermanagh switched to Sinn Féin.

The euphoria did not last long. When the British proposals became public in August, northern Sinn Féin members were downcast to see partition incorporated in them. Deputations from northern councils controlled by Sinn Féin and nationalists began to stream to the Dáil to emphasise the importance of the 'essential unity' de Valera had stipulated when negotiations reconvened. Tyrone and Fermanagh county councils passed resolutions refusing to recognise the northern parliament. The Dáil responded in September by sending Michael Collins to Armagh, the area he represented in the Dáil. He addressed a large crowd, said to number over 10,000, but neither his speech nor reassurances from de Valera when he met deputations could convince northerners.

Nevertheless, when the terms of the Treaty became known in December, northerners west of the Bann were generally satisfied. Article 12 of the Treaty, which stipulated a Boundary Commission, seemed to offer only one outcome. The Commission was to determine the boundary of Northern Ireland 'in accordance with the wishes of the inhabitants'. Naturally it was assumed that since the majority of people in Tyrone and Fermanagh and substantial numbers along the six-county line in Derry and Armagh opposed partition, any commission taking their wishes into account would reduce Northern Ireland to an economically non-viable rump. Sinn Féin members in Tyrone and Fermanagh were keenest in support of the Treaty. Their colleagues in Derry and Armagh were as divided as they knew their counties must be under any interpretation of the Boundary Commission. Those in Belfast knew that whatever happened they would be partitioned off from the rest of Ireland and fervently hoped the Boundary Commission would cut so large a chunk out of the North that partition could operate for only a short period.

Unlike its colleagues in the rest of the country, Sinn Féin in the North remained remarkably united in its initial response to the Treaty. It was in favour. The northern press also supported the Treaty, and Sinn Féin's main supporter among the northern Catholic bishops, Dr Mac-Rory of Down and Connor, the diocese that included Belfast, came out publicly in favour in a sermon on Christmas Day. Apart from the hope held out by the Boundary Commission, another reason for this favourable response was probably the unionists' hostility to the Treaty: if unionists thought it was bad, it must be good for nationalists. It was only after the vote in the Dáil in January 1922 and the withdrawal of de Valera and his anti-Treaty supporters that similar divisions also emerged in northern Sinn Féin.

Pro- and anti-Treaty factions appeared, but the line of division was caused by a dispute completely different from that which produced the murderous conflict in the new Free State. Whereas in the Free State the argument in republican ranks arose out of the oath of allegiance to King George required by the Treaty, in the North the argument developed from discussions on which policy to follow towards the northern parliament. Northern Sinn Féin was faced with a dilemma: recognise the northern parliament and its emerging institutions, and thereby recognise partition, or withhold recognition and resist partition?

Meeting with northern Sinn Féiners at the Mansion House on 7 December 1921, Eoin MacNeill, the Speaker of the Dáil, recommended non-recognition. MacNeill called it 'a practical programme of passive resistance'. There would be no recognition of the northern state's courts, no paying rates or taxes, nor would any republican recognise 'the educational authority of the Belfast Parliament'.

On first consideration it seemed a commendably attractive policy. It was authentic 'Sinn Féin think' of the old Griffithite type. Elected bodies, peacefully occupying the high moral ground, would declare themselves independent of Northern Ireland and recognise the Dáil. This was what had been happening since the local government elections in 1920. The councils would try to organise an alternative State system within the North's jurisdiction until the Boundary Commission set them 'free'. Theoretically it was a powerful argument, stronger than Griffith's original proposals had been in 1905 because now the British recognised that the Dáil and a provisional government existed outside British jurisdiction.

In reality, of course, it was anything but 'practical' or 'concrete', the words MacNeill had used to describe it. In Fermanagh, when the county council refused to recognise Northern Ireland, the police, now under Belfast control, closed the council down within five minutes of the decision; the northern parliament imposed a commissioner. It was clear that the same would happen to any council that followed Fermanagh's example. It would also mean that any such council could not put its case to the

Boundary Commission for inclusion in the Free State. East of the Bann, where unionists controlled all institutions, 'non-recognition' was not an option.

In any case, MacNeill's proposals were purely academic in the face of the reality of ferocious violence being visited on northern nationalists by the Specials and loyalist murder gangs – on occasions the same men – in the Treaty's aftermath. The violence was so serious that, as early as the second week of January 1922, it forced the British government onto the scene to try to broker a deal between Collins and Sir James Craig, the northern unionist leader, to bring it to an end. In the course of lengthy negotiations from January to April, Collins tried to cobble together some arrangement that would at once safeguard the lives and property of Catholics in the North and commit Craig to accepting the consequences of the Boundary Commission clause.

Central to the talks was the attempt to have Catholics enrolled in the Specials, the precursor to what would become, on 31 May 1922, the RUC. Most Sinn Féiners in the North bitterly resented any such suggestion, especially given the circumstances whereby the Specials were engaged in nightly acts of terrorism across the North. How could they join such a body? The more substantial political objection was that joining the Specials meant recognising not just the existence of the northern state but its juridical authority. Even worse, it required an oath of allegiance. Thus the proposal, which Collins and Griffith both argued for, combined the ingredients which were certain to cause a split in the republican movement in the North: recognising partition and swearing an oath of allegiance.

In the event, the so-called Collins–Craig pact collapsed. This was partly because Craig was unable to deliver hardline elements in his own unionist party, partly because there was no will on the Sinn Féin side to implement it and partly because of the duplicitous policy Michael Collins followed, which rapidly resulted in the deaths of many more Catholics and the destruction of Sinn Féin in the North. Exactly what Collins was up to has proved impossible to elucidate with any certainty because the actions he ordered seem mutually contradictory and because he was killed in August 1922 and took his intentions with him to the grave.

The facts are these. At the same time as he was negotiating with Craig to produce a pact whereby Catholics could be involved in security and policing in the North, Collins was organising a renewed IRA campaign in the North in collusion with anti-Treaty forces in the Free State. What were his reasons? Preserving the existence of his new Free State and the unity of the republican movement in Ireland seem the most obvious answers. Achieving both at the expense of the northern state must have seemed an acceptable price. But did the price include the inevitable consequences for northern nationalists? Could Collins possibly not have foreseen what would happen to Catholics in the North given the events of the first three months of 1922? After all, it was as a result of those terrible months that he was trying to make a deal to prevent further destruction and death among those same people.

The answer is that Collins could have been in no doubt of the danger to Catholics. He had spies in the old RIC in various parts of the North who provided accounts of the grisly events and named the members of murder gangs within the Specials. Secondly, he had established a Northern Advisory Committee drawn from Sinn Féin representatives, IRA leaders and clergy in the North who were well-informed about the situation in the North. On 11 April 1922, along with members of the Provisional Government, Collins attended a meeting of the committee in Dublin. On the government side those present with him included Arthur Griffith, Richard Mulcahy, WT Cosgrave, Kevin O'Higgins and Eoin MacNeill. Three bishops attended as members of the Northern Advisory Committee: Dr MacRory of Down and Connor, Dr Mulhern of Dromore and Dr McKenna of Clogher. There were also priests from Enniskillen, Omagh and Belfast who supported Sinn Féin. A substantial turnout of northern republicans was also present: Cahir Healy from Fermanagh, Dr James Gillespie from Cookstown, George Murnaghan, a solicitor from Omagh, and Dr Russell McNabb from Belfast Sinn Féin. The IRA was represented by the chief of staff Eoin O'Duffy, Thomas Morris and Seamus Woods, OCs respectively of the Second and Third Northern Divisions, Frank Crummey and Frank McArdle from Belfast.

The northerners laid out in detail the parlous circumstances of Catholics in the Six Counties and the desperate conditions in Belfast. The minutes of the meeting run to over fifty pages. If there had been any doubt prior to this, Collins could not have left that meeting without a very clear picture of the situation in Belfast and the North as a whole. Yet, unknown to his colleagues in the provisional government who attended the meeting, he was in the process of organising a major IRA offensive against the new six-county state. An IRA meeting in Clones on 21 April ordered 'operations by every division having territory inside the six counties' within two weeks. The campaign burst on the North at the beginning of May in widespread attacks on RIC barracks in east Tyrone and south Derry, followed by murders, explosions, arson attacks and mayhem in Belfast and in counties Derry, Antrim and Down.

Following a weekend of tremendous violence in Belfast, which resulted in fourteen dead and many injuries, the IRA assassinated the Northern Ireland Unionist MP William J Twaddell in broad daylight on 22 May. The following day Craig introduced internment, with 200 initial arrests. At its height in 1923 there were over 700 men interned, most on the *Argenta*, a prison ship moored in Belfast Lough. As usual in these sweeps, the IRA seemed to elude the raiders. Men like Frank Crummey, Seamus Woods, Frank McArdle and Dr McNabb, alert to the prospect of arrest, went on the run if they were not in hiding already. But internment dealt a fatal blow to Sinn Féin in the North. Virtually all the party's major figures who had been prominent since 1917 were jailed. Cahir Healy, Dr Gillespie and other members of Collins's committee arrived on the

Argenta along with Sinn Féin councillors and party members. By the end of June, Sinn Féin as an organisation had ceased to exist outside jail.

Since he was under no illusion about the ruthlessness of the leaders of unionism and their armed forces, why did Collins leave his northern colleagues open to such depredation? Many possible reasons suggest themselves. For a start, he must have been aware that, while Craig was unlikely to be able to persuade his own party to accept a pact that included Catholics and gave republicans a role in policing, there was equally strong opposition within Sinn Féin to a pact. The first attempt at a pact in January had caused considerable dissension in the republican movement, yet Craig had not been able to deliver. The risk Collins took had been for nothing.

The second attempt in April was asking for even further steps towards accepting the northern state. Sam Heron, secretary of the Belfast executive of Sinn Féin, had made it clear that the majority of the party in the city was against it. Belfast Sinn Féin compared the proposal to join the Specials with the suggestion that southern nationalists should have joined the Black and Tans during their 'reign of terror'. If that was inconceivable, why should northern nationalists be asked to act differently? The same attitude obtained in rural areas. But if joining the Specials would cause a split in Belfast, the very place the pact was chiefly designed to calm, then there was no point in Collins proceeding.

Secondly, official and freelance violence against Catholics in the North was so appalling and the attitude of the unionist rulers so callous that there was a growing demand for the IRA to retaliate. Five days before the IRA campaign was launched, the Northern Advisory Committee, meeting in Belfast on 26 April, appealed to Collins to renew IRA attacks, not knowing that he had already ordered the onslaught on the North. In mid-May at the last meeting of the committee, even after some terrible reprisals by the Specials, there was support for the resurgent campaign. The committee asked the provisional government for a 'campaign of destruction inside the six-county area'. They wanted to make the area ungovernable.

It may be that Collins shared the opinion that the only way to compel Craig to accede to demands for a pact involving nationalists was to destabilise the North, in the words of George Murnaghan from Tyrone, 'to squeeze the northern area so small … it can't exist.' Perhaps, but it is unlikely. The new unionist regime in the North had 48,000 armed Specials at their disposal. Collins knew the strength of the IRA in the North in spring 1922 was just 8,500, with 800 in Belfast. Not all of the 8,500 men were available for active service. Not all possessed weapons.

Collins, however, had bigger fish to fry. His main preoccupation was the widening divide in the republican movement throughout Ireland. The North was marginal to this big picture but the plight of northern nationalists was the only issue about which there could be any possible agreement between the pro- and anti-Treaty factions. Collins was vulnerable on partition. De Valera had begun to use the intensifying violence against northern Catholics as a stick to beat Collins. He also derided the pact with Craig as a 'scrap of paper'. For the first time the accusation began to emerge that the Treaty had caused partition and that acceptance of the Treaty meant accepting partition. The anti-Treatyites began to accuse Collins and the provisional government of abandoning northern Sinn Féin and the nationalist population. What better way to unite the pro- and anti-Treaty factions of the movement than by combining to fight for their northern brethren?

In May northern members of Sinn Féin asked repeatedly for help and appealed for unity. The developing violence of the anti-Treaty IRA in the South was a source of great alarm and dismay to them. A fortnight after the renewed IRA campaign in the North began, Sinn Féin's Belfast executive begged the Dáil to unite 'in the name of the persecuted minority'. So awful were the reports from the North that they contributed to bringing together the leaders of the pro- and anti-Treaty sides in a remarkable show of unity. On 18 May a delegation of northerners visited the South, led by twenty-four-year-old Frank Aiken (commander of the Fourth Northern, the North's most powerful IRA division, drawn from Armagh, Down and Louth and which had been heavily involved in the fighting), and met with Collins, Griffith, de Valera and Rory O'Connor, the leader of the anti-Treaty Military Executive. The northerners demanded a 'united civil government supported by a united army'.

There seems little doubt that the pleas of the visiting delegation had a major effect in producing the Collins–de Valera electoral pact two days later. Neither the pro- nor the anti-Treaty side could afford the blame for deserting the northerners in their hour of need. It was as a result of that pact that the two Sinn Féin factions fought the first Free State general election in June as a national coalition panel. The northern campaign, involving the anti-Treaty IRA, had allowed Collins to present one unifying issue to pull together the republican factions. It was a temporary respite. The antagonisms were too sharp and deep. By the end of June the newly mandated government was at war with Rory O'Connor's anti-Treaty IRA.

The North, the Boundary Commission, destabilising Craig's government, preventing the consolidation of partition – all were forgotten in the desperate struggle to prevail over the 'Irregulars', as the anti-Treaty IRA was quickly described. The campaign in the North may have provided Collins with the necessary political and military cover to embarrass the anti-Treatyites into uniting and given him the breathing space to have his government ratified, but it destroyed the republican movement as a political and military force in the North. By mid-June the northern campaign had been snuffed out in deadly fashion by the unionists. The net effect of the campaign Collins had ordered to begin in May was the sacrifice of two northern divisions of the IRA: the Second Northern, based in counties Derry and Tyrone, and the Third Northern, mainly located in Belfast, but taking in County Antrim and north County Down. The First

Northern, based in Derry City, also suffered serious losses.

Collins must have realised that those would be the results of his order. It can never be known whether he viewed the loss of the northern IRA and the destruction of Sinn Féin in the Six Counties with equanimity or whether he had other plans, which could not then be carried out in the Civil War that erupted on 28 June when his forces began to shell the Four Courts in Dublin. Whatever his intentions, the results would have been the same. The new Northern Ireland government quickly crushed what they regarded as a rebellion. The recently passed Special Powers Act, which allowed virtually unlimited stop-and-search powers, the searching of premises without warrant, internment without trial and other more brutal measures, including flogging, was used against nationalists unremittingly and with considerable zeal. Almost overnight Sinn Féin disappeared as a political force in the North.

Although Sinn Féin may have ceased to be a political force, it did not vanish altogether. Individuals flying the party's flag stood in elections in the North after 1922 but they were just that, individuals, with only a tenuous connection to any wider group. The votes for those standing under the Sinn Féin banner slumped in 1924. No candidates were elected. Northern nationalists resumed their pre-1918 support for a more moderate form of nationalism.

By coincidence, and resulting from entirely different causes, Sinn Féin as an organisation in any meaningful sense of the word had been wound up in both parts of Ireland by July 1922. Offices were closed, committees ceased to meet, *cumainn* folded, records ceased to be kept. The party simply fell apart.

De Valera was still president of Sinn Féin, a title he continued to use to enable him to masquerade as the leader of a national organisation or, as he would have claimed, of *the* national organisation, 'the nation organised'. By mid-1922 it was, of course, nothing of the kind. The title and the party name merely constituted a means of keeping de Valera in the public eye. Instead of being 'the nation organised', Sinn Féin was, in de Valera's mind, the means to resuscitate his political ambitions and catapult him to national leadership.

It proved an impossible hope. During the autumn and winter of 1922–23, de Valera was frustrated at every turn. The officer board of Sinn Féin, chiefly in the persons of Jennie Wyse-Power and Páidín O'Keeffe, both firm supporters of the provisional government, stymied every attempt by de Valera and his supporters to take over the organisation. The newly established Executive Council of the Free State, the Cabinet in effect, began to crack down mercilessly on anti-Treatyites of every description, military or political. De Valera and his colleagues who had been elected to the Second Dáil were hunted throughout the State with the same vigour as the anti-Treaty IRA, the Irregulars. In ways reminiscent of the years 1919–21, meetings were broken up, documents seized and anyone or any organisation suspected of being opposed to the new Free State government relentlessly harassed. It was clear that there could be no serious attempt at re-establishing Sinn Féin until the Civil War was over.

It was not until 11 June 1923, therefore, that a meeting was held at the Mansion House to inaugurate a new Sinn Féin. De Valera had been unable to persuade the redoubtable Jennie Wyse-Power or any other of the party's officers to reconvene the adjourned *ard fheis* of spring 1922, nor could he get the Standing Committee to meet. In the end, he and his associates simply set up their own new committee structure and membership and called it Sinn Féin. De Valera's position as president of Sinn Féin lent some credibility to the actions of the 150 or so at that Mansion House meeting.

De Valera now led a party of republicans, some so uncompromising they were even dubious about using the name Sinn Féin because it had monarchical connotations! One of the first actions of this new – third – incarnation of Sinn Féin was to pass a resolution agreeing to abstain from the Dáil that had been elected in June 1922 and to recognise only the Second Dáil, elected in summer 1921, on the grounds that that was the last election in which the Irish people voted as a nation. It then set up an election committee to fight the next Free State elections, which were due in summer 1923.

From this modest start de Valera's new party expanded rapidly and did far better in the elections than most people had expected, except perhaps the party members themselves. The Civil War had caused so much bitterness in many parts of the country, particularly in the southwest, that a substantial proportion of voters was looking for an opportunity to vote against the Cumann na nGaedheal government. De Valera's Sinn Féin put up eighty-five candidates: to the consternation of many in the government it got forty-four elected. It polled 27% of the vote – 6% more than anti-Treaty candidates in summer 1922. De Valera's line had been vindicated. The name Sinn Féin obviously still counted for something. There was indeed a place for an anti-Treaty party with a populist message.

Unfortunately, the party was not going to bring that message into the Dáil. Instead, the new Sinn Féin entered the political never-never land that hardline republicans continued to inhabit until 1986, refusing to recognise any legislature on the island of Ireland. De Valera had managed to extricate himself from the dilemma of whether to participate in Leinster House by the expedient of getting himself arrested while addressing a meeting in Ennis in August 1923, ten days before the election. He remained in custody until July 1924, thereby leaving the fortunes of his new party in the hands of republican ideologues. He must have known that had he been at liberty it would have made no difference to the party's prospects: he would have been unable to change the minds of these diehards.

De Valera must also have spent his year in jail thinking of ways to get off the hook of abstention. He knew he had to if he were ever going to exercise any influence on the country. The new Free State government was working, and people expected that the representatives they elected would represent them. Incredibly, at its first election outing in 1923, de Valera's new Sinn Féin party had won sufficient seats to form a coalition government. The forty-four Sinn Féin TDs elected, had they taken their seats in the Dáil and combined with TDs elected to represent farmers' interests and other independents, would have outnumbered the sixty-three Cumann na nGaedheal TDs.

They had done so well that a belief grew among some of the republican leadership that Sinn Féin, standing as abstentionists, could gain a majority in the next election and renegotiate the Treaty. De Valera knew that this was a forlorn hope. After two by-election defeats in Dublin City and county in the spring of 1924, it had become clear to him that people were not voting for abstentionists. Impeccable republican candidates, such as Sean Lemass and Sean MacEntee, standing in places where republicans should have cruised home, were not sweeping in on the first count. People had switched allegiance. De Valera emerged from jail in July 1924 convinced he had to wriggle off the abstentionist hook. The clinching electoral argument came in March 1925 when republicans won only two out of nine by-elections held on the same day.

Abstention meant the government could ignore the threat posed by de Valera's new Sinn Féin. Yet for de Valera to end abstention would mean overthrowing a whole cartload of cherished theological dogma, starting with the oath of allegiance. To get into government de Valera knew the party would have to swallow its pride and take the oath. Finding a way into the Dáil would be the first step to dismantling the arrangements Cumann na nGaedheal had signed up to in 1922. De Valera toyed with the fanciful notion that Cumann na nGaedheal might agree to drop the oath if Sinn Féin agreed to recognise the Dáil. He never managed to explain why the government should make it easy for dangerous political opponents to enter the political arena. It did not matter. Even that ploy failed among the dyed-in-the-wool republicans in his new Sinn Féin. In

1926 he attempted to persuade the Sinn Féin *ard fheis* to agree to enter Leinster House if there were no oath. They would not hear of it. When this proposal failed by two votes, de Valera resigned as Sinn Féin president, the position he had held since October 1917. He left the movement, taking with him the bulk of the able, ambitious young men in it, and in May 1926 set up a new party: Fianna Fáil.

The rump of Sinn Féin, led by people like Mary MacSwiney, sister of the lord mayor of Cork, Terence MacSwiney, who had died on hunger strike, the fanatical Fr O'Flanagan, Count Plunkett, Austin Stack and the ideologue JJ 'Sceilg' O'Kelly, argued among themselves about whether they should contest the next Free State general election, even on an abstentionist basis. Fianna Fáil presented formidable opposition to the diehards. De Valera had quite simply stolen republicans' clothing and would wear them for the rest of his career. He used the language of pre-Treaty Sinn Féin, sounding more republican than republicans, but his approach was shot through with pragmatism. De Valera was going to do what he had to do to get into power. Fianna Fáil took up farmers' concerns and added a populist mix of social and economic issues to the apparently uncompromising republicanism of its manifesto.

De Valera was also adept at tugging the strings that stirred nationalist sentiment. The very title of his new party, Fianna Fáil – 'Soldiers of Destiny' – had been the slogan of the Volunteers (founded in 1913) and had been embroidered on their cap bands. The fact that the party's name dated from pre-1916, was in Irish, and that de Valera regularly spoke Irish at public meetings meant that he was asserting continuity with the Irish Ireland past of the republican movement, an essential move for anyone claiming the mantle of national leader. It was exactly what Sinn Féin had always done. From the very outset, de Valera accused Cumann na nGaedheal of being impostors who had stolen the trappings of true republicanism and discarded them. In the minds of its leader and members, only Fianna Fáil had a right to ownership of Irish republicanism.

It appeared that the people believed de Valera. In its first election in June 1927, Fianna Fáil won forty-four seats, only three less than Cumann na nGaedheal. What remained of Sinn Féin got a paltry five of its much reduced slate of fifteen candidates elected. De Valera and Fianna Fáil had made off with the people who should have been Sinn Féin's voters.

Another political blow to Sinn Féin soon followed. On 10 July 1927 minister for justice Kevin O'Higgins was assassinated on his way to Mass. Among a series of measures introduced to deal with the crisis this murder caused, the government introduced a bill requiring all election candidates to declare before nomination that they would take their seats if elected. It meant Sinn Féin could no longer stand for elections because it continued to refuse to take the oath of allegiance or recognise the State and therefore would not sign any declaration committing candidates to take seats if elected. Sinn Féin consigned itself to political oblivion by its ideological intransigence. Sinn Féin, now a remnant of a remnant of a national movement, remained outside parliamentary politics in the Free State until the 1950s.

Arthur Griffith, author of *The Sinn Féin Policy*
and founder of Sinn Féin.

Michael Collins, member of the Sinn Féin party executive
and commander-in-chief of the IRA.

Eamon de Valera, president of Sinn Féin, 1917–22 and 1923–26.

A group of TDs at the first session of Dáil Éireann, convened on 21 January 1919. All were members of Sinn Féin and some were also Volunteers.

A group of TDs from the second session of the First Dáil, convened on 10 April 1919. All were members of Sinn Féin and a number were also members of the Volunteers – soon to be called the IRA – notably Michael Collins and Cathal Brugha (seated second and third from the left in the front row). Fr Michael O'Flanagan, vice-president of Sinn Féin, stands in the second row, on the far right.

Dáil Éireann meets in public at the Mansion House, Dublin, on 17 August 1921
to discuss Lloyd George's proposal for talks on Dominion status for Ireland.

THE

RESURRECTION OF HUNGARY:

A PARALLEL FOR IRELAND

WITH APPENDICES ON

PITT'S POLICY AND SINN FEIN

By ARTHUR GRIFFITH.

———

"The case of Ireland is as nearly as possible parallel to the case of Hungary."—WILLIAM SMITH O'BRIEN.

"It is impossible to think of the affairs of Ireland without being forcibly struck with the parallel of Hungary."—SYDNEY SMITH.

"Whenever the people of England think one way in the proportion of two to one, they can outvote in Parliament the united force of Scotland, Wales, and Ireland, although they should think in the other way in the proportion of five to one. And if England thinks one way in the proportion of three to one, she can outvote Scotland, Ireland, and Wales together, although they were each and all to return the whole of their members to vote against her."—GLADSTONE.

"A country is prosperous, not in proportion to its fertility, but in proportion to its freedom."—MONTESQUIEU.

———

THIRD EDITION.

———

Dublin :

WHELAN AND SON.

1918.

Frontispiece of the third edition of Arthur Griffith's 1904 booklet, *The Resurrection of Hungary: a Parallel for Ireland*, which became known as *The Sinn Féin Policy.*

A THING OF THE PAST.

JOHN REDMOND—"Bad luck to that infernal machine with the foreign name. Ever since it come on the road I have lost any fares I had. I can't afford to give the poor baste a feed of oats. I'm to blame meself. Me ould yoke is a bit slow, and it's out of date. I was wan time in comfortable circumstances."

Cartoon depicting John Redmond as an old-fashioned jarvey driving an empty trap symbolising parliamentarianism, while Sinn Féin roars off into the distance with a full complement of passengers in a modern *charabanc*.

Countess Constance Markievicz, member of the Sinn Féin party executive, in full Irish Citizen Army uniform complete with Webley revolver. Elected to the Dáil in 1918, Markievicz became the first woman Cabinet minister.
She was the abstentionist TD for Dublin South between 1923 and 1927.

Sir Edward Carson KC, MP, leader of the Ulster Unionists, inspects a unit of the Young Citizens Volunteers, the youth wing of the UVF, at Balmoral Show Grounds on 6 June 1914.

6. PROTECTING THE FLAME
The Lean Years, 1926–62

After de Valera formed Fianna Fáil in 1926 and made off with the bulk of Sinn Féin's members and voters, Sinn Féin went into rapid decline, then became lost in the political wilderness. By the outbreak of the Second World War in 1939 Sinn Féin had been reduced to the status of a sect composed of ageing, embittered ideologues comforting each other. In 1948 came transformation. A newly reorganised IRA took over, pushed aside the people who believed they had guarded the flame of republicanism and established senior IRA men at the head of Sinn Féin.

The new leaders intended the party to be the IRA's political ancillary, endorsing a new military campaign directed for the first time against Northern Ireland, an area republicans refer to studiously as the 'Six Counties' because they do not recognise its existence as a state. The campaign, waged from 1956 to 1962, failed utterly, but during the 1950s a reinvigorated Sinn Féin, with new life pumped into it by the IRA, demonstrated that there still existed, in both parts of Ireland, a substantial vote for a republican party prepared to take up populist issues and follow a radical set of socio-economic policies.

It could be argued that 1948, when the IRA took control of the dying embers of Sinn Féin and blew oxygen onto them, was a turning point marking the end of a separate phase in Sinn Féin's history. On the surface that may appear to be the case. There were indeed many changes in 1948, but they were superficial. The reality was that the men directing the republican movement after 1948 did not make a break with the past. They still looked back to the War of Independence and Civil War. Some of them had fought in both. They tended to be contemporaries of senior figures in Fianna Fáil, like Sean Lemass, who was forty-nine in 1948 and Frank Aiken, fifty years old that year. The real break with the past came in 1962 when a new generation took over the leadership of republicanism after the failure of the 1956–62 campaign. It was this new leadership that attempted to point the movement in an entirely new direction.

Republicans, of course, argue strongly that there was continuity between 1926 and 1962. Continuity is extremely important in republican dogma; the first group to split from the present IRA after the 1994 ceasefire called itself the Continuity IRA. The fragment who clung to the name Sinn Féin after 1926, and their successors over the decades, asserted their continuity with the past and the purity of their republican principles. They rejected the political present they lived in. Adversity, not irrelevance, was their explanation for diminishing numbers. They claimed that since membership of Sinn Féin guaranteed persecution in the Free State and Northern Ireland, few people were prepared to give the necessary level of commitment to their political beliefs that such a threat involved.

Those who did adhere to the name maintained the unshakeable belief that they alone were the emerald-green incorruptibles. Being consigned to the fringes of politics merely confirmed them in this belief. In their view, all the others had forsaken republican principles and left the movement for filthy lucre, for position and for power. As for the voters, what else could be expected of them? Voters were fickle. A strange attitude for a political party, but Sinn Féin could afford to take that view because it existed in a political never-never land where it did not have to respond to the electorate or articulate voters' wishes.

For those left in Sinn Féin after 1926, the great betrayer was de Valera. He it was who had supplied the vocabulary for republican ideology since the hated Treaty, the man who had sworn unswerving, undying allegiance to the republic, who had justified and encouraged the Civil War, who had recognised the Free State. De Valera may have taken Sinn Féin's voters and most of its leading activists with him when he left, but he did not leave the party completely bereft. He bequeathed the vocabulary and ideology he had articulated so well since 1921. Sinn Féin eagerly accepted the bequest while reviling its source.

Sinn Féin and the IRA also acquired ownership of the terms 'republican' and 'republican movement', descriptions by which they remain known to the present day. Although Fianna Fáil was and is officially known as 'the Republican Party', the name sounds like an afterthought: it never stuck. It was those who rejected the Treaty who continued to be called republicans.

The pre-1924 de Valera line that Sinn Féin adopted took on the rigidity of dogma, a word de Valera himself used at the Sinn Féin *ard fheis* in November 1925 when delegates refused to contemplate entering the Dáil even if the oath were removed. As he sought to relinquish his pre-1924 line, de Valera said he could not 'conscientiously carry on if [entering the Dáil was] held as a matter of dogma by the *ard fheis*'. Sinn Féin split on that particular dogma in 1926 and it controlled the thinking of republicans until the 1980s.

What were the origins of this dogma that republicans used to explain and justify their actions from the Treaty split onwards? What did the people who remained in Sinn Féin after 1926 believe? Why could they not participate in the Free State's politics? What truth is there in the claims, even today, of those who cling to the name Sinn Féin that they are the rightful successors of the party in lineal descent from 1921 and all others are either apostates or impostors?

In attempting to answer these questions a useful starting point is how de Valera saw Sinn Féin. This is what he wrote in 1923 to the republican stalwart and Sinn Féin activist Fr Thomas Burbage:

> [national] self-recognition, self-reliance, always acting as if Ireland was without question a sovereign independent State and the people of Ireland the exclusive source of all authority, and the complete ignoring of any right claimed by England to interfere in our affairs. This is what the words Sinn Féin mean to me.

Anyone reading this will immediately realise how difficult it is to reconcile the position laid out in that letter with an oath of allegiance to King George V. Such an oath is at odds with the idea of 'a sovereign independent State', or 'the ignoring of any right claimed by England to interfere', or the continuing right the Treaty accorded to the British Navy to use Castletownberehaven and Cobh in County Cork and Lough Swilly in County Donegal, known as the 'Treaty ports'. Just as obviously, partition and its consequences – namely the continuing British military presence in the North, northern MPs sitting at Westminster, the Westminster parliament continuing to legislate for the North – all provided equal, if not greater, impediments to national sovereignty.

Most republicans today, as in 1923, would agree with most of de Valera's statement of what Sinn Féin means. Certainly his points about national self-reliance and independence still strike a chord, though another aspect of his description would have caused some difficulty. That is his stipulation that 'the people of Ireland [are] the exclusive source of all authority'. Herein lies the crux of the problem. Then, as now, not all republicans would agree with that statement. De Valera himself had difficulties with the concept at times, despite paying lip service to it. After all, de Valera once said, 'Irish people have no right to be wrong.'

The issue was more than a question of how to interpret the views of the Irish people. For many republicans it was whether the result of an election could override the policy of the republican movement and determine its actions. The mentality that produced such a question

originates in the very beginnings of the republican movement: the establishment of the Irish Republican Brotherhood (IRB) in 1858, leading to
the Fenian rising nine years later. For the men involved in that organisation, the Irish republic existed as an ideal to which they swore allegiance.
The president of the Supreme Council of the IRB was the president of
that ideal republic. For members of the IRB, the Supreme Council constituted the legitimate government of the Irish people because they believed
the British administration in Ireland was inherently illegitimate.

The concepts of nationhood that the IRB promoted and the mentality or attitude about government authority the IRB created were
vitally important to republicans' view of the Irish State. In the nineteenth
century the IRB encouraged the mentality that there did exist some
alternative authority to that of the British administration, a belief which
denied that the British had any right to exercise authority in Ireland.
Thanks to the IRB, an attitude existed in Ireland for decades before Sinn
Féin courts emerged in 1917 that it was perfectly acceptable for there to
be an underground, or alternative, source of authority to Dublin Castle.

What is the relevance of the IRB's nineteenth-century mentality to
those remaining in Sinn Féin after 1926? Quite simply, it is that for the
people who comprised the final splinter of the great national Sinn Féin
party of 1917–21, there was nothing incongruous about a small group of
dedicated, some would say obsessive, people regarding themselves as the
only true embodiment of the Irish republic, the keepers of the truth, in
the face of apparently insuperable odds. The people in Sinn Féin after
1926 would have seen themselves in the same tradition as the IRB. They
would also have comforted themselves with the clear memory of how
tiny and unrepresentative the republican movement was before 1916, and
that Sinn Féin as an organisation hardly existed outside Dublin in those
years.

The Rising and the War of Independence had also fatefully reinforced the belief that force was the only way to get things done, the only

certain route to success. Most Irish people, and all republicans, accepted as an article of faith that without the Rising there would not have been the political sea change that produced the election landslide of 1918, and that without the military campaign of 1919–21 there would have been no Free State. Only force had made the British concede. The powers of the Free State were a long way beyond the insipid Home Rule offered by Britain in 1912. The fact that more had been achieved by force in the five years since 1916 than in the previous fifty years by parliamentary methods seemed impossible to refute. Those remaining in Sinn Féin were certain that one more push would do it. The Irish people would come in behind them.

How Sinn Féin was going to accomplish any of this after supporting the losing side in the Civil War and watching the IRA maintain an ambivalent relationship with Fianna Fáil was never explained. Initially republicans, including de Valera, had entertained the notion of winning a general election in the Free State as abstentionists, but by 1925 that was clearly impossible. With no prospect of securing a majority as abstentionists and transforming the Dáil into an instrument of their own, the ideologues in Sinn Féin were left only with ideology. Ironically, it was the members of Sinn Féin – the organisation the IRA accused of being full of compromisers and politicians – who refused to compromise or act like politicians, while some of the hardest men in the IRA, like Lemass and Aiken, not only compromised but changed tack and became the toughest defenders of the new State.

For those who stuck with Sinn Féin after 1926, however, what was important was not the fact of independence but the form and nature of that independence. For them, independence meant an Irish Republic, nothing else, nothing less. They remained oblivious to all criticism, to all attempts to demonstrate the absence of logic in their position, to sneers about the unreality of their aspirations. Sinn Féin adhered strictly to the dogma and constitutional theology that had been established by the end of 1922. From that date all the elements were in place that would constitute the stance of the republican movement until recent years. Thus, as the new provisional government set about establishing a society with democratic norms, asserting the supremacy of the legislature over the military and of the government over the party, Sinn Féin continued to behave in the manner to which it had become accustomed during the War of Independence. In doing so it transferred its rejection of British rule to a rejection of the new Irish government run by fellow Irishmen. It thereby inaugurated decades of hostility, paradoxically not directed against Britain nor even against the Northern Ireland government, but against its own indigenous government. Sinn Fein set out to convince the population of Ireland to overthrow the first elected Irish government in history.

It was not an outlandish proposition. The size of the vote received by de Valera's Fianna Fáil in 1927, when the party peacefully entered the Dáil, showed that a substantial number of people in Ireland were far from satisfied with the political results of the years 1918–23. The Cumann na nGaedheal government was deeply unpopular. Much bitterness remained about the conduct of the Civil War. Sporadic violence still erupted in the new state. Large numbers of men remained in jail. Most people still felt disgruntled that the 1921 settlement had fallen short of their aspirations and that the British government had partitioned the island. There was widespread disgust that the Cumann na nGaedheal government had accepted the travesty that the Boundary Commission turned out to be when there was no change at all in the positioning of the border: 'Not an inch', as the northern Unionist Party leader Sir James Craig famously said. Nevertheless, there was an independent government, freely elected by the majority of the Irish people, and two major parties competing to form that government. Despite all its shortcomings, most people wanted to get on with building the new Free State. An era was over.

Sinn Féin, however, did not accept this view. By abstaining it gave away the chance of demonstrating what electoral support existed for rejecting the aftermath of the Treaty. Why did republicans stop time at the Second Dáil and regard that body with such reverence? Their answer was that it was the last time the people of the island of Ireland voted in the same election, that is to say, expressed national self-determination. Given a free choice, as they were in 1921, the voters endorsed overwhelmingly the demand for independence. In republican dogma, no one had the right to accept anything less; a treaty accepting less could not be ratified.

Supporters of the new Free State found it easy to present a whole series of objections to the republican position that the Second Dáil was the inviolable expression of the will of the Irish people. They pointed out that in May 1921 most people did not have a choice because in the twenty-six counties there were no contests. The only candidates were Sinn Féin candidates and they were all elected unopposed. Besides, anti-Treatyites had participated in the 1922 election as members of the Sinn Féin panel concocted by the de Valera–Collins pact. In that election the voters had endorsed the Treaty. Anti-Treatyite Sinn Féiners on the panel won thirty-six seats compared to pro-Treaty Sinn Féiners' fifty-eight seats. Many republican heroes were defeated, some heavily: Countess Markievicz, Dan Breen, Kathleen Clarke and Seamus Robinson, famous for his exploits in Tipperary alongside Dan Breen, all lost. Free Staters snidely remarked that with such results it was understandable for Sinn Féin to declare the election illegitimate and to claim that it was carried out at the behest of the British to ratify a treaty the Dáil had no right to make.

Free Staters derided republican allegiance to the Second Dáil on the fundamental grounds that it was that Dáil which, in December 1921, had ratified the Treaty republicans so abhorred. What was the logic in republicans giving their allegiance to that Dáil, of all bodies? If they recognised the legitimacy of the Second Dáil, why not accept its decisions? Republicans responded that the Dáil had no power to endorse the Treaty because its representatives could not agree to anything less than a republic in negotiations with the British. Those accepting the Treaty had betrayed the self-determination of the Irish people exercised in May 1921. Then why do Sinn Féin not recognise the Third Dáil, elected in June 1922, when anti-Treaty Sinn Féiners took part in elections to it, not saying at the time they would not recognise it? Sinn Féin supporters respond in quasi-theological terms. The Second Dáil was never dissolved. It had been decided to hold a final session just before the Third Dáil convened and hand over powers but, because the Civil War had broken out, the newly elected Third Dáil did not convene until 9 September 1922. Republicans therefore argue that not only was the Third Dáil illegitimate as a 'partition parliament', but that the Second Dáil had never gone out of existence and had never transferred powers to its successor. And so the argument goes, around in a circle, to this day.

The fact is that all these arguments which both sides have hurled at each other down the years are redundant. Republicans had been defeated in the Civil War. Nothing could change that. The Free State existed. Its institutions existed. Arguing who was right and who was wrong in 1921, though it continues to be a popular pastime, never convinced anyone on the opposing side of the error of their ways. The republicans who rejected the Treaty and those republicans who rejected the Free State were irreconcilable. Logical or pragmatic objections to their position have no place in territory where absolutism reigns supreme. Purity of doctrine became a refuge for Sinn Féin after 1926. It was all it had left. People defeated politically and militarily could take solace in the fact that they had found high ground no one else wanted. No flood of new recruits joined. No young people, except their own children, supported them. It was obvious even to the most casual observer that Sinn Féin had no future as the challenger to the existence of the Free State. As for its challenge to the Northern Ireland State in 1922, that had been instantly crushed with ruthless brutality in the Six Counties.

As the years dragged on, Sinn Féin was driven to increasingly threadbare and hair-splitting explanations to justify not recognising the Free State. Some prominent members did not believe the explanations themselves. As early as 1924, Countess Markievicz derided republican 'Second Dáil' meetings, usually consisting of a dozen or so people, as play-acting and a sham:

> It is nonsense to call ourselves a Government when the people have turned us down. We have the majority against us and until we have the majority of the people with us again we are not a Government.

Such criticisms had no effect. Mary MacSwiney told Markievicz that the right of the majority did not 'extend to the surrender of the independence of the Nation', a variation of the line that the people have no right to be wrong. Sinn Féin after 1926 was composed of the sort of doctrinaires and fundamentalists more usually found in religion than politics, though Marxism also has its share. Like Marxism, republicanism became for some a secular religion. They also fell into the same kind of pointless disputes about principle common to Marxist splinter groups. Could you apply for a Free State passport and remain a republican? Could you become a lawyer, which meant taking an oath of allegiance to the Free State, and remain a republican? Could you accept any employment or any money at all from the government you did not recognise, and remain a republican? Could you even apply for a driving licence? People Sinn Féin could ill afford to lose were expelled over the years for all these 'crimes' against dogma.

Outsiders dismiss all this as a fantasy world. Yet to the people concerned in the fourth version of Sinn Féin which limped on after 1926, it was no more fantastic than the nineteenth-century claim of the Supreme Council of the IRB to be the government of the republic of Ireland. In fact, it was less so in some respects since, unlike the IRB, some of them had been elected as republicans to the Second Dáil.

So it was that the nineteenth century repeated itself. Tiny groups of people engaged in clandestine, subversive political activity, peaceful in Sinn Féin's case but always supporting and encouraging violent action by the IRA. The techniques, tactics and thinking that Irish nationalists had used prior to 1921 were faithfully deployed again, but this time with the bizarre twist that they were directed not against a British imperial administration but against a freely elected Irish government. Of course, Sinn Féin denied the Free State was any such thing. It claimed, increasingly unconvincingly, that the Free State government was not independent but had been set up by England as a puppet and therefore it was still the British government in Ireland, but in disguise. Sinn Féin after 1926 continued to refuse to recognise the Free State government as the lawful government of Ireland, just as Arthur Griffith's Sinn Féin had rejected Britain's right to rule in Ireland.

Only a dwindling number of people in Ireland was prepared to give any credibility to Sinn Féin's views about the new State. About 200 people turned up to its *ard fheis* in 1926. The following year it was 120, in 1928 about 100. By 1930 there were forty at the *ard fheis*. Attendance in the 1930s settled down around sixty. The party, if it could so still be described, moved into rooms at 16 Parnell Square, Dublin, above Robinson's Tea Rooms. It was able to hold the 1931 *ard fheis* in the drawing-room there. As the years went by, Sinn Féin's activities became confined to members giving lectures to each other, writing articles and issuing statements to the press attacking the latest perfidy of the Free Staters. Few noticed.

The party officers played musical chairs. The same names recur: JJ O'Kelly, or 'Sceilg' as he was commonly known, 'Ceann Comhairle' of the Second Dáil and later president of Sinn Féin; Mary MacSwiney, sister of Terence, grim, implacable, with a black cloche hat crammed on her head; Brian O'Higgins, purest of pure republicans and Sinn Féin president in 1932, but who resigned from the party in 1934, along with Mary MacSwiney, in protest at Sinn Féin allowing people who took Free State pensions to remain members; Fr O'Flanagan, the radical, veteran campaigner, indefatigable writer and polemicist and Sinn Féin president from 1933 to 1935; Cathal Brugha's widow, Caitlín, and the ancient Count Plunkett. The fifty or sixty people who turned up at Sinn Féin *ard fheiseanna* in the 1930s formed a little clique interested in politics but not in the politics of the Free State.

In the 1930s Sinn Féin directed its energies against fellow Irish people instead of against the British government or the new Northern Ireland state. Members devoted their attention to futile efforts at undermining the Free State, hoping, but never really expecting, to overthrow it. They were consumed with hatred and contempt for their former comrades, castigating everything they did. In short, they continued to fight the Civil War, with words in the case of Sinn Féin, but with low-intensity violence in the case of some IRA men.

After 1923 republicans never presented a real threat to the existence of the Free State or its government. On the contrary, the IRA's sporadic violence and the undercurrent of carping discontent Sinn Féin maintained actually meant neither Cumann na nGaedheal nor Fianna Fáil governments needed to explain why they were not making any progress in prosecuting the aims they had all once agreed upon, that is, uniting the country and securing a republic. The actions and attitude of republicans made it easy for successive Free State governments to concentrate on consolidating the twenty-six-county state rather than completing the 'unfinished business' of the years 1916–21. The unpalatable truth for Sinn Féin after 1926 was that anyone who wanted to be active in developing the potential of independence was in the Fianna Fáil party which Sinn Féin reviled as traitorous.

It has been pointed out already that when de Valera established Fianna Fáil in 1926 he took most of Sinn Féin with him, or at least its most forward-looking and able members. Since many individuals in the anti-Treaty movement held dual membership of Sinn Féin and the IRA, that also meant most of the forward-looking and able members in the IRA. The establishment of de Valera's new party meant that, whereas in 1923 Sinn Féin *cumainn* and local IRA units tended to be the same men, after 1926 local Fianna Fáil *cumainn* and local IRA units were practically synonymous. Indeed, one of the reasons for Fianna Fáil's early success in elections, particularly in the greater Dublin area and Cork City, was that the IRA brigades in those cities, despite being barred by a general IRA order, organised electoral personation for the new party.

The fact that the IRA, under its chief of staff Frank Aiken, remained if not completely loyal to Fianna Fáil, then at least not antagonistic, had a crucial consequence for Sinn Féin after 1926. The IRA's continued association with Fianna Fáil meant that Sinn Féin was fatally weakened because it had no muscle at its disposal. When Fianna Fáil entered government in 1932, Aiken left the IRA. His successors as chief of staff in the 1930s, Andy Cooney and Maurice (Moss) Twomey, also toed the Fianna Fáil line and maintained a curious arms-length relationship with the party until 1936 when there was a final parting of the ways between Fianna Fáil and the IRA.

The final straw for Fianna Fáil was the murder, on 24 March 1936, of the retired Royal Navy officer Vice-Admiral Henry Boyle Somerville for giving references to local recruits to the British Navy. This atrocity was followed a month later by the murder in Dungarvan of John Egan, who had recently left the IRA. Fianna Fáil could not be in government and retain any association or perceived sympathy with the IRA while it carried out such actions. De Valera acted immediately. Maurice Twomey was arrested and the IRA banned. The traditional republican demonstration at Wolfe Tone's grave at Bodenstown was prohibited and the prohibition powerfully enforced. After 1937, with the new constitution ratified, de Valera and Aiken made it brutally plain that the IRA would receive no quarter if they opposed the Free State government.

Sinn Féin provoked no such wrath. During the ten years following the appearance of Fianna Fáil in 1926, the ageing, declining numbers of people in Sinn Féin thrashed about searching for a role, but they had lost initiative and direction. They became hopelessly introspective, concentrating on petty quarrels about the meaning of republicanism rather than on doing anything about achieving a republic. One indication of their lowly status was that when the Cumann na nGaedheal government, hostile to any manifestation of anti-Treaty republicanism, banned the IRA and a raft of other republican groups in 1931, it ignored Sinn Féin.

Perhaps most telling of all is that the dominant group in the republican movement, the IRA, seemed to share Cumann na nGaedheal's view of Sinn Féin's irrelevance. During the years between the Civil War and the Second World War, as the IRA searched for a role and a direction, its leaders set up various organisations as political fronts. In 1929 it was Comhairle na Poblachta, an umbrella movement attempting to bring the IRA, Sinn Féin and Cumann na mBan together. In 1931 it was a new, left-leaning movement, Saor Éire, established to promote republican ideals with a dash of socialism. In 1936 the IRA set up Cumann Poblachta na hÉireann, some of whose leading members, including its chairman, Pádraig MacLógáin, abstentionist MP for Armagh South, were also figures in Sinn Féin.

On none of these occasions did it occur to them to use Sinn Féin as a political front. Obviously the IRA considered Sinn Féin had no role to play in advancing the republic. Sinn Féin, beyond holding an annual reunion it called an *ard fheis*, had to all intents and purposes ceased to exist. If it were not fighting elections and did not recognise the State, what function did a political party have? The cruellest blow fell in December 1938 when the seven surviving members of the 'Second Dáil' formally transferred their 'authority' to the IRA. They did not deem it necessary to tell Sinn Féin either before or after the fact.

Soon after receiving the 'laying on of hands' from the 'Second Dáil', the IRA also fell on hard times. The years of the Second World War,

1939–45, marked the lowest ebb for the republican movement, North and South. Under the impact of draconian emergency legislation in both parts of the island, the IRA virtually ceased to exist as an organisation outside jail. During the war years Sinn Féin existed in deep freeze. Members laboured under government and police suspicion and under censorship in the Free State, while, in the North, unremitting hostility from the Stormont administration had long before driven the party underground so that its survival remained problematic.

By the end of the war in 1945 Sinn Féin counted for nothing as a political force, North or South. Its members, mainly elderly, confined their activities to commemorations of past glories, which took the form of little more than social occasions, opportunities to meet old friends and agree on past wrongs, read statements over windswept graves of dead heroes and martyrs, say a decade of the rosary and hope that something might turn up.

Sinn Féin suffered further defections in 1946 when some of its members were attracted into a new republican-leaning political party, Clann na Poblachta. It seemed inevitable that Sinn Féin would reach a terminus when its surviving members died. Yet, amazingly, the republican movement, in an image constantly evoked in its propaganda, once again rose phoenix-like to launch a six-year military campaign against the North from 1956 to 1962. In the same period Sinn Féin, as the IRA's civilian wing, won Westminster constituencies in the North and Dáil constituencies and council seats in what had by then become the Irish Republic.

Once again the republican movement transformed itself, pulled itself up by its bootstraps and in doing so demonstrated conclusively that there exists a niche in Irish politics for people of its political persuasion. If the movement could get it right, there was electoral support in Ireland waiting to be tapped. Getting it right remained the perennial problem. What sort of Sinn Féin did the electorate want? What did votes for Sinn Féin mean: support for a campaign of violence against the North, or against Britain; disaffection with the Free State government expressed in a temporary protest vote; a new surge in national consciousness? Should the movement take a more strident approach on Irish unity? Should it concentrate on social and economic issues? Republicans incessantly argued and debated the answers among themselves.

In 1945 the prospect of 150,000 votes in the North and 65,000 in the South – as was to be achieved in the 1955 Westminster general election and the 1957 general election in the South respectively – would have seemed impossible fantasy. How did the movement reach such figures from having been on its uppers in 1945?

For the IRA, the approach of war in 1939 and the emergence of a new leader, Seán Russell, had the effect of providing it with a single direction, which it had lacked since Fianna Fáil went into government in 1932. Under Russell's leadership the IRA swung away from the course it had followed since 1922, namely a low-intensity continuation of the Civil War, attacking or undermining the institutions of Free State governments for betraying the republic. Instead, in 1939 the IRA issued a preposterous declaration of war on England, which few noticed and no one took seriously. It then inaugurated a bombing campaign in England. As the real war loomed, the IRA, acting on the false premise that 'my enemy's enemy is my friend', sought to enlist the help of Germany. It was a calamitous course of action. By mounting attacks on English targets and seeking German aid, the IRA instantly caused not only intense embarrassment but real danger for de Valera's government. De Valera had been at pains to show the British they had nothing to fear from Ireland. He was not going to involve Ireland in the war on the same side as Britain or allow British troops back into the country because he firmly believed such a course of action would renew the Civil War. His solution to the problem, which was an uncanny reminder of the difficulties John Redmond had faced in 1914, was neutrality. It was a high-risk strategy. Like Redmond, de Valera had to do everything in his power to show that Ireland presented no threat to a British Empire at war. The lunatic stance the IRA had adopted was the last thing he needed.

As Britain's plight grew more desperate in 1940 with the U-boat onslaught in the Atlantic, there was always the chance that prime minister Winston Churchill would authorise an expedition to retake the 'Treaty ports' to use as bases for the war in the Atlantic and as safe havens for hunted ships. De Valera was determined that England would have no excuse to invade and reoccupy any part of the Free State. It was essential, therefore, that Ireland was not seen as England's back door. De Valera's way of showing that Ireland represented no danger was to crack down on the IRA in as public and draconian a manner as he could manage. Ireland would not stab England in the back. This time, England's danger would not be Ireland's opportunity.

The IRA's bombing campaign in England had begun in January 1939. By the end of the year it had caused seven deaths and 200 injuries. De Valera could not let it continue. The IRA campaign presented a bigger threat to the integrity of the Free State than it did to Britain, as the bombs might give the British government a pretext to invade. De Valera set out to crush the IRA. The Offences Against the State Act, in force by June 1939 alongside the Unlawful Organisations Order, equipped his government with enormous powers. He showed he meant business by moving PJ Ruttledge, a former IRA adjutant-general, from the ministry of justice and replacing him with the much more hardline Gerald Boland.

Over the next six years Boland practically wiped out the IRA in the Free State. He arrested IRA men in droves. Imprisoned men went on hunger strike but, after an initial wobble in the case of John Plunkett, a brother of the executed 1916 leader Joseph Mary Plunkett, de Valera stood firm and made it clear that he would let hunger strikers die. Three did. Other IRA men were executed by firing squad or by hanging. During the war years twenty-six IRA men died in one way or another in

England and Ireland. Over 500 were interned in the Curragh, a bleak military camp in County Kildare, and over 600 were jailed under the terms of the catch-all Offences Against the State Act. In December 1944, Charlie Kerins, the IRA chief of staff, was hanged. By that time there was no GHQ staff or Army Council. Gerald Boland pronounced the IRA dead.

Sinn Féin had continued in desultory fashion, but heavily circumscribed by the same kind of wartime restrictions the IRA faced. Its few members were unable to publicise republican grievances or gain any public support for the plight of IRA men in jail. Restrictions imposed during the 'Emergency', as the Second World War was known in the Irish Free State, prevented dissemination of any material the censor deemed injurious to the State. The last republican publication, Brian O'Higgins's *Wolfe Tone Weekly*, had been banned in 1939.

Perhaps one of the chief reasons for Sinn Féin's continuing survival through the war years was that its president, Margaret Buckley, was a woman in her sixties. It would have been rather difficult for the State to intern her as a threat to its existence. Her colleagues were of much the same vintage. In 1937, at the age of fifty-eight, Mrs Buckley had succeeded Cathal Ó Murchadha, Second Dáil TD, as president of Sinn Féin. She remained in the post until 1950. Originally from Cork, she had joined Inghínidhe na hÉireann in 1900, had been involved in the War of Independence in Cork and had been a judge in republican courts in 1919. She took the anti-Treaty side and was interned in Mountjoy and Kilmainham, where she went on hunger strike. She was released only in October 1923. By the time the Second World War broke out in 1939, her age and her record were wholly typical of those who stayed in Sinn Féin after 1926, railing against the Free State, de Valera, Fianna Fáil, the Special Branch and all other institutions of the new State. Yet no one among the ageing members in Sinn Féin had the slightest notion of what to do to change any of it.

Symptomatic of the time warp people like Margaret Buckley lived in was the case Sinn Féin fought through the courts in the 1940s. It became known as the Sinn Féin Funds case. Buckley ultimately lost in 1948 after five years of legal proceedings. The case arose from an attempt by Buckley to acquire money vested in the High Court in February 1924 by the party's joint treasurers. The stated view of the treasurers in 1924, both Treaty supporters, was that they took the action they did because the party no longer existed. More likely they acted to prevent de Valera, then leading the rump of Sinn Féin, from getting his hands on the money, which amounted to £8,610. Buckley, as president of Sinn Féin, set out with her fellow Sinn Féin plaintiffs, the inevitable JJ O'Kelly, along with Diarmuid Ó Laoghaire and Séamus Ó Ruiséal, to prove that they, as the officers of Sinn Féin in 1942, were the legal owners of the money. The case turned on whether the Sinn Féin they represented in the 1940s was the same organisation as the one whose treasurers had vested the money in the High Court in 1924.

In the end, the judgement went against Buckley, largely on the technicality that when de Valera and his republican supporters had called a meeting in 1923 to try to resurrect Sinn Féin, they had ignored Sinn Féin's existing officers and Standing Committee who, under the party's rules, were the only people empowered to call a meeting. Therefore, in Justice Kingsmill Moore's judgement, there was no legal continuity between the post-Rising Sinn Féin and the post-Civil War Sinn Féin.

Although they lost the case, when the judgement was finally handed down in 1948 it rather vindicated Buckley and her colleagues. The judge accepted that the people in Sinn Féin in 1948:

> … appeared to me perfectly sincere, believing not only in the righteousness but also in the rightness of their claim. Moreover they adduced considerable evidence to show that they faithfully represent one approach to the Irish Republic which was prevalent in the Sinn Féin of 1917–1922, the approach typified in Cathal Brugha amongst others and which I have termed transcendental

… It would appear that all the required steps were taken to preserve the continuity of the organisation and that present-day Sinn Féin is legally the same organisation as that which was born in 1923.

But not, it will be noted, the same organisation as existed *before* 1923. Buckley could take comfort in one respect at least, namely that de Valera had left Sinn Féin in 1926, and it was the party of which she was president in 1948 that owned the mantle of republican continuity, not Fianna Fáil. The magic word 'continuity' had been used in the judgement. Such small triumphs were important to Sinn Féin in the endless finger-wagging arguments about the Treaty. Buckley would have hoped for the court to have gone further and to have found that the Treaty supporters had already left Sinn Féin in 1922, and that the technical matter of a pro-Treaty majority on the party's Standing Committee in 1922 did not entitle them to set aside the republic. It was not a view the court was likely to accept.

The case provides a good example of how Sinn Féin remained obsessed with the rights and wrongs of the past, of events twenty-five years earlier when time had seemed to stop. Needless to say, Sinn Féin went through agonies deciding whether to pursue the case in the first instance because it would mean recognising the Free State courts. Not surprisingly, given the record of the group in the 1930s, some of its few remaining adherents resigned when Margaret Buckley resolved to proceed.

In the meantime, back in the real world, while the case was being argued in court, de Valera had no intention of letting Sinn Féin get its hands on the money, which by now had accumulated to about £24,000, any more than the treasurers of Sinn Féin in 1924 would have countenanced de Valera getting hold of the money in the party's account then. Having brought the IRA to its knees between 1939 and 1946, de Valera was not about to allow Sinn Féin access to that kind of money, the equivalent of over half a million euro today. With cavalier disregard for the fact that the matter was *sub judice*, in March 1947, a year before the judgement, de Valera brought in the Sinn Féin Funds Bill, which, in effect, confiscated the money and decreed it would be used for such nebulous purposes as promoting the Irish language and providing for 'needy people'. As for Sinn Féin, not only did it lose the case but costs were awarded against it.

The timing of the judgement and de Valera's anxiety to keep Sinn Féin and the money apart was no coincidence. Historian Peter Novick claims that a nation's collective memory is jolted by what he calls 'memory spasms' caused by anniversaries. Whether or not such a general law can be proved to exist, there is no doubt that Ireland's 'memory spasms' would constitute crucial supporting evidence for Novick's thesis. An important spasm took place in 1948. In some ways it was a double *frisson*. The year marked the 150th anniversary of the United Irishmen's rising of 1798 and the centenary of the 1848 debacle at Ballingarry, County Kilkenny, which is sometimes referred to without much justification as the '1848 rising'.

Commemorations of these events produced the usual articles, parades, speeches and so on, all of which served to raise national consciousness. The events of 1848 also recalled the Great Famine (1845–49) and the mass deaths, emigration and appalling hardships suffered by Irish people. Naturally, Britain had a less than glorious role in the events of 1798 and 1845–49. In 1947–48, Free State political parties competed to outdo each other to sound as republican as possible, to identify and connect themselves, their founders and their inheritance with the struggle the people of 1798 and 1848 had been waging. They all agreed that the United Irishmen were heroes, their aim still a just and laudable goal, in fact, it was 'unfinished business' which people in 1848 and, for that matter, 1916 had been carrying on.

In practical political terms the consciousness raising that took place in the immediate aftermath of the war was demonstrated in a number of ways. The most obvious continuing source of grievance was partition. Opposition to partition was a way to unite people within the Free State.

They may not necessarily have agreed with the policies of the Fianna Fáil government or, indeed, those of the Fine Gael opposition, but one item everyone could agree on was the injustice of partition, which was England's fault. All parties accordingly threw themselves into agitation to end partition, which would, of course, finish the business inaugurated by Wolfe Tone and his colleagues 150 years before. How ending partition would be achieved was never clarified, but helping the separated northern nationalist brethren certainly salved a lot of consciences in the years after the war.

Other factors contributed to the resurgence of support for a campaign for Irish unity. With the war over, the British prime minister, Winston Churchill, was defeated in the general election of 1945. A Labour government was elected. Naively, most Irish people and many Irish politicians assumed that a Labour government would automatically look favourably on the reunification of Ireland. Most Irish people in Britain voted Labour. Many Labour MPs were of Irish extraction; some, including the future prime minister, Harold Wilson, depended on voters of Irish extraction to get elected, or at least to make their seats safe. Surely the Labour government would undo the injustice of partition? Churchill, the old imperialist, one of the men who had inflicted partition, had shored up the northern state and armed and funded its security forces, was gone. Clement Attlee commanded a thumping Labour majority. Surely now justice would be done?

The British government did not see matters in quite the same way. They had just fought a six-year war, the first three years of which had seen Britain with its back to the wall. The public perception was not only that the Irish Free State had not helped but that de Valera's government was, if anything, rather sympathetic to Germany. On the other hand, the North of Ireland had proved invaluable as a safe landfall for Atlantic convoys, a westerly base for aircraft and a haven for ships and aircraft alike to limp home to, hundreds of miles and tonnes of valuable fuel closer to the Atlantic than

Britain. American troops, too, had fond memories of Northern Ireland.

It was an almost eerie repeat of 1919. Was the British government about to sell out the region that had provided succour on its western shores in Britain's time of need to a place that had stayed studiously neutral and had hampered the war effort? Virtually no one in Irish politics seemed to understand the emotion and sentiment generated in Britain about Ireland's role, or lack of it, in the great world struggle. Virtually no one in nationalist Ireland appreciated that Attlee's government was not likely to view an anti-partition campaign with anything other than indifference. On the contrary, it was probably the worst conceivable time to launch such a campaign.

Ill-considered though the timing was, the Anti-Partition League was founded in January 1946 and instantly attracted support in the Free State from Fianna Fáil, Fine Gael and senior figures in the Catholic Church. In the North, the major figures leading it were the Stormont Nationalist MPs James McSparran, Thomas Campbell KC and the veteran republican Cahir Healy. At last it seemed that there was a truly national political organisation again. Funding was to be provided for nationalist candidates in northern elections. There was talk of finding places for northerners in the Oireachtas. Once again northern nationalists would feel part of Irish politics. It was a long way from the chilly reception their representatives had received when they met de Valera in 1940 to ask for guidance about how to respond to the war.

Despite the coincidence of approaching anniversaries in 1948, the warmth of the Fianna Fáil government's sudden embrace of northern nationalists in 1946 and their newly agitated *animus* about partition must have come as a bit of a surprise to those on the receiving end. Of course, none of it was prompted by entirely altruistic motives. De Valera and his Cabinet had spotted a threat heading towards them from a hitherto unprecedented direction: republicanism. The hundreds of IRA men and IRA suspects interned and convicted during the war years had thrown up the inevitable support groups from among their families, friends and sympathisers around the country. Out of these groups and the committees which organised them had emerged a new political movement led by the formidable Seán MacBride, barrister, former IRA chief of staff, son of Major John MacBride who was executed in 1916, and the famed Maud Gonne.

MacBride's movement quickly took the form of a new political party, Clann na Poblachta, founded in July 1946. The establishment of this new party sent shivers through Fianna Fáil. For some of Fianna Fáil's leaders it was uncomfortably reminiscent of the founding of their own party in 1926. Clann na Poblachta was unashamedly republican. Its members included many ex-IRA men, like MacBride himself. It had emerged out of public unhappiness, not to say shame, about the treatment of IRA prisoners, some of whom Seán MacBride had defended in court. The new party also offered a radical social and economic programme, just as Fianna Fáil had in 1926. Its leader was an intellectual who looked spare, ascetic and vaguely exotic, just like de Valera. He had impeccable republican credentials, just like de Valera. Unfortunately for Fianna Fáil, he was also twenty years younger than its leader.

Fianna Fáil leaders knew that there was a deep disquiet, even embarrassment, about the way imprisoned IRA men had been kept in solitary confinement, naked, denied exercise and allowed to die on hunger strike. The party sustained a nasty shock in the presidential election of June 1945 at the support for Dr Patrick McCartan, a republican candidate with virtually no organisation. McCartan was a northerner, originally from the republican stronghold of Carrickmore in County Tyrone. He was a veteran IRB figure, prominent in the organisation for a decade before 1916. He had been imprisoned in 1917. He had fought the Armagh South by-election for Sinn Féin in 1918 when de Valera had campaigned for him. Standing to draw attention to the plight of the prisoners and Fianna Fáil's failure to advance the cause of the republic, McCartan polled 200,000 votes, enough to prevent Fianna Fáil's candidate, Seán T O'Kelly, from getting an overall majority. Even more ominously, McCartan's republican voters gave 118,000 of their transfers to the Fine Gael candidate as compared to a derisory 27,000 to O'Kelly. Clearly there was a republican constituency in the country to be worked on. Clann na Poblachta looked well placed for that work.

The new party was bad news not only for Fianna Fáil, it also posed a serious threat to what was left of Sinn Féin. With Seán MacBride's past as IRA leader, his party's republican platform and its critique of Fianna Fáil, Clann na Poblachta seemed an attractive way for old republicans to get their own back on de Valera and their former comrades for walking out in 1926 and finding a route into the Dáil. Now, twenty years later, why not undermine them in exactly the same way? However, that would have meant another chunk of ideological republicans, or physical force republicans, or both, had taken the constitutional path and recognised Dáil Éireann. Sinn Féin, squeezed between the Clann on one side and the IRA on the other, looked doomed.

In fact, the emergence of Clann na Poblachta and its rapid political success proved to be a boon for Sinn Féin. Senior figures in the IRA, newly reconstituted in 1947, saw Sinn Féin as the only political party that shared the IRA's political outlook. The Clann's acceptance of de Valera's 1937 constitution and its entry into government were two of the factors which brought Sinn Féin and the IRA together in a mutual embrace that eventually turned them into inseparable Siamese twins.

Despite Boland's claim that it was dead, the IRA had begun to reconstitute itself as soon as the war was over and de Valera released the IRA internees and prisoners. Reorganisation was to be a slow, grinding task with many setbacks. No sooner had the five survivors of the 1938 Army Executive met and elected an Army Council in 1945 than the Special Branch arrested most of them; they spent 1946 in jail. Yet when they emerged in December 1946 they began again: a new Army Council, a new chief of staff, a new GHQ staff.

During 1947 the new Army Council considered their position at length: the mistakes and failures of the thirties and the war years. What should future strategy be? They began to organise units around the country. The key figures were Tony Magan, Tomás MacCurtáin and Pádraig MacLógáin, sometimes known as the Three Ms, sometimes as the Three Macs. These three men ran the republican movement for the next ten years.

MacLógáin had always been a physical force man. He had been in the IRB in 1913 and had been jailed by the British in 1917. He had commanded the IRA in south Armagh during the War of Independence and had represented the constituency as an abstentionist republican MP in the thirties. By 1945, based in Portlaoise where he ran a pub, his days of military combat were over. He confined his activities to plotting and planning. Unlike Magan and MacCurtáin he never sat on the Army Council, though he was quite prepared to take other senior positions in the IRA. For example, it was he who chaired the first army convention after the war.

Tomás MacCurtáin was an enormous man with an enormous beard to match. The son of the murdered mayor of Cork, he had taken the anti-Treaty side in the Civil War, had been sentenced to death by hanging, reprieved and spent years in jail, most of them in solitary confinement.

Tony Magan, who was to become chief of staff, was the dominant figure of the three. In many ways he embodied what had by the 1960s become the chief criticisms of the IRA in particular and the republican movement in general. A strict Catholic, and by all accounts a daily communicant, Magan was an austere, narrow-minded, conservative man. He set out to build a new IRA. In his mind its members would be half-monk, half-warrior, rather like the ideal set out in the 1930s for members of Franco's Falange in Spain. Like ardent Falangists, many IRA men of the 1950s were devout Catholics with strong social consciences, members of Catholic organisations, such as the Legion of Mary and the St Vincent de

Paul society, parish confraternities and sodalities, all of which, coinciden-
tally, were useful sources of recruits. These were the kind of men Magan
wanted. A vehement anti-Communist, Magan would allow no tincture of
left-wing thinking or radicalism into the movement. IRA volunteers also
had to be paragons of virtue: no drinking, no womanising, no reason for
attracting the attention of the authorities. They would be examples to
their community.

After a year's organising and ruminating, the Army Council was
ready to hold the first general army convention since before the war. It
took place in September 1948 with about fifty delegates in attendance. A
number of crucial decisions was taken which mapped out the direction
for the republican movement for many years to come. First, it was generally accepted that continued military activity in the Free State would not
only achieve nothing but could end in the complete destruction of the
movement, given the experience of the previous decade. It was therefore
agreed that there should be no military operations in the twenty-six
counties. The target would be the British presence in Ireland. Following
on from that, the second resolution was that the IRA's objective should be
a successful military campaign against British forces in the North. The
third major decision set the tone for the IRA's relationship with Sinn Féin
for the foreseeable future. The convention agreed that the IRA should
not be isolated from the political world as it had been since the 1920s. Of
course, there had been republican political parties in the 1930s but they
had been splinters from the main IRA and had never been approved
because membership might have meant involvement in politics in the
Free State. Such involvement would have contradicted the key item of the
IRA's political ideology: abstention.

Abstention remained the IRA's bottom line and its defining political
stance. The organisation rejected all political institutions on the island as
bodies imposed by Britain in defiance of the self-determination of the
Irish people expressed in 1921. Therefore any political party the IRA

became involved with had to share that view. In 1947 the IRA expelled any members who had joined Clann na Poblachta for the very simple reason that the Clann had recognised the Dáil.

The only party that was completely at one with the IRA on the nature of the State was Sinn Féin. The single point of contention between Sinn Féin members and the IRA was the IRA's claim to be the government of the Republic with authority vested in it in 1938 by the survivors of the Second Dáil. Senior people in Sinn Féin were still smarting from the way that tiny group of survivors had slighted the party in 1938 by handing 'authority' to the IRA without even consulting Sinn Féin.

However, even within the IRA there was some disquiet about the claim to be the government of the Irish Republic. At the 1948 convention, a man as senior as Tomás MacCurtáin proposed that, since the IRA was not sufficiently representative of the Irish people for it to be regarded as the government of the Republic, it did not have the right to kill anyone on behalf of the Republic. His proposal was, of course, defeated but qualms remained. Still, it was pointless to make a major issue of the problem as no one could foresee circumstances in the immediate future where the IRA's claims to be the Irish government would be put to the test. In 1948 it did not look as if the IRA was about to kill anyone on behalf of the Republic, let alone mount a campaign against the British forces in the North. In any case, such an arcane issue was hardly a reason for Sinn Féin to reject the IRA's overtures. The party had no intention of doing so. The approach from the IRA was the first recognition the party had enjoyed for over twenty years. Sinn Féin was happy to be taken over after years in the wilderness.

Another attraction for the IRA was the name 'Sinn Féin' with its historic connections and its political continuity. If the IRA endorsed the party, it would mean there was no need to think of a new name or explain what the party stood for. It was all familiar ground. Furthermore, there would be no opposition from Sinn Féin. There were so few members in

Sinn Féin by 1948 that it would not be a question of the IRA infiltrating Sinn Féin, it could simply take it over.

According to Ruairí Ó Brádaigh, Sinn Féin president from 1970 to 1983, in an interview with the author in December 2000, the extent of the Sinn Féin organisation in 1948 was pitiful: a few Sinn Féin *cumainn* in Dublin, one in Cork and one in Glasgow. It was not a case of the IRA paying court to Sinn Féin so much as the IRA saving Sinn Féin from oblivion. Sometime late in 1948 or early 1949 the Army Council issued instructions for IRA members to join Sinn Féin. As Ó Brádaigh said, by spring 1949 you could read little bits in the republican newspaper, the *United Irishman*, which had started publishing again in 1947, 'appealing for people to join Sinn Féin and the IRA and that everyone [in the movement] should be a member of Sinn Féin. So this is the first mention of Sinn Féin by IRA sources, so evidently they had decided that Sinn Féin was the political body.' Just as the anti-Treaty IRA had, in effect, set Sinn Féin up again in 1923 after the party's collapse in the winter of 1922, so it was again in 1948 that the IRA, having rejected Sinn Féin in the thirties as an irrelevance, decided to re-establish Sinn Féin as its political ancillary.

There were important differences, however, between 1923 and the IRA's takeover of Sinn Féin in 1948. In 1923, de Valera and a number of his colleagues had been and still considered themselves to be senior figures in Sinn Féin. Among the IRA's leaders in 1948 only MacLógáin had any connection with Sinn Féin, a group the IRA had regarded as an irrelevance since the 1930s. In 1923 de Valera had hoped to use Sinn Féin as a political vehicle to attract enough abstentionist votes to gain a majority over Cumann na nGaedheal and rewrite the Treaty. In 1948 the IRA's leaders had no intention of entering the political process by using Sinn Féin as a vehicle or a front and certainly did not intend to put up candidates in an election. They had decided they needed publicity for their political aims. Their dilemma was, however, that after the Fianna Fáil legislation of the thirties and the Offences Against the State Act of 1939, the

IRA, and any associated organisation that could be construed as a threat to the State, was illegal. As a political party Sinn Féin was legal, therefore it would be the mouthpiece for the IRA and the IRA's public face. The IRA would determine Sinn Féin's policy and control the party. It continued to do so until the 1990s and even after 2001 IRA policy on decommissioning acted as a constraint on Sinn Féin's political decision-making.

Very quickly the IRA pushed aside the Sinn Féin officers who had flown the flag since the 1930s. At the 1949 Sinn Féin *ard fheis* men prominent in the IRA emerged as senior figures in the party. Tom Doyle, IRA adjutant-general in the early 1940s, became Sinn Féin's general secretary and later joint vice-president alongside another prominent IRA man, Michael Traynor. At the 1950 *ard fheis* Pádraig MacLógáin, one of the IRA's three leading figures, replaced Margaret Buckley as president. The IRA adjutant-general, Charlie Murphy, became general secretary. Sinn Féin was on the move again, this time as the IRA's glove puppet. From being stalled in 1947, Sinn Féin made rapid strides on the political scene in the immediate post-war years, helped by the resurgence in national feeling that was officially encouraged by the Fianna Fáil government. Veteran IRA men swelling Sinn Féin's ranks in 1949 did not constitute the only new members. For the first time in years, young people appeared at *ard fheiseanna* representing *cumainn* from around the country. In November 1950, for example, Ruairí Ó Brádaigh, aged eighteen, attended his first *ard fheis*. The re-launch of the party could not have come at a better time. It coincided with rising discontent in the country. People were in the mood for change. Just as in all its various manifestations at different times in the twentieth century, Sinn Féin was able to capitalise on the mood of disaffection in the late 1940s.

If Fianna Fáil's leaders thought the 200,000 votes in June 1945 for the republican candidate Dr Pat McCartan an aberration, they were quickly disabused of the notion. Clann na Poblachta won some council seats in June 1947 and then, to the consternation of Fianna Fáil, the Clann won two Dáil by-elections in October, one of which sent its leader, Seán MacBride, into the Oireachtas. De Valera decided to call a quick general election in February 1948 before Clann na Poblachta could develop any further. It was to no avail. In the election the Clann won ten seats with 173,000 votes, enough to deprive Fianna Fáil of an overall majority in the Dáil.

The election campaign heightened republican issues which had been to the fore in 1947, the chief one being partition. Clann na Poblachta fought its campaign against a backdrop of 1798 commemorations and nationalist agitation led by the Anti-Partition League. With a number of recognisable ex-IRA figures in its ranks, most notably MacBride himself, the Clann looked as if it had cornered the republican end of the electoral market. All the other parties were making republican noises in the election, but after Fianna Fáil's treatment of republicans during the war, only the Clann had any credibility.

Once again it seemed Sinn Féin had missed the boat. As abstentionist, it declined to enter the political fray to take advantage of rising national sentiment. The Clann seemed to have taken the helm and was sailing the republican ship away. Just as in the 1920s, however, the party that sounded most radical, most republican, the party that attacked other parties most vociferously as 'partitionist' and accused them of betraying the nation, very quickly joined in running the very State it criticised most severely. Almost immediately Clann na Poblachta did the unthinkable for republicans: it went into government with Fine Gael, the most conservative party in the State, led by Richard Mulcahy, the man who had commanded the Free State Army in the Civil War. MacBride was able to veto Mulcahy as taoiseach because of that background. He accepted Fine Gael's alternative, John A Costello, but the Clann was in government with Fine Gael nonetheless.

It was precisely what the purists in Sinn Féin and the IRA had confidently predicted. Once you got into electoral politics you were on the road to compromise, which led inexorably to recognition and acceptance of the Free State and all its institutions. There was, no doubt, a logic to this argument, which drew attention to the contradictions in Clann na Poblachta's position. In the spring of 1948 leading figures in the Clann were making speeches that sounded indistinguishable from editorials in Sinn Féin's newspaper, the *United Irishman*. Yet they were in government with Fine Gael, the party of the 'seventy-seven murders' as republicans referred to it, harking back to executions of IRA men in Civil War days. In 1948 Fine Gael, previously known as Cumann na nGaedheal, still stood for the antithesis of republicanism, at times even calling itself the party of the Commonwealth. For Clann na Poblachta to go into government with such a party seemed apostasy. It seemed to have been seduced by the allure of power.

Nevertheless, Seán MacBride could claim that his republicanism exercised an important influence on the government. In fact, all the major parties were paying lip service to republicanism in 1948. MacBride's Clann might have 'sold out', but they had got into power by mouthing republican rhetoric and mixing it with radical social and economic policies. Sinn Féin was on the margins, was abstentionist, yet at the same time was acting as a republican conscience for the other parties. In the atmosphere of the time, all the parties felt they had to pay obeisance to the emotions Sinn Féin could conjure up at occasions like the annual republican pilgrimage to Bodenstown. Even the taoiseach, John A Costello, said his 'principal objective' was to end partition. No major party in the Free State could discard nationalist rhetoric.

Perhaps in an attempt to steal Fianna Fáil's guise, perhaps to put an end once and for all to the accusations that the government was doing nothing to complete the 'unfinished business' of 1916, Costello announced out of the blue, during a visit to Canada in September 1948, that he intended to declare a republic. Furthermore, he introduced the bill himself in the Dáil in 1949 to make sure his radical republican minister for Foreign Affairs, Seán MacBride, did not get any credit for it. The hasty decision may have been popular in the Free State but it produced a series of unlooked-for consequences in Northern Ireland and Britain.

First, it provided the pretext for a quick election in Northern Ireland in February 1949, which confirmed Sir Basil Brooke's grip on power. Costello's announcement provided Brooke with the simplest of all platforms: 'No surrender!' Costello's government organised financial help for northern nationalist and anti-partition Labour candidates in the election through the Anti-Partition League. Nearly £50,000 was raised in collections, mainly outside church gates, which led unionists to call it the 'chapel gate election'. More important by far for the long term was the reaction in Westminster. Lest anyone should think that the declaration of a republic strengthened the Free State's claim to the Six Counties, in June 1949 the British government passed the Ireland Act, which declared that 'in no event will Northern Ireland or any part thereof cease to be part … of the United Kingdom without the consent of the Parliament of Northern Ireland.' It was simply a statement of the political reality, but the act produced uproar in the new Republic. It was regarded as deliberately provocative, an unnecessary reinforcement of partition, a slap in the face for the anti-partition agitation recently endorsed by all the main parties in the Free State. The people reacted with marches and protest rallies, leader writers penned stentorian editorials, politicians fulminated in speeches and the Oireachtas passed an all-party resolution condemning Britain's action – all of which simply demonstrated the impotence of the Irish government to make the slightest difference to the facts.

Combined with the heady rhetoric of 1948–49, what the Ireland Act also did was convince a number of young men that the only way to make progress against British arrogance and unionist intransigence was through violence. The events of 1949 led them to believe that the IRA and Sinn Féin's propaganda was correct, whereas the policies of the major parties were fraudulent. The heady political atmosphere created in the post-war years – the Anti-Partition League, the 150th anniversary of the

1798 rebellion, the election campaign of Clann na Poblachta full of republican rhetoric, the establishment of the republic and, finally, the Ireland Act – drew in scores of young men who took the politicians' speeches seriously and wanted to do something definite. The republican rhetoric continued with an enthusiastic anti-partition campaign mounted by Fianna Fáil around the country and in England. The campaign was topped off with an extensive 'anti-partition tour' by the opposition leader, de Valera, which took in America, Australia and New Zealand. He also visited India, which had just been partitioned and had also declared a republic but, unlike Ireland, had remained in the Commonwealth.

Sinn Féin benefited enormously from all this agitation. According to Ruairí Ó Brádaigh, there were *cumainn* 'in every province if not in every county' by November 1950. Dublin City had six *cumainn*, which met weekly, as did Dublin's *comhairle ceanntair*, the body to which all the *cumainn* in a district sends representatives. The party was strong in Cork and north of the border, in County Armagh in particular, so much so that there was a north Armagh *comhairle ceanntair* and a south Armagh *comhairle ceanntair*.

It was easier for people to join the party in the Republic because the hostility to Sinn Féin had palpably relaxed since 1948. MacBride in government had helped, of course. So had a view among politicians that the growth in republican sentiment had been advanced by the poor treatment of IRA prisoners during the war. The new coalition government had released all prisoners and by September 1948 had returned the bodies of executed IRA men to their families. The 1948 decision by the IRA army convention that there would be no military action in the Free State had also helped. Fearful of suppression after its reorganisation, the IRA was very anxious that the government should be aware of this decision so it was repeated in speeches at Bodenstown and regularly in Sinn Féin literature.

As always, none of these circumstances applied in the North where

Brooke's government reacted to the surge in anti-partition agitation by cracking down on any manifestation of republicanism. After all, the IRA was promising a campaign against the North where, to all intents and purposes, Sinn Féin had ceased to exist during the war years. There had been sporadic IRA activity but, using wartime legislation as well as the draconian Special Powers Act (1922), republicans had been ruthlessly rounded up and interned, their propaganda banned and possession of it classed a criminal offence. In a conversation with the author in August 2000, the prominent Belfast republican Jimmy Drumm said that there was 'nobody in Sinn Féin' in Belfast in 1946–47; 'Young men from Dublin started it up again.' In fact, it was mostly 'young men from Dublin' who started up the IRA and Sinn Féin all over Ireland after the war. Reorganisation in the North, such as it was, was just part of the drive.

The public decision to focus on Northern Ireland caused difficulties for republicans reorganising in that jurisdiction but, like many other decisions the republican movement took, it was primarily motivated by southern exigencies. In this case, it was quite simply the need to survive as a movement in light of the merciless response of Fianna Fáil in the war years, which had brought the movement to its knees. Although self-preservation lay behind the policy change, there is no doubt that the decisions the IRA took in 1948 and 1949 were a major and long overdue *démarche*. Trying to undermine or subvert the Free State was pointless, stupid and irrational. It was not so much a policy as a long huff against former comrades that did more damage to the republican movement than to those former comrades.

The decision to eschew military action in the south had important consequences. Allied with the resolution to mount a campaign against British forces in the North, what the decision really meant was that, in the long term, the struggle moved North. The new IRA leadership, which also ran Sinn Féin, concentrated on the North both militarily and politically, and continued to do so for the next fifty years. The tactics changed many times, but in 1948 the republican movement ceased to view the Dublin government and its institutions as the primary target. They did not like them, they did not recognise them, but they devoted their efforts to overthrowing the regime in the North, an impossible task, many would have thought, in view of the massive military and paramilitary resources available to the Stormont government.

The 1948 IRA convention resolution stating the objective of a military campaign against British forces in the North became publicly known in the IRA's Easter statement of 1949. Naturally, it was regarded as hot air. It was the sort of belligerent language people expected in the prevailing climate of excitement and hostility towards Britain and the North in the aftermath of Costello's unilateral declaration of intent to establish a republic, even if it would not be *the* Republic. But the IRA was, in fact, deadly serious. From 1951 its leaders began secretly planning to acquire weapons and *matériel* which would be used in the campaign against British Army bases in the North.

It took five years before the campaign could be launched. Acquiring arms involved a series of raids on barracks in England and in the North, during which some of the best new recruits to the movement were captured and jailed. Targets included: Ebrington Barracks in Derry in 1951; the Officers Training Corps School in Felstead, Essex, 1953; Gough Barracks in Armagh, 1954; Royal Inniskilling Fusiliers' Barracks in Omagh, 1954; Eglinton Naval Air Base outside Derry in 1955; and Arborfield Barracks near Reading, Berkshire, in 1955. Some of the leading figures involved in executing these raids came to dominate the IRA and Sinn Féin in one form or another until the 1980s: Ruairí Ó Brádaigh, Seán MacStiofáin, Seán Garland and Cathal Goulding becoming the most prominent.

In the meantime, while all this IRA activity was being planned and carried out, the newly revamped Sinn Féin was presenting its case to the electorate at every opportunity. In the Republic not many such

opportunities arose. Electoral forays had to be confined to council elections because the legislation brought in by WT Cosgrave in 1927 to
stymie de Valera's new Fianna Fáil required Dáil candidates to promise to
take their seats if elected. Sinn Féin's results were far from encouraging.
The party put up two candidates for Cork Corporation and one for Mayo
County Council in September 1950 but failed to have any elected.
Clearly there was no correlation between support for the sentiments of
republican rhetoric and support for republican candidates. No doubt if
asked, the average voter in Mayo or Cork would have answered that he or
she was opposed to partition, but the relevance of partition as an issue in a
council election in the far west or far south of the country would not be
immediately obvious.

As a single-issue party Sinn Féin was going nowhere. It might be
thought that there was a simple lesson to be learned from Fianna Fáil or,
more recently, from Clann na Poblachta, namely that, for electoral success,
a party needed more than to be 'sound' on the national question: an
attractive radical programme was essential as well. That was all very well
for a party whose leaders wished to be elected. It was not the case for Sinn
Féin. The IRA men who directed Sinn Féin regarded politics other than
'the national question' as a dangerous distraction, and, worse still, the route
to participation in the State. Besides, many of them were also strongly
opposed to radical politics, believing it smacked of Communism, that
great bugbear in Ireland in the 1950s. There would be no radical
programme.

In public the IRA paid lip service to Sinn Féin's role in the overall
republican movement. One of Sinn Féin's vice-presidents, Criostóir
O'Neill, told the gathering of the faithful at Bodenstown in 1949:

> The republican movement is divided into two main bodies, the
> military and the civil arms, the IRA and Sinn Féin. Each has an
> important task to do. In the final analysis the work of either is as
> important as that of the other.

Such a public declaration of commitment to equal status was far from the truth. It may have been designed to enhance Sinn Féin's status in the public eye and give the party an appearance of independence, but the reality was quite different. The IRA leaders saw Sinn Féin merely as a support group and a mouthpiece for the IRA, an organisation in which people, mainly men past military age, could act as cheerleaders for the IRA. They could write, organise, distribute pamphlets, sell newspapers, carry messages to IRA units, speak at rallies and so on. Success at elections was neither here nor there. Election campaigns simply kept the republican movement in the public eye.

As in so many ways, the North was different on the electoral front too. There, partition was a burning issue of immediate relevance, especially to nationalists living near the border. Many northern nationalists in the 1950s could clearly remember life before the border. They yearned to be reunited with the rest of the country. Many farms straddled the border. Parishes stretched on both sides of it and the border thus disrupted parish life. Many towns in the Free State, such as Dundalk in County Louth, Castleblayney in County Monaghan and Sligo town, were the natural urban centres for people near the border. Towns in the North, like Newry and Derry, suffered economically from being cut off from their natural hinterland. Many northerners worked in the Free State. Often people from the Free State worked in the North, though the unionist government, fearing large-scale immigration into the North, had required work permits. With improved health and educational services, which the post-war Labour government funded, unionists had a paranoid fantasy of being swamped by hordes from the South who would out-vote them. In short, in border areas partition was a real, everyday problem.

It was less so in the greater Belfast area, where partition did not create immediate physical problems for nationalists. However, the unionist security apparatus and the endemic discrimination made for chronic disaffection and discontent for city nationalists just as for those across the North.

If partition was the one issue Sinn Féin campaigned on, there were plenty of people in the North for whom it was also the sole issue.

Sinn Féin's electoral profile in the North was also helped by the different types of election which took place. Stormont had introduced legislation for its own elections that forced prospective candidates to take an oath forswearing organisations proscribed by the Special Powers Act, thereby effectively disbarring Sinn Féin from standing. In 1953 new legislation required candidates for Stormont elections to take an oath of allegiance *before* nomination, thus completely ruling out Sinn Féin. The party itself had, of course, been banned at various times since the 1920s and was again proscribed in 1956, although individuals were able to stand for election – at considerable personal risk, it must be said.

However, Westminster elections offered an opportunity. Not facing any disagreements about the nature of the State or the identity of its inhabitants, the United Kingdom had no rules surrounding the nomination process to Westminster elections, or 'imperial elections' as they were known in the North, which would inhibit Sinn Féin. Nor were unionists able to interfere with Westminster arrangements, which had to be on the same basis throughout the United Kingdom.

What tended to happen in the North therefore was that Sinn Féin let nationalists stand for Stormont elections, which they did in a shambolic, disorganised fashion but usually picked up a dozen or so seats. When it came to Westminster general elections, however, Sinn Féin stepped in to try to use them as an index of support for ending partition. Often it was prepared to back an abstentionist candidate, though it naturally preferred to field its own man. But if a nationalist candidate who promised to attend Westminster stood in a winnable constituency, Sinn Féin stepped in and split the vote to prevent him going to Westminster. It was an unspoken arrangement that did not always work, for some men elected on an abstentionist ticket occasionally found a reason to go to Westminster, usually on a one-off basis, though attendance was the exception. This division of labour, so to speak, between nationalists and republicans operated for most of the period of the Stormont regime.

The one exception was West Belfast, an overwhelmingly Catholic, working-class constituency that naturally contained large numbers of nationalists and republicans but regularly returned left-wing, labour candidates. From 1943 to 1955, with a short break in 1950, West Belfast returned Jack Beattie, a Protestant and a Labour man who was staunchly anti-partitionist but who nevertheless participated fully at Westminster where he successfully embarrassed the unionists on many occasions. Following an interlude of a decade after 1955 the constituency reverted to form, and in 1966 elected Gerry Fitt of Republican Labour, who represented it until Gerry Adams of Sinn Féin defeated him in 1983.

From time to time Sinn Féin used Westminster elections for another purpose: to draw attention to prisoners. Its first chance to do this after the war was in the February 1950 election. Hugh McAteer of Derry, a senior IRA figure in the North and former IRA chief of staff in the war years, and Jimmy Steele, a well-known Belfast IRA man and former adjutant of Northern Command, stood in Derry and West Belfast respectively while interned in Crumlin Road jail. McAteer had a free run among nationalists in Derry and polled well in what was a guaranteed unionist seat.

Unfortunately for Sinn Féin, Jimmy Steele ran up against the redoubtable Jack Beattie in West Belfast. Furthermore, Beattie was locked in a fierce contest against a rancorous sectarian candidate, the Rev Godfrey McManaway, Stormont MP for Derry City. In the heated atmosphere of 1950, following hard on the heels of the Stormont election of 1949, McManaway defeated Beattie 33,917 to 30,539. Steele polled a derisory 1,482 amid accusations that he had split the vote. He had not, as the figures show, but the figures also show the paltry size of the Sinn Féin vote in West Belfast, even for a local prisoner candidate. It would be another five years before Sinn Féin scored what would be its greatest successes with prisoner candidates in the North until the election of hunger-striker Bobby Sands in 1981.

The opening years of the 1950s were tetchy, nasty, sour years. Repressive legislation from Stormont, like the 1951 Public Order Act and the 1954 Flags and Emblems Act, which in effect banned the Irish flag, constricted any possibility of nationalist protest. There was growing unease against a background of IRA arms raids in Britain and against British Army bases in the North. The B-Specials, the Protestant, loyalist militia, were armed with .303 rifles and Sten sub-machine guns and were on active service, and a squad of 100 or so RUC men, known, amazingly for a UK police force, as RUC Commandos, had been specially trained to deal with riots and other perceived threats to unionism. They were assiduous in breaking up nationalist rallies and parades in nationalist districts, from Derry in the northwest to the Mournes in south Down, and forcing Orange marches through the same districts. An end to partition seemed further away and the Stormont regime seemed more secure than ever, though, under Sir Basil Brooke, the administration continually acted as if Britain were about to cut it adrift any week.

Nationalist politics were in the doldrums. Unionist reaction was unremitting and unyielding. In the Westminster election of May 1955, however, an opportunity arose to register a protest, to show that nationalists still existed, to stand up and be counted at no personal cost. In October 1954 the IRA had raided the barracks of the Royal Inniskilling Fusiliers in Omagh for weapons for their planned campaign in the North. The raid degenerated into a pantomime of blunders. Eight men were arrested and convicted under the Treason Felony Act of 1848. In the 1955 British general election, the IRA decided to field Sinn Féin candidates across the North. The candidate it proposed for Mid-Ulster had been imprisoned for the Omagh raid, which took place in the Mid-Ulster constituency. It was a winnable nationalist seat. Would nationalist voters in Mid-Ulster endorse a man in jail for violence perpetrated in the constituency?

A tradition had grown up whereby nationalist candidates were selected at open conventions composed of councillors, local worthies and representatives from parishes, often including clergy. Nothing was more symbolic of the absence of structure and organisation in nationalist politics. At two of these conventions, Sinn Féin's Phil Clarke was selected for Fermanagh–Tyrone South, a nationalist seat, and Tom Mitchell, one of the leaders of the Omagh raid, for Mid-Ulster. Both men were serving ten years for the raid. Both men duly won their elections in no-holds-barred contests. Amid allegations and counter-allegations of personation and a host of other voting abuses by both unionists and Sinn Féin, and after a knife-edge count, Mitchell won by 260 votes and Clarke by 261, in both cases out of a total of over 60,000 votes cast. No nationalist candidates had stood in any of the twelve seats across the North, leaving the field to Sinn Féin. It scored a resounding success. It polled 152,310 votes, the biggest vote against partition since 1921 and the biggest nationalist vote in the North prior to the combined SDLP/Sinn Féin total in the 1982 assembly election.

The vote in Mid-Ulster and Fermanagh–Tyrone South was not a one-off. Since both men had been convicted under the Treason Felony legislation, they could not legally be elected. Clarke was unseated by petition and the unionist candidate declared the member for Fermanagh–Tyrone South. Mitchell, however, was declared disqualified and a by-election was held in August 1955. Mitchell won again with an increased majority. As a convicted felon, he was disqualified again. Meanwhile it was discovered that Charles Beattie, the unionist candidate declared elected following Mitchell's disqualification, was also ineligible because he held office under the Crown. Another by-election had to be held in May 1956. Mitchell went forward for the third time. The Unionist Party, afraid of being made to look ridiculous, declared that they were standing aside. The Nationalist Party, seeing their chance, nominated Michael O'Neill, a former Nationalist Mid-Ulster MP. With the prospect of a split vote, unionists stepped back in immediately, fielding George Forrest as an independent, but in reality he had the full support of the Unionist Party. O'Neill, always unhappy at Sinn Féin's intervention, refused to stand down and assured Forrest's election. The result was: Forrest 28,605 votes, Mitchell 24,124, O'Neill 6,421.

What to make of all this? Republicans naturally concluded that there was extensive support for the activities of the IRA. After all, nationalist people in Tyrone had three times preferred the Sinn Féin candidate in free elections. Tom Mitchell had not been an ordinary candidate, or indeed an ordinary prisoner, but a man who had attacked the main British Army barracks in the constituency and yet he was twice elected, on the second occasion with a 90% turnout. In the second by-election in 1956 he had out-polled his nationalist rival by a margin of four to one. The election of the two prisoners could be explained away as a sympathy vote; perhaps people believed the men would be released if elected. But what about the 100,000 votes in the other ten constituencies? Surely it indicated that the climate was right for the planned IRA campaign?

Others seemed to agree that there was a reservoir of support for aggressive action. The IRA arms raids had not been the only republican military actions. Splinter groups and what, in GAA parlance, were called 'solo runs' had been hitting the headlines in 1955. One republican splinter group, Saor Uladh, or 'Free Ulster', led by the egregious Liam Kelly from Pomeroy in County Tyrone, whom the IRA had expelled in 1951, carried out a gun and bomb attack on Roslea RUC barracks in November 1955. Earlier in the year, Brendan O'Boyle, another man the IRA had expelled for excess zeal, died when a bomb he was transporting in his car detonated prematurely as he drove to plant it at the Stormont telephone exchange.

All this republican activity, coupled with the massive vote for Sinn Féin in May 1955, spooked unionists. In response to republican attacks, the unionist administration beefed up the RUC Commando unit eventually to 500 men, about a sixth of the total RUC complement, renamed it the RUC Reserve Force and supplied members with heavy military equipment, such as mortars, hand grenades, Bren guns and, staggeringly, anti-tank bazookas. Two hundred B-Specials were called up for full-time duty. Invoking the Special Powers Act in 1956, Stormont ministers banned Saor Uladh and its political wing, Fianna Uladh, and Sinn Féin. Clearly Sinn Féin's electoral success led unionists to regard the party as a real threat to the state. There was to be no outlet for any manifestation of republicanism in the North.

Given this background of simmering violence and frustration and the huge Sinn Féin vote in 1955, the IRA could be forgiven for believing that its long-planned military campaign would provide the coping stone for a republican revival which seemed to be swelling across the island. The IRA leaders had been dithering for a year about when to begin their onslaught. The delay had caused individuals to leave and go on 'solo runs' or to join more impetuous groups, like Saor Uladh, which carried out an ambitious set of attacks one night in November 1956.

At last the IRA launched its campaign, which it called Operation Harvest. In the early hours of 12 December 1956, four IRA columns, totalling about 120 men, split into small units and struck targets in each of the Six Counties, using explosives to destroy bridges, a BBC transmitter and military buildings (though perhaps that is too grand a term for the B Special hut wrecked at Newry). It was the culmination of five years of planning and preparation.

Performing its allotted role as the IRA's political mouthpiece, Sinn Féin issued a statement in which it said Irishmen had again risen in revolt against British aggression in Ireland: 'The Sinn Féin organisation say to the Irish people that they are proud of the risen nation and appeal to the people of Ireland to assist in every way they can the soldiers of the Irish Republican Army.' Would they? Was there the level of support which could justify and sustain the campaign?

At first it seemed that there was. A series of IRA attacks on northern installations took place in December 1956. In one, which became the most famous of the campaign, two IRA volunteers, Fergal O'Hanlon from Monaghan and Sean South from Limerick, were killed and most of the others on the operation wounded. The attack, against Brookeborough RUC barracks, was a fiasco but the IRA men immediately became heroes. A wave of emotion swept across the country. It is generally agreed that 50,000 people attended Sean South's funeral on 4 January 1957. The following week a republican rally at College Green in Dublin, addressed by the leading IRA figure Tomás MacCurtáin, attracted a huge crowd. Emotions ran high, North and South.

Costello's government was alarmed. The taoiseach decided to stem the rising tide. He had warned the IRA to desist the day after its campaign began in December. Again, the day after South's immense funeral, Costello issued another stern warning and in the next few days the Special Branch arrested most of the IRA Army Council and GHQ staff, including MacCurtáin, Magan, Charlie Murphy and Sean Cronin, the man who had planned Operation Harvest. But the funeral, the big Dublin rally and other gatherings organised by Sinn Féin showed there was more to the campaign than the couple of dozen men arrested. Seán MacBride believed he saw an opportunity to play the republican card and recover the ground his party had lost in the 1954 election. He tabled a censure motion in the Dáil at the end of January criticising the government for their treatment of the IRA and harassment of republicans. The government fell and a general election was called for 5 March 1957.

Unfortunately for MacBride, the IRA also saw the election as an opportunity. Full of confidence as a result of the northern elections in 1955 and the mass public support for men killed in action, it decided to nominate nineteen Sinn Féin candidates and throw all the resources of the movement behind them. Its decision was vindicated. Four were elected: John Joe McGirl in Sligo–Leitrim; Einachan O'Hanlon, the brother of

Fergal, for Monaghan; John Joe Rice in Kerry; and Ruairí Ó Brádaigh in Longford-Westmeath. Sinn Féin polled 65,640 votes, its best result since 1927, though it has to be said that it was also its first result since 1927 because it had not contested any election across the twenty-six counties in the interval. On the face of it, the election was a stunning success for Sinn Féin, apparently an endorsement of its campaign in the North and an expression of sympathy for the movement's aims.

In reality the election's outcome had disastrous consequences for Sinn Féin because it brought back to power de Valera who would show the republican movement short shrift, regardless of their 65,000 votes. By entering the election Sinn Féin had, of course, cornered the republican vote – the public now had the real thing to vote for, which meant Clann na Poblachta's vote evaporated. Seán MacBride lost his seat and his party vanished. MacBride's opportunism, besides ruining his own party, had resulted in the return of a Fianna Fáil government with an overall majority. Sinn Féin's four TDs, needless to say, did not take their seats, which meant that there was no republican voice in the Dáil. Not that it would have dissuaded de Valera from acting against republicans even if there had been.

Taoiseach again, de Valera had no qualms about confronting the IRA. On 7 July 1957, three days after the IRA killed an RUC man at Forkhill in south Armagh, he introduced internment. The Stormont administration had, of course, begun interning republicans within days of the IRA campaign starting the previous December. Now there was no hiding place for the IRA; the Irish Special Branch had incomparably better intelligence than the RUC Special Branch. It was not long before internment on both sides of the border began to take effect, so much so that by the end of 1958 de Valera felt it safe to release internees and in March 1959 the Curragh internment camp was closed. The campaign had failed but it seemed only the IRA failed to realise it.

If its lack of military success was dispiriting, there was always the electoral success of Sinn Féin as a consolation to show that, while the

Dublin government might join Stormont in repressive measures, a substantial proportion of the electorate North and South still sympathised with the republican cause. After three years of the campaign a new chance arose to demonstrate their support in the Westminster election of October 1959. Again, the Nationalist Party gave Sinn Féin a free run in the North's twelve constituencies. The results were profoundly shocking for republicans. Yes, Sinn Féin could claim intimidation of its workers and censorship and harassment but that had always been the case, perhaps even more so in the Mid-Ulster by-election in 1956. Adverse conditions had not prevented the voters turning out. How then to explain that in the 1959 general election Sinn Féin's vote was sliced almost precisely in half: from 152,310 in 1955 to 73,415 in 1959. Only Tom Mitchell's vote in Mid-Ulster, at 24,170, held up, but it was not enough. He lost. Elsewhere republicans did very badly. In nationalist Fermanagh–Tyrone South they polled 7,348, a mere quarter of the 30,529 votes Phil Clarke had garnered in 1955. It was a similar story in Armagh, down from 21,363 to 6,823.

Two years later, in October 1961, it was the same pattern in the Republic of Ireland. Full of optimism despite the reverses in the North, Sinn Féin put up twenty-one candidates, two more than in 1957. Just as in the North, the party's vote was halved: down from 65,640 to 36,393 with no TDs elected. Fourteen Sinn Féin candidates lost their deposits. The military campaign had failed and there was obviously no political support for it. De Valera's government was as rock solid as Brookeborough's in the North. Violent republicanism had no electoral support.

Finally the IRA accepted defeat. On 26 February 1962 it dumped arms. The IRA statement announcing the end of the campaign said:

> The decision to end the resistance campaign has been taken in view of the general situation. Foremost among the factors motivating this course of action has been the attitude of the general public whose minds have been deliberately distracted from the supreme issue facing the Irish people – the unity and freedom of Ireland.

It was the end of fourteen years of reorganisation and planning that had begun in 1948, and of a campaign that lasted on and off for six years, from December 1956 to February 1962. The balance sheet? The IRA had mounted almost 450 operations, 341 of them in 1957. Eight IRA men were killed, as well as two republican supporters, two members of Saor Uladh and six RUC. Thirty-two British soldiers were injured. Hundreds of men were interned for four years and about 200 convicted. Damage in the North amounted to almost stg£1 million and extra security cost stg£2.5 million. The whole exercise had achieved nothing.

What of Sinn Féin during this period? The IRA had saved it from oblivion in the immediate post-war years but the price was that Sinn Féin ceased to be an independent organisation in any sense. Pádraig MacLógáin, one of the top three in the IRA, was president of Sinn Féin throughout the period 1950–62, with the exception of 1953–54 when Tom Doyle[1] was president.

Throughout the years 1950–62 the membership of Sinn Féin's *ard comhairle* was dominated by the IRA. The chief of staff, Tony Magan, was a member for most of the time and, apart from Tom Doyle who was a member when not president, there were: Michael Traynor, a Dublin shop-owner originally from Belfast, former adjutant-general, member of GHQ and the Army Council in the 1930s; Charlie Murphy, IRA adjutant-general who was also Sinn Féin's general secretary; and Paddy Doyle, a senior IRA man from Belfast. Just to be sure Sinn Féin would not stray from the IRA line, there was a coordinating committee of members of the Army Council and Sinn Féin *ard comhairle* chaired by MacLógáin, of which the majority were IRA. No opportunity for any dissent was available.

It was during this time that the IRA and Sinn Féin became, in what was to be a phrase constantly repeated in the 1990s by Conservative secretaries of state for Northern Ireland, 'inextricably linked'. There was no doubt in anyone's mind which organisation was in control. Both sets of security services in Ireland regarded Sinn Féin as auxiliary or ancillary to the IRA. Sinn Féin members might be beyond 'military age' but were often prepared to carry out auxiliary activities for local IRA units. They provided safe houses, they drove cars, they ran errands and they did intelligence work. Some members of Sinn Féin, most commonly those at the very top, remained leading members of the IRA. Tony Magan was a good example. Virtually all Sinn Féin candidates in subsequent elections were current or former IRA men.

One of the best illustrations of the duality of membership is what occurred after Costello's government arrested the majority of the Army Council and GHQ in January 1957. Éamon Mac Thomáis, officer commanding the Dublin IRA, had eluded the Special Branch sweep and had contacted MacLógáin and Michael Traynor. Together with MacLógáin, president of Sinn Féin, and Traynor, a member of the *ard comhairle*, he set up an emergency Army Council. Within a week the new stop-gap Council had emerged comprising, among others, Traynor and Tom Doyle, both Sinn Féin *ard comhairle* members. The campaign continued uninterrupted. The men arrested in January under the Offences against the State Act had received between three- and six-month sentences. They began to be released in March and took up where they left off as those on the emergency IRA Army Council who were primarily Sinn Féin dissolved back into Sinn Féin.

Little wonder, therefore, when de Valera brought in internment in July 1957 that one of the first places raided was Sinn Féin headquarters on Wicklow Street, Dublin, where they arrested most of the *ard comhairle*, leaving only the seventy-eight-year-old Margaret Buckley. Within days, Buckley was the only member of the Sinn Féin leadership not in the Curragh. The attitude of the northern security forces was obviously even more hostile. Sinn Féin had been illegal again since 1956. Within days of the onset of the IRA campaign, members of Sinn Féin were on the run from internment sweeps. As far as Stormont was concerned, Sinn Féin and the IRA were one and the same organisation and were treated as such.

Why should it have been otherwise? Sinn Féin gave total support to the IRA and in its public statements urged others to support the IRA's military campaign in the North. In other words, it was indistinguishable from the IRA. The IRA men who controlled and directed the party would not allow a separate political line to develop in case it led to involvement in politics. Abstention was the watchword. It was also the dogma that hamstrung Sinn Féin as a political party and prevented it developing policies relevant to the time. But then, that was the reason the IRA took over Sinn Féin in 1948. It was the only political party that did not recognise the authority of any parliament, whether in London, Dublin or Belfast, to legislate for Ireland. By 1962 it was plain that the people of Ireland had rejected such a stance and had no belief in physical force as a way to unite the country. It was time for a new approach.

7. VEERING TO THE LEFT
Flirting with Marxism, 1962–70

For at least three years before February 1962 – when the IRA formally accepted that the campaign against the North was over – the republican movement had been in a sorry state. Rival camps within the organisation were at loggerheads, many members had resigned or walked away. Even a man of the standing of Tomás MacCurtáin, one of the 'Three Ms' who had run the movement since the 1940s, left in 1959, disgusted with the poisonous, debilitating feuding. The signs of defeat were everywhere.

Sinn Féin, its *ard comhairle* now run by IRA leaders, had been downgraded to a rubber stamp for the IRA. It had nothing to offer politically, North or South. In the North its function was to act as a convenient rallying point where northern nationalists could register their numbers and disaffection when a Westminster election was called, after which the party would promptly vanish until the next general election. In other words, Sinn Féin's political role in the North was to display the impotence and disorganisation of nationalists. As late as 1964, Sinn Féin, while still adopting an abstentionist line, polled 98,000 votes, as usual failing to win a seat and thereby reassuring unionists that they had nothing to worry about.

In the IRA, recriminations had come to a head in 1958 during internment in the Curragh camp and continued after the internees were released. Bitter disputes about leadership, internal discipline, how the campaign was being pursued and, in the end, disputes about not very much had riven the leadership. Since both Sinn Féin and the IRA overlapped at the top, the demoralisation infected both wings. Sinn Féin's disastrous showing in the Republic's October 1961 election was the last straw for some members. Men were prepared to die in the campaign against the North but the message from the voters was that they did not care.

In many ways the initial disputes had emerged from the generation gap between the top leaders and the second rank. MacLógáin was born in 1897. He had been on hunger strike with Thomas Ashe in 1917. Magan was of the same vintage. Both men were rigidly conservative and unbending in every aspect. Their view of the world had been formed in the years 1916–23. They would not and could not change. Younger members accused them of blowing hot and cold on the border campaign, and then of being quiescent in the Curragh camp, making no attempt either to escape or even to disrupt the camp's routine.

In the months after 1957 when the veteran IRA leaders were interned, new, younger men had taken over. The change in leadership was confirmed in June 1959 at an army convention dominated by pointless arguments and tedious monologues from the ousted veterans about who had done what and when in the Curragh. When MacLógáin and Magan did not get their way they withdrew their names as candidates for the Army Council. A new IRA Army Council was elected. For the first time in more than a decade neither MacLógáin nor Magan was a member.

Of course, the new appointments to the Army Council did not affect the officer panel of Sinn Féin, which was elected at its own *ard fheis*. Pádraig MacLógáin hung on as president and others of the older generation, like Magan and Michael Traynor, remained on the *ard comhairle*. Could these disgruntled old men be allowed to dominate Sinn Féin and perhaps turn the party into a new power base for themselves from which they could criticise the IRA as part of their continuing effort to vindicate their conduct in the Curragh?

After Sinn Féin's rout in the Republic's 1961 election it certainly did look like it. MacLógáin and Magan may have seen such action as a preemptive strike, even as self-preservation. MacLógáin, in particular, had been stunned by Sinn Féin's poor showing in the 1961 elections. The bad result had been all the more unexpected because the party had performed reasonably well in the Republic's 1960 local government elections, winning sixteen county council seats and fourteen urban district seats. MacLógáin became concerned that the new IRA leaders would use the 1961 results to accuse him of incompetence and of failure, as president of Sinn Féin, to get the appropriate electoral support for the IRA's military campaign, which people in the movement had expected after the party's surprising successes in the 1957 election.

The plan MacLógáin and Magan seem to have hatched was to reverse what they had done in 1948, namely to separate Sinn Féin from IRA control and run it themselves as an independent party. They, of all people, must have known that such a move was unacceptable to the IRA for the very reasons that had led them to take over Sinn Féin fourteen years earlier. The IRA simply wanted Sinn Féin as a political megaphone. Still, the veterans pursued their plan. MacLógáin resigned from the IRA in April 1962 and began to gather signatures within the Sinn Féin *ard comhairle* to call an Extraordinary *Ard Fheis*. There is no doubt what the outcome of such a meeting would have been. Already, word of the murky internal squabbles had reached the press. A lot of dirty linen would have been washed very publicly. In the atmosphere of 1962 the movement would likely have been split irrevocably.

As it was, MacLógáin and his supporters were outvoted and outmanoeuvred. After failing to get the necessary number of signatures for an extraordinary general meeting, they resigned from the *ard comhairle*. MacLógáin was out of the republican movement after nearly fifty years' service. In July 1964 he shot himself with a 9mm Walther in the garden of his bungalow in Blanchardstown, County Dublin. Despite the fact that he was a weapons expert with an extensive illegal collection of small arms, the coroner returned the strange verdict that his death was self-inflicted but with the strong likelihood that it was inflicted accidentally.

It really was the end of an era. Once again, Sinn Féin had virtually ceased to exist. In 1948 the IRA had taken it over and had run it to be the IRA's legal political mouthpiece. When the IRA began to fall apart in 1958, Sinn Féin, led by the same men as the IRA, also started to collapse. By 1962 the IRA campaign was formally and officially over and many observers at home and abroad thought it was time to write off the republican movement. The *New York Times* commented: 'The IRA belongs to history, and it belongs to better men in times that are gone. So does the Sinn Fein (sic). Let us put a wreath of red roses on their grave and move on.'

Nothing was further from the minds of the new leaders of the IRA and Sinn Féin, respectively Cathal Goulding and Tomás MacGiolla. They accepted that the failure of the border campaign marked the end of fourteen years of planning and organisation. Perhaps more importantly, they acknowledged that the policies pursued since 1948 had also failed. It was time for a root-and-branch reassessment of the republican movement's aims and objectives. The outcome of that reassessment led to an attempt by its leaders to bring about the most radical realignment in the movement since its foundation, to move away from its fixation with the constitutional issue and concentrate instead on changing Irish society through radical socialist politics. It was necessarily a delicate process, the aims of which were never made fully known to the membership at large nor even to all those at leadership level. Rank-and-file members viewed the implications of the process with deep suspicion. They may not have been able to see the full picture, but they did not like the part of picture they could see.

Internal arguments about what direction should be followed persisted throughout the 1960s. Up until the movement split following the emergence of the Provisional Army Council in December 1969, dissension and discontent surfaced regularly and publicly at *ard fheiseanna*. What line to take? Continue with militarism, turn exclusively towards radical, left-wing, quasi-constitutional politics, or combine both? It is clear that 1962 was a turning point. The disagreements of the 1960s show how difficult it was for the new leadership to persuade the movement to turn, particularly when the leaders themselves were divided. Ultimately the leadership failed to create a revolutionary movement cast in the mould of the radical 1960s and the movement split along fault lines that had surfaced as early as 1964.

A brief look at the mindset that had guided the republican movement in the 1950s will illustrate the size of the task confronting anyone attempting to radicalise Sinn Féin and the IRA. When the IRA had taken over Sinn Féin in 1948, its leaders had drawn up, among other policies, the Social and Economic Programme of Sinn Féin. Amazingly, it was based on the papal encyclical *Rerum Novarum*. This was remarkable not just because its inspiration was a papal encyclical but because that encyclical had been issued in 1891, sixty years before Sinn Féin's policy document was produced after the 1951 *ard fheis*. Obviously the much more enlightened 1931 encyclical *Quadragesimo Anno* was too radical for them!

Rerum Novarum, which conservative Catholics had thought pretty revolutionary when it was issued, dealt with the social problems caused by industrialisation and asserted the Church's right to pronounce on social issues and relate them to moral questions. In other words, it fitted in exactly with the controversies about welfare legislation raging in the Republic in 1951. Sinn Féin's newly drafted policy placed it firmly on the side of the Catholic Church in those controversies. Just to be sure that there was nothing in it that ran counter to Church teaching, Sinn Féin had the document cleared by friendly clerics. The men leading Sinn Féin in the 1950s opposed the Welfare State and believed, along with the Catholic hierarchy, that a proposal like the Mother and Child Scheme promoted by Dr Noel Browne in 1951, which would have provided some free State medical care, weakened moral resolve and induced a dependency culture. Sinn Féin, under MacLógáin's leadership, fully supported the position adopted by the hierarchy, led by the archbishop of Dublin Dr John Charles McQuaid – a cleric notorious, even in those times, for his unbending conservatism.

Men like MacLógáin and Magan had vivid memories of Episcopal thunderbolts hurled in the poverty-stricken 1930s against any leftward tendencies in the republican movement. They were keenly aware that any such tendency would immediately lead to accusations of Communism, which would be fatal to the movement's prospects of public support, with the main parties in the State instantly seizing upon any clerical denunciation as a brush for painting republicans red.

A desire to avoid providing political opponents with any ammunition was only one reason for eschewing left-wing policies. The truth was that 'The Three Ms' and others on the Army Council and Sinn Féin *ard comhairle* in the 1950s were devout Catholics and deeply conservative. They fully subscribed to the religious ethos of the Free State. IRA chief of staff Tony Magan was a deeply religious man. While interned in the Curragh he established the Legion of Mary among the men. At least two senior IRA men, one of whom was a member of the Army Council in the early 1950s, resigned from the movement to become priests. Despite their attitude to the Noel Browne scheme and strange though it may seem to outsiders, many men who were devout Catholics joined the IRA out of a concern for social justice, which they believed the Irish Republic, as then constituted, could not possibly provide. For example, Seán South, killed in the Brookeborough raid, was a member of the Irish-speaking branch of the Legion of Mary, *An Réalt*.

For many, but not all, of the new leadership who had taken over in 1959, removing MacLógáin and Magan also meant removing the influence of their constricting, hidebound Catholicism too. It proved a huge task, which was never completed for the simple reason that, since members of the republican movement lived in Ireland in the 1950s, most of them agreed with MacLógáin and Magan. As Professor Joe Lee observed in the *Sunday Tribune* in May 2001, there are 'probably few western countries in which there was so uniform a value system' as Ireland in the 1950s. The Catholic Church was dominant in public morality. Partition had left the Church, like the political value system, with little incentive to take account of any alternative views. Outside Dublin, members of Sinn Féin, broadly speaking, fully shared that value system. Many others in the IRA did not: they set out to convert the movement to their view.

It was an uphill task. By 1962 Sinn Fein was composed mainly of middle-aged men beyond military age, led and controlled by elderly men who also led the IRA and who permitted the party no independence of thought or action. Most bright young men who joined the republican movement took one look at the men leading them and, with a couple of exceptions, made their excuses and left quickly. When someone like Sean Cronin, former army officer and later a New York university professor, joined in 1955, he immediately soared to the top. Some clever and able people, like Seamus Sorahan SC, sympathised with the party but remained on its fringes. An association with Sinn Féin was death to any career, and so it has remained.

As is so often the case with the republican movement, the impetus for change came from the IRA men in jail. By 1962 the best men in the movement, the only ones capable of initiating change, had joined the IRA in the 1940s or early 1950s out of idealism and altruism, and had ended the 1950s in prison. When they had first volunteered they had been deeply dissatisfied with Irish society, with its poverty, inequality, injustice and backwardness. In jail they had the time to think, reflect, discuss and write. They came to believe that the structures of government, North and South, had to be torn down and rebuilt from new.

First of all, of course, the border would have to go. They took to its logical conclusion the official line of the Irish government, published and reinforced by the Anti-Partition League, that partition was the source of all evil in Ireland. The British government should declare its intention to leave and all would be well. It was at this point that the views of the jailed IRA men departed from the Irish government line. For them, partition was only part of the problem. It exacerbated and perpetuated all that was wrong with Irish society because both the Stormont administration and the Dublin government were reluctant to initiate radical reform in case such action would be seen as an admission that something was wrong. So getting the British to leave was only the beginning; until there was a united Irish Republic there could be no radical change in Irish society, North or South. It would not be a simple matter of absorbing the North into the South. Both would have to be changed.

Unfortunately, the older IRA leaders were fixated on ending partition and avoided other contemporary issues, vigorously opposing any social or economic policies that smacked of radicalism. An apocryphal story told to illustrate their conservatism alleges that the Army Council in the border campaign rejected the use of condoms as timing devices for bombs, despite the fact that condoms were very suitable for this usage because acid melts through rubber in a predictable time. While it is certain that, had the situation ever arisen, Magan and his fellow Army Council members *would* have taken that position as they would never have permitted the use of contraceptives for any purpose, the story is unfounded. In the Republic of Ireland in the 1950s, condoms were as rare as hens' teeth; besides, even if they had been available, no one could imagine any IRA man actually going into a shop to ask for them.

One of those who set out to bring change was Cathal Goulding, IRA chief of staff from September 1962. Goulding, forty years old that year, had been sentenced to eight years in jail for leading the arms raid on Felstead School Officer Training Corps depot in 1953. A Dublin small building contractor who came from a republican family with political traditions going back to Fenian times, he was a flamboyant character who regarded himself as a bit of a bohemian and a left-wing intellectual. He was friendly with the Behan family and frequented the same haunts as Brendan and Brian Behan.

Roy Johnston, a computer scientist and academic, who played a prominent role in trying to change the direction of the republican movement in the 1960s, told the author in a conversation in September 2001 that Goulding had always held left-wing and radical political views. However, Ruairí Ó Brádaigh, in an interview with the author in December 2000, claimed that Goulding was converted to socialism while in jail in England. Ó Brádaigh said that because he had an IRA record in Ireland dating from the 1940s, Goulding was sent to Wakefield prison in Yorkshire while the other members of his unit, being first offenders, were sent to Wormwood Scrubs. At Wakefield, Goulding met the East German atomic spy Klaus Fuchs, a dedicated Communist, and fell under his spell. Ó Brádaigh said: 'I had known Goulding before in 1950–53 and then when he came out [in 1959] he was quartermaster-general and I worked pretty closely with him and I could see he was different.'

Whatever the truth, as one of the chief advocates of a leftward move for the republican movement, Goulding was in a prime position as chief of staff to promote such a move. Tomás MacGiolla, president of Sinn Féin from 1962 to 1970, was another advocate. An accounts officer with the Electricity Supply Board in Dublin, MacGiolla had become friendly with Goulding when he was released from jail and returned to Ireland. The two shared the same left-wing views. MacGiolla had been interned in the Curragh in 1958 and during his time there had become convinced of the futility of purely military action. He concluded that the republican movement's policy had to be 'bread today' rather than 'roses tomorrow'. In other words, he advocated political involvement in the fullest sense, which would mean breaching the sacred dogma of abstentionism. Needless to say, he kept the full extent of his conversion to himself for a few years.

Perhaps Roy Johnston was the person who had most influence on republican thinking in the 1960s. Like MacGiolla, he too warmed to Goulding and they became firm friends. Johnston had lived and worked in England, where he had been a member of the Connolly Association. On his return to Ireland he involved himself in left-wing politics as a founder member of the Irish Workers' League, effectively the Communist Party in Ireland. What Johnston managed to do was to develop a set of theories which attempted to reconcile Irish republicanism with Marxism, or at least socialism. It was exactly what men like Goulding and MacGiolla were looking for.

Another influential figure at the time was Anthony Coughlan. Like Johnston he was an academic, a lecturer at Trinity College, Dublin. Unlike Johnston, Coughlan never joined the republican movement but produced papers and presented plans on social and economic issues which members of the movement found attractive.

Seán Garland, another 1950s veteran, was also a strong supporter of the swing to the left. Garland was a legendary figure in the IRA. He joined the British Army in the North to acquire intelligence for the IRA for its arms raids. He played a prominent part in the raid on Gough barracks, was involved in the attempt to rescue Goulding from Wakefield prison and was wounded in the Brookeborough raid during which Seán South and Fergal O'Hanlon were killed. By the 1960s he was a hardline Marxist.

It can readily be seen that the men advocating socialist policies in the movement were a narrow Dublin clique. Those like them who held important positions in the IRA and Sinn Féin did not represent the views of the membership as a whole. The distance between Dublin and Leitrim or north Kerry was not measured in miles alone but in years. Apart from unremitting hostility in rural parts of Ireland to socialist ideology, many of those remaining in the IRA after 1962 expected to hear plans for the next military campaign in the North. Young recruits wanted to know when weapons training would begin. The new leadership had to proceed carefully.

Opposition came not just from those keen on military action or opposed to socialism. Others were leaving because they were unhappy with the trend towards constitutional politics. Apparently insignificant issues mattered a lot. For example, some left because they were ordered to apply for permits to sell Easter lilies in 1963. Green, white and orange badges depicting Easter lilies were symbols of the 1916 Rising and were worn by republicans throughout Ireland each Easter. In the past there had been running fights with the Gardaí about unauthorised sale of Easter lilies. Refusing to apply for a permit was one of the last, comparatively harmless ways left open to republicans of refusing to recognise the 'Free State'. Being ordered to jump through that hoop was too much for some of the older members.

In Belfast there was dissension among northern nationalists about the supine attitude towards the unionist authorities recommended by the Dublin leadership. Following a dispute in 1963 about whether the Irish tricolour should be carried along the Falls Road in a march to com- memorate the 200th anniversary of Wolfe Tone's birth, thereby defying an RUC ban. The new leadership recommended compliance and a number of IRA veterans, led by Billy McKee, OC Belfast, resigned. He was replaced by Billy McMillen, who supported the Goulding line, as did the new second in command in Belfast, Jim Sullivan.

At a more senior level similar resistance to change quickly emerged. Just as at the grass roots, the objections were not simply about whether to engage in political action in the Republic or the North. The bugbear of Communism was an important issue; Roy Johnston was the chief suspect. Through his friendship with Goulding he had been catapulted to the top of the IRA and was co-opted on to the Army Council in 1965 as Director of Education. The year before he had been in trouble with conservative republicans for objecting, in an article in the *United Irishman*, to the prac- tice of reciting a decade of the rosary (and in some cases all five decades plus the prayer, *Hail, Holy Queen*) at republican ceremonies, especially at commemorations of dead heroes. Johnston called such performances sectarian. Seán MacStíofáin, future Provisional IRA chief of staff, refused to allow the edition of the paper with the offending article to be sold in south Kerry, where he was in command.

Later that year, MacStíofáin tried to have Johnston expelled from the movement by showing, quite correctly, that IRA rules barred Communists from membership. Ruairí Ó Brádaigh remembers the meeting as taking place in 1965 and the issue arising out of suggestions that had been made at an Extraordinary *Ard Fheis* that Sinn Féin should enter 'the three parliaments', that is, stand for election in the Republic, the North and Westminster. Ó Brádaigh said: 'I remember Goulding's reply so well. He said, "I think Johnston is the greatest thing that ever hit this movement and if he goes, I go".'

While such disputes produced passionate arguments within the republican movement, the vast majority of the population of Ireland remained oblivious to what was going on. Most people would have agreed with the *New York Times* that Sinn Féin and the IRA were finished and done with. For most Irish people, their only contact with the republican movement would have been the sight of a man wearing a dingy tweed jacket adorned with two badges: one, a pioneer pin, which signified that he had taken a religious vow to abstain from alcoholic drink; the other, a gold *fáinne* showing that he was a reasonably good Irish language speaker; he would be offering copies of the *United Irishman* for sale outside a Catholic church or at the GPO in Dublin. Almost no one bought a copy of the paper.

It was an image of the movement that men like Cathal Goulding, Roy Johnston and Tomás MacGiolla desperately wanted to shed. The world had moved on. Change was coming, even to Ireland. The Catholic Church was changing under a new pope, John XXIII, who had convened a Council of the Church known as Vatican II to enable the Church to meet the challenges of the modern world. John F Kennedy, an Irish-American Catholic, had been elected president of the USA; he visited Ireland in June 1963. The Beatles played to a rapturous crowd at the Adelphi cinema in Dublin the same year. Surely the republican movement could also change? Could it not throw off some of its deadening dogma, which was more appropriate to the 1920s than the 1960s? How to dispel the image of republicanism as a sect?

Some facts were crystal clear to the men pushing for change in Sinn Féin and the IRA. First, there was a substantial republican vote in the country, North and South. The core vote of around 200,000 in the twenty-six counties had remained remarkably stable. In 1923 Sinn Féin polled 290,000 votes in the Free State. In 1927 Fianna Fáil got 299,000 votes. In 1945 Dr McCartan got 200,000 votes. In 1957 Sinn Féin, with only nineteen candidates, got 65,000 votes. On that showing, if it had fielded candidates across the Republic, it would have come close to 200,000. The second fact that arose out of those figures was the simple conclusion de Valera had reached in 1925, namely that voters in the Free State did not support abstentionist candidates except in special circumstances. Fianna Fáil's 299,000 votes in 1927 – essentially the same people who had voted Sinn Féin in 1923 – zoomed to 566,000 in 1932. The huge increase could only be explained by two factors: Fianna Fáil's candidates were going to go into the Dáil if elected, and the party had presented social and economic policies the voters had found attractive. Clann na Poblachta, with ninety-three candidates, had managed to get near the total republican core vote of 200,000 in 1948 for the same reasons. Abstentionist Sinn Féin could attract a respectable protest vote – whether in 1945 to register objection to the treatment of IRA prisoners, or in 1957 in despair at the dire economic conditions in the country – but the party could not build on it. Without entering the Dáil it remained a protest vote.

Tomás MacGiolla, president of Sinn Féin from 1962, and others around him were convinced that Sinn Féin had to take any seats the party won. They believed that the extensive poverty and unemployment in the Republic were fertile ground for a left-wing party. The evidence of the 1950s tends to support that opinion. There has always been a strong correlation between support for Sinn Féin and economic distress in rural areas. The four Sinn Féin TDs elected in 1957 were from Longford–Westmeath, Monaghan, Kerry South and Sligo–Leitrim, all counties with traditionally strong republican votes, but also counties with a great deal of poverty and a general air of hopelessness. To many people in those constituencies it did not matter whether their TDs took their seats or not. Voting for Sinn Féin, a party that rejected the State, was a way of protesting at the State's betrayal of them by its failure to provide them with a living.

The 1950s were a terrible decade in Ireland. By 1961, census returns showed that the population of the twenty-six counties had fallen to 2.8 million, the lowest since the Famine; the Irish marriage rate was the lowest in the world; and emigration was catastrophic – between 1951 and 1961, 412,000 people emigrated. For two years in a row in the mid-1950s, the Republic was the only country in the western world in which Gross Domestic Product, the total volume of goods and services consumed, actually fell. For those with jobs, wages were poor. Sixty percent of Irish workers earned less than £10 a week in 1960. In Britain the figure was 10%. Occasionally there were minor disturbances in Dublin arising from protests against unemployment. Dismal marches with drooping banners trailed through the capital's main streets as early as 1953. In the face of this social and economic disaster, partition lay a long way down most people's list of priorities. Even de Valera, in his last speech as party leader to a Fianna Fáil *ard fheis* in 1958 did not mention partition. The IRA's quixotic activity along the border had been utterly irrelevant. When it called it off in 1962 many people did not even notice.

How was Sinn Féin to connect with these deprived and poor people, its natural supporters, and marshal them, direct their discontent? How was Sinn Féin to extricate itself from the political ghetto it had walled itself into? The men at the head of the republican movement in the early 1960s believed the movement had to address the social and economic issues of the day. The people no longer believed that ending partition was the panacea for the country's ills. Holding a single policy devoted to righting the wrongs of the previous forty years, and directing force against the North to achieve it was just plain stupid. How would it improve the life of anyone in Leitrim or Mayo? Ruairí Ó Brádaigh, who would have been one of the more conservative of the leaders in the 1960s, said that in 1962, 'Everyone agreed it was back to the drawing board. Everyone felt that, "Look, scrub it, we've to start writing a new page and we have to try and learn … We can't just start building up to do exactly the same thing, because the world has moved on."'

From 1963 the republican movement developed a strategy that would involve it in the pressing concerns of the 1960s. It meant transforming the republican movement into a revolutionary socialist organisation with an extreme left-wing agenda. The republican movement publicly and privately still made obeisance to the use of military force to unite Ireland, but the new leaders no longer believed in it and did not intend to pursue its use for that purpose. Force would still be used, but against the police, against property and to defend protesters. The new strategy was such a complete departure from traditional republicanism that few in the leadership (including Ó Brádaigh) realised the full implications of what was envisaged.

The best glimpse at what was planned comes from a document the Gardaí seized in spring 1966 from Seán Garland, a senior IRA man and one of the leading reformers. It was read out in the Dáil in May 1966 and was published as an appendix to the Scarman Report into the disturbances in Northern Ireland in 1969. The Scarman Tribunal, acting on self-serving RUC information, dates the document erroneously to 1968.

In 1971 the (by then Official) IRA issued a statement to the Tribunal admitting that the document was theirs but denying it represented the movement's policy and was merely a discussion paper. However, its contents are remarkably similar to the policies the republican movement followed in the 1960s.

The proposals outlined in the paper emphasised the need to move away from military training and to concentrate on social and economic objectives. It concluded that new recruits were leaving the movement because once they had received military training they became disillusioned when they never got the chance to use it, and were not prepared to engage in political activity. That would have to change, with political training coming first. 'The basic movement will be a political, national and social-revolutionary organisation with an open membership and legal existence.' Recruitment would be on that basis alone, utilising 'the appeal of the Social and Economic Programme'. The IRA would remain the dominant structure 'to function within the revolutionary organisation as a backbone.' It would deal with 'the military aspect of the revolution'. Elections were not to be contested until everyone in the movement was satisfactorily trained 'to give a good account of themselves'. When 'our strength is sufficient' both Dáil and Stormont elections would be contested. Sinn Féin did indeed stop fighting elections of any kind in the South after 1965, and after 1966 in the North.

The paper recommended that branches or *cumainn* be organised, where possible, in factories to give leadership to factory-workers. A local *cumann* would have separate groups to work through, that is infiltrate – tenants' associations, youth groups, credit unions, co-ops and so on. Those involved in this would be specialised groups reporting back to the local *cumann* so that activities could be coordinated. In other words the movement would operate on several levels, some legal and open to anyone, others secret and subversive, with the controlling level, the IRA, prepared to use revolutionary violence. Only an elite at the top would have a panoramic view of what was happening and why. In short, Sinn Fein's plan proposed a conspiracy against the Irish people in general and against some of its own members in particular.

At the *ard fheis* in 1964 the party adopted a new Social and Economic Programme that indicated a swing to the left. Ruairí Ó Brádaigh explained that by 1964 Sinn Féin had decided to concentrate 'on local issues and the whole idea of egalitarianism', to object to 'economic pene- tration from England with their chain stores and that type of thing'. There was emphasis on rural co-operatives and support for a 'Save the West' campaign designed to halt the flight from the land and end emigration. The campaign was to follow the lines of Fr McDyer's approach in Glen- columcille in west Donegal: encouraging home industries and self- sufficiency. Considering that nearly 200,000 agricultural workers had left the land between 1946 and 1961, Sinn Féin's new policies were clearly attempting to address pressing contemporary issues.

The Sinn Féin Social and Economic Programme was a 1960s ver- sion of the Irish Ireland economics Arthur Griffith had laid forth in 1905. It ran completely counter to what the taoiseach, Sean Lemass, and the sec- retary of the Department of Finance, Dr TK Whitaker, were advocating in the 1960s, namely an open, free-trade economy. Sinn Féin opposed the Republic's 1965 Anglo-Irish Free Trade Agreement and expressed con- cern about the early overtures the government was making to what was then called 'the Common Market'. Sinn Féin objected to 'foreigners' buying Irish land or businesses, ignoring the fact that only foreigners had the capital to provide investment that might lead to employment. It objected to foreign 'river lords' who for historical reasons were mainly English, retaining fishing rights, even though fishing brought in much- needed money for locals who acted as ghillies and as porters and staff in hotels frequented by visiting fishermen. In Mayo and Galway locals staged protest fish-ins to highlight the fact that foreign absentees owned the rights. In the matter of ground rents demanded by 'absentee landlords'

Sinn Féin had a better case. In the west and south the party mounted campaigns to refuse such payments. For example, around Midleton in County Cork, Sinn Féin ran a strong and popular campaign.

Instead of creating organisations associated with the name Sinn Féin or led by known republicans, the movement adopted a tried and trusted strategy that republicans had been using successfully since the 1870s and that the document seized from Garland had advocated: infiltration. They threw themselves into what had become the fashionable radical political activity of the western world at the time – protest. Republicans took part in sit-ins, sit-downs, fish-ins and other demonstrations of passive resistance. Borrowed from the black civil rights movement in the USA, such 'protests' were designed to expose injustices, with the participants demanding 'rights' of various kinds.

In Ireland, as in other democratic states, the authorities did not know how to react to this form of political activity. Largely non-violent, the protesters could make police look like stormtroopers. Police personnel tended not to be trained to deal with any form of public protest other than a riot and often reacted as if they were facing a riot. For the activists, protests were extremely effective in obtaining publicity for their cause and their organisation if not in achieving the changes they claimed to seek. Protests helped portray the State as brutal and oppressive and reactionary.

The proliferation of television cameras played an important role in publicising such events. Protesters were filmed being dragged out of buildings and carried off streets by gardai. They were escorted off estates where they had been engaged in 'fish-ins'. Republicans helped organise agitation about 'foreign' landlords. In Westmeath, in Ruairí Ó Brádaigh's bailiwick, the duke of Mecklenburg, a wealthy refugee from East Prussia, bought an estate and then bought up neighbouring family farms until he had amassed several thousand acres. Even the writer Peadar O'Donnell, renowned for his campaigns on behalf of tenant farmers in Donegal in the 1930s, arrived on the scene to lend his expertise and reputation to the protests. By the mid-1960s, there was hardly any such demonstration, North or South, without republicans participating in it, organising it, policing it.

Whereas in rural areas republicans became involved with land and fishing rights, in urban areas they agitated for housing and jobs, but mainly the emphasis was on the demand for councils to build cheap, rentable accommodation. Cutbacks in public expenditure in the early 1960s caused a housing crisis, especially in Dublin, with people living in over-crowded, extremely sub-standard conditions. The worst consequence of this situation in the capital was the deaths of four people in Bolton Street in 1963 when a condemned building in which they were living collapsed.

Just as in rural areas, it was not always obvious that the protesters were republicans. Sinn Féin never used its own name when initiating a group. Yet there was hardly a tenants' or residents' association that did not count a republican or two among its committee members. Republicans were prominent in the Dublin Housing Action Committee. They were always available to attend meetings, to travel and volunteer for action. They were always ready to second any motion proposed by another republican or anyone else for that matter, as long as the proposal fell in with republican strategy. They were always prepared to take on the authorities and provide muscle if required. In the North, republicans, including the teenage Gerry Adams, were involved in wholly ineffectual protests against the redevel-opment of the lower Falls district that proposed demolishing dozens of tiny, cramped streets and housing their residents in multistorey flats, which later became notorious as Divis Flats.

This swing to populist, left-wing activism was not confined to what came to be known in later years as 'pressure groups' agitating on local issues. Republicans targeted universities too. Their means was to set up student societies called Republican Clubs. Like any other student political society, Republican Clubs invited guest speakers and organised debates on the issues of the day. What was significant about Republican Clubs was the distinctive left-wing direction they took. Famous, or to some people notorious, icons of left-wing republican tradition came to speak at the club in Trinity College, Dublin; men like George Gilmore and Peadar O'Donnell.

Gilmore, sixty-five years old in 1963, was born in Belfast but had been brought up in Howth and Foxrock, the son of a wealthy accountant. He had been the leader of the Anti-Treaty IRA in Dublin in the 1920s. He had been reviled as a Communist in the 1930s after he visited the USSR in 1930. Along with Peadar O'Donnell he had left the IRA in 1934 and established the Republican Congress, an attempt to marry republicanism and socialism with the aim of promoting a Workers' Republic in Ireland. Bitterly opposed by the IRA, the Catholic Church and Fianna Fáil, the Congress lasted only one year.

His partner in these endeavours, O'Donnell, was seventy in 1963. His background could not have been more different from Gilmore's. Born on a small farm in Donegal, he had become a teacher but by 1918 was a full-time official for the ITGWU (Irish Transport and General Workers' Union). A member of the IRA from 1920, he opposed the Treaty and took the same route as Gilmore to the far left. O'Donnell had considerable literary powers and he wrote seven novels and three volumes of autobiography. He edited the IRA's newspaper, *An Phoblacht*, in the 1920s and the literary magazine, *The Bell*, from 1946 to 1954. To have these bogeymen of the Irish establishment speaking at Trinity was indeed revolutionary.

They were not alone. Other republicans of a left-wing bent appeared not only at university Republican Club meetings but outside universities at what became another receptacle for Sinn Féin infiltration: Wolfe Tone Societies. The first Wolfe Tone Society emerged in October 1964. Others grew out of various local committees organised in 1963 to commemorate the bicentenary of the birth of Wolfe Tone, the founder of Irish republicanism.

The brains behind the first Wolfe Tone Society in Dublin seems to have been Roy Johnston, supported by Anthony Coughlan. The aim of the society was 'a united, independent and democratic Irish Republic in accordance with the principles of the 1916 Proclamation and the Democratic Programme of the First Dáil.' The emphasis on the Democratic Programme is significant. Drafted by Thomas Johnston, leader of the Irish Labour Party, the Democratic Programme, which the Dáil had adopted in January 1919, was openly socialist in tone. At the time it had caused serious misgivings among senior figures in the republican movement, including Michael Collins, who tried to have it suppressed. After it was passed by the Dáil it was promptly shelved and played no part in policy in the Free State. The inclusion of the document in the aims of the Wolfe Tone Society was a clear indication of the left-wing priorities of the society's members.

All these new ventures were put into operation in the North, too, without any recognition of the unique circumstances there. On the contrary, the republican leadership believed the North especially suitable territory for the new policy and Wolfe Tone Societies duly appeared there. They organised seminars, presented discussion papers and tried to raise consciousness about traditional republican values and publicise them. In tune with the sentiments of the time in the USA, Britain, France and Germany, members concentrated on issues such as justice, rights and equality. They provided an important intellectual stimulus for the realignment of Irish republicanism away from militarism, not least because they attracted some respectable intellectuals and left-wing activists from both sides of the border. In the North of Ireland one of the most remarkable aspects of the societies was that they included both Catholics and Protestants, remarkable because it was highly unusual for northern Protestants to be associated with anything that advocated republicanism, which a society named after Wolfe Tone must of necessity do.

Nevertheless, it is important to keep all this activity in perspective. It is true that Republican Clubs in universities were enormously popular. In Trinity College the club quickly acquired the biggest membership in the university. The club in Queen's University, Belfast, also attracted large numbers for what was a risky commitment in a unionist-controlled educational establishment. Republican Clubs were also formed in nationalist areas across the North. It was quickly obvious, not least to the RUC, that they were run by Sinn Féin. Just as the IRA had found it convenient to use Sinn Féin as its political mouthpiece because it was a legal political party, so the republican movement used Republican Clubs in the North as its mouthpiece because Stormont had again proscribed Sinn Féin in the run-up to the 1964 British general election. Still, despite their later prominence and expansion in the North, it should be remembered that until the late 1960s most people had never heard of Sinn Féin.

As for Wolfe Tone Societies, they were tiny talking shops. The leading lights in the Dublin society, the dominant one in the country, were Johnston and Coughlan, who wrote papers and published articles trying to produce a coherent and systematic argument to connect republican ideas to contemporary political issues. In Belfast the society never had more than a dozen members. Usually half that number attended meetings. Proceedings were often fruitless and argumentative, mainly because of the ramblings of one of the members, an eccentric Englishman, Michael Dolley, a professor of numismatics who taught medieval history at Queens. Like his academic interests, Dolley had only a tenuous connection with the real world. Other members, however, had a firmer grasp of the realities of life in the North. Jack Bennett, a former member of the Communist Party of Northern Ireland, Fred Heatley, a civil rights activist, Liam Burke, former IRA adjutant general in the 1940s and Alec Foster, former headmaster of the Royal Belfast Academical Institution, one of the North's most prestigious Protestant grammar schools, found it interesting to discuss papers on republicanism and republican history. Such a motley collection of people meeting together was exciting and extraordinary. It appeared to confirm that northern society was changing dramatically.

The emergence of these clubs and societies in the North was taking place against a rising sense of hope among northern nationalists. Groups like the Belfast Wolfe Tone Society encouraged people to believe their hopes were justified. Events provided further support. In March 1963 Captain Terence O'Neill had become prime minister of Northern Ireland, succeeding Lord Brookeborough who had been in that office for twenty years. O'Neill was anxious to reform the North after Brookeborough's stultifying period of rule. The new prime minister genuinely believed that if he held out the hand of friendship to nationalists and included them in the affairs of the State, they would become reconciled to living in Northern Ireland. In October 1964 Harold Wilson won the British general election and became the first Labour prime minister since 1951. Nationalists hoped a Labour government, led by a man who had resigned his junior government office in protest against the 1949 Ireland Act, would look sympathetically on their grievances.

For the men striving to lead the republican movement away from its obsession with the single issue of partition these political developments were an exciting vindication. It appeared as if they might offer the prospect of the sort of changes which dovetailed perfectly with the policies being advocated by Johnston and Coughlan. Developments at lower political levels in Britain and Northern Ireland also fitted their ideas, especially the growing emphasis on demanding rights and equality as a way to bring about political change. In 1964 Conn McCluskey, a Dungannon doctor, and his wife, Patricia, set up the Campaign for Social Justice (CSJ), documenting and publicising discrimination in housing and jobs and drawing attention to unionist gerrymandering of political boundaries. In London in 1965 two left-wing Irishmen in the Streatham Labour Party, Paddy Byrne and Bill O'Shaughnessy, founded the Campaign for Democracy in Ulster (CDU). They demanded 'full British democratic standards for the people of Northern Ireland, to which they are entitled as British subjects.'

Ominously for unionists, Paul Rose, a Manchester Labour MP, became president of the CDU. Sixty other MPs sponsored the CDU, which was formally launched in the House of Commons at a meeting chaired by Lord Brockway and attended by a score of MPs and other interested people from Northern Ireland, like Mrs McCluskey of the CSJ. The CDU demanded a Royal Commission to investigate the functioning of the Government of Ireland Act 1920 and the 1949 Ireland Act. Nobody could accuse the gathering of being a republican front any more than was McCluskey's CSJ.

So why then were republican modernisers like Roy Johnston delighted with developments in the North from 1963 to 1965? How did they suit Sinn Féin plans? Johnston argued that there was a way to produce a united, independent Ireland that did not follow the 'classical European path of nation building'. The classical path aimed at developing the cultural and ethnic distinctiveness of a nation as a way of uniting its people and raising their consciousness, exactly what Arthur Griffith's Sinn Féin strove to do. Johnston understood that such a process was divisive and threatening to unionists. Any policy that emphasised culture or ethnicity would lead nowhere in the North of Ireland. Therefore the path that had been followed in the rest of the country, and indeed in most of the rest of Europe in the nineteenth century, was not appropriate.

Instead, Johnston argued that the way to unite people in the North was by concentrating on social and economic issues, which slotted into the republican movement's new direction in the South. The aim would be to show people, Catholic and Protestant, that it was in their social and economic interest to have a united, independent Ireland. Only then could they build a prosperous society free from the results of economic imperialism and dependence on England. In conventional Marxist terms, uniting the northern working class in agitation for jobs, houses and equal rights would be the first phase of the struggle. Once the working class, Catholic and Protestant, was united, they could move on to the next phase, taking on the Northern Ireland State, not with the traditional military assault republicans had been employing, but again making only social and economic demands in case unionists, suspecting a republican plot, shied away and split working-class solidarity.

Naturally, therefore, Johnston and others who subscribed to such ideas were gratified when members of the British Labour Party, northern Catholics and liberal Protestants appeared to make common cause in the early to mid-1960s. The CSJ and CDU were music to the ears of reformers in Sinn Féin. With O'Neill as northern premier, Harold Wilson in Downing Street and sympathetic Labour MPs visiting Northern Ireland, it seemed that the network of organisations demanding reform was entangling unionism.

Republicans, following their infiltration strategy, had the sense either to keep out of these organisations or, when they joined, to keep in the background. That way, if an organisation had republican membership, no one could say republicans were orchestrating events, because they were not. Leading figures in the societies were well aware that they had republicans in their membership. Even if they were not fully aware of the movement's strategy, they were naturally determined to keep republicans at arm's length or at least out of prominent positions, partly because they wanted to retain control of their own committees and partly because they did not wish the organisation to be discredited as a republican front. Neither did republicans: it would not suit their purpose.

Fred Heatley, fully aware of who was or was not a member of the republican movement in the Wolfe Tone Society in Belfast, said the society was 'an autonomous adjunct of the republican movement'. He and some of the other members were interested in discussing theoretical republicanism, but were not in the republican movement nor were they prepared to allow the republican movement to take them over. They were happy to debate issues with known republicans like Liam Burke and attend the same meetings as them, but that was as far as it went.

However, although republicans were only a minority in the Wolfe Tone Societies, they were able to use the societies as a vehicle to carry their ideas of mass struggle north where they had more success in a short time than they ever imagined possible. It was republicans who produced the plans for a civil rights movement in the North, had the plans accepted and who had a major influence in the role that movement played in northern politics from 1967 to 1972. The proposal for a civil rights movement came from the Dublin Wolfe Tone Society, intellectually dominated by Roy Johnston and Anthony Coughlan, but also numbering among its membership IRA chief of staff Cathal Goulding.

In 1966 the Dublin Wolfe Tone Society suggested a sort of convention of Wolfe Tone Societies to examine general policy. They met in the Maghera home of a well-known republican, the County Derry solicitor Kevin Agnew. At that meeting, on Friday, 13 August, a lengthy paper, largely written by Anthony Coughlan but with crucial contributions from Roy Johnston, was presented. Since Coughlan was not present at the meeting and Johnston has a stammer that tends to occur when he reaches words he wants to emphasise, Eoghan Harris, then a Cork-based writer with republican views, read the paper to the meeting.

The paper followed the predictable lines that Johnston and Coughlan had been advocating for some years. It dealt with ways of uniting Protestant and Catholic workers and organising them into joint action. Much emphasis was laid on the role of trade unions in demonstrations and agitation with thinly veiled suggestions of infiltration. Part of the strategy bore striking resemblance to the paper seized from Garland three months earlier. It was out of this Maghera meeting that a subsequent seminar on civil rights was organised in November in Belfast. The Belfast seminar decided to establish a civil rights body, which was duly constituted in January 1967 as the Northern Ireland Civil Rights Association (NICRA) along the lines suggested by the Dublin Wolfe Tone Society's paper. The committee included a wide range of interests: trade unions, of course, and political parties, Republican Clubs, of course, and the CSJ. A small subcommittee of three, which included Billy McMillan, OC of the Belfast IRA, was nominated to draw up standing orders. The proceedings were observed with some satisfaction by members of the National Council for Civil Liberties from London, a satisfaction not shared by the RUC who looked askance at the personnel involved.

And so was constructed a huge castle in the sky. As applied to the North, the Marxist theory was nonsense and its practice dangerous. Johnston and Coughlan had no idea of the strength of emotion that existed among unionists in the North. The leadership of Sinn Féin and the IRA ignored warnings, even from men sympathetic to their views – like Belfast IRA man Billy McMillen – that trade unions in the North were not fertile ground for the sort of infiltration that worked among trade unions in the Republic. Northern unions had always been sectarian. The result was that, within a year, the scheme that was to unite Protestant and Catholic workers in the North and show them that it was in their social and economic interest to unite to claim equality and justice, became the source which split the two communities in the North wider apart than they had been since 1921. The split reawakened the visceral hatreds that had simmered beneath the surface of northern society for generations.

It was not just that the men articulating rights-based agitation as a way to advance Sinn Féin's agenda had ignored the misgivings expressed by people within the republican movement in the North. They blithely ignored the evidence that the signals on their track in the North had turned red even before 1967. All the hopeful signs that things might improve in the North with the arrival of Terence O'Neill, the change of government in Britain, O'Neill's meeting with taoiseach Sean Lemass in 1965, O'Neill's promises of reform and the liberal noises many middle-class unionists were making, all these had blinded the Dublin-based theoreticians in the republican leadership to what was actually happening on the streets of Northern Ireland.

Each positive sign for the objectives of the republican modernisers was countered by an opposite and more powerful negative sign. One curious blind spot was the way the actions of northern republicans on the streets contradicted Johnston's argument that cultural and ethnic issues should be played down in case they antagonised the unionist working class. Beginning in 1963 with republican attempts to commemorate Wolfe Tone's bicentenary with parades and bands, a welter of significant dates followed each other in the 1960s, most particularly the 1966 celebrations of the fiftieth anniversary of the Easter Rising, which nationalists of all descriptions joined in enthusiastically but which republicans marked with their usual attempts to march through towns behind the Irish tricolour. On top of everything else came two British general elections, in 1964 and 1966, with all their attendant tensions, which led to rioting and communal disturbances.

O'Neill's administration at Stormont became very nervous about all the displays and demonstrations. By 1967 they stepped in to prevent any manifestation commemorating the centenary of the Fenian rising. By then it should have been obvious that it was too late for Johnston's theories, yet this was the very year they came into operation in the North. By 1967, not only had the unionist working class, held in fond regard by Johnston and others in the Sinn Féin leadership, become extremely twitchy but many members of O'Neill's own party were concerned about the rising level of republican activity, admittedly none of it violent. Already in 1966, Gusty Spence, a convicted thief and former British soldier, had pulled together a gang on the Shankill Road that called itself the Ulster Volunteer Force (UVF) after the 1913 group that organised resistance to Home Rule. By June 1966, Spence and his gunmen had shot dead two Catholics, wounded two others and killed an elderly Protestant widow with a badly aimed petrol bomb.

The most powerful negative public signs were usually associated with the Rev Ian Paisley, then a little known fundamentalist Presbyterian preacher who had dabbled in 'direct action' of his own since the early 1950s when he threatened to lead thousands of loyalist shipyard workers through the Catholic County Derry town of Dungiven if an Orange march through the town were banned. Now, in the early 1960s, he became the public face of unionist reaction.

Thus, when the liberal Pope John XXIII died in June 1963, Belfast City Hall, in keeping with the new approach of the new Northern Ireland prime minister, flew the Union Jack at half-mast in respect. Paisley preached a furious sermon against the gesture and led an impromptu (and illegal) protest march to City Hall. In 1964 Paisley threatened to march into the republican heartland of Divis Street in West Belfast and remove an Irish tricolour from the office of Billy McMillen, the republican candidate in the Westminster general election. To pre-empt him, the RUC removed the flag forcibly, leading to the worst rioting on the Falls Road for thirty years. In January 1965 when Sean Lemass drove to Belfast to meet Terence O'Neill, Paisley was waiting for him at the gates of Stormont to throw snowballs at his car. In 1966 Paisley was convicted of unlawful assembly and breach of the peace for his behaviour while protesting at the Presbyterian General Assembly against their 'Romeward trend'.

While it is easy to single out Paisley as the cause of trouble, it is a fallacy to assume that if it had not been for the antics of Paisley in the mid-1960s, or if the Stormont administration had taken a stronger line against him, all would have been well. The harsh truth is that if Paisley had not existed, it would have been necessary to invent him. Some other extremist cleric or hardline unionist would have appeared on the scene, and indeed Paisley had rivals for the role of 'Saviour of Ulster' whom he saw off. The fact is that Paisley was simply articulating in a more coarse and brutal fashion the views of some members of Terence O'Neill's Cabinet and of a substantial number of his party's Stormont MPs. Their views were that unreconstructed unionist supremacy was the only way to secure the ethnic survival of the North's Protestant community and, secondly, that their survival was under threat from a republican conspiracy all the more dangerous and insidious because on this occasion republicans were not engaged in military action. The only response to this threat was that no concession of any kind should be entertained and that every manifestation of republicanism, real or imagined, was to be suppressed.

The involvement of Protestants in organisations demanding fundamental change in the North, which so encouraged republicans, incensed Paisley. As far as he and his supporters were concerned, liberal Protestants in NICRA were what Lenin called 'useful idiots'. That was Lenin's description of middle-class intellectuals and liberals who demanded rights and justice for Bolshevik revolutionaries in Russia or Communist parties in western Europe, blissfully unaware that those same revolutionaries planned to destroy them. Paisley believed that liberal Protestants and unionists were being duped by the IRA before being cast aside. They were worse than republican spokesmen because of the credibility they provided for republican fronts.

Senior figures in O'Neill's Unionist Party, most notably Bill Craig, minister for Home Affairs, who was in receipt of RUC Special Branch reports on republicans in NICRA, agreed with Paisley. Others, including Terence O'Neill, regarded Paisley as a dinosaur, a useful and frightening reminder of the sort of society Northern Ireland had been in the past. Many young people saw him as a figure of fun. He was a gift for impressionists in the local entertainment scene. Few commentators imagined that his strident, vituperative opposition to Terence O'Neill was an authentic reflection of the opinion of a significant section of the unionist population who proceeded to vote for him in 1969 and have done so ever since.

Resistance to change was not confined to the extremes of unionism. Within the republican movement men like Cathal Goulding and Tomás MacGiolla were finding the going tough. They faced three principal grounds of criticism. First, and most easily dealt with, was the complaint that there was no military action. Young hotheads could be given two answers: that action was being planned and would happen in due course, or that action was being planned in conjunction with other strategies. The 'other strategies' fairly obviously involved 'direct action', such as attacks on property and protests at which local IRA units could employ strong-arm tactics. It was hardly a satisfactory response but it placated most objectors. Some recruits would always want to have a crack at the British. From time to time some did. Throughout the 1960s there were freelance activities, though most were connected with the 'other strategies', such as burning the property of foreign investors or the blowing up of a large fishing boat at Rossaveal, County Galway. The action that gained the most publicity was blowing up Nelson's Pillar in Dublin in March 1966. Like all the other incidents, it was a merely a one-off gesture.

The other two grounds for criticism were much more serious: resistance to any suggestion of abandoning abstentionism and, secondly, to the increasing Marxist tone of party literature, first apparent publicly in the columns of the *United Irishman* after 1962. Although senior figures in the IRA had agreed in 1962 that the movement should involve itself in contemporary Irish social and economic issues, the problem was how to get Sinn Féin to agree this switch explicitly at an *ard fheis*. Any such agreement would necessarily imply that Sinn Féin would have to abandon abstentionism. The movement would split. To avoid such an outcome, MacGiolla, Goulding and the modernisers moved step by step.

The first step was to develop a radical policy on bread-and-butter issues. That took two years. In 1964 the Social and Economic Programme was adopted at that year's Sinn Féin *ard fheis*. Nevertheless, there was enough disquiet about talk of entering the Dáil that an Extraordinary *Ard Fheis* was convened in May 1965. It rejected a policy of recognising Leinster House. Following this, Sean Caughey from Belfast, Sinn Féin's vice-president, and Des Foley, editor of the *United Irishman*, both resigned from the movement.

Foley, a Kerryman, had become the editor of the *United Irishman* when he was released from Crumlin Road jail in 1962. He had completely revamped the paper, discarding the old-style Gaelic script in the title. Hagiography about 'republican' heroes was exchanged for articles with a mainly far-left socialist analysis of social and economic issues. The membership of Sinn Féin was less than supportive of the changes in their newspaper. Foley finally left the republican movement in 1967.

Sean Caughey from Belfast was another man impatient with the lack of speed of reform. He had played a prominent role in civil rights agitation from 1962 and became secretary of the Northern Ireland Council for Civil Liberties when it was formed in that year. In 1965 he wanted Sinn Féin to recognise both Stormont and Dublin parliaments.

The effect of that 1965 Extraordinary *Ard Fheis* was to label people in the movement according to which side they had taken in the debate. Either you were a 'Leinster House person', that is to say you favoured ending abstention, or you were not. The lines of division within the republican movement were being drawn tighter.

Doubters who criticised Sinn Féin's explicit left-wing policies could be countered with the argument that the policies did not signify Marxism but were in fact in the true mainstream republican tradition of James Connolly and Liam Mellowes, that is, republicans had always been on the side of the underdog, had opposed huge estates and absentee landlords and so on. In the last analysis, however, the most militant and critical republicans did not care too much about the party's social and economic stance. For them, the sole aim was to achieve a united Ireland. Crucial to that aim was the principle of not recognising any partition parliament because that implied Britain had a right to be in Ireland. Sinn Féin's social and economic policies were a secondary matter because, if Sinn Féin was an abstentionist party, then its social and economic policies could not be put into practice anyway, which, of course, was precisely the issue that concerned MacGiolla, Goulding and their supporters. Ending abstention would be the big test.

Although defeated in 1965, Tomás MacGiolla, who as president had been straddling both views in an attempt to maintain unity, felt that enough progress had been made for him to be able to say at the 1966 *ard fheis* that if Sinn Féin won a majority in an election in the Republic, the party would enter the Dáil, though, of course, he added, with the purpose of radically changing the Oireachtas. He said he believed a majority for Sinn Féin was possible within five years. There was no mistaking the direction in which the leadership intended taking the movement. The following year at Bodenstown, traditionally the occasion when changes of policy were announced, Cathal Goulding made it clear in his speech that the obsession with removing partition had been a mistake and that the republican movement had to win popular support. That would require a radical set of policies. Placing these before the Irish people would be the priority, not ending partition. Given the occasion, Goulding naturally had to reiterate the traditional republican position that Irish people retained the right to use force to achieve their aims, but there could be no mistaking that the leader of the IRA was leaning towards participating in constitutional politics, even if he had not said it in so many words.

From 1965 a grim tussle ensued within the republican movement to achieve a change in the IRA's standing orders and in Sinn Féin's constitution to allow the party to recognise Leinster House and take any seats it won in the Dáil. In Sinn Féin's case such a change required a two-thirds majority at an *ard fheis*. That majority proved impossible to secure. It was clear that even discussion of the issue could provoke a split in the movement. Goulding and MacGiolla could only look on as spectators while events in the North unfolded in a way they imagined would advance their policies. The whole process in the North seemed to them tailormade for the policies they were advocating, including going one step further than recognising Dáil Éireann: the hitherto unimaginable prospect of attending Westminster.

Sinn Féin had stood aside in West Belfast in the 1966 British general election with the result that Gerry Fitt, leader of the tiny Belfast-based Republican Labour Party, was elected. With the help of sympathetic British Labour MPs he had quickly begun to wreak havoc. First he had the so-called Westminster Convention, which prevented Northern Ireland's affairs from being discussed in parliament, set aside. A gregarious, articulate, likeable, working-class figure, he organised tours to Belfast and across the North for his new-found Labour MP friends. Using material supplied by the CSJ, he began to expose unionist discrimination and gerrymandering while at the same time using rhetoric that reached out to the Protestant working-class in his constituency. The leaders of the republican movement could only look on in envy as he seemed to demonstrate the validity of their arguments. In reality, Fitt had become a hate figure among hardline unionists who whipped up working-class loyalist fears about his intentions.

Fitt's success cut no ice with traditional republicans either. Despite Goulding's rhetoric in the 1967 *ard fheis* he could not get abstention ditched. By the time of the 1968 *ard fheis* in December, the president, Tomás MacGiolla, was no more likely to have the necessary majority to pass the annual motion to overturn abstention. Knowing it would fail, the *ard comhairle* had decided that Seán Garland, one of the most committed supporters of the leftward move, would propose an amendment to the motion to end abstention. The amendment suggested that a commission should be established to examine the issue of abstention and report back to a subsequent *ard fheis*. There were high hopes among the modernisers that when the commission submitted a positive report, as it was confidently expected to do, it would be endorsed by the movement. Younger members of Sinn Féin were champing at the bit. Seamus Costello, who seconded Garland's motion, believed he had an excellent chance of election in Wicklow if only abstention could be voted down in time. (The next election in the Republic was due to take place in June 1969.)

Once again, events in the North overtook the republican movement's plans. Northern Ireland had burst on the world's television screens on 5 October 1968 with the now infamous pictures of the RUC batoning all and sundry – men, women, MPs, old, young, fit, disabled – at a civil rights march in Derry. Unionism was in crisis. In November, Terence O'Neill had announced a comprehensive package of reforms that seemed to concede all the demands of the civil rights movement on voting, allocation of housing, review of the Special Powers Act, an electoral boundary commission and, unbelievably, the suspension of Derry City Council and its replacement by a commission. Immediately, O'Neill's premiership came under threat from his own hardliners. He had to sack his strongman, minister of Home Affairs, Bill Craig. The North looked as if it were collapsing into anarchy, with violent attacks by police and B-Specials on marchers belonging to the Trotskyite student organisation, the People's Democracy, in January 1969. By the end of January, Brian Faulkner, another member of O'Neill's Cabinet, had left the sinking ship. Not many people had noticed the modernisers' travails at Sinn Féin's *ard fheis* in December 1968.

In the midst of this huge crisis for unionism and Northern Ireland, George Forrest, unionist MP for Mid-Ulster, died in January 1969. What was Sinn Féin to do? Surely it had to connect with the people? How could it stand idly by and keep up its abstentionist policy? Yet it was trapped by its own procedures. Garland's commission had not reported. Even if it had, a special *ard fheis* would have had to be convened to endorse any proposal of ending abstention. Mid-Ulster was a republican constituency which, thirteen years before, had repeatedly elected Tom Mitchell as MP despite his being in jail. Northern republicans had spotted a once in a lifetime opportunity. Now there was a chance to send a republican to Westminster to join Gerry Fitt. Perhaps if a Sinn Féiner won Mid-Ulster it would finish Stormont? If their candidate were abstentionist the seat would be lost to a unionist and republicans would be blamed.

Furthermore, they would be accused of halting the momentum for change in the North created by the civil rights movement over the previous year and, what's more, a civil rights movement republicans had been instrumental in creating.

By the end of January 1969 there was still no sign of Sinn Féin's commission filing a report. Sinn Féin's candidate, Kevin Agnew, was already in the field, but inevitably as an abstentionist republican candidate. There was every likelihood that Austin Currie, Nationalist MP for Tyrone East, would stand as a civil rights candidate. If that happened, the unionist would be elected. Bursting with frustration, six leading republicans in Tyrone resigned from the movement. They said 'the abstentionist policy bears no relevance to conditions in 1969'. Among the six were prominent IRA men, including Kevin Mallon from Coalisland, convicted in 1957 of the murder of RUC Sergeant Ovens. In the 1970s Mallon became a legendary figure in the Provisional IRA. Another of the six, Tomás O'Connor, was a member of Sinn Féin's *ard comhairle*. No one could accuse these men of not being sound on the national question.

Their action forced the hand of the Dublin leadership, which had Agnew withdrawn in favour of an agreed candidate, Bernadette Devlin, who would take her seat if she won. The events leading up to the selection of Bernadette Devlin, her subsequent stunning victory and brilliant performance at Westminster are a perfect illustration of the ineptitude of the republican leadership and how divorced it was from political reality, how slow to respond to a challenge and how steeped in useless dogma.

It was not simply a matter of being hung up on the dogma of abstention. Revolutionary socialism now held them in as tight a grip. The Goulding–MacGiolla leadership seemed mesmerised by the international events of 1968: *les évenements* in Paris which saw off de Gaulle, the Prague Spring, the Grosvenor Square riots in London, as well as events in Derry. The leaders of Sinn Féin and the IRA became convinced that mass, direct action on the streets was the way to change society. Their statements became ever more left-wing, Trotskyite even. At Easter 1969 they announced 'economic resistance, political action, military action in pursuance of a 32-county Workers' and Small Farmers' Republic.' It put them to the left of Chairman Mao. It sounded practically hysterical.

Over the next few months prior to the Republic's general election, the Irish Labour Party and others on the left managed to convince themselves and, it should be said, a fair number in Fianna Fáil, that the mood of change sweeping the rest of Europe would affect Ireland. There was going to be an abrupt swing to the left. In line with its new policy, Sinn Féin was not contesting the election, preferring 'direct action', but there was a general belief that there would be radical changes in the Republic. To keep its existence in the public eye, on 11 June 1969, a week before the Republic's election, the IRA burned down four German-owned farms in Meath, an action that seemed completely at odds with the emphasis on non-violent means which republicans had professed in the North in the previous three years. As it was, despite fears to the contrary and great hopes on the left, republican activity, direct or otherwise, made no impression whatsoever on mainstream politics in the South. Nor did Labour. Fianna Fáil increased its majority in the general election.

In the North, Sinn Féin had no role at all to play. The party had been banned since 1964 and in 1967 Republican Clubs were also banned. The civil rights movement had seized the initiative in confronting unionism, and during 1968 and 1969 their mass demonstrations brought the Stormont administration to its knees. Seamus Rodgers of Donegal Sinn Féin said the civil rights movement had done more in a few weeks to damage unionism than decades of IRA activity; he obviously knew very little about how events in the North were organised.

NICRA decided the time and place for every civil rights march. However, in cooperation with NICRA, republicans organised the marches. Often they advised on the route. On the first march, from Coalisland to Dungannon, the route was suggested by Austin Currie, and senior republicans, including Kevin Mallon, planned the logistics. Virtually all the stewards, over sixty of them, were IRA men. Just as in the South, republicans played a role in sit-ins and other demonstrations. The most famous in the North, the 'squat' at Caledon in County Tyrone to publicise the injustice of allocating a house to a single Protestant teenage girl, was initiated by Brantry Republican Club and joined by Austin Currie, the local Stormont MP. It was local republicans who barricaded the house. The family who squatted in the house were republicans and their granddaughter, Michelle Gildernew, was elected MP for Fermanagh–Tyrone South in June 2001 to represent the area in which her grandparents could not get a house.

In Derry, republicans had linked up with a loose network of left-wing groups to produce a formidable agitation for more housing. From 1966 they had taken direct action to prevent eviction of families from the Creggan. In other words, republicans fortified the houses with the family and resisted the police, just as Cathal Goulding had intended. Their actions were an embarrassment to nationalist councillors who had managed to pull out all the stops to guarantee alternative accommodation for the families threatened with eviction. Derry seemed full of 'action groups', such as the Derry Young Republican Association, the People's Action League, the Derry Unemployed Action Committee and the Derry Housing Action Committee, which was the body that invited NICRA to hold a civil rights march in the town in October 1968. The committees comprised a hotchpotch of socialists, from mainstream Northern Ireland Labour to Trotskyites like Eamon McCann, but republicans were in all of them.

As 1969 wore on, with escalating loyalist violence, people in nationalist areas began to look for more from republicans than background support. They began to look to the IRA for defence. They looked in vain. Under Goulding the IRA had been run down. His idea was to create instead a sort of citizens' army that would engage in politico-economic activity. Its role, as described in the captured 1966 document, would be to defend demonstrators from police action or attacks by reactionaries, whoever they might be. It was the sort of action the Derry groups excelled in. Citizens' Defence Committees would be organised to defend areas. It would have to involve action by all the population of the district, not just Catholics as such. The IRA could not be seen to be defending Catholics for that ran counter to the Marxist analysis of the leadership. In the ghettoised demography of working-class Belfast and Derry this policy was a fantasy. In any case, it was all academic, for there were few or no weapons and the only people who knew how to use them were men beyond combat age who, in most cases, had left the movement because they disagreed with its direction since 1962.

When the North exploded in August 1969 the IRA was in tatters and without military direction. There were nominally about sixty IRA men in Belfast, though most had never seen action. There were perhaps ten in Derry. The reaction in Belfast and Derry when men discovered that there were no guns available from sources in the Republic was blind rage. Within a week of the August pogrom in West Belfast, the republican movement in the city had split. Men who were to form the Provisional IRA – Joe Cahill, Seamus Twomey, Jimmy Drumm, Billy McKee, Leo Martin, Billy Kelly, John Kelly and the twenty-year-old Gerry Adams – challenged Goulding's supporters. The challengers were supported by Daithí Ó Conaill, a revered 1950s veteran and close friend of Ruairí Ó Brádaigh who had travelled to Belfast. At first the challenge was unsuccessful, but very quickly it became clear that although a deal had been cobbled together to keep the peace, the dissidents, led by Billy McKee, were the dominant faction in Belfast.

Almost as if they were oblivious to what had happened in the North, the IRA Army Council met in October 1969 to consider the report of the Garland commission, established at the Sinn Féin *ard fheis* the previous December. It had completed its report in March 1969 recommending, as expected, an end to abstention from Leinster House, Stormont and West-minster. The IRA accepted the recommendation by twelve votes to eight and called a special army convention for December, which endorsed the decision. It now remained for Sinn Féin to pass an appropriate resolution at its *ard fheis*, which was scheduled for January 1970.

Events had made it irrelevant. Already the northerners, including those in Tyrone, had decided, in a complete reversal of their position the previous spring, to have nothing to do with politics. The people had risen. They could overthrow Stormont by force of arms. The door was rotten; one last kick would knock it down. By December 1969 they had set up a Provisional[1] Army Council under Seán MacStíofáin's leadership and had started to muster support around the country. They claimed that the IRA meetings in October and December had been rigged to secure an anti-abstentionist majority. By the time of the Sinn Féin *ard fheis* in January 1970 the dissidents were confident that although Goulding and MacGiolla would get a simple majority for ending abstention, they would not get the two-thirds majority they needed. They were right. The pro-posal to end abstention was carried by 153 to 104, eighteen short of the two-thirds required. In a pre-arranged move, Sean MacStíofáin led the opponents of the Goulding leadership out of the Intercontinental Hotel in Dublin, the venue of the *ard fheis*, and held a meeting in Kevin Barry Hall, Parnell Square, which had been booked previously in for the pur-pose. The Provos, as they were to be known, had arrived.

8. THE YEARS OF AGITPROP
Sinn Féin backs the War, 1970-81

T he 1970s was the most terrible decade in Ireland in the twentieth century. During those ten years over 2,000 people died as a result of the Troubles, which had erupted in the North in the 1960s. Most of them died in Belfast, mainly in north and west Belfast, but many also died in Dublin, Monaghan and other parts of the Republic. The newly formed Provisional IRA was responsible for over 1,000 deaths in that dreadful decade. In 1972, the worst year of the Troubles, almost 500 men, women and children died.

In early 1970 neither the Provisional IRA nor its political mouth-piece, Provisional Sinn Féin, had much of an existence outside west Belfast. Its new Dublin-based leaders had almost no followers. There were, of course, pockets of support around Ireland where various individuals in the republican movement, emotionally spurred by the events of August 1969, gave their backing to the breakaway group, which as yet had no organisation on the ground. They tended to be made up of two age groups: young hotheads and men over the age of forty. Curiously, this is almost exactly the same breakdown an IRA member gave in 1999 when describing the people who split from the main movement in autumn 1997 to form the Real IRA. He said they were 'the very old and the very young': young men who wanted action and older men who could not accept the radical changes in the movement they had been part of for most of their lives.

Some members of the republican movement, both modernisers and traditionalists, were glad when the split finally happened in 1970. They had regarded it as inevitable given the growing tensions since 1965. Others, both inside and outside the movement, viewed the Provisionals as a dangerous, backward-looking offshoot from a republican movement that had spent the best part of ten years trying to jettison irredentist violence and rhetoric and to turn it into a movement which, in 1969, was on the verge of entering electoral politics in both parts of the island.

Within two years, however, the roles were reversed. People flocked to join the Provos, as they quickly became known. In a forlorn effort to assert its authority, the republican movement from which the Provisionals had broken away in December 1969 began to call itself the Official IRA and Official Sinn Féin. To no avail. By 1972 the 'Officials', North and South, were a discredited rump, themselves regarded as a faction by what was now the main body of the movement. From Easter 1970 the Provos used the slang word 'Stickie' or 'Stick' as a derisory term for the Officials. The term was first coined in Belfast when the Official republican movement decided to wear adhesive paper badges depicting the Easter lily, the symbol of the 1916 Easter Rising, which they stuck to their clothing rather than pinning it on in traditional fashion, as the Provos continued to do. The Officials were on the defensive ideologically from the instant the Provos appeared.

Ten years later, from their origins as a tiny, geographically limited group, the Provos – comprising both the Provisional IRA and Provisional Sinn Fein – had mushroomed into a national movement with supporters in every town in Ireland, 100,000 votes in the North and councillors in many parts of the Republic, including Dublin. How did the small group of militarist dissidents who came together off Parnell Square in 1970 spawn a new Sinn Féin that commanded support unprecedented since 1921?

The meteoric rise of the Provos and the equally rapid decline of the 'Stickies' have spawned a variety of conspiracy theories purporting to explain these phenomena. The most fashionable and persistent notion has been that Fianna Fáil invented the Provos, funded them and armed them because Fianna Fáil feared the rise of left–right politics in Ireland and was especially concerned about the growth of radical republicanism at the end of the 1960s. Traditional republicanism, it was claimed, was more in Fianna Fáil's line: that, at least, they knew how to deal with. In other words, the suggestion is that senior figures in Fianna Fáil shared exactly the same fears as right-wingers in the republican movement, such as Seán Mac-Stíofáin, Dáithí Ó Conaill and Ruairí Ó Brádaigh and other less prominent members who had left the movement in the 1960s. This *canard* was given legs by the appearance of Fianna Fáil ministers as defendants in the 1970 Arms Trial and by nods and winks from those supposedly 'in the know about what really went on' behind the scenes. The allegation has been kept in the limelight by people influential in the media who themselves were members of the Official republican movement or sympathisers. It is a fantasy.

One of the major flaws in the argument is that it fails to explain why anyone in Fianna Fáil would be panic-stricken about the rise of left-wing radicals in the Republic when Fianna Fáil had increased its majority in the general election in June 1969 while so-called left-wing republican radicals did not even contest that election. Even the moderate left-of-centre Labour Party lost votes and seats. In short, not only was there no threat whatsoever to Fianna Fáil, after June 1969 no one in the party had any reason to think there might be. Why should anyone in Fianna Fáil care about Marxists in a tiny marginalised organisation whose members had no seats in the Dáil nor any likelihood of winning one? In fact, being able to castigate opponents publicly as Marxists was an electoral advantage to Fianna Fáil.

Did anyone in Fianna Fáil sympathise with the plight of northern nationalists in 1969? Yes. Did anyone in Fianna Fáil supply money to northern nationalists and republicans after August 1969? Yes. Would senior figures in Fianna Fáil have supplied guns if they had been allowed? Yes. Does that mean they founded the Provos? Absolutely not. In fact, the first contacts Irish army officers and members of Fianna Fáil made with republicans were in spring 1969 as the temperature began to rise in the North. The contacts were with the existing IRA leadership under Cathal Goulding. There was no one else to contact. The same is true of contacts after August 1969. Even in Belfast, the republican leadership still gave allegiance to Cathal Goulding and Tomás MacGiolla until they were ousted some months later. The fiction that Fianna Fáil invented the Provos to forestall a left-wing lurch in politics in the Republic was concocted by Goulding and his entourage to explain the demise of their own political strategy.

The Provos grew out of what happened in August 1969 in west Belfast, Derry, Newry, Armagh, Coalisland, Dungiven, Crossmaglen and a number of other smaller towns, but principally out of events in west Belfast. There, Protestant mobs supported by the armed Protestant part-time militia, the B-Specials, poured into Catholic streets off the Falls Road, burning houses and driving people out. Armoured police vehicles directed heavy machine-gun fire into flats occupied by Catholics, killing a child in its bed. The most notorious incidents were the burning of Bombay Street in the Clonard area of west Belfast and the murder there of a teenager in broad daylight on 15 August.

In 1972 the Scarman Tribunal, established to investigate the events of 1969 and named after the English judge who chaired it, reported that, apart from ten dead and 154 wounded by gunfire across the North, 745 people in Belfast had been injured and 179 homes and other buildings had been demolished. The tribunal found that 'in Belfast the permanent displacement of families reached major proportions'. Scarman concluded that around 1,800 families had moved home, of these 1,500 were Catholic and 300 Protestant. He calculated that 0.4% of Protestant households and 5.3% of Catholic households in the city were displaced, and that 83% of the premises damaged were occupied by Catholics.

After these events, republicans in Belfast needed no urging from Fianna Fáil or anyone else to organise in their own defence. Clonard, where Bombay Street is located, is considered the womb of the Provos. As the Provisional IRA slogan had it: 'From the ashes of Bombay Street rose the Provisionals.' Never again, they promised, would Catholic areas be left undefended. In its inception in Belfast, therefore, the Provisional IRA was a Catholic defence organisation. No assistance from Fianna Fáil – even if it had been forthcoming in the fashion the apologists for the Marxist-leaning republican movement claim – was necessary.

The same response was evoked among the nationalist population in Derry that same August after what became known as the 'Battle of the Bogside'. Clashes provoked by the annual march of the loyalist Apprentice Boys through the city on 12 August quickly escalated into a pitched battle between the police and youths from the Bogside. Stones and petrol bombs were hurled into police ranks by the well-prepared Bogsiders. Soon barricades were thrown up and the Bogside was under siege from the RUC and loyalists. It was deliberately in order to stretch police resources – 'to take the heat off the Bogside' in the phrase of the time – that various groups, including the Northern Ireland Civil Rights Association (NICRA), encouraged people to engage in street protests across the North. Those protests in aid of Derry led to Protestant mobs in several places, especially Belfast, pouring onto the streets in the belief that there was a republican insurrection across the North.

The behaviour of the RUC that weekend in the various nationalist towns where riots occurred – baton charges, discharge of small arms, the use of CS gas, firing heavy calibre machine-guns and acting in concert with the undisciplined B-Specials and loyalist gangs in trying to suppress the local nationalist population – was the culmination of over a year's skirmishing between the police and civil rights marchers. After that weekend, when units of the British Army were deployed to replace the exhausted RUC, the North's nationalist population never again trusted the police. It is no coincidence that the places where the new Provisional republican movement emerged and retained its strongest support were exactly those towns which suffered serious disturbances during the weekend of 12-16 August 1969. Newry, Coalisland, Dungiven, Crossmaglen, Armagh and the countryside around them, as well as Belfast and Derry, became synonymous with Provo activity for the next twenty-five years. Of course, it is also true that the populations of those towns tended to have republican predilections anyway and that is why many of their inhabitants were out on the streets 'protesting' about events in Derry.

The men who established the Provisional republican movement in 1970 immediately overturned the policy that had been laboriously constructed during the 1960s by Goulding and MacGiolla. The emphasis placed on political development was swept aside. All efforts were bent to acquire weapons for defending Catholic areas. Soon, however, the Provisional leadership in Dublin had decided that the events in the North provided a once in a lifetime opportunity to overthrow Stormont by making the Six Counties ungovernable. Their belief was that this would result in the British negotiating a withdrawal from Ireland. The arrival of British troops, who superseded the RUC in strong nationalist areas, appeared therefore as an encouraging sign. Not that the republican movement welcomed the deployment of British troops, rather their appearance on the streets was, to republicans, an admission that Northern Ireland as a political entity had failed. It appeared to republicans that the unionists and their police force were no longer in control. A new arrangement would have to be worked out dealing directly with the British government, an arrangement that republicans were convinced would result in the departure of the British troops.

Indeed, the aim of abolishing Stormont was one of the reasons the

new Provisional republican movement gave for walking out of the Sinn
Féin *ard fheis* in January 1970. A week after its first public appearance, the
caretaker executive of Provisional Sinn Féin issued a lengthy statement,
written mainly by Ruairí Ó Brádaigh, justifying its actions. The statement
gave five reasons for the walk-out, beginning with the attempt to change
Sinn Féin's constitution to recognise Leinster House, Westminster and
Stormont. Second was the 'extreme form of socialism being pushed on
the Movement'. Naturally the failure to protect northern nationalists was
an important justification: 'Despite repeated warnings from last May on,
sufficient priority was not given to this matter,' the statement said. Failure
to seize the opportunity to get rid of Stormont was another reason given
for the split:

> We find absolutely incomprehensible from any Republican stand-
> point the campaigning in favour of retaining the Stormont parlia-
> ment in August, September and October last [1969] when it was in
> danger of being abolished altogether by the British government. In
> any future struggle for freedom it would surely be preferable to
> have a direct confrontation with the British government on Irish
> soil without the Stormont junta being interposed.

The final justifications for walking out, which take up most of the
rest of the statement, were accusations about the 'internal methods', such
as vote-rigging, that the leadership had used within the movement from
1965 to 1969 and the expulsion of any member who 'dared to criticise
ultra-left policies'.

Despite the tone of the statement and the heated verbal exchanges,
the division within the movement was not as clear-cut as the walk-out
might have led people to believe at the time. A lot of personal *animus* had
developed in the late 1960s in the republican leadership. It now poured
out in public recriminations by Ó Brádaigh and MacStíofáin, much of it
directed against Roy Johnston. Veterans of the 1950s, like Ó Brádaigh and
Ó Conaill, saw the failure to deal with the onslaughts in the North in

August 1969 as an opportunity to overthrow a leadership they had become increasingly disenchanted with over the previous three or four years. The emergency in Belfast and Derry had also brought back into the organisation in those cities a number of veterans, most of whom, like Billy McKee and Jimmy Steele in Belfast and Sean Keenan in Derry, had either left or been expelled for opposing the leftward trend in the movement in the 1960s. For these men, the turmoil of August 1969 meant they could now repossess the republican movement and restore it to the shape and function with which they were familiar. For such men the break was definite and irrevocable.

Younger members, North and South, however, were not necessarily opposed to the socialism being advocated by MacGiolla, Goulding and Johnston. But, as well as the revolutionary socialist rhetoric, the northerners wanted guns to defend their districts. If Goulding had been able or willing to supply them, the outcome for the republican movement might have been very different. But he had deliberately run down the IRA. What weapons he had he was not prepared to hand out for he was totally opposed to the notion of the IRA as a Catholic defence force, which was exactly what beleaguered Catholics in the North wanted it to be.

Many young people who subsequently became prominent in the Provisional IRA in the 1970s, including Martin McGuinness in Derry, did not join the breakaway movement until well into 1970. In Belfast, Gerry Adams in particular had subscribed to the philosophy that the republican movement had adopted in the 1960s. He had been involved in housing agitation and opposition to the proposed multi-storey Divis Flats in the lower Falls district from where his family, like hundreds of others, had been re-housed to the Ballymurphy estate in the process of redevelopment. Like many republicans he had also taken part in civil rights marches. As he explains in his book, *Before the Dawn*, the situation within the republican movement in Belfast at that time was confused. There were 'three broad tendencies: first the [Belfast] leadership; second, the older people who had come back in response to the crisis; and third the younger people on the ground', like Adams himself.

Far removed from this confusion was the Dublin leadership of the movement, which relayed its instructions to the Belfast leadership. The leaders were pulling levers that were no longer attached to anything. They continued to press ahead with their plan to end abstentionism and to set up a broad front of radical activists, the so-called National Liberation Front, described by Adams as 'common cause with all organisations and individuals which opposed the British imperial intervention in our country'. As Adams says, 'the pogroms changed everything … At the very least, the leadership should have recognised the need for urgent new priorities and suspended its pursuance of the new departure in republican strategy until a more settled time.' Such as 1986, perhaps?

Like many others, Adams teetered between both factions in Belfast until 1970 when he came down firmly on the side of those who wanted to organise armed defence of nationalist districts. This was in defiance of the Belfast leadership, now a minority among republicans in the city, which was still making a futile effort to carry out the instructions of the central leadership in Dublin. Matters were made even more complicated by the British Army and some British politicians negotiating with the existing Belfast leaders, like Billy McMillen and Jim Sullivan, not knowing that these men's authority was slipping away by the moment.

Not only was the new Provisional IRA organising throughout Belfast, so was its political wing, Provisional Sinn Féin. Naturally, in the circumstances of the time, the dominant organisation was the newly developing military wing. While that dominance continued into the 1990s, it was at its peak until about 1975. Most young men who were attracted to the republican movement opted to join the IRA.

Danny Morrison, a prominent figure in the IRA in the 1970s, in an interview with the author in August 2000 said: 'Most people wanted to join the IRA so the people who went into Sinn Féin were over military age or women and they were looked down upon as the "poor relations".' However, for men over military age, and particularly for women who wanted a role, there was plenty to do in Sinn Féin. One such party member was Patricia Davidson, a leading Sinn Féin organiser in Belfast from the origins of the Provisional movement to 1979, when she and her husband were arrested. In May that same year her husband was seriously wounded.

Patricia Davidson was secretary to Professor Frank Pantridge, Northern Ireland's most prominent cardiologist, who was based in the Royal Victoria Hospital in west Belfast. Her mother was English. She had been on holiday at the home of relatives in England when the trouble broke out in Belfast in 1969:

> Well, when I came home towards the end of August, I came home to barricades and sheds[1] at the bottom of streets with people doing vigilante and watching out and things like that, it just sort of developed along from there. There were just things going on in the community you couldn't avoid because you got leaflets around telling you they were going to have this meeting, that meeting, and then it just snowballed really from there.

Asked what Sinn Féin's role was, Ms Davidson's response is simple and direct: 'Agitation and publicity'. It was difficult because, 'bearing in mind that Sinn Féin was a proscribed organisation at that time, so that everything that was done was done in houses and undercover and you would sneak about and do whatever you could do, and I did a lot of work from my own home.' What made such activity easier was that from August 1969 residents in nationalist areas in Belfast and Derry barricaded themselves in. The districts behind the barricades, mainly the lower Falls, Ardoyne, the Markets and Short Strand in Belfast, and the Bogside and Creggan in Derry, were in effect run by republican-dominated street committees: in Belfast, the Central Citizens' Defence Committee (CCDC) and in Derry, the Derry Citizens' Defence Association (DCDA).

Throughout 1970 Stormont's unionist ministers made strenuous efforts to have the British Army remove these barricades. Republicans were equally determined to maintain them, partly because of the powerful influence they gave the resurgent IRA over the community behind the barricades, partly because of the leverage they provided in negotiations with the British Army who had taken over policing in nationalist areas, and partly because of the intense embarrassment their presence caused to the Stormont administration and the feeling of crisis and abnormality they sustained. In Derry, the area behind the barricades had immediately been declared 'Free Derry'. The existence of such places, which the British security forces called 'NO-GO areas' with the implication that barricades had to be manned to stop hostile crowds invading those districts, was a standing affront to unionists.

In the hothouse atmosphere behind these barricades the Provisional republican movement gathered strength and developed rapidly, nourished on a rich diet of rumour, introspection, atavistic fears and ill-conceived actions by the British Army and the RUC. In Derry, 'Barricade Bulletins' were printed and circulated. Belfast had its own bulletins distributed by Sinn Féin members, like the *Vindicator* and *Phoenix*, run off on Gestetner machines, sometimes illicitly in schools or office premises where Sinn Féin members worked.

Soon, the new Provisional organ, *Republican News*, was on sale door to door. Provisional Sinn Féin *cumainn* emerged in Belfast. According to Patricia Davidson, the first was the Padraig Pearse *cumann*, established in Clonard in early 1970 by Proinsias MacAirt, a veteran republican who had rejoined the movement in 1969. After that came the Liam McParland[2] *cumann* in Ballymurphy, probably organised by the Adams family, the leading republicans in Ballymurphy. From May 1970 *cumainn* developed rapidly, first in west Belfast, then throughout nationalist areas of the city.

By Easter 1970, after serious rioting in Ballymurphy and also in Derry, the die had been cast in relations between the nationalist community and the British Army. Looking back at those events, many people imply that there was a concerted plan by republicans to provoke riots and draw the British Army into confrontation with the population, thereby forfeiting the goodwill troops had enjoyed since their arrival in August 1969. The same people also discern the hand of the ubiquitous Gerry Adams in such activities, mainly because Ballymurphy was his stamping ground.

It is true that Adams was a prominent figure in Ballymurphy and that his family was a famous republican family. It is also true, as he admits himself, that he played a role in organising protests against a 'hearts and minds' campaign that the British Army tried to implement. Adams met his future wife, Colette McArdle, while protesting against a disco the British Army had arranged in their barracks near Ballymurphy, hoping to attract local girls. He said: 'We aimed quite consciously to prevent collaboration with the British forces … We continued this low intensity agitation through the spring of 1970.'

What is also true is that the behaviour of the British soldiers in nationalist districts was provocative, coarse, brutal and stupid. Many of the NCOs had seen action against anti-imperialist groups in British colonies, most recently in the Crater district of Aden in 1966–67. Some had memories of Malaya and Cyprus in the 1950s. In Belfast they adopted the methods and attitudes appropriate to colonial disputes. The troops were officered by men acting at the behest of Stormont's unionist ministers who constantly kept the general officer commanding British troops (GOC) under pressure to take determined action against republicans, which, in effect, meant against the entire population of certain districts. The prevailing view at Stormont continued to be that the events of August 1969 were an insurrection against the unionist regime, that the insurrection had still to be quelled and that it was the British Army's job to do so. In pursuit of that aim, 'law and order' had to be restored: that required NO-GO areas to be eliminated. The first step towards that end would be army patrols in nationalist areas which were not securely barricaded off, places like Ballymurphy. These patrols would eventually 'prove' that the Queen's writ ran in all areas.

'Foot patrols' by the British Army quickly led to a deterioration of relations with the nationalist population. Completely untrained in any form of policing, soldiers, usually the same age or younger than the people they stopped in the street, often reacted to verbal abuse or even mere defiance with beatings. They carried long batons like baseball bats and used them lavishly on local youths. They arrested large numbers of teenagers, male and female, and often beat them in barracks before handing them over to the police for prosecution. They routinely lied in court, identifying youths and middle-aged men as rioters, which would result in a prison sentence, usually four to six months. Whenever reaction to foot patrols developed into a riot, the soldiers fired large quantities of CS gas indiscriminately into narrow streets.

The army set out, in their own words, to 'dominate' areas. Colonel Evelegh, commanding officer at Springfield Road barracks in the heart of the Falls, put it thus in his memoirs: 'Ultimately these Catholic areas could only be governed by the British by the methods, however mollified, (sic) that all occupying nations use to hold down all occupied territories.' That was not what Catholics had thought the British Army had arrived to do, though it was the role that republicans had predicted they would adopt. By spring 1970 the army, far from being perceived as protecting Belfast Catholics, was acting as the agent of the unionist administration in controlling them.

Exactly the same process was taking place in the Bogside and Creggan in Derry: large-scale arrests, beatings, prison sentences and great volumes of CS gas. Months of worsening relations between the people of the Bogside and Creggan and British soldiers culminated in a major riot after a republican parade at Easter 1970. What is intriguing about the circumstances in Derry, however, is that there is no evidence of the sort of conscious republican effort to stop 'collaboration' that there was in Bally-murphy in west Belfast. Derry republicans did not oppose the military's 'hearts and minds' campaign, which began virtually the moment troops arrived in August 1969. It was only after the riot at Easter that the Official IRA threatened British troops. Nevertheless, in Derry the soldiers quickly came to regard the nationalist population, that is, the overwhelm-ing majority of the city, as a problem to be contained. The Bogside seemed the best place to contain them.

As in Belfast, no one can point to a Provisional organisation in Derry that could have organised large-scale riots or any sustained opposition to the newly arrived British troops. The first meeting to establish a Provi-sional organisation in Derry took place in Donegal in mid-February 1970. Dáithí Ó Conaill, who lived in Donegal, was the dominant figure behind this development which placed Derry veteran Sean Keenan in control of Provisionals in the city. By the end of the month the Padraig Pearse *cumann* had been set up in Derry. In Belfast, the Provos called their *cumainn* Sinn Féin from the outset, disregarding the fact that Sinn Féin was an illegal organisation. In Derry, confusingly, the new movement stuck to the nomenclature adopted in the 1960s to avoid prosecution. Therefore at the start, new *cumainn* (republican clubs) sounded as if they were *bona fide* republican bodies. In Derry there was none of the animosity that existed in Belfast between individuals in the new Provisional organisation and the existing republican movement. For example, members of the newly formed Provisional wing in Derry marched alongside Officials at com-memoration parades and picketed military and police barracks jointly.

While simultaneous rioting intensified on the margins of the Bog-side and in Ballymurphy in Belfast in spring 1970, there is no evidence that this activity was in any way coordinated between the cities or by the new republican leadership. On the contrary, the Provisionals in Derry did not even know the names of the Provisionals in Belfast. Who had split? Who had remained with the Goulding leadership? Who was new? The only evidence of coordination is rather in the behaviour of the British Army. By February 1970 they had obviously decided to get 'tough' with nationalists, both in Belfast and Derry. The results of this decision – street fighting, CS gas and arrests – were clear for all to see. At the end of May 1970, GOC General Sir Ian Freeland announced that petrol bombers could be shot. It was obvious that the army was dancing to a unionist tune. The Stormont prime minister, Sir James Chichester-Clark, was by that time desperate to have normality restored as a British general election loomed. Rev Ian Paisley had announced his candidature for the safe unionist seat of North Antrim and was constantly attacking Chichester-Clark for weakness and concessions to republicans.

Paisley duly won the seat, which he has held ever since. The Conservatives won the general election. The effects were immediate. The Conservatives had an instinctive affinity with the Ulster Unionists. The restraints that Harold Wilson's Labour government had imposed on the Stormont administration and the British Army were now removed. There followed very quickly the first of a series of major events which, over the following two years, would give the Provisional movement a series of boosts that expanded its power base exponentially.

On 3 July 1970, the British Army sealed off a large part of the lower Falls area in west Belfast after an arms find in the district triggered serious rioting. Petrol bombs, nail bombs and hand grenades had been used, followed by gunfire; then a full-scale gun battle took place between the army and local republicans. Ironically, it was an Official IRA arms dump that had been discovered, the area being the heartland of the Officials in Belfast; ironic because it was the Provos who would benefit, with Provisional Sinn Féin gaining one of its first Public Relations successes as a result of what followed.

The British Army imposed a curfew that officially lasted from 10pm on Saturday, 3 July until 9am on Monday, 5 July and began comprehensive house-to-house searches in the area. First, it should be said that there was no legal basis for the curfew – the GOC, General Freeland, had simply decided to teach republicans a lesson. It should also be remembered that the area was densely populated and contained a large proportion of families with young children and babies. It was one of the poorest districts in Ireland, a place where, in 1970, there were few fridges and people did not keep large supplies of food in their homes. Many of the houses, built in the nineteenth century, had no sanitation or hot running water. The army would not permit anyone to leave their home. Supplies of baby food ran out quickly. Many homes were wrecked in the searches, which were carried out with some ferocity by the Black Watch, a Scottish regiment just arrived off the Liverpool boat that very day and notorious in nationalist Belfast from then on. The unit was itself riven by the same sectarianism that divides the North of Ireland. During the weekend of the curfew four people were killed; three, including an amateur photographer from London, were shot by soldiers, and one man crushed by a Saracen armoured car. Twenty soldiers were wounded in the exchange of fire.

Although the army claimed that the curfew ended at 9am on Monday morning, it was in fact broken by hundreds of women and children who marched down the Falls Road carrying food, mainly loaves of bread, piled up high in prams. The march was organised by Provisional Sinn Féin's Máire Drumm, later the party's vice-president, and constituted the organisation's first propaganda coup. The young soldiers manning the knife-rest barriers at the boundary of the curfew area were faced with a phalanx of determined middle-aged women looking remarkably like their own mothers, and allowed themselves to be brushed aside. The women swept triumphantly through. The whole scene was captured on television.

On their way back out of the curfew area after delivering their food, the women reported, for the benefit of journalists and television crews, the horror stories of British Army brutality that had taken place over the weekend. So outraged were people in west Belfast at the tales of woe that thousands of women, most with no republican connections, marched down the Falls Road that afternoon, disdainfully pulled aside the army's barricades and thus ended the curfew. The occasion is regarded as one of the turning-points of the Troubles. It was a public relations disaster for the British Army, confirming it in the eyes of nationalists as an oppressive force acting on behalf of unionism. For many nationalists what set the seal on this perception was the news that the army had taken Lord Brookeborough, a worthless political hanger-on and the son of the former prime minister of Northern Ireland who was hated by the nationalist community, on a sight-seeing tour of the curfewed district in a Land Rover so that he could see for himself the fabled Falls district and its cowed denizens, a sight never before vouchsafed to any unionist.

By the time of the Falls Road curfew in July 1970 it would have been crystal clear to the security forces that they were facing far more than simply inter-communal strife. It should be said in this context that the British Army had been just as robust with loyalist mobs trying to attack Catholic districts in spring 1970 as they had been with nationalist rioters. But the army did not act as a police force in loyalist areas or maintain a twenty-four-hour presence in them. They did so in nationalist areas partly because the RUC no longer operated there but increasingly because the Provisional IRA was using those areas as bases for storing equipment and *matériel* and planning attacks. It was no secret that the attacks would be designed to bring down the Stormont administration; the president of Provisional Sinn Féin, Ruairí Ó Brádaigh, said so. People were experimenting with bombs. Already IRA men had died in a premature explosion in Derry. IRA units in Belfast had rifles that they had already used to lethal effect in Ardoyne and the Short Strand.

Sinn Féin's role in these circumstances was, as Patricia Davidson said, 'agitation and publicity': to stir up opinion in nationalist districts, to write and distribute propaganda and to organise opposition to the presence of British troops, to protest, protest, protest. By the summer of 1970 *cumainn* had sprung up all over Belfast. According to Davidson, a *cumann* was based on an IRA company area, so in west Belfast, C company would have been based in Clonard and the Clonard Martyrs *cumann* was organised in that area. The lower Falls was D company area and the Charlie Hughes *cumann* emerged there, and so on. However, Jim Gibney, a senior Sinn Féin man today but an IRA man in the 1970s, denied this. In an interview with the author he said that *cumainn* were based on districts, depending 'on the strength of the organisation. Whatever the natural geographical area is you'll find a *cumann* in that area.'[3]

Who was in Sinn Féin? In the early stages it was mainly women. Davidson says: 'There would have been some men. The proportion would have been two-thirds/one-third, if I was to make a guess for numbers. Two-thirds women.' Gibney agrees: 'There were very few males of active army age in Sinn Féin. The backbone of the organisation would have been women and again later prisoners' wives, prisoners' relatives.' The age range was from sixteen upwards. Those men in Sinn Féin who were of 'military age' were, in Davidson's words, 'not of a background that would have been suitable for the IRA. Let's put it that way. You would have had people maybe with criminal records. Well, they just wouldn't have been looked at by the IRA. But they were people who were allowed to join Sinn Féin. But it was a primarily feminine organisation. The primary human body of it would have been women.'

Sinn Féin was and is overwhelmingly working-class, particularly in the North. Since it was an illegal organisation, membership could mean jail and a criminal record. Davidson herself ended up with a suspended nine-month sentence in 1971 and consequently lost her job as Professor Pantridge's secretary. Few people were ever charged simply with membership alone, which would have been very difficult to prove. The RUC usually preferred more serious charges, such as promoting the aims and objects of an illegal organisation 'with intent' or 'under suspicious circumstances'. Therefore people in Sinn Féin, the activists, tended to be those with nothing to lose, the have-nots; Patricia Davidson was an exception. In many Catholic areas of Belfast and Derry most members, both men and women, were unemployed following the collapse of heavy engineering and the recent rundown of the linen and cotton textile industry.

In many ways Sinn Féin took on the role of the *sans-culottes*[4] in Paris in the 1790s, a role that in both cases is difficult to categorise. The Paris *sans-culottes* were much more than mindless rioters. Simon Schama, in his history of the French Revolution, *Citizens,* points out that there was never more than 10% of the population of any of the poor, working-class districts of Paris active in riotous politics. The *sans-culottes* were often skilled artisans and able speakers who played a leading role as motivators in the riots, people who nowadays and in the 1970s would have been called 'community leaders'. In the republican areas of Belfast after 1970, their modern counterparts led the 'active' 10% who came onto the streets – amounting to 300–400 rioters at most in any republican district in the city. It could have been as few as forty to fifty in Coalisland, Strabane, Armagh and other small northern towns. Few of the rioters or protesters would have been members of Sinn Féin: only the leaders and organisers and instigators.

The districts which have borne the brunt of the violence from 1969 until the present day are exclusively working-class. It was republicans who organised to defend those areas after the onslaught in 1969 and it was behind the barricades in those areas that Sinn Féin grew, first as an IRA support organisation, then as a protest movement. Sinn Féin's leaders and members for the most part had no interest in electoral politics. In June 1970 Gerry Fitt, now of the SDLP, was re-elected MP for West Belfast with over 30,000 votes. There is no doubt that a lot of Sinn Féin people voted for him and continued to do so until Sinn Féin entered electoral politics in 1982.

The Provisional movement was hostile to electoral politics. Danny Morrison said that Sinn Féin was not just 'non-electoral' but that it was 'anti-electoral'. Becoming involved in elections could lead to recognising partition parliaments or arguing about abstention, which was one of the main reasons the movement split in 1969. Besides, those arguments would have been regarded as pointless distractions in the frenzy of the early 1970s. The party disowned Albert Price in 1974 when he stood in West Belfast in that year's February general election to draw attention to the plight of his daughters, Dolours and Marian, on hunger strike in jail in England following conviction for the IRA bombing of the Old Bailey. Price got just over 5,000 votes; Fitt polled nearly 20,000.

Nevertheless, although republicans were opposed to involvement in what they called 'partitionist elections', Sinn Féin's role in those working-class districts of Belfast and Derry was political with a small 'p'. The part they played quickly undermined the existing political structures. From August 1969 British Army officers talked to IRA commanders directly, by-passing the local nationalist politicians like Fitt and Paddy Devlin in Belfast and John Hume and Eddie McAteer in Derry. It was clear that Fitt and Hume and the others carried no weight behind the barricades. Almost immediately the IRA was negotiating on behalf of the people in those districts and Sinn Féin members acted in support, relaying information to people door-to-door. Individuals built up reputations in those early years of the Troubles which, ten years later, would lead to their being elected with massive votes by the same people they had helped and worked among in the difficult times.

As the conflict intensified, the British government made more serious mistakes, which have been well chronicled. If the Falls Road curfew was the first major error that boosted the Provos in Belfast, internment in August 1971 and Bloody Sunday in Derry in January 1972, which resulted in fourteen dead and many wounded, alienated the whole of nationalist Ireland. Each of those two traumatic events produced an influx into the Provisional IRA that made it the dominant force on the military side, finally eclipsing the Officials everywhere and bringing hundreds into

Sinn Féin. Patricia Davidson says that Sinn Féin in Belfast could not have grown any bigger after internment and that it was Bloody Sunday that brought in the numbers in rural areas. That may have been so in west Belfast, but in other parts of the city people who had no previous association with republicanism joined the IRA and Sinn Féin in the days after Bloody Sunday. Others became tacit sympathisers.

The effects of internment and Bloody Sunday, occurring just five months apart, are well known. There was a huge and immediate increase in violence, which led to the demise of Stormont in March 1972. There were 342 people, all Catholics, arrested in the first internment sweep in August 1971, 105 of whom were released within two days, indicating the level of intelligence on which the British Army's action was based. Nevertheless, arrests continued for another three years. Sinn Féin came into its own as a protest movement. Here is Patricia Davidson: 'From internment it really went crazy. You'd have every shade of opinion wanting to gravitate towards Sinn Féin because we seemed to be the organisers. There were leaflets, protests, demonstrations, taking over buildings, God, it was enormous, and organising within the community ... self-help groups, mothers' groups, it just seemed to be like an alternative thing.' The Catholic community withdrew its cooperation from the northern state. A rent and rate strike began, also supported by the recently formed Social Democratic and Labour Party (SDLP).

Sinn Féin picketed police and army barracks and organised protest marches, including one along the M1 motorway, a route that began in west Belfast. They never got very far, but succeeded in having the motorway closed with associated traffic chaos. News of the torture techniques, known as sensory deprivation, which the British Army used against selected internees, quickly became known and photographs of men beaten by soldiers were published. Sinn Féin members carried copies of these photos as they stood in protest outside barracks. The Irish government took up the men's cases. Sinn Féin organised visits for relatives to the internment camp at the disused airfield called Long Kesh, outside Lisburn. Soon Sinn Féin was organising busloads of people to try to picket Long Kesh. Almost every day some action of the British Army seemed to offer a chance for what Davidson called 'agitation and publicity' or, in the language of the 1970s, *agitprop.*

These were the years in which the groundwork was laid which would make Sinn Féin into the organisation it became in the early 1980s, the years when its members established themselves as community leaders in nationalist, working-class districts across the North. Thanks to the big milestones of internment and Bloody Sunday, by 1972 the Provisional movement had established itself in all major nationalist areas as the premier republican organisation. After a bomb attack killed five civilians and a chaplain at the Parachute regiment headquarters in Aldershot in England in revenge for Bloody Sunday, the Official IRA declared a ceasefire and continued on the path Goulding and MacGiolla had mapped out before the upheavals in the North. They concentrated on political development in the Republic and on eventually entering the Dáil.

It was to be some years before Provisional Sinn Féin developed any political thinking. During the height of the violence, from 1971 to 1973, the party appeared to be simply a notice board for the IRA. Ruairí Ó Brádaigh would use Sinn Féin *ard fheiseanna* to announce republican policy, which was, in effect, IRA policy, namely that Britain should leave the North or the 'war' would continue. It was only in 1973, three years after Provisional Sinn Féin was founded, that the first stirring of political activity began with the opening of the Republican Press Centre run by Tom Hartley at 170 Falls Road. According to Jim Gibney, that was 'the first expression of a republican point of view anywhere in Ireland outside Dublin and the head office.' Still, however, political personalities could not operate openly. Those speaking to the press in the Centre did not use their own names. For some years, spokesman Danny Morrison was known to journalists simply as 'Peter'.

There was no distinct Sinn Féin message. Political leadership among republicans was, in fact, in the hands of the Trotskyite People's Democracy (PD), which had originated among students at Queen's University in 1968. People like Michael Farrell and Bernadette McAliskey (née Devlin) were the voices of protest about internment and security-force behaviour that republicans listened to. There were no others who had access to the media, nor indeed any others as articulate. As Jim Gibney describes it:

> You had Michael Farrell and you had Bernadette McAliskey. So there was a political leadership of sorts which organised the political support base of the people who came out onto the streets. You know, People's Democracy were to the fore. They dominated the scene politically from about 1970 to about the 1975 period. They were the recognised political leadership of what we loosely called the anti-imperialist movement in this city and elsewhere.

It was the PD members who took the lead in speaking about internment at public protests. That was not simply because they were articulate. They were the public expression of republican opposition because Sinn Féin was illegal and its senior figures liable to be interned. However, republicans grew increasingly unhappy with this state of affairs. As Gerry Adams wrote in his autobiography, the PD formed the Northern Resistance Movement in October 1971 to campaign against internment, and Adams spoke at some of their meetings, but 'it struck me that all of the potential for mobilisation was ours while PD had the theory'. Sinn Féin had no political profile. Its people were still the *sans-culottes* in the back streets.

Gradually, from 1973 on, as the British and Irish governments began to edge towards the political negotiations which culminated in the Sunningdale Agreement, people in the republican movement began to feel the need for their own spokespersons. Gibney again:

> There was tension between republicans and the PD, because the PDs' position would have been to have critical support for the

armed struggle, but also to be critical of the armed struggle. And republicans, in those days you know, couldn't take criticism very lightly and so there was always tension at that time ... And there was pressure coming from republicans for a republican public leadership to emerge who would, in a sense, replace PD as the public expression of how republicans are feeling at that particular time because the prisoners were in jail and Fergus [O'Hare, a PD activist] was speaking on their behalf or John McAnulty [another PD figure] was speaking on their behalf. What republicans wanted was a Sinn Féin person to speak on their behalf.

There were important Sinn Féin figures in Belfast, of course, the most senior being Máire Drumm. Another important person was Marie Moore, whose career spans the whole period from the emergence of Provisional Sinn Féin to her election as deputy lord mayor of Belfast in 1999. But the problem remained: Sinn Féin was illegal. Open political activity was impossible. Only when Merlyn Rees, the Labour secretary of state for Northern Ireland, legalised Sinn Féin in May 1974 did a range of options begin to unfold. Over the next three years a number of crucial events in Sinn Féin's development took place.

For some time the British government had been anxious to involve republicans in the political process. They had even hoped, naively, that Sinn Féin could be persuaded to take part in the elections to the new Sunningdale assembly in February 1974. That such a hope could even have been entertained was a measure of how little the British appreciated the complexities of the republican position. Nevertheless, with better intelligence, a series of contacts with the IRA Army Council throughout 1974 culminated in a ceasefire in 1975. Paradoxically, this ceasefire did not produce the switch to political involvement that the British administration in the North had hoped for, at any rate not in the short term. Nor did it lead to British withdrawal, as IRA leaders deluded themselves into believing was on the agenda. Rather it caused great tensions within the IRA at leadership level and between North and South and proved to be a catalyst for change in both the IRA and Sinn Féin's role in the republican movement.

During the ceasefire a number of able young IRA men from the North were in jail, the most prominent of these being Gerry Adams. These young men, who had come through the crucible of the early 1970s, were aware of some of the sporadic contacts between the British and leading IRA men since 1973. They were very suspicious of the ceasefire and were deeply frustrated because they did not know the full story behind it. They were also aware that during the ceasefire the IRA was fraying badly at the edges and losing momentum and direction. What added to their frustration was the growing gap between North and South and between the older generation of leaders, like Ó Brádaigh and Ó Conaill, veterans of the 1950s, and themselves. They also resented the southerners acting on behalf of people from the North where the front-line, so to speak, was located.

The events of 1975 were all the more exasperating for Adams because in 1972 he had been released from internment and flown to London as a member of an IRA delegation that met the first northern secretary, William Whitelaw. Adams was present in his capacity as the most senior IRA commander in Belfast (before his capture in March that year). Martin McGuinness, the ranking officer in Derry, was also flown to London for the meeting so that the two men spearheading the IRA's campaign in the North's two main population centres could have their say. Now, in 1975, in jail, Adams had to witness helplessly the inept performance of Ó Brádaigh and Ó Conaill, powerless to influence them.

On 16 August 1975, Gerry Adams wrote his first article for *Republican News*, under the pen-name of 'Brownie', at the invitation of his friend Danny Morrison, now the paper's editor. From then until 1976 Adams used this column as a vehicle for advocating greater political involvement by Sinn Féin. His approach was very careful, constantly referring back to republican heroes of the left, like Liam Mellowes and James Connolly, to demonstrate the continuity in the movement of his ideas and the orthodoxy of his arguments. But the aim was unmistakable. It was to connect

Sinn Féin politically to the people who supported the republican movement. Of necessity he had to move cautiously. Any hint of 'electoralism', as it was called, would bring down condemnation on him. The ground had to be prepared. As Adams later wrote:

> Sinn Féin's political programme based itself upon the defence of the nationalist people in the North ... Of course republican ideology also opposed any participation in the partitionist parliament in Dublin. Apart from the theoretical basis of the position, in practice it meant that Sinn Féin was abandoning this ground to other parties ... However the failure to consolidate politically the support flowing towards Sinn Féin, or even to establish a more durable way of quantifying support than the holding of demonstrations, left crucial room for the political establishment in the south to manoeuvre.

In the North the policy left electoral politics to the SDLP, which meant that the British and Irish governments could ignore Sinn Féin because there was no way of measuring their support. Yet, thanks to the British, Sinn Féin in the North knew they had extensive support. As part of the ceasefire the British agreed to set up 'truce incident centres'. As Jim Gibney said:

> This was the development that brought Sinn Féin out of the back streets and put them into public thoroughfares. So, in an ironic sort of way, it was the relationship between the British and the IRA back then that led to the first public expression through these truce incident centres of republicans coming out of the back streets, the smoke-filled rooms, onto the main roads and I think that there then begins this sort of network. Sinn Féin moved into these buildings after they were no longer in use [in a ceasefire situation] and so therefore Sinn Féin becomes a point of contact in these buildings.

In these centres there was a direct phone-link to the British so that republicans could raise any infringement of the ceasefire immediately with the army or the Northern Ireland Office (NIO). The instant consequence of the centres, scattered all over republican areas of Belfast and the North was to cut out the SDLP. Even if republicans contacted SDLP representatives, say about someone being arrested, those representatives had to go through the normal channels, whereas republicans could simply ring their designated contact. It was in these centres that Sinn Féin first began to deal with local constituency problems even though it had no elected representatives. Years later, in the 1980s, people in republican districts still called the Sinn Féin office 'the incident centre'.

When the truce collapsed in 1975 another issue immediately emerged that would prove to be the one which drew Sinn Féin into politics, North and South, in a way and at a level no one could have then imagined. By Christmas 1975 alarming rumours were circulating in republican circles that political status for prisoners was about to be withdrawn. The British government had telegraphed this plan far ahead in 1975, but republicans did not seem to believe they were serious. A whole new prison, the Maze, had been completed with state-of-the-art cells and equally modern security systems; inmates would call it the H-blocks after the shape of the units of cells. No longer would prisoners be housed in compounds, or cages as republicans called them, which had all the appearances of Second World War German POW camps. Instead, each prisoner would be alone in his cell or with one other cellmate. They would have to wear prison clothes, do prison work and be subject to the same prison rules as any criminal.

The scene was set for a huge confrontation. It was, and remains, the most fundamental tenet of republicanism that it is legitimate to use force to oppose the presence of British rule in Ireland and therefore that those engaged in using force are patriots and freedom-fighters, not criminals. There had been hunger strikes in 1917 in opposition to British attempts to impose criminal conditions on republican prisoners. The so-called 'special category status' enjoyed by paramilitary prisoners in Long Kesh had also been won by a hunger strike in 1972. Only the British administration in the North of Ireland seemed not to realise how important was the issue they were raising. It was part of a profoundly stupid, ill-conceived policy that failed in all its respects and provided the republican movement with the means for transforming itself from a small, ghetto-based sect into a national movement with a minimum of 100,000 votes in the North of Ireland and substantial sympathy in the rest of the island, and which led eventually to a seat in the Dáil in 1996.

The British policy was two-pronged: Ulsterisation and criminalisation. The Ulsterisation prong meant a reduction in the role of British troops and their replacement by the overwhelmingly loyalist local militia, the Ulster Defence Regiment (UDR), and the RUC, itself over 90% Protestant. This policy would remove the appearance of a colonial problem with British troops patrolling large parts of the North of Ireland. It would also reduce casualties among expensively trained troops who ought to have been manning tactical nuclear weapons at the Fulda Gap in West Germany.

The second prong, criminalisation, was a plan to characterise the IRA as a small, unrepresentative group of evil men defying the will of the vast majority of the population. Their actions would be classed as purely criminal and they would be sentenced as such. The proposal was inherently absurd and could only have been devised by officials who had no connection with the nationalist population of the North, which was indeed the case. Quite patently the IRA prisoners were members of their close-knit communities and enjoyed widespread sympathy and support for their actions that extended well beyond their communities. The immediate problem for the republican movement was how to produce the evidence for this support and translate it into effective political action which would defeat the criminalisation policy. For a long time they had no success.

The sequence of events is well known. Those prisoners convicted after 1 March 1976 were required to conform to prison rules. The first man convicted, Kieran Nugent, famously said that the prison authorities would have to 'nail the prison clothes' to his back. So the prisoners went naked except for a prison blanket. A grim struggle ensued between them and the prison authorities who made life as difficult as possible for the rebellious inmates. Failure to conform meant denial of all privileges: no visits, no food parcels, no remission. No information about the prisoners was coming out. Danny Morrison, in effect propaganda chief of the movement at the time, recalls:

> Kieran Nugent disappeared. Like, Kieran Nugent was on the blanket for weeks before we knew. We couldn't find out where he was. His mother didn't know where he was. Even by November 1976 we didn't know how many people were on the blanket.

As the authorities responded to the prisoners' refusal to conform with more and more restrictions and petty violence, the prisoners also reacted. Both sides climbed a ladder of intransigence. After assaults by warders, the prisoners refused to leave their cells and refused to wash, and the 'dirty protest' began. Republican inmates smeared excrement over the walls of their cells. The IRA began to kill off-duty prison warders. The outside world looked on in horror.

The developments in the prison from 1976 to 1978 coincided with other important developments for Sinn Féin. The attempt by Gerry Adams, through articles in *Republican News* from 1975 onwards, to develop a political stance connected with the community in which republicans lived has already been mentioned. He was not alone. According to Adams, men in Long Kesh discussed 'communication with the base of our support, the role of newspapers, bulletins, co-ops, tenants' associations and women's organisations as means of empowering people.' Messages about strategy passed to and fro. A group of young Belfast republicans, some IRA like Jim Gibney and Gerry Kelly, who was in and out of jail with Adams, others members of Sinn Féin, agreed with him. Among this group were Danny Morrison, who gave over the columns of

Republican News to the emerging ideas, and Tom Hartley, who excelled himself in the incident centre on the Falls Road and in the republican press centre. According to Patricia Davidson the telex machine was 'Tom Hartley's baby. Nobody was allowed near that. That was his. Oh, the statements were flying.'

In 1974 Sinn Féin had set up a Belfast Executive of six people to organise a boycott of the assembly elections and they remained in post after the elections. They were Danny Morrison, Patricia Davidson, Marie Moore, Paddy McParland, Gerry Brannigan and Billy Donnelly. Things had eased after the party was legalised. Davidson says:

> It [the Executive] reported to the *comhairle ceanntair*, but it was autonomous in the sense that it could take action. It could see a particular thing that would require intensive action and a bit of intelligence to be brought to bear on it and it would have moved on its own. Many of these people met in each others' houses to organise and allowed their houses to be used as *ad hoc* advice centres and extensions of the incident centres.

As a result of these Belfast developments, Sinn Féin was in a position in 1976 to organise its publicity, to present policies and rebut accusations and attacks by the NIO and its massive publicity machine. It was lucky for Sinn Féin's young turks that they were ready. In August 1976, a car containing IRA men being pursued by British soldiers ploughed into a mother and her three children, killing the children and seriously injuring their mother after the driver was shot dead. Out of the horrifying accident arose the Peace People organisation, led by an aunt of the dead children and a friend. Tens of thousands of people marched for peace along the Falls and the Shankill. There was colossal international publicity, all of it awful for republicans. The two women leading the Peace People won the Nobel Peace Prize in 1977. The republican movement was rocked back on its heels. It needed all the ingenuity of Danny Morrison and his team to mount any kind of defence. He says: 'I was sort of like a fireman, just came in whenever there was a crisis and wrote the odd piece.'

Morrison remembers it as a time of great pressure. There were the violent interrogations at the notorious Castlereagh holding centre, the growing number of prisoners 'on the blanket', and the Peace People. He saw his role as 'taking on the Peace People, the SDLP and the Catholic Church', all of whom appeared to have ganged up on republicans in 1976. He needed all the help he could get from the other members of the Belfast Executive. In the welter of hostile propaganda it was virtually impossible for Sinn Féin to develop any support for its prisoners. The Relatives' Action Committees (RAC), which the leadership had set up in response to the criminalisation policy introduced in 1976 was struggling to be heard.

Alongside the mainly unsuccessful effort on behalf of the prisoners, Sinn Féin pressed on with a political policy to which virtually no one except the NIO paid any attention. Sinn Féin's first attempt at proposing political structures, originally devised in jail, was a scheme for people's councils or the 'people's assembly'. When the proposal was sent out of jail to Sinn Féin in 1977 it resulted in the laughable charge of treason being levelled against Tom Hartley and others of the Belfast Executive, including Patricia Davidson. The charge said more about the NIO's paranoia at Sinn Féin's influence than about the content of the proposals. All told, about sixty members of Sinn Féin were arrested on various charges, including membership of the IRA.

Patricia Davidson remembers her solicitor coming to her and Marie Moore while they were on remand and asking did they want the good news or the bad news. They asked for the good news first. 'Well,' he said, 'you might or you might not get bail. We'll have to work on it.' 'Now,' he said, 'that document is seditious and the bad news is, on that you can still be hanged.' What was the document? It was a 1977 version of Arthur Griffith's Sinn Féin proposals to set up an alternative system of government and boycott the British government. It involved people's courts and community structures run in nationalist areas of the North that would be entirely independent of the British administration. Treason? Of course the charges all came to nothing. It was part of the harassment of Sinn Féin, which grew intense under the bumptious and aggressive northern secretary Roy Mason, who believed he had the IRA on the run.

Despite the pressure from the Peace People demonstrations and the attentions of the British administration in the North, the efforts of Gerry Adams, Danny Morrison and others in the Belfast leadership to develop street-level politics had begun to bear fruit within the republican movement. The first public sign was the 1977 Bodenstown speech given by veteran Belfast republican Jimmy Drumm, a man who had probably spent more years in jail than any other republican. His wife, Máire Drumm, former Sinn Féin vice-president, had been shot dead in her hospital bed the previous year, having been refused a visa to travel to the USA for treatment. It was a carefully worded speech, crafted by Adams and Morrison, pointing out the limitations of the current leadership's policy of armed struggle in the North and nothing else.

Later in the year, it became clear that Bodenstown 1977 had heralded a shift in emphasis in Sinn Féin's role. In December that year Seamus Twomey, the IRA chief of staff who had been on the run since 1973, was arrested in Dun Laoghaire and an IRA GHQ staff report was found with him. It is worth quoting the section relevant to Sinn Féin.

> Sinn Féin should come under Army organisers at all levels.
>
> Sinn Féin should employ full-time organisers in big republican areas.
>
> Sinn Féin should be radicalised under Army direction and should agitate about social and economic issues which attack the welfare of the people.
>
> Sinn Féin should be directed to infiltrate other organisations to win support for and sympathy to the movement.
>
> Sinn Féin should be re-educated and have a big role to play in

publicity and propaganda department, complaints and problems
(making no room for RUC opportunism). It gains the respect of
the people which in turn leads to increased support for the cell.

It could have been written by Gerry Adams except for the crudeness
of the style. It was exactly what the northern group had been advocating
and had actually been putting into practice since Adams had emerged
from jail in 1977. Disillusioned and depressed by the long, destructive
ceasefire that had been on and off since Christmas 1974, Adams knew
there had to be a more complex approach. As he wrote: 'If the struggle was
limited to the armed struggle, once it stopped, the struggle stopped.' Now
he had a strategy in place to prosecute 'the struggle' on a variety of fronts.
Furthermore, Adams was also in a position to exercise control over it. He
probably became chief of staff after Seamus Twomey was captured,
though his tenure was short since he was re-arrested the night after the La
Mon hotel atrocity in February 1978 when twelve people were killed in
an IRA blast incendiary. Two months after Adams was released, in September 1978, he was elected vice-president of Sinn Féin. He was also a
member of the IRA Army Council again.

By 1978 the work of the previous three or four years had come
together in such a way as to allow Sinn Féin to maximise its influence. The
party was organising housing associations, tenants' associations and community associations across the North and beginning the same process in
the Republic. Sinn Féin had a strongly developing network in the North
and a skeletal one in the South. Unwittingly, the British government had
handed Sinn Féin a superb cause that would enable the party to use all the
skills and expertise it had developed since it was legalised: the plight of the
prisoners in the H-blocks. On top of and alongside the growing community involvement which Adams's new policies had initiated, the deteriorat-
ing state of the prisoners was an issue people could support whether or not
they supported Sinn Féin or the armed struggle of the IRA. Sinn Féin was
no longer, in public at any rate, a one-issue party.

However, the campaign on behalf of the prisoners made little progress at first. It was a matter of burning concern in republican areas but the
general public seemed not to notice. Republicans were unable to make
any impact on a British government that was slowly sinking into a minority in parliament and therefore unable to take any radical decisions about
Ireland, even if they had wanted to. Under the guidance of the experienced master parliamentarian Enoch Powell, Unionist MP for South
Down, the Ulster Unionists used the Labour government's precarious
position to their full advantage. The IRA campaign seemed to have settled down to a war of attrition: 1978 saw one of the lowest death tolls of
the Troubles: eighty-eight. Certainly in 1978 the IRA was no closer to
making the British withdraw than it had been when the Provos were
founded, perhaps further away.

Only with hindsight can the importance of the Relatives' Action
Committees (RAC) be discerned. In an uncanny repetition of what had
happened in the Free State in the mid-1940s when Clann na Poblachta
grew out of relatives' committees established to protest about conditions
of republican prisoners in Mountjoy jail, the RAC in the North allowed
Sinn Féin to broaden the base of its support and ultimately to produce a
national campaign. Like the relatives' committees of the 1940s, the RAC
had to contend with censorship and harassment, but the committees
brought in people who had not been republicans before their sons or husbands or other relatives were jailed. Now, they had different attitudes and
outlooks.

It was Jim Gibney who first spotted the RAC's potential. Gibney is a
clever, highly articulate, sharp-thinking man who does not come from a
republican family. He has little knowledge of the history of the republican
movement and in the course of our conversation was constantly surprised
and interested by parallels from the past. A supreme pragmatist, he
strongly advocates what works rather than what, in his own words, 'republican theology' would dictate. He kept close contact with left-wing

organisations and read the articles in their papers. He was struck by a debate on the far left about militarism versus mass struggle, which argued that Sinn Féin was losing out and limiting its appeal because it supported only armed struggle.

Gibney suggested that the RAC should distance themselves from Sinn Féin in order to widen their support; that they should invite in people from trade unions and other groups, like community and tenants' associations; in short, that the RAC should not be a sect composed solely of Sinn Féin members and prisoners' relatives. He also spotted that another avenue of expansion was in the Republic, but that to go south some other body would be needed, since obviously there were few or no people in the Republic with relatives 'on the blanket'. He therefore argued for the National H–Block/Armagh Committee to be established:

> And then it's a *national* organisation. It has a *national* appeal. And that was one way of us trying to break out of the straitjacket of the North in which we'd been confined. We'd confined ourselves as much as being confined by the issue which was political status which was related to the six counties. But yes, the formation of the National H–block/Armagh Committee was an important development in terms of bringing the story to the nation, the message to the nation.

The National H–Block/Armagh Committee was careful also to make its appeal as broad as possible, soon avoiding demanding political status *tout court*, but devising 'Five Demands' concerning clothing, visits, food parcels, etc., which, in effect, amounted to political status but could be presented as the humanitarian rights of any prisoner. People did not have to be republicans, did not have to agree with the Republican intention that IRA violence was political to support the committee's demands, especially in view of the degradation going on in the prisons. Powerful public figures, like Cardinal Tomás Ó Fiaich, came close to supporting the demands, and Ó Fiaich was personally sympathetic to the RAC in the

North. Many trade union branches supported the National H-Block committee, as did tenants' associations and community groups which had been infiltrated or set up by Sinn Féin, North and South, along the lines of Adams's plans as laid out in the 'Staff Report'.

Despite all, whatever progress the RAC and the National H-Block committee might have been making ground to a halt in June 1979 with the election of the most right-wing Conservative British government since the 1920s, under the leadership of Margaret Thatcher. To make matters worse, one of her closest confidants and likely northern secretary, Airey Neave MP, had been murdered in March 1979. Although the INLA (Irish National Liberation Army) had carried out the murder, Mrs Thatcher made no distinction between republican armed groups: they were all undifferentiated terrorists to her. There would be no concessions to the prisoners.

The antipathy of the British establishment towards republicans was exacerbated on 27 August 1979 when the IRA killed eighteen soldiers in a double bombing at Warrenpoint. The dead included sixteen members of the Parachute Regiment, for which republicans harboured a special loathing after Bloody Sunday and because of the regiment's scandalous and unremitting brutality in nationalist districts. On the same day, 209 kilometres away at Mullaghmore harbour, off the coast of County Sligo, an IRA team killed Lord Louis Mountbatten, a cousin of Queen Elizabeth II, along with two members of his family and a local boy, Paul Maxwell, who were accompanying him on a boat trip. His death had a huge impact in Britain. The last viceroy of India, he had been commander of the British Mediterranean fleet in the Second World War, First Sea Lord and chief of the defence staff. After these events, to expect any clemency from a Conservative government in Britain simply demonstrated how far removed republicans were from any understanding of the mentality of British Conservative politicians.

So it was that over a year later conditions in the prisons were even worse. By 1980 some prisoners had been 'on the blanket' for four years and on the dirty protest for two years. At home their relatives, who had not seen the prisoners for years in some cases, were frantic with worry as horror stories seeped out of the jail. Many of these relatives had never been involved in politics in any way. Their first knowledge that their son, brother or husband was in the IRA was often when the front door was kicked in during the early hours of the morning by the police or British Army. When the prisoners themselves took the decision to go on hunger strike in autumn 1980 their families were gripped with fear and apprehension. The decision was also greeted with some consternation among the republican movement on the outside. The plight of the prisoners was now driving the whole movement. The IRA Army Council was no longer in complete control of the struggle, and from the moment the first hunger strike began in 1980 the Army Council never since fully recovered that control.

By Christmas 1980 the hunger strike had ended amid recriminations between the British and the IRA about what deal had or had not been made concerning the clothes prisoners would be permitted to wear. The prisoners felt they had been tricked. In early 1981 they resolved to go on hunger strike again, this time fortified with the experience of their previous attempt. Bobby Sands, the Officer Commanding IRA prisoners, had decided he would lead it and stood down as OC in case his judgement might be clouded as he weakened. He began his hunger strike on 1 March 1981, the fifth anniversary of the removal of special category status.

It was immediately apparent to republicans on the outside that support had flagged. Jim Gibney:

> We found it very difficult in the early days of the second hunger strike because people were exhausted by the whole issue: the blanket protest, the prison protest in Armagh and the first hunger strike. People just prayed fervently that it was over after the first one. When the second one started, our job of mobilising support was

extremely difficult. There's no doubt about it. Go back and look at the photographs. The protests were small. It was an uphill battle.

The British administration had also learnt. The NIO advised Humphrey Atkins, Mrs Thatcher's ineffectual northern secretary, not to issue bulletins about the health of the prisoners as had been done during the first strike. The periodic health checks in 1980 had been a great help to Sinn Féin's publicity machine under the powerful propaganda management of Danny Morrison. Now there was no information, not even a recent photograph of Sands, available to the press. The prison service adopted the official position of not commenting on 'individual prisoners'. Neither the prisoners nor Sinn Féin were making any headway.

Then, on 6 March, Frank Maguire, the Fermanagh–Tyrone South MP died. Contrary to what is often claimed, the Fermanagh–Tyrone South seat was always a matter of concern to republicans. Their main concern, as it had been since 1921, was to keep it out of the hands of a nationalist who would attend Westminster. Maguire had been an 'agreed' or unity candidate, which was a euphemism for someone who agreed with abstention and was acceptable to both nationalists and republicans. Sinn Féin did not automatically boycott Westminster elections in winnable seats. It used them to show how many voters supported its position, unchanged since the days of Arthur Griffith, that Irish elected representatives should not go to Westminster. It was entirely normal therefore that republicans should be instantly interested in the by-election. Republican prisoners had fought and won many by-elections in Irish history, including one in Fermanagh–Tyrone South in 1957.

Jim Gibney, who knew nothing about this history, immediately spotted the opportunity.

> When Frank Maguire died, I immediately, instinctively, thought we should put Bobby Sands up as the candidate, and I said to Gerry Adams – I had heard about Frank's death that morning, I was to see Gerry that afternoon – and I said, 'Listen, I need to see you now.

Bobby Sands, the first hunger striker to die in 1981, whose election as MP for Fermanagh–Tyrone South swept Sinn Féin into electoral politics in Ireland.

Martin McGuinness, aged thirty-two, Sinn Féin's candidate in the Derry constituency in the 1982 assembly elections. He was elected on the first count.

Gerry Adams and Martin McGuinness at a Sinn Féin press conference
chaired by Tom Hartley, one of Sinn Féin's leading strategists
and a member of the party's *ard comhairle*.

Gerry Adams makes his
victory speech in Belfast
City Hall in June 1983 after
winning the West Belfast
seat in the general election
from the sitting MP Gerry
Fitt (*behind*) who had
held it since 1966.

An taoiseach Dr Garret FitzGerald and British prime minister Margaret Thatcher sign
the official copies of the Anglo-Irish Agreement at Hillsborough Castle in November
1985. Tánaiste Dick Spring, although not in the photograph, looks on from behind Dr
FitzGerald. Behind Mrs Thatcher (again, not visible) stands Sir Robert Armstrong,
British Cabinet secretary and one of the Agreement's architects on the British side.

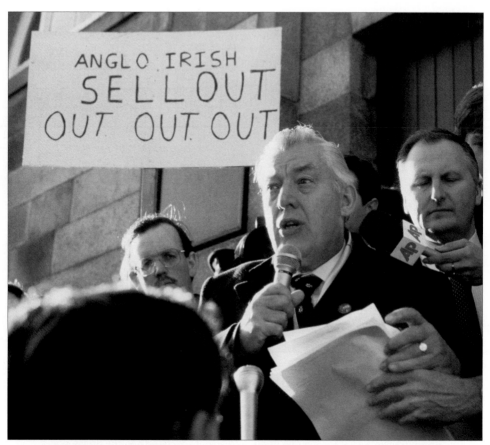

Rev Ian Paisley leads an anti-Agreement protest outside Hillsborough Castle. Much was made of the symbolism of Unionist MPs locked out of the northern secretary's official residence while Irish and British ministers signed the Anglo-Irish Agreement inside.

Delegates at the 1986 Sinn Féin *ard fheis* in the Mansion House, Dublin, vote to end abstention from the Dáil while supporters look on from the gallery.

The parting of the ways: following his defeat in the *ard fheis* vote on abstention, Ruairí Ó Brádaigh gives a less than cordial handshake to Gerry Adams. The two men's facial expressions say it all.

Martin McGuinness walks in the first rank behind the coffin of Derry IRA man Charles English who was killed in August 1985. Either Martin McGuinness, or Gerry Adams, or both, walked in the cortège of every IRA person killed from the early 1980s on. Often both men carried the coffin.

Gerry Adams carries the coffin of Thomas Begley, known as the 'Shankill Bomber', who died in October 1993 along with nine Protestants when one of his bombs exploded prematurely. Adams's action provoked outrage among unionists at a delicate moment in the peace process. Also carrying the coffin is Sinn Féin's general secretary, Tom Hartley (*left*).

Danny Morrison, Sinn Féin's director of publicity in the 1980s and the party's most gifted spin doctor, was the man who coined the phrase 'the Armalite and the ballot box' to describe republicans' dual strategy.

This is what we should do. Let's *do* this.' Now what was motivating me wasn't so much that I thought that this would give us an entry into electoral politics. What was motivating me was, 'We've got to break through this censorship thing' [the absence of health bulletins, etc.]. I hadn't even got to the point of thinking we'd win. In my head was, 'If we announce we're putting Bobby Sands up, it's going to be loads of publicity. It's going to make our job of building support on the outside all the easier'.

Gerry Adams corroborates this version in his autobiography. He and Gibney travelled to Fermanagh to talk to the Maguire family and to persuade them not to field Frank's brother, Noel Maguire, as a candidate.

The announcement by republicans that Sands was the candidate threw the SDLP into disarray. If they stood aside, did that mean they endorsed the hunger strike? If they contested the election they would be routed. On the other hand, suppose the SDLP split the vote sufficiently to get a unionist elected? The party's favoured candidate, Austin Currie, deeply unpopular among republicans, had been beaten two to one by Frank Maguire in 1979, but he had still got 10,000 votes. As Danny Morrison said:

> The alternative was that the SDLP stopped Bobby Sands getting it. Bobby Sands dies and people turn to the SDLP and say, 'Youse bastards'. They'd be faced with that.

At a four-hour meeting of the SDLP party executive, of which the author was a member, no one could present a viable plan. The SDLP in Fermanagh had no organisation and what few party members there were in the county opposed contesting the election. Individuals who were likely candidates passed the privilege around, establishing what a founder member of the party, Paddy O'Hanlon, dubbed 'the Gethsemane principle'. No one accepted the chalice. It was decided to wait to see what Noel Maguire would do. To run and come third behind Noel Maguire and Bobby Sands would also be disastrous for the SDLP.

Noel Maguire withdrew. When nominations closed, Bobby Sands was the sole nationalist candidate. It was a defining moment in nationalist politics in the North. The SDLP had publicly acknowledged that it could not beat Sinn Féin in Fermanagh–Tyrone South. The SDLP never again produced a candidate with a chance of winning the seat. By standing aside, the SDLP had also yielded the initiative to Sinn Féin. The hunger strike was a supremely emotional issue but the SDLP had no political argument to oppose it. It was a matter between Sinn Féin and the British: an ideal position for republicans.

Sinn Féin, its propaganda and publicity expertly and adroitly marshalled by Danny Morrison, exploited the emotionalism surrounding prisoners in the nationalist community to its limits. Many people could envisage one of their own relatives on hunger strike. How many parents could say for certain their teenage son was not in the IRA? The Sinn Féin line was: 'Lend us the seat. It will save Bobby Sands's life.' There was a widespread belief in the Catholic community as a whole that if Sands became an MP the British government would not let him die. It should be said that this was a belief shared in many other countries where the progress of the hunger strike was being followed closely.

When Sands was elected with 30,492 votes – 51% of the vote – it changed everything in the North of Ireland. Unionists watched in amazement as over 10,000 people who had voted SDLP two years before switched, along with virtually every other nationalist voter in the constituency, to vote for a convicted IRA man. Despite strident claims to the contrary, Sands's election made it impossible for the British government to argue convincingly that Sands, or indeed any of his fellow hunger strikers, were mere criminals. The vote, which Sinn Féin had maintained during the campaign was specifically to demonstrate support for prisoners' demands and to save Sands's life, was instantly claimed by Sinn Féin as evidence of support for the republican position on everything. When Sands died in May 1981 and over 100,000 people walked behind his coffin, including the Iranian ambassador, many dignitaries from Europe and further afield, alongside members of the SDLP, Catholic clergy, IRA men and ordinary individuals who were not members of any political organisation, it was obvious to any observer that a political earthquake had taken place. It was now clear beyond peradventure that Sinn Féin and the IRA were not, as the NIO insisted, a 'small group of evil men'.

Even before his death, Sands's election had borne in on some of the hardest men in the IRA that there was something more to be pursued than armed struggle. Gibney again:

> When the result came through I was in a house in Sebastopol Street [off the Falls Road] with probably one of the most senior IRA men around at the time and the nine o'clock news came on and it had a map of Ireland on it with a wee graphic, and there was this wee flash in the middle of Fermanagh–Tyrone South. Main item on the news: 'Hunger Striker Bobby Sands has won Fermanagh–Tyrone South.' And this guy sitting beside me turned round and he says to me, he says, 'That's worth twenty bombs in England.' Now, that might have just passed by that man's head. But the fact of the matter is there was an election result, and for this IRA man, this senior IRA military man to say that, it just showed you the impact that had on him. Now, when he went out of the door it might have left him. I don't think so. I think for a lot of republicans that election result changed the world, changed the world.

The fact that the IRA campaign had continued unabated through the second hunger strike, that sixty-one people died, had no impact on the nationalist electorate. In the by-election caused by Sands's death his election agent, Owen Carron, was elected for Fermanagh–Tyrone South. In an even higher poll, Carron won more votes, 31,278, than Sands. It seemed the armed struggle did not limit Sinn Féin's appeal to a nationalist electorate, which included a substantial slice of SDLP supporters. After the election of Bobby Sands many republicans suddenly wanted to fight every election, North and South.

9. ARMALITE AND BALLOT BOX
Becoming an Electoral Force, 1981–86

I n the five years between 1981 and 1986, the young men leading the IRA in the North took over the republican movement. In retrospect it was inevitable that they would. They were young – all in their early thirties – capable, smart, ruthless, streetwise, politically astute and masters of the constitutional procedures of the movement. They had the inestimable advantage that they operated where the action was, in the 'war zone', as they called it. At the time, though, the outcome of their tussle for control of the movement did not seem so clear-cut.

The northerners moved slowly, carefully, crabwise at times, anxious not to be seen to criticise the leadership of Ó Brádaigh and Ó Conaill, cautious in case a sudden move on their part produced a reaction to them, but, above all, determined to provide no excuse for a split. They had to move slowly because, given the hierarchical structure of the republican movement, there could not be a *coup* without a split. The northerners' accession to power had to be a process and that process had already begun in the 1970s following the collapse of the IRA ceasefire in 1976. From then on, the men of Northern Command beavered away to reorganise Sinn Féin in the North to complement their control of the IRA. Like so many other developments in republicanism, it was the hunger strike that enabled the northerners to take the dominant position on the whole island.

The deaths of ten men on hunger strike in 1981 and Sinn Féin's subsequent entry into electoral politics North and South constitute such an obvious watershed in modern Irish politics that the series of decisions republicans took in the years following 1981 now appears almost to have been pre-ordained. It was far from the case. Those arguing for Sinn Féin's entry into electoral politics did so with some trepidation. Bobby Sands's election and death did not swing opinion in the republican movement instantly and unanimously behind 'electoralism'. As for changing the sacred policy of abstention, that did not seem to be an issue after the electoral successes of 1981. If Sinn Féin picked the right constituencies, the votes apparently were there, North and South, abstention notwithstanding. It was only when the southern electorate swiftly disabused Sinn Féin of this notion that thoughts turned to ending abstention.

In 1981, however, the immediate response of many republicans to the end of the hunger strike was a sigh of relief. They could get back to the business of the armed struggle, which the hunger strike had knocked off centre stage. It is true that violence had continued unabated during 1981. In that year there were 118 deaths, seventy of them caused by the IRA, but violence had taken on a different form during the hunger strike. The republican movement had bent much of its effort to support the prisoners. From April onwards, as the condition of Bobby Sands deteriorated and other men joined him on hunger strike, regular, intense rioting turned the streets of a number of northern towns, but especially republican districts of Belfast and Derry, into scenes of wanton destruction with burnt-out buses, lorries and cars littering the roads.

Sinn Féin organised hundreds of demonstrations in support of the hunger-strikers and the prisoners' so-called Five Demands. Almost invariably the demonstrations ended in a riot. During the year nearly 30,000 plastic bullets were fired by soldiers and police in north and west Belfast alone. Republican communities were in a ferment. Who would be the next man to go on hunger strike? What district, what part of the

North would he come from? Which mother's son would he be? The security forces adopted a policy of containment, that is to say keeping protesters bottled up in their own areas and preventing demonstrations spilling onto main thoroughfares or into town centres. Republican districts felt more like ghettos than they had since the early 1970s. Street violence was endemic. Unionists moved away from adjacent neighbourhoods. Polarisation sharpened.

All kinds of ingenious protests were devised to draw attention to the prisoners. The letter 'H' proved to be a wonderfully simple symbol. Even three-year-olds took to scrawling it on every flat surface available, oblivious to its significance. Individuals at public events would suddenly produce placards with 'H-block' on them. Groups of men and women would, without warning, walk into the roadway in nationalist areas with pictures of the hunger strikers and stand on the white line marking traffic lanes. The energy expended drained away resources from the armed struggle.

Would that drain not be a continuing problem if the republican movement were to move into 'electoralism'? After all, the whole movement had been on a war footing since 1970. IRA leaders believed that Britain could be persuaded to leave by armed force, in other words, that the North of Ireland was a military or security problem. Indeed, in the early 1970s a couple of years had been declared, prematurely, the 'year of victory'. If that war effort were diluted, on what basis would resources be divided? Jim Gibney was well aware of the issue:

> Well, that attitude was in there and it wasn't just an attitude in 1981. There has always been a tension in the modern republican movement derived from history, about the relationship between political development and military development. And because resources and personnel are limited, there's always been competition.

Asked did the IRA always win the competition, Gibney replied, 'Yes, I think so'. He then went on to expand that answer at length:

You know what it was like in the 1980s. In that climate, the IRA was engaged in armed struggle, willing to kill British soldiers and blow places up, so your ability to attract people in a community into a political organisation like Sinn Féin is very limited. With a British fort in the middle of the area, with the soldiers raiding homes and arresting people and when there's men dying on hunger strike, people are naturally going to join the IRA instead. So when the war is on, the tendency is that the IRA becomes the biggest and strongest organisation. Sinn Féin may not be the poor cousin but it doesn't get the same attention, personnel, etc, that the IRA would have. That's just the nature of things. The attitude that the IRA is more important and should get everything was clearly there. But the leadership of Sinn Féin had a duty to their own organisation, with their own independent system of raising finances, getting resources, ensuring a supply of posters, leaflets, etc. If you look back at that period, you'll find that, despite the competition for personnel and resources, Sinn Féin had, in fact, a very effective system of raising money in these areas here where it relied on and had big support.

How was this competition resolved? It is clear both from Gibney's first response and his longer, more considered reply that when the chips were down the IRA came first 'when the war is on'. The war certainly was 'on' in 1981 and everyone in the republican movement presumed, with very good evidence, that it would continue. How then did Sinn Féin obtain anything? The answer is quite simple. The men leading and directing the republican movement, that is, the IRA Army Council, decided that Sinn Féin's role should be enhanced, that it should be involved in elections.

It has already been established here that the enhancement of Sinn Féin's role began some years before the 1981 hunger strike. The 'Staff Report' seized from Seamus Twomey in December 1977 and referred to in the previous chapter is evidence for that. It is worth recalling the language in that document. It is perfectly obvious that it was the IRA that was directing the extent of Sinn Féin's involvement: 'Sinn Féin should be directed to infiltrate', 'Sinn Féin should be re-educated', Sinn Féin should do this and that, but always with the proviso, 'under Army direction', Sinn Féin should come 'under Army organisers', and so on.

The 1977 'Staff Report' and the developments over the next five years were important victories for the group of young northern IRA men who looked to Gerry Adams for leadership. They were mostly Belfast based, but Martin McGuinness from Derry also played an important part in redesigning the republican movement. The young northerners made a crucial advance in autumn 1976 with the re-establishment of Northern Command, led by McGuinness. There had been a Northern Command in the IRA during Second World War, but since the establishment of the Provisional IRA in 1970 the southern-based central leadership had directed it.

Allowing a Northern Command to emerge conceded control of the campaign in what republicans called 'the war zone' to the young northerners, a decision that was simply facing the facts. But this decision also meant that Northern Command would control Sinn Féin in the North, thus enabling the northerners to advance their ideas on street politics alongside a rejuvenated military campaign. Danny Morrison says:

> I think the big change in all this pressure on the leadership [after the failure of the 1975 ceasefire] led to the founding of a Northern Command in autumn 1976 and I would actually place a lot of the politicisation that was subsequently to occur from that moment.

According to Morrison, there was 'a conscious effort' by the northern leadership in 1977 to beef up Sinn Féin, to put into practice the ideas of 'Active Republicanism', which Gerry Adams had been advocating in his 'Brownie' columns in *Republican News*. Morrison agrees with Gibney about the difficulty in attracting quality recruits to Sinn Féin:

> The problem about it was the biggest magnet was the IRA. You

couldn't get anybody to go into politics. So that meant the republican leadership [by which he means the IRA] had to send *cadres* into Sinn Féin in a sense because that was the only way Sinn Féin was going to have respectability and it needed that internally. Now, this isn't to repudiate or run down the people who were working there incredibly hard down the years and getting their houses wrecked and selling *Republican News*, because the act of selling the paper was also political … When you're involved in a conflict there's a need for fundamentalism and that means when you want something done you have to have a very disciplined attitude to getting it done. Sinn Féin wouldn't have held together properly prior to 1977. They always looked to the IRA for guidance. They would have been shaped.

Therefore with hindsight it can be seen that from 1976 power within the republican movement began to swing northwards. Morrison sums it up:

So I would say as a result of all that, the 1975 ceasefire, Northern Command being set up in late 1976, you could see the powers switching to northerners and that document you're talking about, the Twomey document, certainly there was a big input from Northern Command into it.

Morrison says the Army Council and leaders of Sinn Féin knew what the northerners were up to:

I presume poor Dave O'Connell probably knew what we were at and so did Ruairí [Ó Brádaigh]. But they were stuck in the South and we had credibility because of our profiles and what we were doing, and because we were based in the North.

Nevertheless, a large gap yawned between enhancing the role of Sinn Féin to engage in 'Active Republicanism', that is, street and community politics, and engaging in 'electoralism'. The republican movement remained, in Morrison's words, 'not just non-electoral, but anti-electoral'. The IRA actively 'discouraged' people from voting, using methods which included firing shots at a polling station in north Belfast during a 1979 election. Indeed this opposition to elections spancelled Sinn Féin's first chance of building on Bobby Sands's success in the North's local government elections in May 1981.

Apart from traditional hostility in the IRA to elections, one of the reasons for trying to make it impossible to hold elections in the North was that, after the collapse of the power-sharing executive in 1974, there had been no institutions in Northern Ireland. A Constitutional Convention set up by the British in 1975 had, by 1976, come to nothing. The political vacuum that existed fortified republicans' hostility to electoralism. Elections to any regional institution lent credibility to Northern Ireland and smacked of a return to Stormont, the overthrow of which republicans claimed as their greatest success. To republicans, elections in the North looked like part of a counter-insurgency strategy, a means of restoring 'normality' or creating political opposition to armed struggle. Without institutions, Northern Ireland looked like a colony being held by an occupying army. The IRA leadership still held out hope that the British would be brought to the negotiating table by violence. If elections to northern institutions were allowed to take place then the IRA's perceived route to the negotiating table would be blocked.

Some northerners wanted to extend their opposition to elections. They toyed with the idea of exporting the theories of 'Active Republicanism' to the South, of creating an alternative State within the state composed of the network of tenants' associations and community groups that Sinn Féin was building in urban areas in the South, as they were in republican districts in the North, along the lines of the Adams's inspired 'Staff Report'. These community groups would negotiate with the State on behalf of their districts. To this end, some northerners entered a proposal on the *Clár* at Sinn Féin's 1980 *ard fheis* to prevent Sinn Féin candidates standing in council elections in the South, something which republicans had been doing since the 1940s. Sinn Féin delegates from the Republic were having none of it: it was defeated.

Not all northerners took such a hard line on elections. Francie Molloy and Jimmy McGivern, both from east Tyrone, wanted to contest the upcoming local government elections in the North in 1981 and accordingly proposed a motion at the 1980 *ard fheis*. Danny Morrison and Jimmy Drumm were nominated by the *ard comhairle* to speak against the motion. Jim Gibney remembers Ruairí Ó Brádaigh denouncing the proposal and declaring that if anybody were to bring forward a motion of that nature again, he would personally seek their immediate expulsion from the party. Not only was the motion defeated, but defeated in such terms that it was impossible for Sinn Féin to field candidates the following May.

Ruairí Ó Brádaigh claims that he and Dáithí Ó Conaill had been in favour of fighting elections in the North since the late 1970s and that it was the northerners, and Gerry Adams in particular, who had opposed the idea. According to Ó Brádaigh, he and Ó Conaill were in favour of fighting the first direct European elections in 1979 but lost at the *ard comhairle* by one vote, 'and Adams was the principal person against it'. Whatever the truth, clearly there was a debate within the movement, but the leadership was not prepared to take a decision in the autumn of 1980 without thoroughly preparing the ground and certainly not with the first hunger strike looming.

Danny Morrison admits there was uncertainty:

> Privately a few of us would have been thinking about it [elections] in '78, '79, but we had no idea how to move from there to there. The whole movement was hostile to electoral politics and politicians, and we shared that view. We had no idea how to get from there to there without causing a split. There was no way.

Quite simply, Bobby Sands inadvertently solved the problem for the movement. Those who had been advocating the fighting of elections were vindicated by his victory in April 1981. But it was too late to ride the wave of popular emotion into the local government elections on 20 May.

It would have required an Extraordinary *Ard Fheis* to overturn the decision of the previous October forbidding Sinn Féin's involvement in the
elections. Ruairí Ó Brádaigh, Sinn Féin president, was not going to facili-
tate those wanting to contest the elections:

> It wasn't that the *ard comhairle* couldn't, but they [the northerners]
> had tied the *ard comhairle* by an *ard fheis* decision which said that we
> couldn't contest local elections in the six counties. Now this was
> deadly. How could you get an Extraordinary *Ard Fheis* together in
> time to reverse the decision? I was very firm. You go by the book.
> No putting a coach and four through the constitution.

In some ways, however, the inability of Sinn Féin to contest the local
elections was useful. The party threw its weight behind National
H-Block/Armagh candidates and could observe, at no risk to Sinn Féin,
how they performed. If they did well, Sinn Féin could claim its candidates
would have done better. If they did badly, well then it was because they
were not real Sinn Féin candidates. In the event, as Ó Brádaigh said, 'the
result was that anyone that got up and said, "Brits Out, H-Block" got
elected.' Across the North, H-Block candidates of various stripes polled
51,000 votes and thirty-six were elected. In Belfast four H-Block councillors were elected, two PD and two Irish Republican Socialist Party
(IRSP), the political wing of the INLA.

Sinn Féin knew immediately that the results were of tremendous
significance. Two nationalist icons in Belfast, Gerry Fitt and Paddy Devlin,
had been humiliated. Fitt, the MP for West Belfast since 1966, one of the
founders of the SDLP and its leader until his resignation from the post in
1979, had been re-elected for West Belfast in 1979 with over 16,000 votes.
In 1977 he had polled over 3,000 votes in the council area in which he
had been born and had pulled in two other candidates on his transfers. In
1981 he polled a mere tenth of that, a pathetic 300-odd, and had lost his
council seat. Paddy Devlin, another founder of the SDLP, had polled the
highest vote in local government in the North in 1977, over 7,000. In

1981 his vote slumped to 1,200, though he clung onto his seat. Both men had been swept aside by unknowns from the PD. Sinn Féin knew the votes would have been there for the taking had the party been able to field candidates.

One area where Sinn Féin was not curtailed by the 1980 *ard fheis* ban on elections was the Republic. In spring 1981 a general election was looming. The taoiseach, Charles Haughey, leader of Fianna Fáil, was fully aware of the emotional charge the hunger strike in the North transmitted to politics in the Republic. Given what had happened in the North, it was obvious that republicans would put up prisoner candidates in the Republic too. Although they had been born and lived in the North, the Irish constitution recognised such candidates as Irish citizens with full rights to stand for election to the Oireachtas. Nervous of their impact on key constituencies, Haughey changed his mind twice about announcing the date for the election. Finally he called it for 11 June.

Sinn Féin announced it was running nine prisoners, four of them on hunger strike. Although Sinn Féin laboured against the Republic's censorship of the electronic media, which banned from the airwaves spokespersons for subversive organisations or those sympathetic to such organisations, there was plenty of coverage on the British media that the majority of the Republic's population could view or listen to without let or hindrance. Even so, it was grassroots organisation that counted. Gibney's brainchild, the National H-Block/Armagh Committees, came into their own, along with the community agitation network that Sinn Féin had been developing for four years. Sheer Anglophobia also played its part in the campaign as prisoner after prisoner died. England seemed once again to be rejecting the reasonable demands of the whole of Ireland as voiced by the leader of the Catholic Church in Ireland, the Irish Commission for Justice and Peace and in fairly well publicised requests from Charles Haughey's government for some accommodation.

The election results had both a long- and short-term impact on the

Republic. H-Block candidates polled almost 40,000 votes and two won seats in the Dáil, Kieran Doherty for Cavan–Monaghan and Paddy Agnew for Louth, both border constituencies with substantial connections with the North and containing a large number of voters who held traditional republican views about partition and the British. Joe McDonnell, another hunger striker, missed election in Sligo-Leitrim by 315 votes. He died on 8 July. The two H-Block TDs and the 40,000 votes scattered among the other constituencies were sufficient to cost Charles Haughey the election. Garret FitzGerald, leader of Fine Gael, became taoiseach. Haughey never forgave Mrs Thatcher and tried to exact revenge the following year during the Falklands War when, as taoiseach again, he took an anti-British line at the United Nations.

The long-term results were more important. Garret FitzGerald became convinced that the policies of the British government towards the North of Ireland were so dangerously misguided that they could end up destabilising the whole island. The emotional surge in the June 1981 election had alarmed many politicians in the South, but was particularly startling for a man like FitzGerald who took a pleasure in psephology.[1] He decided, correctly, that there was a republican vote in the South to be tapped if Sinn Féin could find the right divining rod. Only a radical change in the attitude of the British government could cut off the well-spring of support, otherwise any government in the Republic would be vulnerable to a swing to Sinn Féin provoked by some ill-conceived British decision.

Sinn Féin drew the same conclusion as FitzGerald about its voting potential in the Republic, but of course the party took a different view regarding the solution to the problem. Since the party supported the IRA's analysis of the Irish problem, that meant Sinn Féin essentially agreed with Mrs Thatcher that the problem was a military one. Mrs Thatcher believed the solution was to defeat the IRA. For Sinn Féin the solution was to be able to show that a substantial percentage of the Irish people, North and South, supported the republican position that the British should leave and furthermore that the IRA was right to use armed struggle against the British Army to force it to leave. If the IRA could show that Sinn Féin had widespread electoral support, then the IRA could claim that electoral support was for the IRA's policy. The military campaign would be endorsed by the people.

So it was that on Hallowe'en 1981 Danny Morrison found himself at Sinn Féin's *ard fheis* adopting exactly the opposite position from the one he had argued the previous year. It was during his speech on that occasion that he produced the famous question:

> Who here really believes we can win the war through the ballot box? But will anyone here object if, with a ballot paper in one hand and the Armalite in the other, we take power in Ireland?

Whereas in 1980 the leadership had been undecided about elections, by the time of the 1981 *ard fheis* a year of electoral success North and South had convinced them of the benefits of participating. According to Danny Morrison, the group around Adams wanted a position 'where the leadership was free to make whatever decisions were relevant at the time' because it was an open secret that the new northern secretary, Jim Prior, intended some kind of political initiative. However, despite the stunning successes in elections North and South, which continued right up until Owen Carron's victory in Fermanagh in August 1981, there was concern that the outcome at the *ard fheis* would not be clear-cut. Morrison says:

> We went to the *ard fheis,* but things weren't great because what you have to understand is a lot of Sinn Féin was made up of Army people. They had separate roles, or somebody was in there to do a Sinn Féin role, but they were still members of Óglaigh na hÉireann. We were a bit nervous because now what we were wanting was to move into electoral politics, not under H-Block but as Sinn Féin, and a lot of people were thoroughly opposed to it. So at the *ard fheis* Adams says to everybody: 'You all have to speak here. We need to

carry this through.' So when I got up it was near the end and the Armalite/ballot box came out, just off the cuff. There wasn't anything planned about it. In fact, I think most of the press had gone home at that stage. They hadn't even realised how important this debate was and the only person sitting there, I think, was Vincent Browne, and he wrote down what I said. So it was passed. And as far as we were concerned it was just, 'That's brilliant!' The leadership now had a free hand.

Nevertheless, there had not been the careful preparation of grassroots reaction which later became a feature of Gerry Adams's political leadership. The decision was very obviously northern-driven. Some senior members of the movement, among them Ruairí Ó Brádaigh, were taken aback by the speed and apparent lack of concern for the consequences with which electoralism was embraced. On the other hand, some found the extent of support amazing. According to people at the *ard fheis*, Martin McGuinness, listening to speeches enthusiastically endorsing fighting elections and listening to Danny Morrison's peroration, turned to another member of the *ard comhairle* and asked, 'What the fuck is going on here?' It was not that he did not know what had been planned because he was very close to Adams. Besides, as chief of staff of the IRA since 1978 and *ex officio* a member of the Army Council, he would have been privy to the strategy. What disconcerted McGuinness was that Morrison had let the cat out of the bag by revealing publicly the dual strategy of electoralism and militarism that had been hammered out by a small group at the top of the movement. Stating it so openly was a shock because the Army Council had not sanctioned its revelation. But Morrison's clarion call engendered a delighted response among *ard fheis* delegates.

If some of the northerners were astonished by the enthusiasm in the hall, the southern-based leaders of Sinn Féin, Ruairí Ó Brádaigh and Dáithí Ó Conaill, the men who had built the movement from 1970, were aghast. In an interview with the author, Ruairí Ó Brádaigh objected to 'the volatility of it', as he described the zeal for elections:

> These were people who had been totally opposed to every kind of election. We pointed out at the time, it is one thing to contest elections, but we shouldn't be tied to every election: we should just assess elections and take what suits the objective conditions on the ground.

To Ó Brádaigh's horror the young northerners had their eyes on general elections in the Republic, not simply selecting key constituencies on an issue like the hunger strike. The northerners, as could be expected, may have correctly analysed the conditions in the North but they were hopelessly at sea when it came to politics in the Republic. Ó Brádaigh knew better from long and bitter experience. No one was listening to him. In the 1981 *ard fheis* the northerners had swept the boards.

It was not long before the new exponents of electoralism came a cropper. FitzGerald's government fell early in 1982 on the budget. Sinn Féin's *ard comhairle* decided to put up candidates in the ensuing election. Ruairí Ó Brádaigh found himself in a minority of two on the *ard comhairle* along with Charlie McGlade, a Belfast republican living in Dublin. O'Brádaigh argued, quite correctly, that the 1982 election was completely different. As he said:

> Last summer we were centre stage. Ulick O'Connor wrote, 'In the summer of '81 the Taigs in Belfast made the world their stage.' This is now because the budget fell down. It's about the price of children's shoes and milk or something like that. Where are we centre stage on that? You know, as a national liberation movement? We're not there, and we're going to do very badly.

Of course the enthusiasts for election on the Sinn Féin *ard comhairle* did not intend to fight every constituency, merely selected ones in the 'war zone'. It should be explained that Northern Command's remit, as well as covering the North, extended into the border counties in the Republic: Donegal, Sligo, Leitrim, Cavan, Monaghan and Louth, places where H-Block candidates had stood the previous year. The plan was to throw the party's weight into Cavan–Monaghan and Louth, the two constituencies where Kieran Doherty and Paddy Agnew had won seats in 1981. The idea was to have a re-run of 1981 with prisoner candidates.

Ó Brádaigh was correct in his assessment of the southern electorate. Sinn Féin's chief hope in the election in February 1982 was Seamus McElwaine, former IRA OC of Fermanagh, who was serving life for the murders of a UDR man and a policeman. From Knockascullion, near Scotstown in Monaghan, he was a local candidate who seemed well placed, on the basis of the 1981 results, to do well. In the event, he polled less than 4,000 votes. Overall, Sinn Féin, standing in the Republic for the first time in many years in its own name, polled less than half the votes the H-Block candidates had received during the high emotions of the hunger strike. The party retired temporarily from Dáil elections with a bloody nose to reconsider its position. Sinn Féin wisely decided not to contest the general election held in November 1982. A rethink of the party's role in the Republic was long overdue.

There were no such problems in the North. Once again the British administration played into republicans' hands. Appointed in September 1981, the new northern secretary, Jim Prior, a heavy-hitter in the Conservative Party, had rapidly resolved the issues about prisoners' clothing and their other demands and then immediately set to work to produce new political institutions in the North. He faced several major problems. First, Mrs Thatcher had exiled him to Northern Ireland from Westminster because he was at odds with her over economic policy; he was a 'wet' in the parlance of the time. Mrs Thatcher did not want him to make a success of the North as she undermined or countermanded all his efforts to reach an acceptable accommodation between the two communities.

An even more important obstacle to success was that by trying to set up some arrangement in the North, Prior was running counter to settled Irish government policy which both Fianna Fáil and Fine Gael had been operating since 1979, namely that Ireland should act jointly with Britain in dealing with the North. The policy had been formally inaugurated in May 1980 at a meeting in Downing Street when the taoiseach, Charles Haughey, famously presented Mrs Thatcher with an Irish Georgian silver teapot, the result being that the process became known as 'teapot diplomacy'. In December 1980, after a groundbreaking meeting in Dublin between Irish and British Cabinet ministers, an important communiqué was issued that mentioned 'the totality of relationships within these islands'. Joint studies between officials of the two governments had begun on issues of mutual benefit to the two states, and the plan was to examine the results of these studies at regular meetings between cabinet ministers from Ireland and Britain.

Now, while much of the programme had been derailed by the hunger strike and its aftermath, the programme still remained the Irish government's policy. Both Haughey and FitzGerald in their periods as taoiseach aimed to get Mrs Thatcher back on board. Prior's plans played no part in any of that, nor was Thatcher about to let him dovetail his plans into the programme. As a result, Prior's proposals dealt exclusively with the North. Worse still, when in early drafts he had attempted to include elements attractive to nationalists, Mrs Thatcher had told him to go away 'and take the green edges off it'.

Prior's chances were further handicapped by the general election in the Republic in February 1982 that returned Charles Haughey to power, full of rancour about Mrs Thatcher and her handling of the hunger strike which had cost him the 1981 general election. Haughey was not going to cooperate with any scheme concocted by one of her ministers, especially since the Irish government had not been consulted about it and since it threatened to shunt Irish policy on the North into a siding. As the Falklands crisis slid towards war, Anglo-Irish relations entered a period of acrimony unequalled since the early 1970s.

Prior's scheme, which became known as 'rolling devolution' because it was designed to 'roll' towards ever stronger devolved powers, could not therefore have been launched against a worse political and diplomatic background. As it was, when the details became known, the proposals were completely unacceptable to the SDLP. Aside from having no Irish dimension to them, the proposals gave unionists a veto on progress towards power-sharing. Given the attitude of Haughey's government, there was no prospect that Dublin would encourage reluctant northern nationalists to play ball. John Hume, the SDLP leader, announced that Prior's rolling devolution was 'unworkable'. Haughey agreed. Prior found himself in the unique position of facing opposition from both Thatcher and Haughey.

But the plan was his political lifeline, his only means of climbing back on board the ship of state at Westminster. Prior doggedly pressed on and thereby set up a contest among nationalists as to who could be the toughest opponent of his plan. There could only be one winner in a contest of that nature. The SDLP could never compete in political extremism with Sinn Féin. Prior's rolling devolution gave Sinn Féin the chance to enter electoral politics on terms ideal for republicans: competing with the SDLP on how best to reject a British proposal. As a result, Sinn Féin did not even have to consider ending abstention: abstaining would be an essential element in rejecting Prior's plan.

For once, John Hume took his eye off the ball. During 1982 he was unwell for periods of time, but for whatever reason he dithered in his response. Instead of rejecting it out of hand, Hume negotiated with Prior about the white paper containing the proposals. It is true that he was faced with a serious dilemma. He could not accept what was on offer. It was not even a pale shadow of the Sunningdale Agreement of 1973. It did not offer guaranteed power-sharing, the bottom line for the SDLP, and there was no institutional link to the rest of the island. However, if Prior pressed on, what should the SDLP do? The party could no longer act without reference to Sinn Féin's intentions. Yet it was inconceivable for the SDLP to act in concert with Sinn Féin since Sinn Féin was wedded to violence. The SDLP did not even reply to letters from Sinn Féin seeking a meeting and suggesting cooperation. In the past, when it was the only nationalist party in the field, the SDLP could have announced a boycott of the elections to Prior's assembly. Obviously if both the SDLP and Sinn Féin boycotted the elections the scheme would collapse with no nationalist participation. Now, if the SDLP unilaterally announced a boycott, could Sinn Féin be trusted not to stand? What if both parties stood on an abstentionist ticket? How could the SDLP differentiate its position from that of Sinn Féin? Would people not vote for the real abstentionists, Sinn Féin?

There were deep divisions in the SDLP about Hume's vacillating response. Prominent figures in the party, like Agriculture spokesman Paddy Duffy from Dungannon and Security spokesman Michael Canavan from Derry, a close colleague of Hume's, strongly advised Hume to tell Prior to drop the plan as soon as he announced it because the SDLP would boycott it. The scheme was published at Easter 1982 and months went by, on into the summer, with no definite response from the SDLP other than the repeated use of the word 'unworkable'. By the summer it was too late to reject it. The plan had gone through Westminster.

Sinn Féin was delighted. There was nothing in it for nationalists. They knew the plan was a disaster for the SDLP. The SDLP could not participate in something Hume had denounced. Sinn Féin had set the agenda early on. The party's response was clear and definite from the outset. Sinn Féin opposed Prior's scheme root and branch. It announced that it would boycott the elections but that it would contest them if the SDLP did. Sinn Féin, of course, would not take any seats it won. What would the SDLP do? Danny Morrison, who was to become Sinn Féin's director of elections, saw it like this:

> The SDLP were trapped into an abstentionist position and that was happy for us because we were concerned about the counter-insurgency side of politics. You know, we just wanted the Brits to

rule out every option [by having each one rejected] so that none of their options were working until they had to come round to our way of thinking, or move towards our position regardless of what happened subsequently.

For the SDLP – a party that had come into northern politics on a participatory basis – to fight an election on an abstentionist policy was to place it at the worst imaginable disadvantage. At a four-hour meeting in Dungannon in August 1982, after much agonising, the SDLP at last decided to contest the election but to abstain from the new assembly. Paddy Duffy and Michael Canavan, who thought the SDLP should have announced a boycott of the whole scheme the moment Prior published it, left front-line politics that summer.

Sinn Féin threw itself into an election made for it. Despite much visible activity, however, the party was not as well organised as many observers believed. Since the Sinn Féin founded in 1970 had never fought an election in the North, and since prominent candidates were members of the IRA or had been on the run, there were certain technical problems. For example, some, including Danny Morrison, were not on the electoral roll until the summer of 1982. The same was true for hundreds of sup-porters in every constituency. Republicans tended to ignore the state. This was all very well as a matter of principle, but when pragmatism supervened and people intended to take part in one of the state's most fundamental processes, namely an election, the scruples of principle had to be set aside pretty quickly.

To be nominated for election required, needless to say, a proposer, a seconder and a number of assentors, altogether about a dozen people. Their names would be made public. In the violent society of Northern Ireland, to be known as someone who endorsed the candidature of a senior figure in Sinn Féin meant presenting yourself as a target for loyalist murder gangs or for visits by the RUC Special Branch. There was not exactly a headlong rush. Danny Morrison remembers with a chuckle: 'We had to be a bit creative with some of the signatories.'

Sinn Féin had further difficulties in finding candidates and deciding which constituencies to contest. The problems continued until nomination day. Contrary to the belief that all decisions in the republican movement are centralised, there were disputes, familiar to all political parties, about the carve-up of constituencies. The most intractable was in Mid-Ulster where the supporters of two potential candidates, Sean Begley from Omagh and Francie Hurson from Galbally, were at loggerheads. Sinn Féin had decided to field three candidates in this strong republican constituency, but while the candidate for the west of the constituency was agreed, the two others were not. In the end, when agreement could not be reached between supporters of Begley and Hurson, the party parachuted in Danny Morrison on nomination day. Morrison was left on the afternoon of nomination day running around Carrickmore trying to collect the necessary signatures. It was vital to get him nominated because he was the party's twelfth candidate, the magic number which qualified a party for radio and TV time in election broadcasts, and therefore an absolutely crucial goal for Sinn Féin. Morrison made it in the nick of time.

The twelve candidates were spread over just seven of the North's twelve constituencies, obviously the most nationalist ones. The election would therefore be a direct confrontation with the SDLP in nationalist heartlands. All Sinn Féin's top people were candidates: Gerry Adams, Martin McGuinness, Danny Morrison and Owen Carron, Bobby Sands's successor as Fermanagh–Tyrone South MP.

The results sent a shiver through the political establishment North and South. Sinn Féin had five men elected to the Prior assembly: Gerry Adams, Martin McGuinness, Danny Morrison, Owen Carron and Jim McAllister from south Armagh. The party polled 64,000 votes or 10% of the vote – 2% more than the total of H-Block votes the previous year. Percentages are of interest to politicians and commentators. It was the raw figures that hit the headlines, the vote in each of the seven constituencies.

In West Belfast, Gerry Adams topped the poll with one-and-a-half quotas and almost twice as many votes as the SDLP candidate. In Derry, Martin McGuinness was also elected on the first count, only 4,000 behind the SDLP leader John Hume. In several constituencies Sinn Féin narrowly missed a second seat.

The SDLP, with fourteen seats, was five seats down on its 1973 assembly number, exactly the same number Sinn Féin won. The election showed features which persist to this day in PR election contests between Sinn Féin and the SDLP. Firstly, the major one is that Sinn Féin's seat total is minimised since no other party transfers to it. Sinn Féin candidates tend to top the poll and sit there, often being overtaken in subsequent counts. Proportionately, Sinn Féin should have got two more seats in the 1982 election if it had received the transfers. Secondly, while only a small minority of SDLP voters transfer their preferences to Sinn Féin, on the other hand a substantial number of Sinn Féin voters transfer to the SDLP, which also receives transfers from the Alliance Party and therefore tends to maximise its number of seats.

It was also clear from this first election contest between the two parties that Sinn Féin had brought out a new vote. Although the SDLP share of the vote was down slightly in percentage terms, the party gained 2,000 votes over its total in 1981 because there was a higher turnout. Therefore, although some SDLP voters had switched to Sinn Féin, they only amounted to a fraction of Sinn Féin's 64,000 votes. Who were Sinn Féin's voters? The figures show the biggest concentration of support was among the urban working-class, particularly first-time voters and young men in working-class areas, a category of people who normally do not vote in similar constituencies elsewhere in the western world. The party also picked up a traditional rural republican vote from people who had until this time boycotted elections in the North.

The image of Sinn Féin bursting onto the electoral scene was magnified because the first result was from West Belfast, a densely packed constituency whose result in a PR election was easiest to calculate because of Adams's massive vote. Therefore on the six o'clock television news on the evening of the count, the first shot was of Adams's face and his victory celebrations in, of all places, the unionist bastion of Belfast City Hall. The story was repeated on the nine o'clock news and went around the world.

Thanks to Jim Prior and his ill-conceived scheme, Sinn Féin now had elected representatives. The policy of the northerners in the republican movement had been vindicated. They had shown that the 1981 vote for the hunger-strikers was not a one-off, an emotional spasm. The October 1982 assembly vote for Sinn Féin was bigger; 35% of nationalists in the North supported it. Sinn Féin had defeated SDLP candidates comprehensively in cockpit constituencies like West Belfast and Fermanagh–Tyrone South and had given them a run for their money in places like North Belfast. If the British government did not take Sinn Féin seriously as a political threat after that showing, the Irish government most certainly did.

The most alarming spectre haunting Irish politicians was the possibility that Sinn Féin would overtake the SDLP as the majority party representing northern nationalists. That would mean the triumph of the republican argument that the majority of northern nationalists supported the armed struggle being waged by the IRA against the British presence. From the point of view of republicans that would, in Danny Morrison's words, 'rule out another option' for the British. Of course, in terms of real politics it would mean that the British government would not negotiate; there would be no political developments at all. The consequences could destabilise the whole island.

For many years, and particularly since John Hume had become party leader in 1979, the SDLP had been, in effect, the Irish government in the North. Many of the policies the SDLP advocated on the North emerged from Iveagh House and the Irish Department of Foreign Affairs. It was a fundamental tenet of SDLP policy never to criticise the Irish government, or indeed any Irish political party, in case it became the Irish government. As a result, successive Irish governments enthusiastically endorsed the SDLP and its politicians. Why would they not? After all, the SDLP enunciated faithfully the Irish government's policy on the North and towards Britain.

Were Sinn Féin to eclipse the SDLP, all that would end. Sinn Féin was beyond the control of the Irish government. Nationalists in the North would be seen to have repudiated the Irish government's policy on the North of Ireland. Leaving aside the embarrassment of such a situation for Dublin, the most disconcerting aspect of Sinn Féin was its support of the IRA's campaign of violence. If Sinn Féin were to become the party representing most northern nationalists, how then could any Irish government press the case for northern nationalists to the British, the targets of the violence?

Accordingly, when the dust from the elections to Prior's assembly had settled, the Irish government bent all its efforts to shoring up the SDLP and constitutional nationalism in the North. The man driving this effort was Garret FitzGerald, who was taoiseach again after yet another general election in the Republic in November 1982, the third in seventeen months. FitzGerald set out to mend the damaged relations with Britain caused by Haughey's stance on the Falklands War, but also to construct some means of undermining the seemingly unstoppable growth of support for Sinn Féin among northern nationalists, and especially among young northern nationalists.

Officials in the Department of Foreign Affairs had already devised a plan to enable the SDLP to have something constructive in its manifesto for the assembly elections. This plan envisaged a conference of Irish parties to produce an agreed position on the North to put to Britain. FitzGerald ran with this proposal, not least because it had the support of his officials, but also because the SDLP had inserted it as a manifesto promise in the assembly elections. The result was the New Ireland Forum.

The Forum met in Dublin Castle between May 1983 and May 1984. All parties in Ireland with elected representatives were invited except, of course, Sinn Féin because of its support for violence. It goes without saying that unionists rejected all blandishments to take part, although individuals did attend the Forum unofficially to present the unionist case. The Forum performed a number of useful functions. It provided an arena for the SDLP where party members elected to the assembly could engage in representative political activity. It placed them on a par with TDs from the parties in the Dáil – Fianna Fáil, Fine Gael and Labour – which all participated in the Forum and thereby gave an aura of respectability to the SDLP and portrayed the party as a component of the Irish political scene. In that respect the New Ireland Forum was a huge step forward for northern nationalists since it represented the first explicit political recognition of them by an Irish government since partition. It sent the unequivocal message that the SDLP was the respectable northern party and Sinn Féin the pariah.

However, if the intention had been to give the SDLP a leg-up in the obstacle race against Sinn Féin, the Forum had no effect at all on republicans. It was a long time before it convened: nine months after the 1982 assembly elections. It did carry out serious and important business. It produced a redefinition of Irish nationalism that was agreed by all parties in the Dáil and the SDLP. But its most important achievement was a seminal report issued in May 1984 that formed the basis of negotiations with the British government, which led ultimately to the Anglo-Irish Agreement of November 1985.

The problem was that this was all high politics. Certainly republican leaders were annoyed at such a blatant attempt to favour the SDLP and sideline Sinn Féin, but they knew it had no impact whatsoever on their supporters. The attitude of Sinn Féin voters was best demonstrated in a radio *vox pop* interview about the Forum. One interviewee in Ardoyne, when asked what he thought about the Forum, helpfully told the interviewer that it used to be a 'picture house that's now converted into the Star drinking club'. The New Ireland Forum, sitting in Dublin in the ornate surroundings of Dublin Castle, was a long way from Ardoyne. Its sessions were esoteric, its proceedings necessarily lengthy and convoluted. Its results, if any, would naturally take a long time. It caused no problems for Sinn Féin, whose leaders had in the meantime found a huge gap left by the SDLP in the North.

From the time the northern secretary, Roy Mason, had dissolved the Constitutional Convention in 1976, the SDLP had had no full-time, paid elected representative apart from its leader, Gerry Fitt. When Fitt left the party in 1979, there was no one. John Hume, the new party leader, received a salary as an advisor to Dick Burke, the Irish EC commissioner, but the other leading party figures had to try to find jobs where they could. Seamus Mallon, SDLP deputy leader and a former headmaster, eked out an existence as a substitute teacher. Others, like Austin Currie, could find no permanent work. The party became badly demoralised. The election results in 1981 and 1982 plunged members deeper into despondency. There was no incentive for nationalists to become involved in elected politics. As a result the SDLP had left large parts of the North unrepresented. Belfast, with its four Westminster constituencies, was the worst lacuna. For example, no SDLP candidate stood in Ardoyne in the 1977 local elections, thereby handing a guaranteed seat to unionists as Sinn Féin at that time was hostile to elections. Ardoyne was not the only place where the SDLP had no organisation. Independents began to emerge across the North. Without paid representatives, the SDLP simply could not do the job a political party is supposed to do.

Sinn Féin eagerly filled the gap after the assembly elections in 1982. Since both SDLP and Sinn Féin were abstaining, neither party's representatives received any salary or facilities from Stormont. For the SDLP therefore, nothing had changed. In some respects the representative issue became even worse because the SDLP's assembly members spent as much time as they could at the New Ireland Forum in Dublin, where they received expenses and where life was a good deal more congenial than being part-time politicians in the North.

By contrast, Sinn Féin's assembly members threw themselves into the business of representation with all the fervour of converts. They were full-time representatives, all on the dole or receiving allowances from the movement, or both. They quickly built up a reputation for good representation. They lived among their electorate. They worked out of the old incident centres that had been set up during the 1975 truce, where armies of volunteers manned the premises six days a week. By 1983 Sinn Féin had twenty-eight offices across the North, including some in constituencies where the party did not have an assembly member. The SDLP had none. Strenuous efforts eventually produced one in West Belfast, but it could only be manned on a part-time basis and even then with no regularity. How could voters contact the SDLP?

Sinn Féin soon discovered the SDLP was a paper tiger. In large parts of Belfast the party had no members at all, or only a paper membership. The same was true in many places in the North where republicans found they had no competition for electoral support in great swathes of nationalist territory. Prominent SDLP figures had stood as well-known celebrities in their districts on the basis of their reputation in the civil rights movement or some such activity in the 1960s or early 1970s. People had automatically voted for them as the only nationalist candidate. In reality, until 1982 the SDLP had never had to fight an election, just as the Ulster Unionist Party (UUP) had not had to fight an election before Ian Paisley's Democratic Unionist Party (DUP) emerged to challenge them for the unionist vote. Sinn Féin found virgin territory for organisation. They wasted no time building an election machine.

From 1982 every poll in the North would see two sets of elections: one for supremacy within unionism and one for supremacy within nationalism. The first test for the new republican machine came ten months after the Prior assembly elections in the form of the British general election of June 1983. The North's twelve constituencies, established at partition in 1921, had been increased to seventeen as a result of a deal done by Enoch Powell on behalf of the Ulster unionists to keep the Labour government in power for a couple of extra months in 1978.

Sinn Féin fought fifteen seats, including no-hopers like East Belfast, in order to maximise its vote. The SDLP had to fight all seventeen seats for the same reason. Both parties were prepared to lose deposits rather than reduce their total vote by even a few hundred. As it turned out, the SDLP needed every vote it could muster to stay ahead of Sinn Féin. The headline-grabbing result of the election was Gerry Adams's win in West Belfast, where he unseated the veteran Gerry Fitt. Despite the intervention of an SDLP candidate, Adams had a majority of 5,400. Next to that result was Danny Morrison's performance in Mid-Ulster where he came within seventy-eight votes of the DUP's Rev. Willie McCrea.

Overall, the Sinn Féin result marked another huge stride forward for the party. It polled 102,000 votes or 13.4% of the electorate. Though the SDLP also increased its vote from the assembly elections, its share of the vote slipped to 17.9%. Sinn Féin's support among northern nationalists had now jumped to 43%. It did not take a mathematical genius to calculate that at this rate Sinn Féin could overtake the SDLP by the end of the decade if there were no major political development to halt the republicans' onward march. Could taoiseach Garret FitzGerald convince Mrs Thatcher of the necessity for action in time?

In the North there was political stalemate. The polarisation caused by the hunger strike had, if anything, deepened with the arrival of Sinn Féin on the electoral scene. Unionists reacted with dismay to the fact that over 40% of nationalists supported a party that, in the words of a resolution at a Sinn Féin *ard fheis,* gave 'unambiguous support to the armed struggle'. There had also been a serious deterioration in the security situation after autumn 1982 when a series of incidents took place in which republicans had been shot dead by RUC men from a shadowy Special Branch unit called E4A. The men had all been unarmed and subsequent investigations showed that senior RUC officers had ordered a cover-up. Nationalist confidence in the organs of the State was further undermined.

There is no doubt that this growing disaffection helped Sinn Féin's electoral performance. Voting Sinn Féin was a protest vote. For young people in republican ghettos it was a way of hitting back at Mrs Thatcher, of expressing alienation. The alienation was not confined to the young. The British Army had been on the streets of nationalist districts since 1969. By 1982 there was not a man over thirty in republican areas who had not been humiliated by British soldiers in front of his wife, children or neighbours. Each policeman walking in a nationalist area needed an escort of eight soldiers, a recipe for continuing friction with a sullen population.

Sinn Féin strategists took full advantage of the resentful sentiments evoked by such a heavy military presence. When Mrs Thatcher told journalists in the run-up to the June 1983 general election that she would be very concerned at a strong vote for Sinn Féin, the party rushed out an election poster with the slogan, 'Give Mrs Thatcher a headache – Vote Sinn Féin'.

Being the darling of both governments did the SDLP no good at all, especially since the party's special relationship buttered no parsnips in nationalist areas. If the SDLP seemed to have reached a ceiling in electoral terms, Sinn Féin's northern leaders still had electoral ambitions, but their ambitions extended across the whole island. The amazing and satisfyingly rapid results of their electoral strategy in the North were not being repeated south of the border. The poor result in the February 1982 election had been a setback. What was wrong? What was different? What had to be changed?

First, the process of taking control from the old guard had to be completed. It was not enough to run Northern Command and, as a consequence, Sinn Féin in the North. The northern leaders needed to run the whole movement in order to implement their policies in the South. The policies were more than simply engaging in 'Active Republicanism'. Sinn Féin members had been pursuing this policy with some effect since the late 1970s in impoverished urban districts in the South. That kind of grassroots activity was fine for getting councillors elected and it had certainly borne fruit, particularly in Dublin. But what Adams and his supporters wanted was to get TDs elected. In the early 1980s there was no question of their taking seats. Simply to have one or two elected could have a powerful impact in the Republic's PR voting system, as the results in June 1981 had illustrated.

The northerners also believed that Sinn Féin's national policy document, *Éire Nua* (New Ireland), needed changing. They believed this was an indescribably stupid policy for a number of reasons. It proposed carving up the country into four provinces, partly so that unionists could have a powerful role in a nine-county Ulster. Each province would have a provincial assembly called a Dáil, which would have more power than Stormont. The Oireachtas would become the national parliament of a federal state. There were many other refinements dealing with community councils and reorganisation of cities, but to pragmatists in the movement it was a non-starter.

Such a policy might have its theoretical merits, and its authors, Ó Brádaigh and Ó Conaill, set great store by it as a means of persuading unionists of Sinn Féin's concern for their welfare in a united federal Ireland, but it is doubtful if a single unionist ever read it. *Éire Nua* was all very well if the party were not fighting elections and trying to get people to vote for its candidates. If Sinn Féin were to fight elections, *Éire Nua* was a hopeless basis on which to canvass support. How could Sinn Féin candidates – people who were going to abstain from the Dáil – persuade people to vote to dismantle the State? Surely the first priority was to negotiate British withdrawal from the North? Would the Irish government be included in the negotiations for British withdrawal? How, at the same time, could the Irish government be asked to hand over three counties to a new provincial assembly of Ulster? How could a couple of abstentionist TDs persuade an Irish government to support Sinn Féin's *Éire Nua* policy in any negotiations? It was preposterous.

There were even simpler objections. Northerners had always detested the policy. Jim Gibney remembers 'vehement [his emphasis] opposition to it among internees' when Sinn Féin adopted *Éire Nua* in 1972. They were also opposed to federalism. Gibney says:

> It looked to us as if it was being claimed that it was OK for the Unionists to run a nine-county provincial parliament. Our feeling was: 'Hold on a minute, these people have abused us for years. That plan would just give them more power to abuse more people.' So there was a very strong hostility to that policy among [northern] republicans.

As soon as they had the strength and had prepared the ground, Adams and his supporters dumped *Éire Nua* at the 1982 *ard fheis*. Still, they did not get the two-thirds majority needed to remove it from the party constitution, an indication that the northerners would not find it easy to make far-reaching changes quickly. The attack on *Éire Nua* was a sore point with Ruairí Ó Brádaigh and something he never accepted. The policy was his pet scheme. He says he felt so strongly about its rejection that in 1983 he handed over the leadership of Sinn Féin to Gerry Adams:

> This is terribly important to us, and that's the reason people like myself and Ó Conaill stepped down from the leadership in '83 after *Éire Nua* was thrown out because we thought it was going to make the task so much harder if you back the unionists politically onto a cliff edge. We [Republican Sinn Féin] don't believe in a steamrollering unitary state.

By the time Ó Brádaigh 'stepped down' from the leadership in 1983 he had no choice. The northerners were in the majority: they controlled the *ard fheis*. Patricia Davidson says that by the late 1970s northern delegates made up half the hall at *ard fheiseanna*. By 1983, with the surge in membership after the hunger strike and the election successes, northern *cumainn* were in a comfortable majority.

The National H-Block/Armagh Committees had strengthened northerners in their conviction that there was urgent need for change. Travelling around the country in 1981 and 1982, canvassing and speaking at meetings, the new leaders from the North had learnt that their ideas about the south and Sinn Féin's position there were completely wrong. Danny Morrison had noticed it even earlier when, while on the run in 1978, he spent time in the south. He had imagined Sinn Féin in the South were well organised politically. After all, the party there always had twenty or so councillors, including county councillors. On one occasion he suggested to Ruairí Ó Brádaigh that they should attend a protest meeting against building a nuclear plant at Carnsore Point, County Wexford:

> So we went to it. I'm in the audience. Ruairí gets up to speak. He's booed. Right? People either cough over him or boo. To me it was an eye-opener that we were not in touch with people. I thought we were. Because I remember the Dublin government refused to celebrate the sixtieth anniversary of 1916. So Sinn Féin organised it in Dublin. So you had April 1976, like 50,000 people on O'Connell Street. Of course from the North you were completely misreading it. You were saying, 'We've tonnes of support down there.' Now the thing is there was more support for the IRA. Right? I was at meetings in Fine Gaelers' houses. People who were putting up republicans on the run. A Fine Gael councillor. I actually stayed in his house. So the point I'm making is, I was misreading the degree of support.

When the leadership analysed the reasons the party was confined to certain areas of traditional support in the Republic and doing so badly in general elections, they came up with a number of answers. Jim Gibney, one of the strategists close to Gerry Adams and by 1982 Sinn Féin's national organiser in touch with all levels of the party, was in an ideal position to see the party's problems in the South:

> Federalism had a part to play, the North–South divide had a part to play and the generation gap [in the movement] had a part to play. But more importantly, in all of that, I think, was the ideological issue of how to build a political party on this island as a whole when the institutions of State in the major part of the island are being ignored. That was the thought that came crashing in after the elections in the North with Bobby Sands's success and after the local government elections with people in the system. At the same time, they were refusing to participate in the system in the South which was regarded as barren territory. People began to say, 'No, no, that's not right.' We have to accept that the mass of people view the southern institutions as legitimate. Whatever we might think about them, we have to change our approach if we want to build across the island as a whole. I think the core of the problem is the policy of abstention. That's the primary issue.

Clearly Adams and the men around him – Martin McGuinness, Danny Morrison, Tom Hartley, Jim Gibney, Joe Austin and Richard McAuley – had by 1982 formed the opinion that abstention in the South had to go. How to do it? It had split the republican movement in 1969 and had been the major reason for the Provisional movement coming into existence. Could it be done without splitting the movement again? It was another four years before Adams and his group felt strong enough to make the decisive move.

Although Adams, and those who thought like him, controlled both the IRA and Sinn Féin by 1982, their dominance in the movement was based on the successful marriage of the Armalite and ballot box. It had worked well in the North, but even so, there was discontent in the IRA about the direction policy was taking. Sinn Féin was assuming an ever larger role in the movement and consuming more and more money and time. IRA men were being used to pack Sinn Féin meetings to ensure the new policy was implemented and in case older republicans, who tended to dominate Sinn Féin *cumainn,* objected to the republican movement's developing political involvement.

Several of the IRA men sent to see that the leadership's policy was endorsed had never been at a Sinn Féin meeting prior to 1982. Inevitably, the feeling grew that the IRA should be carrying out attacks on the British Army instead of spending time at Sinn Féin meetings, that the IRA was being reined in for fear that 'bad operations', that is, ones in which civilians were injured or killed, might prejudice Sinn Féin's electoral prospects. Danny Morrison admits this was an issue:

> I wanted to reassure people that you could have an armed struggle and electoral strategy running parallel, although in my heart I knew there was a ceiling because people were not going to support bad IRA operations where civilians were killed, whereas they might have an OK attitude towards soldiers being attacked. Or, even if they didn't have an OK attitude, they didn't see it as interfering with them voting Sinn Féin because they could clearly distinguish in their minds between Sinn Féin and the IRA.

The successful marriage of the Armalite and ballot box was therefore not simply a matter of winning elections. The question arose: which was more important in the last analysis, the Armalite or the ballot box? For the IRA the answer was clear, but some senior figures were concerned that the required clarity was not forthcoming from the leadership. Would the IRA's military campaign always have to be tailored to suit the next election campaign?

Gerry Adams's response to this concern was to ask the IRA to give his strategy a try for a couple of years from 1983. As the MP for West Belfast, an IRA leader and the man who had devised the strategy that brought Sinn Féin over 100,000 votes in the North, he could hardly be refused.

His strategy was to fight all elections in Ireland. In 1983 he could not disclose beyond a few close associates that it was also intended that Sinn Féin should take any seats won in the Republic.

There were several reasons for going completely political in the South, all of them compelling. Firstly, as Gibney, Morrison and others, including Adams, certainly appreciated, people in the Republic supported the institutions of the State and did not see the point in voting for abstentionists. Secondly, even one elected TD could have the potential of holding the balance of power in the Dáil. The Provisionals' great rivals, the Official Republican Movement, had shown what could be done when their political wing, Sinn Féin the Workers Party, succeeded in getting Joe Sherlock elected to the Dáil in June 1981. In turn, Sherlock had helped elect Garret FitzGerald as taoiseach. Thirdly, the republican movement was seriously lopsided by the early 1980s in that the IRA campaign was obviously restricted to Northern Ireland and England, and Sinn Féin's electoral support was mainly in the North too. The republican movement was also led by men from the North. With no electoral presence to speak of in the bulk of the island, how could it claim to be a national movement? How could it claim to represent the Irish people without sounding absurd? How could it have any influence on the Irish government? Fourthly, Sinn Féin had to demonstrate that it was not a one-issue party, a movement that simply harped on about the constitutional issue. That was of no importance to the majority of people in the South. Campaigning on the basis of 'Brits out' in Ballymun or Waterford was a nonsense and the northern leaders knew it. They had to develop social and economic policies relevant to the voters in southern constituencies and get elected on those policies.

Taken together, all these reasons required radical shifts in republican ideology, the most important of which was abolishing the abstention policy. Even to set foot on that road was difficult because the Sinn Féin constitution banned discussion of the issue of abstention at *ard fheiseanna*.

At the 1983 *ard fheis* where he became Sinn Féin president, Adams took the first step on the road to full electoral participation. The party constitution was changed so that 'no aspect of the constitution and rules be closed to discussion'. This was ostensibly to enable a motion to be discussed that would allow Sinn Féin candidates in the 1984 European elections to take their seats in the European Parliament; obviously there was no objection to the European Parliament's legitimacy despite the fact that the party opposed the EC. Everyone knew Sinn Féin had no chance of winning a European seat. In reality, the resolution opened the way to discussing abolishing abstention from the Dáil at the next *ard fheis*.

In his acceptance speech as Sinn Féin president on 13 November 1983, Adams set out to reassure delegates. He told them that Sinn Féin's attitude to armed struggle is that it 'is a necessary and morally correct form of resistance in the Six Counties against a government whose presence is rejected by the vast majority of the Irish people.' He also told the *ard fheis*: 'We are an abstentionist party. It is not my intention to advocate change in this situation.'

Others in the movement knew different. In the North, and in Belfast especially where IRA men regularly drank together in republican shebeens and GAA clubs, the rumour mill was grinding at full speed, producing conspiracy theories about the leadership's intentions. The belief grew within the IRA that military activity was being deliberately reduced. In 1983 there were fewer killings – eighty-seven – than in any year of the Troubles until then; in 1984 there were seventy-one. Adams was nearly numbered among the dead himself when in March of that year a loyalist murder gang riddled his car with bullets, wounding him and three other occupants of the car. The driver, Bob Murray, was unhurt and kept driving to the hospital on the Falls Road where he deposited his injured passengers. The body armour Adams was wearing saved his life. The murder attempt did not deflect him from his electoral policy, but the criticism from his more militarist colleagues did slow his progress. There were rumblings about the need to call an army convention to discuss the current state of the movement.

It was not until the 1985 *ard fheis* that Adams and his colleagues felt secure enough to make their next move. Earlier in the year they had seen off a strong challenge in Belfast from important IRA men, including Ivor Bell. Bell was a former Belfast brigade commander, former member of Northern Command, former member of the Army Council and one of the delegation that had met Willie Whitelaw in London in 1972, a delegation that included Gerry Adams and Martin McGuinness. In March 1985, Bell and three others were expelled from the IRA for 'factionalism'. Northern Command threatened to execute them if they tried to form a new organisation. One of those expelled had been the adjutant of the Belfast brigade until 1984.

Matters had come to a head when the four had used their influence to prevent the IRA donating a large sum, believed to run to six figures, to Sinn Féin's election campaign for the local elections in May 1985. As a result, the party had to reduce the number of candidates it had planned to field. Those expelled had been foremost in complaining about the reduction in IRA operations and the sidelining of veterans like themselves. Despite the draconian measures the IRA took against them, others joined them in leaving the movement. One of them was Bob Murray, Sinn Féin's finance officer in Belfast and the man who, the previous year, had been driving Adams's car when it had come under attack.

The departure of such important IRA figures could not be ignored. After the elections in May 1985 there were some concessions to satisfy the objections they had made about a slackening of the military campaign. IRA operations rose significantly in the summer, so that by the end of the year *Republican News* could boast that in 1985 the IRA had used the largest tonnage of explosives of any year of its campaign. To some extent, therefore, it was possible to answer the criticisms from the military wing at the 1985 *ard fheis,* though not to silence them completely. Equally important, the northern council elections had been a success for Sinn Féin despite the IRA faction's attempted financial sabotage. The leadership could claim, with some justification, that the Armalite and the ballot box were still happily wedded.

The 1985 elections had been another crucial step in Sinn Féin's electoral progress. They were the party's first run out in local government in the North, therefore the republican leadership had been anxious to do well. Sinn Féin had put its toe in the water in a number of carefully engineered by-elections in 1983 and 1984 and had found the water enticing. In 1985 the *ard comhairle* modestly predicted about forty seats for the party, knowing full well that that would have been a disastrous result. But Sinn Féin had learnt to understate its electoral predictions so that when the actual result emerged it looked as if the party had done better than anyone expected. The fifty-nine seats it won reaffirmed Sinn Féin as a force to be reckoned with in northern politics.

Sinn Féin's appearance in the North's council chambers completed a cycle. The party had now fought elections in 1982, 1983, 1984 and 1985 at local government, regional assembly, Westminster and European levels. The share of the vote was holding up at around 12%, and Sinn Féin could claim to represent about one-third of northern nationalists. In the South, however, the party had difficulty raising the share of the vote to 2%. It seemed legitimate to ask whether abstention was not the main reason for this poor showing. Resolutions proposing the removal of the clause were entered on the *Clár* for the 1985 *ard fheis*.

It was a clever move. There was deliberately no push for change from the leadership. Adams did not speak on the motion, but many of his close associates did: Richard McAuley, Tom Hartley and Danny Morrison. They hammered away at abstention as a tactical position rather than as a matter of principle. They claimed that boycotting Stormont elections had also been merely a tactic, but that standing in 1982 had prevented the SDLP from entering Prior's assembly. Tom Hartley told the *ard fheis* that the only principle that mattered was 'the principle of success'. The motion was defeated by twenty votes. The whole exercise was a useful dress rehearsal. During 1985 the leadership had discovered the extent of opposition within the IRA and had decided how to deal with it. The debate at the *ard fheis* showed the northerners what the strength of the opposition was in Sinn Féin and where it was coming from. It showed them what needed to be done to defeat the opposition in the following *ard fheis*. They set to work on that task immediately.

Some have argued that the timing of the move to abolish abstention in 1986 was as a result of the Anglo-Irish Agreement in November 1985 and the subsequent dip in Sinn Féin's vote in the North in Westminster by-elections. It has even been suggested that Gerry Adams became convinced by the Anglo-Irish Agreement of the need for political involvement. Nothing could be further from the truth.

The Agreement was signed on 15 November 1985 at Hillsborough, the official residence of Britain's northern secretary, amid cries of outrage from unionists milling around outside the gates. It was the fruit of the work Garret FitzGerald and the tireless Irish officials from Foreign Affairs had put in with the British since 1984. The terms gave the Irish government a consultative role in Britain's northern policy, inaugurated regular meetings of an intergovernmental conference and established a full-time secretariat based near Belfast that was manned by Irish and British officials twenty-four hours a day. Certainly the furious unionist reaction helped make the Agreement seem more radical than it was, but it had no effect on the ground. From the outset, the British began to frustrate the Agreement's terms. For example, one of the Irish government's priorities was to keep the British Army and the UDR from contact with the nationalist population because the evidence was that contact provided one of the major causes of alienation of that population. All military patrols were to be accompanied by police. This provision was never implemented. All kinds of mendacious excuses were offered by the British, but until the removal of British troops from most streets of the North in 1997, the army and UDR patrolled as they pleased despite thousands of complaints from the Irish. This feature was the most obvious way in which the British government and NIO (Northern Ireland Office) avoided honouring the Agreement.

In the short term however, the Anglo-Irish Agreement provided a huge boost for nationalist morale, again partly because of unionist over-reaction. The major political response from unionists was the decision to resign their seats at Westminster as a way to engineer a 'mini-referendum' on the Agreement in the North. Their resignations forced fifteen by-elections in January 1986. The results were trumpeted by both the Irish and British government as evidence that the Agreement was reducing support for Sinn Féin. Sinn Féin was indeed in some difficulty about how to respond to the Agreement. It did object that it copper-fastened partition, but it could hardly present root and branch objections to something that drove unionists apoplectic.

Both the SDLP and Sinn Féin were anxious to avoid giving unionists their referendum and therefore fought only four selected seats where there was a chance of defeating a unionist. The only nationalist success was in Newry–Armagh where Seamus Mallon, deputy leader of the SDLP, defeated the unionist candidate despite Sinn Féin splitting the vote.

In two of the other three seats, Mid-Ulster and Fermanagh–Tyrone South, Sinn Féin defeated the SDLP. The successful result in Newry–Armagh was classic tribal tactical voting. Many Sinn Féin supporters decided that Seamus Mallon was the only man to beat the unionist and voted for him. They continued to do so in each election until 2001. The issue was nothing to do with support for the Anglo-Irish Agreement. Both governments, however, blithely ignored the difference between contesting fifteen seats and four and announced that Sinn Féin's share of the vote had halved.

None of this had anything to do with the Sinn Féin leadership's plans to end abstention in the Republic, which they had been working on for at least four years by 1986. By the time of the *ard fheis* in November 1986 the years of preparation were complete. The scene was set. The northern leaders had placated IRA opponents. There had been personnel changes in the Belfast brigade. Southerners had been assured that there was no intention of parachuting in northern celebrities to contest Dáil seats. Party organisers had been dispatched around the country to sell the proposal to end abstention in the South. Finally came the signal that made the northern leaders believe they were going to be successful: a general army convention, the first the Provisional IRA had ever called, was convened on 20 September near Navan.

On 14 October the IRA issued a statement to volunteers reporting on the convention. The statement included the following:

> Several sections of the constitution of Óglaigh na hÉireann were amended and, by more than the required two-thirds majority, the delegates passed two particular resolutions. The first removed the ban on Volunteers discussing or advocating the taking of seats. The second removed the ban on supporting successful republican candidates who take their seats in Leinster House.

Following this decision two conclusions were clear. The ensuing Sinn Féin *ard fheis* would pass similar resolutions on its *Clár,* and secondly, of critical importance, delegates at the Sinn Féin *ard fheis* would know there would be no split in the IRA. When the *ard fheis* met on 1 November in its usual venue, the Mansion House in Dublin, the debate on ending abstention was therefore a piece of theatre, the outcome of which everyone knew in advance. Gerry Adams and Martin McGuinness, the undisputed leaders of the republican movement, knew they were going to get their two-thirds majority and Ruairí Ó Brádaigh and Dáithí Ó Conaill, the leaders of the old guard, knew they were going to lose.

Ó Brádaigh failed to rise to the occasion. He made a poor speech full of procedural gobbledegook. His performance was no match for the most powerful speech of the debate. That came from Martin McGuinness, important in itself because of his steely militarist commitment, known and respected by all the delegates. McGuinness went straight to the heart of the issue:

> We are not at war with the government of the twenty-six counties – the reality of this fact must be recognised by us all. And, in accepting this reality, we must also accept that after sixty-five years of republican struggle, republican agitation, republican sacrifice and republican rhetoric, we have failed to convince a majority in the twenty-six counties that the republican movement has any relevance to them. By ignoring reality we remain alone and isolated on the high altar of abstentionism, divorced from the people of the twenty-six counties and easily dealt with by those who wish to defeat us.

In pressing his case he went on to make points which continue to be used against him inside and outside the republican movement to this day.

> Sadly, the inference that the removal of abstentionism would lead to the demise of military opposition to British rule has indeed called into question the commitment of the IRA to pursue the struggle to a successful conclusion. I reject any such suggestion and I reject the notion that entering Leinster House would mean an end to Sinn Féin's unapologetic support for the right of Irish people to oppose in arms the British forces of occupation. That, my friends, is a principle which a minority in this hall might doubt, but which I believe all of our opponents clearly understand. Our position is clear and it will never, never, never change. The war against British rule must continue until freedom is achieved.

McGuinness concluded by appealing to delegates not to support the walk-out he knew was planned. He told the *ard fheis* that the IRA, even though some of the volunteers disagreed with ending abstention, 'will not split, they will not walk away from the armed struggle. If you allow yourself to be led out of this hall today, the only place you are going is home. You will be walking away from the struggle. Don't go, my friends. We will lead you to the Republic.'

The resolution was carried by the required majority and, on cue, just as he had done sixteen years before, Ruairí Ó Brádaigh led about twenty supporters out of the *ard fheis* to a pre-arranged meeting in the West County hotel, Chapelizod, where they established Republican Sinn Féin. History did not repeat itself. This time it was a small, forlorn group, mostly middle-aged and elderly lifelong republicans, who followed Ó Brádaigh. This time there was no surge of young activists as there had been in 1970 after Provisional Sinn Féin was founded. The spotlight remained tightly focused on the existing republican movement led by its MP, five northern assembly members, fifty-nine councillors in the North, thirty-nine in the south and an unknown number of IRA volunteers who constituted, as Martin McGuinness told the *ard fheis,* 'the most dangerous and committed revolutionary force in Ireland for sixty-five years.'

Back in the Mansion House, Gerry Adams and Martin McGuinness stood as the unchallenged leaders of republicanism, political and military, in Ireland. Together they commanded the loyalty of the IRA and Sinn Féin. They had achieved what previous republican leaders, including de Valera, had failed to do and many people in Ireland had thought impossible. They had managed to persuade the IRA to support Sinn Féin in fighting elections in a state they did not recognise, Northern Ireland, and to agree to Sinn Féin TDs taking seats in a parliament whose legitimacy they did not accept, the Dáil. They did it by showing that Sinn Féin could win elections while the IRA continued its military campaign in the North and by claiming politics represented no threat to the IRA.

How would they use the unprecedented power this achievement had given them? Would they choose to make peace or war, to build or to destroy?

10. 'TOWARDS A STRATEGY FOR PEACE'

Sinn Féin No Longer Alone

Under the leadership of Gerry Adams and Martin McGuinness, Sinn Féin had broken the republican movement's greatest taboo, what Jim Gibney had called its 'millstone': abstentionism. One of the main reasons for being able to achieve this feat, which had eluded every Sinn Féin leader since de Valera, was the fact that repeated success for Sinn Féin in northern elections between 1982 and 1985 was accompanied by a resolute and vocal commitment to the use of armed force. The two had to operate in tandem to show that electoralism did not mean ending the armed struggle. Indeed, the price paid to the militarists in the movement for acquiescing in the removal of abstention was an increase in the number of bomb attacks from the summer of 1986.

However, it is now clear that while the end of abstention did mark a decisive break from the past, it represented only one stage in the development of the movement. It is impossible to ascertain precisely when Gerry Adams came to the conclusion that abandoning the republican movement's commitment to political abstentionism could advance the movement's goals faster than the continued use of military violence. What is certain is that Gerry Adams and Martin McGuinness remained convinced in the mid-1980s that while force alone would not drive the British out of Ireland, only force could bring the British to the negotiating table. It took a long time to persuade these men, and even longer to coax the pure militarists in the IRA who disagreed with them, that the movement could succeed in its aims by the use of violence – but without actual armed struggle – against the British forces. In the years immediately after 1986 such persuasion proved impossible.

Faced on one side with the virulent opposition of unionists to the Anglo-Irish Agreement and their refusal even to meet the British ministers running the NIO, and on the other side confronted with the continuation of republican violence, Margaret Thatcher set her face against what she saw as more 'concessions' to nationalism. She had assumed that the Anglo-Irish Agreement would bring measurable improvements in the security situation. When it demonstrably failed to do so, she authorised, from 1987 on, an ever increasing number of ambushes by British special forces, mainly the SAS and 14 Intelligence Company. The result was a large number of IRA members shot dead, often in disputed circumstances.

Against this background, and alongside poor results in elections in 1987, it proved difficult for the handful of people in the republican movement who had advocated change to show that electoralism was taking the movement anywhere. To suggest running down 'the armed struggle' in these circumstances was unthinkable. Nevertheless, in the years between 1986 and 1992 this group would become the leaders of the republican movement and would bring about a series of changes in republican thinking just as radical, though not as dramatic in the short term, as ending abstention. As a result of these changes Sinn Féin moved from being political pariahs – after 1988 banned from the airwaves in Britain as well as in Ireland and shunned by all political parties – to a point where, in the early 1990s, its leaders were involved in talks with British and Irish officials, with John Hume, the leader of the rival SDLP, and with other influential figures in politics and religion. How did such a sea change come about?

In the immediate aftermath of the successful *ard fheis* in 1986, Sinn Féin threw itself into the Republic's general election of 19 February 1987. The results were dreadful: the party polled 1.7% of the vote. Of course, the figure looks much worse than it was in purely statistical terms because Sinn Féin stood candidates only in selected constituencies, and therefore to talk about a share of the vote in the whole State does not have much relevance. Nevertheless, Sinn Féin had exerted a major effort. The party had stood in twenty-nine constituencies, but there was no kind of break-through. Far from it. Sinn Féin lost over twenty deposits. There were no redeeming features. Abandoning abstention had made no difference whatsoever to the party's performance in the Republic. In its defence it was easy to argue that there had been no time to acquaint the electorate with Sinn Féin's new policy between the momentous decision in November 1986 to recognise Leinster House and the general election in February 1987. All the same, it was a blow.

What could not be so easily argued away was Sinn Féin's perform-ance in the British general election in June 1987. Confident in its dra-matic breakthrough in the 1983 general election and the good results in the 1985 local government elections, Sinn Féin fielded candidates in all but three of the North's seventeen constituencies. Its vote fell from 102,000 in 1983 to 83,000 (13.4% to 11.4%). The one bright spot was Gerry Adams's performance in West Belfast where, in a reduced turnout, he increased his vote slightly. Even so, while it encouraged the party faith-ful, a sober analysis could not disguise that West Belfast too was a disap-pointing showing because Adams made no inroads into the SDLP vote.

It was a similar story elsewhere across the North. Sinn Féin made no gains. The SDLP's share of the vote rose by 3% to 154,000 – the party's highest ever vote to that date and all the more telling since the overall turnout was down by 6%. The SDLP won another Westminster seat, bringing their total to three, when Eddie McGrady defeated Ulster Unionism's political guru, Enoch Powell, in South Down. It was the highest number of Westminster seats nationalists had held since partition. North and South, Sinn Féin's electoral strategy seemed to have run into the sand.

The other component of republican strategy – the armed struggle – also suffered serious setbacks in 1987. On 8 May, a few weeks before the British general election, an IRA 'crack unit' based in east Tyrone, a group of men responsible for many murders and explosions, was shot to pieces in an SAS ambush at Loughgall, County Armagh, as they attempted to destroy an RUC barracks. All eight men in the unit were killed, mown down in a blizzard of machine-gun fire along with an innocent civilian who drove into the ambush. It was the greatest loss of life sustained by the IRA in one incident in the period between 1970 and the ceasefire in 1997, and indeed the largest loss of life the movement had suffered since 1921.

Loss of personnel was not the only setback that hit the IRA in 1987. In October, French customs officials intercepted a freighter, the *Eksund*, which proved to be transporting tonnes of munitions from Libya to the IRA. The celebrations of the British security services were short-lived, however, when it became known that the skipper of the vessel was in fact on his fifth trip, having already delivered to Ireland, since August 1985, about 150 tonnes of weaponry, including hundreds of AK-47 rifles, pistols, heavy machine-guns, flame-throwers, rocket launchers and surface-to-air missiles. Most important of all, the Libyan cargoes had also supplied the IRA with tonnes of Semtex plastic high explosive, which is virtually undetectable as it is odourless and so malleable that it can be cut up and hidden to look like cheese in sandwiches. The revelation that the IRA had such an arsenal threw into perspective the 'Armalite and ballot box' strategy. It was clear now to both the British and the Irish government that the republican movement was in a position to prosecute its 'Long War' indefinitely.

The concept of the 'Long War' was yet another strategy developed in prison in the 1970s and gradually put into practice by the IRA in the early 1980s. Put simply, it meant the IRA had accepted that they could not drive the British out of the North by mobilising the whole nationalist community, taking on the British Army and winning. The frenzy of the early 1970s was over. The sort of turmoil at the height of the Troubles when, in 1972 for example, there were over 10,000 shooting incidents and 100 killed in the month of July alone, could not be sustained. The IRA realised that they did not have to 'bomb everywhere', as one of their Belfast leaders said. The purpose of IRA violence would not be to defeat the British. Instead, they would choose targets tactically and for maximum public effect, for what Gerry Adams in his 1986 book, *The Politics of Irish Freedom*, called 'armed propaganda'. It would be a war of attrition, with the IRA picking the targets. Ultimately they believed, as Martin McGuinness said, that they could 'sicken the British'. Instead of driving the British out, they would bring them to the negotiating table. The Libyan arsenal gave the IRA the military wherewithal. The votes of northern nationalists gave Sinn Féin and the republican movement the political clout. All it would take was time.

That was the theory. But in 1987 it was not working out too well in practice. Certainly there had been major 'successes' for 'armed propaganda', such as the killing in April of Lord Justice Gibson, second in seniority to the North's Lord Chief Justice. He and his wife were driving north from Dublin, returning from a holiday, when a 500lb bomb killed them instantly in the no-man's-land between the border and an RUC escort waiting for their car on the northern side. But the problem with 'armed propaganda' is that it is a two-edged sword. Violence cannot be controlled. Politicians regularly make mistakes, but they do not kill anyone by mistake. The IRA did so regularly in what Danny Morrison referred to euphemistically as 'bad operations'. There was nothing new about these occasions. 'Bad operations' had been commonplace in the 1970s: innocent bystanders cut down by flying glass, children killed in crossfire, people murdered in cases of mistaken identity. In the 1970s the IRA would simply issue a statement, often blaming the security forces for not clearing the area where a bomb was planted, or, to the fury of relatives, offer an apology.

By the 1980s it was different. The ballot box meant there were public faces fronting the republican movement. It was very damaging for the elected representatives of Sinn Féin, a party that gave 'unambiguous support to the armed struggle', to have to go on TV and justify some atrocity in which civilians had been slaughtered. As soon as such an event happened, the media would pursue Sinn Féin representatives to inquire persistently if they condemned the outrage. The first major backlash had been in 1983 when a 30lb IRA bomb exploded outside Harrods in London the week before Christmas. The blast killed six people and injured 100 others, including fourteen police officers.

Under enormous media pressure, both Adams, by then an MP, and McGuinness had to qualify the IRA action at Harrods, saying that the IRA had not set out to cause casualties and that 'all ASUs [Active Service Units] in Britain as in Ireland are aware of the need to avoid civilian casualties'. In a lengthy statement the IRA said 'the Army Council did not authorise the specific operation at Harrods', as if that made some difference.

The reaction to the Harrods bomb in 1983 was as nothing compared to the international contumely heaped on the republican movement in 1987 after the IRA's most disastrous atrocity, the Enniskillen bomb. On 8 November a 40lb IRA bomb exploded in a community hall behind the footpath where people gathered on Remembrance Sunday for the annual Poppy Day parade in Enniskillen. The blast killed eleven people at the time, five of them women, and one other victim who remained in a coma for thirteen years until he died in 2000. Sixty-three people were injured, nineteen of them seriously.

Fermanagh's Sinn Féin councillors wilted under a storm of public outrage. The next day the IRA issued a statement expressing 'deep regret'. They then tried to excuse the slaughter with a lie, saying that the device had been accidentally detonated by British Army electronic counter-measures. It was not until 1995 that the IRA admitted that the unit which planted the bomb had used a simple preset timer that was designed to explode the bomb earlier in the morning when police and soldiers would have been carrying out a security sweep of the area. When it failed to go off on time, the unit gave no warning to the public and callously allowed the bomb to explode. The IRA had killed eleven Protestant civilians who had gathered on Remembrance Day for a quasi-religious service. There could not have been a worse sectarian terrorist message to flash around the world.

What made the atrocity even more damaging for republicans was the reaction of one of the survivors, Gordon Wilson, who recounted on television how he had tried to comfort his daughter, Marie, a nurse, as they both lay trapped under several feet of rubble. They could speak to each other, but they could not move. Marie died in great pain as father and daughter held hands. Gordon Wilson told how he had prayed for the people who had murdered his daughter. A devout Methodist, his response of Christian charity to his daughter's death in the Enniskillen bombing was profoundly moving to the public in both Ireland and Britain.

Republicans knew they were in trouble. One senior IRA man told the press shortly afterwards:

Politically and internationally it is a major setback. Our support is in concentric rings. The centre is the republican movement, the next is the nationalist community in the North, followed by the people in the South, then solidarity groups, left groups and finally international sympathy. Our central base can take a hell of a lot of jolting and crises, with limited demoralisation. But the outer reaches are just totally devastated. It will hurt us really badly in the Republic more than anywhere else. We were trying to convince people there that what's happening in the North is a legitimate armed struggle. But the obloquy we've attracted cuts the ground from under us. It allows the Brits to slot us into the category of terrorists. This is probably the worst year the IRA has had for five years.

Gerry Adams's response was along similar lines:

What is clear is that our efforts to broaden our base have most certainly been upset in all the areas we have selected for expansion. This is particularly true for the South and internationally. Our plans for expansion have been dealt a body blow.

How right he was. The following week the South almost came to a standstill for a minute's silence in what was virtually an act of atonement for what had happened in Enniskillen. During the minute's silence RTÉ showed a silent screen with a white dove of peace. Outside the Mansion House in Dublin an estimated 50,000 people queued to sign the book of condolence made available by Dublin Corporation. Dublin's lord mayor took the book personally to Enniskillen.

The stark fact was that as long as armed struggle continued, such incidents were bound to occur. It was not just that Sinn Féin did not control the IRA – it did not – but that in a violent campaign 'mistakes' would always occur and such mistakes tended to be fatal. Senior Sinn Féin leaders like Adams and McGuinness, the party's president and vice-president, obviously realised how damaging disasters like Enniskillen were. In fact,

Adams said the movement could not take another Enniskillen. Though either Adams or McGuinness, and sometimes both, were usually members of the IRA Army Council, it made no difference. Even taking personal command of every single IRA operation, a completely impossible idea, would not prevent fatal errors. It is the nature of violence. All Adams could do was to publicly urge members of the IRA 'to be careful and careful again' when carrying out operations because it was inconceivable in 1987 to propose ending the military campaign.

The truth is that Gerry Adams and Martin McGuinness, like the rest of the republican leadership, believed that without violence the British would not listen to them. At the same time Adams, in particular, was acutely aware how atrocities damaged the republican project and isolated the movement. In response he sought ways not to end the violent campaign but to run it down, to control it more tightly, using the IRA as a threat, a tactic, while pushing Sinn Féin to the fore with demands for political negotiations.

The aim of the republican leadership from the time Adams and McGuinness took complete control in November 1986 was to get into talks with the British without calling a ceasefire. The northern-dominated leadership believed a ceasefire had been a calamitous line of action on the previous occasion in 1975, so debilitating to the movement that it had been one of the main reasons they had ousted Ruairí Ó Brádaigh and Dáithí Ó Conaill from the leadership.

Adams set out his stall in 1986 in *The Politics of Irish Freedom*. Armed struggle, he wrote, was of 'primary importance'. It was 'the cutting edge'. He asserted that it was the only way to make the British pay any attention to Ireland: without it, Ireland would not even be an issue. He claimed armed struggle had been an agent of change. He reiterated the republican view that if it had not been for the campaign of violence the Anglo-Irish Agreement would never have happened. The Agreement was unsatisfactory and Sinn Féin opposed it, but it would never have come about without violence. Sinn Féin also took credit for the abolition of Stormont in 1972 and the frustration of all subsequent attempts at an internal settlement. However, Adams was at pains to point out in his book that armed struggle was 'a tactic'. He wrote that 'armed struggle on its own is inadequate and that non-armed forms of political struggle are at least as important'. In short, he appeared to be presenting simply a more verbose version of Danny Morrison's 'Armalite and ballot box' soundbite.

Closer inspection, however, revealed a lot more to Adams's argument. Naturally, in the run-up to the 1986 *ard fheis* with the crucial motion on abstention coming up, Adams was careful in his book to follow the orthodox republican line on the use of armed force. It was especially important for him to do so because one of the arguments of his opponents within Sinn Féin and the IRA was that abandoning abstention and participating in elected assemblies always resulted in abandoning armed force shortly thereafter. Adams could give no inkling of relinquishing republicans' traditional belief in the right of Irish people to use force to drive out the British. But Adams had nonetheless downgraded armed struggle to 'a tactic'. Conceivably, tactics could change. Different emphasis could be placed on different tactics. He had said other forms of non-armed struggle were on a par with the use of force. He had also pointed to the need to broaden the base of support for republicans. Since one of the main reasons republicans found it difficult to widen their 'base', as they call it, was the use of force, the implication was that force needed, at the very least, to be used selectively.

The opportunity to develop such ideas came early in 1987 after the old guard had walked out of the 1986 *ard fheis* and established their own organisation. With the *Éire Nua* policy dumped, and no serious opposition to the northerners' political analysis, it was time for Adams and his entourage to produce their own policy statement. Entitled *A Scenario for*

Peace, it emerged in May 1987 to act as Sinn Féin's election manifesto for the following month's British general election. On the face of it, the eight-page document offered nothing new. Much of it was a restatement of the traditional republican position that partition was the cause of the trouble in the North, that Britain, a foreign power, was responsible for that state of affairs and that all would be well when the British left because they had no right to be in Ireland. The first step, therefore, should be a British government statement of intent to withdraw from Ireland. In 1972 the IRA had told the northern secretary, Willie Whitelaw, in a meeting in London, that the British should leave Ireland within three years. The 1987 Sinn Féin manifesto asked that the British complete their withdrawal 'within the lifetime of a British Government', that is, five years. So essentially what had changed in the 1987 manifesto?

First the word 'peace' was used repeatedly. It was in the title of the document and occurred in various contexts throughout. Republicans were looking for negotiations in which Sinn Féin would present the movement's position. They did not envisage a military victory. Secondly, and the most important departure, was acknowledgement that unionists existed. Hitherto republicans saw no role for unionists, whom they regarded as the dupes of the British. When the British left, everything would be fine because unionists would realise they are Irish and settle down just as southern unionists had done after 1921. Now, in *A Scenario for Peace*, Sinn Féin tried for the first time to address unionist fears. It was a pretty ham-fisted effort, as party spokesmen would admit today, but it was a beginning. Sinn Féin told unionists that they did not wish to dispossess them or 'foolishly attempt to reverse the Plantation ... We offer them peace. We offer them equality.' What Sinn Féin meant by equality, of course, was that unionists had to accept they were Irish, in the words of the document, 'throwing in their lot with the rest of the Irish people and ending sectarianism'. Unfortunately, in an unwitting illustration of how far Sinn Féin thinking was from reality, the document negated the good impression republicans intended to make on unionists by including what republicans considered the generous offer that: 'Anyone unwilling to accept a united Ireland and wishing to leave would be offered re-settlement grants to permit them to move to Britain.'

Republicans were aware of some of the shortcomings of *A Scenario for Peace*, but they had to consider reactions in their own movement first. There had been a splinter in November 1986 and after the dismal election results in the Republic in February 1987 many were saying, 'I told you so'. One of the defining characteristics of the leadership of Adams and McGuinness has been the slow, tortuous approach to every development to avoid a major split in the movement. The departure of Ruairí Ó Brádaigh had been long expected and successfully managed. An unex-pected split within the IRA was to be avoided at all costs. *A Scenario for Peace* was the first tentative toe in the water and of its nature could not have gone any further than it did. Jim Gibney says *A Scenario for Peace* is:

> The theological republican view of the world, which is, 'We'll negotiate for the British to disengage, the unionists will come to their senses. If they want to leave, we'll help them leave, but those who want to stay, can stay.'

A Scenario for Peace cut no ice with unionists – very few read it. It was dismissed with derision by the SDLP and ignored by the British. Never-theless its publication marks the beginning of what later became known as the peace process. Observing the reaction, the leaders of Sinn Féin who had drafted the document realised they were talking to themselves. *A Scenario for Peace*, into which they had put a lot of work, had failed to make a ripple on the surface of politics. How could they get into talks with anyone, let alone reach the point of negotiating with the British government?

The solution came in the person of Fr Alec Reid, a Redemptorist priest based at Clonard monastery in the heart of west Belfast. Reid, originally from Tipperary and no mean hurler in his day, had been living in Belfast since 1967 and had watched the Troubles unfold at first-hand. The wall of Clonard monastery runs along one end of Bombay Street, the burning of which by loyalists in 1969 is regarded as the *raison d'être* of the Belfast IRA. From his own personal experience, Fr Reid was aware of the poverty and desperation in west Belfast and of the sufferings of the people there at the hands of the British Army, the RUC, loyalist paramilitaries and, not least, the IRA. He had been the central figure in successful mediations between republican factions in the 1970s when the Official IRA and the Provisional IRA flew at each other's throats and on other occasions when he prevented a feud erupting.

Fr Reid's most important contributions were yet to come. In regular contact with the men who were now directing the republican movement, most of whom were based in west Belfast, convenient to Clonard, Fr Reid was uniquely placed to appreciate the change in thinking that had taken place under Adams's leadership. Fr Reid believed, correctly, that there was an opportunity here to engage republicans; to that end he set out to convince politicians in the Republic to talk to them. Fr Reid had been successful at the time of the hunger strike in persuading Cardinal Tomás Ó Fiaich to meet Gerry Adams so that the cardinal could hear the republican position at first-hand. That dialogue developed into regular meetings in the early 1980s. Now, in 1987, Fr Reid had hopes that he could persuade Charles Haughey, once again taoiseach after the February election, to listen to Adams's ideas on how to break the impasse on the North.

Haughey was happy to hear Fr Reid's appreciation of the republican movement's position. Indeed, Fr Reid had kept him apprised of it through 1986, too. A meeting with Adams was, however, out of the question. As taoiseach, where could Haughey meet Adams that would not be public?

And if they met secretly news of it might leak, which would be even worse. With the baggage Haughey was carrying from the Arms Trial in 1970, he judged the political risk too high. He was absolutely right. What would reaction have been in the Republic if it emerged that the taoiseach had been meeting the leader of a movement that in the previous two years had taken delivery of 1,000 AK-47s and a total of 150 tonnes of munitions, which were hidden somewhere in the State for whose security the taoiseach was responsible? What would reaction have been in the Republic if Haughey had been meeting Gerry Adams when the Enniskillen bomb exploded?

Some *entrée* into legitimate politics was nevertheless crucially important for the leaders of Sinn Féin. They wanted to break the carefully constructed *cordon sanitaire* that excluded them from everything, to find some way to have their share of the vote recognised, to show that the party was more than the mouthpiece for the IRA.

Fr Reid had another string for his bow. He approached the SDLP leader, John Hume, with the same message he had presented to Haughey. Like Haughey, Hume had to weigh up the risks. There was a British general election approaching in the summer of 1987 and he could not offer Adams what would be seen as a helping hand in the run-up to the election. After the election it would be a different matter. Hume and Haughey discussed the problem. Haughey had also authorised his advisor on the North, Dr Martin Mansergh, to keep in touch with republicans, which he had done since 1986. From the information at his disposal, Haughey knew there were political opportunities. Whatever passed between Haughey and Hume, the SDLP leader agreed to meet Adams secretly in Clonard monastery late in 1987.

Unfortunately for anyone trying to write about this period, Fr Alec Reid is the very soul of discretion, which is, of course, why he has been so successful in retaining the trust of the republican movement, not to mention senior nationalist politicians in the North and leading politicians in the Republic. Being the soul of discretion means that Fr Reid has only ever given one interview about the period from 1987 on, or for that matter about any period. Nor has he ever written any public account, however cursory, of his dealings. Therefore the exact sequence of events in 1987 and the precise arguments Fr Reid used to persuade the participants must remain unknown.

What is known is that after a number of meetings with Adams, John Hume agreed to a series of formal meetings between his own party and Sinn Féin. The first meeting, in March 1988, was at St Clement's retreat house, high behind the Redemptorist Church of St Gerard's on the Antrim Road in north Belfast. St Clement's is a modern building designed for meetings and seminars. It is set beneath the looming, 1,000-foot high, black basalt Cavehill where, safe from spying eyes, the Belfast United Irishmen were sworn into the movement in the early 1790s. There are superb views across Belfast Lough to the Castlereagh Hills, Stormont and the north Down coast. On a clear day, Scotland is visible on the horizon.

For the meeting Sinn Féin turned out those of its top strategists who were not in jail or on the run: Gerry Adams, Danny Morrison and Tom Hartley, all from west Belfast, and Mitchel McLoughlin from Derry. The SDLP team comprised the party leader John Hume, the party's deputy leader Seamus Mallon MP for Newry–Armagh, Sean Farren, a lecturer in the University of Ulster at Coleraine and former SDLP chairman, and Austin Currie from Dungannon, a founder member of the SDLP and one of those in the party most hostile to Sinn Féin. In some ways the two groups of men symbolised the differences between the two northern nationalist parties. The SDLP men were all about ten years older than the Sinn Féin men. Farren, at forty-nine, was the youngest of the SDLP. Adams, at forty, was the oldest of the Sinn Féin group. None of the SDLP was from Belfast and, apart from Hume who had met Adams several times in the early 1970s, none would have known any of the Sinn Féiners personally. By 1988 Sinn Féin was well on the way to becoming the largest nationalist party in Belfast, taking over from the SDLP in all the nationalist working-class areas. The SDLP's support was predominantly rural.

Sinn Féin had put a lot of work into preparing for the meeting. They presented a revised, beefed-up version of *A Scenario for Peace* called *Towards a Strategy for Peace*; it ran to twenty-one typewritten pages. The reference to resettlement grants for those unionists who wished to leave had been diplomatically removed. Otherwise the document was substantially a restatement of the manifesto of 1987: the British were the problem, their presence was malign, they remained in the North for strategic, imperialist and economic reasons and they must therefore announce their intention to disengage and do so within the lifetime of a parliament.

There was also a robust defence of the 'armed struggle' and a strong attack on the SDLP for its support of the Anglo-Irish Agreement and cooperation with the British government. However, there had been some significant refinements in the Sinn Féin line since 1987. Armed struggle was now 'seen as a political option'. It was 'forced upon the IRA. Neither the IRA nor Sinn Féin want this war but the ineffectualness of all other forms of struggle, the conditions of repression and British attitudes have made armed struggle inevitable.' Having set out their position, the Sinn Féin paper went on:

> The aim of our political struggle in the Six Counties is to popular-
> ise opposition to British rule and to extend that opposition into
> some form of broad anti-imperialist campaign. Our main political
> task is to turn political opposition to British rule in Ireland into a
> political demand for national self-determination. That demand
> will be eventually realised when the will of the British government
> to remain in Ireland will be eroded. Our struggle and strategy has

been to close down each option open to the British until they have no other option but to withdraw.

Sinn Féin put forward a list of seven proposals to the SDLP, including that the SDLP accept that the IRA is politically motivated, that 'IRA volunteers are not criminals' and that the two parties join forces to impress on the Dublin government the need to launch an international and diplomatic offensive to secure national self-determination. On a copy of Sinn Féin's document annotated by one of the SDLP team, which is in the author's possession, in the margin beside this proposal is written the derisive question: 'Like the Anti-Partitionist campaign?'[1]

It was the first Sinn Féin proposal to draw the attention of John Hume and eventually formed the basis for private discussions between him and Gerry Adams which lasted, on and off, for five years and culminated in a joint statement of agreement at Easter 1993. That statement read, 'that Sinn Féin and the SDLP agree with and endorse the internationally established principle of the right of the Irish people to national self-determination.' Hume responded in writing with a series of questions to Adams about what he meant by self-determination and his definition of 'the Irish people'.

The Sinn Féin–SDLP talks continued for six months and were of enormous importance for a number of reasons. Firstly, the fact that the SDLP agreed to meet Sinn Féin at all was a major breakthrough for Sinn Féin, and not just because its support for violence had made previous meetings unthinkable. In 1985 Gerry Adams had publicly asked John Hume to meet Sinn Féin, but Hume had responded along the lines that he would only talk to the organ-grinder, not the monkey, that is, he would meet IRA leaders as the men who took the decisions because Sinn Féin was not an autonomous political organisation. Within days the IRA Army Council had responded and offered a meeting, but it came to nothing because the IRA insisted on video-taping the proceedings. Hume left.

Few people noticed that by 1988 Hume had obviously changed his mind. Sinn Féin was now worth talking to. Secondly, Hume and the SDLP took Sinn Féin seriously. Hume quickly replied to *Towards a Strategy for Peace* in a detailed letter to Gerry Adams. Thirdly, the SDLP stuck to the talks through thick and thin. That may seem a superfluous observation, but the talks began during one of the most ghastly sequences of events in the whole period of the Troubles. Events on the streets would have made it very easy for John Hume to walk away. Indeed, some senior members of his party, like Eddie McGrady, MP for South Down, were dismayed by what was going on.

The talks began just a few months after the interception of the *Eksund*, with its cargo of Libyan arms, and the Enniskillen bomb. As if that backdrop were not bad enough, on 6 March 1988, in Gibraltar, just as the SDLP and Sinn Féin teams were preparing for the talks, the SAS shot dead three members of the GHQ staff of the IRA in controversial circumstances. Mairéad Farrell, Seán Savage and Danny McCann were in Gibraltar to plant a bomb. The target was the Royal Anglian Regimental band who would be playing at a ceremony on 8 March. The snag was, there was no bomb on 6 March when the SAS killed the trio. Furthermore, the IRA members were unarmed. The killings roused strong passions among nationalists north and south of the border.

The following week, to the dismay of the Irish government, people lined the route of the cortège as the coffins were driven from Dublin to Belfast, even though it took place at night. In Belfast thousands turned out for the funerals. As the coffins were being lowered into the republican plot in Milltown cemetery in west Belfast, Michael Stone, a UDA gunman, opened fire with a pistol and threw hand grenades towards the graveside. Hundreds of republican mourners pursued him. One of the best accounts of what followed appeared in *The Irish Times*, written by Kevin Myers, a harsh and unrestrained critic of republicanism:

Unarmed young men charged against the man hurling grenades and firing an automatic pistol. This was not a momentary flash of bravery, a reflex response to a brief and passing danger. This deadly pursuit lasted a long time. The young men stalking their quarry repeatedly came under fire; they were repeatedly bombed; they repeatedly advanced. Indeed this was not simply bravery; this was a heroism which in other circumstances would have won the highest military decorations. Victoria Crosses have been won for less.

Stone killed three men in his lone rampage and injured sixty men, women and children who were struck by bullets, shrapnel and flying fragments of splintered gravestones.

The grisly *danse macabre* was not finished. The victims of Stone's onslaught, one an IRA man, had to be buried. On 19 March, the day Gerry Adams received John Hume's reply to Sinn Féin's *Towards a Strategy for Peace*, the funerals of the three killed took place. Shortly after the coffin of Caoimhín MacBrádaigh (Kevin Brady), the dead IRA man, left the church, a silver Volkswagen Passat with two male occupants ignored Sinn Féin stewards and ended up amidst the funeral cortège after mounting the footpath. The mourners assumed they were facing another loyalist attack like Stone's three days before. Dozens of men attacked the car and their worst fears were confirmed when one of the occupants produced a Browning automatic pistol and fired into the air.

In fact, the two men were British corporals. Their presence at the funeral has never been satisfactorily explained. They were finally dragged from the car, badly beaten and hauled to a nearby GAA ground, Casement Park, where they were stripped and searched. IRA men had by now arrived. They beat the corporals more, threw them into a black taxi and drove them off to shoot them dead behind a row of shops 200 metres away. The whole appalling scene was filmed for television, right up until the taxi drove the corporals off to their deaths, with an IRA man shaking his fist in triumph out of one of the taxi's windows. The images went around the world. They made the people of west Belfast look like savages.

The IRA was delighted. It issued a triumphant statement:

> The Belfast brigade, IRA, claims responsibility for the execution of two SAS members who launched an attack on the funeral cortège of our comrade volunteer Kevin Brady. The SAS unit was initially apprehended by the people lining the route in the belief that armed loyalists were attacking them and they were removed from the immediate vicinity. Our volunteers forcibly removed the two men from the crowd and, after clearly ascertaining their identities from equipment and documentation, we executed them.

The world had watched an entirely different scenario on television as what looked like a lynch mob had set about the two soldiers. Sinn Féin knew how bad the images were. The party issued its own statement, which clearly illustrated the difference between the two wings of the movement:

> What happened was terrible, but it must be seen in the context of the conflict created by the British presence and of the battle of the funerals[2] and especially the Milltown massacre. It was in that atmosphere that the car drove into the cortège. Everyone believed that there was to be a repeat of the Milltown massacre. Despite Sinn Féin's best efforts to restore calm, all pandemonium broke out when the undercover soldiers produced their weapons.

The horrendous catalogue of events in the first three weeks of March 1988, from the Gibraltar killings to the corporals' executions, each incident more unexpected, bizarre and shocking than its precursor, marked for many people the lowest point of the Troubles. There had been incidents which were worse either in terms of the number of casualties or in the tragedy visited on individuals, but taken together the series of horrors that disfigured that month made many people despair. Two days after the corporals' murders the IRA killed a twenty-five-year-old policeman in the Creggan area of Derry. There seemed to be no way out of the endless cycle of death.

It is important to demonstrate in detail exactly what was happening on the streets of Northern Ireland in early 1988. Given the appalling circumstances of March of that year, it is certain that John Hume must have had a clear signal and enough evidence to convince him that Sinn Féin's leaders did indeed want to break the cycle of violence, otherwise he would not have continued the public dialogue between the two parties. It would have been the easiest decision in the world, one understood by most people and applauded by many, if Hume had washed his hands of the republican movement after sending his response to Sinn Féin's *Towards a Strategy for Peace*. Instead, his response was only the beginning of a long, slow process.

Hume focused on the three points in the Sinn Féin presentation that were central to republicans. First, the right of the Irish people to self-determination; second, and what was for republicans the cause of the problem, the role of the British in Ireland; and third, of course, the armed struggle. To Hume a fourth item was critical: the position of unionists and how they were to be included in any arrangements.

On the use of violence, Hume's argument, unsurprisingly, was that it had no justification, it made everything worse, it strengthened unionists' determination and it could not achieve republicans' political aims. It goes without saying that he expected no acceptance of those points in 1988. On the role of Britain in Ireland, Hume argued that, after the Anglo-Irish Agreement, the British were neutral and that if the Irish people agreed on Irish unity as the outcome of self-determination, then the British would endorse that. In Hume's view the only reason the British maintained a large force in Ireland was to ensure that violence would not produce political change or destabilise Britain's neighbouring island.

Hume fastened on a line in *Towards a Strategy for Peace* that said: 'Only the domiciled people of Ireland, those who live on this island, can decide the future of Ireland and the Government of Ireland.' Against this line on the author's copy of the Sinn Féin document, the comment in the margin by the SDLP member reads: 'Exactly – *all* who are domiciled on this island.' Hume readily agreed to define the Irish people in Sinn Féin's words as, 'those people who are domiciled on the island of Ireland'. From that time and for the next five years, Hume hammered away at this line, constantly repeating that the SDLP and Sinn Féin agreed that the Irish people had the right to self-determination, but that the Irish people, who included unionists concentrated in substantial numbers in the North, were deeply divided about how to exercise self-determination. Hume argued that the search for agreement on the exercise of the right to self-determination is the real search for peace in Ireland, and that since it involved *all* the people on the island it should not be pursued by armed force and could not be won by armed force. The agreement of unionists was essential, he maintained, and was therefore obviously a task of persuasion, not coercion.

After six months of exchanging documents and position papers, the talks between Sinn Féin and the SDLP came to an end on 5 September 1988. They ended as they had begun: against a background of intense and horrifying violence. On 20 August 1988 the IRA had killed eight soldiers from the Light Infantry regiment, all aged between eighteen and twenty-one. Nineteen others were injured. The soldiers had been travelling in an unmarked bus along the Ballygawley–Omagh road when 30lbs of Semtex, a massively powerful bomb, exploded at the roadside. Ten days later, on 30 August, the SAS ambushed and killed three IRA men, including the IRA commander in mid-Tyrone, Gerard Harte, his brother Michael, and Michael's brother-in-law, Brian Mullin. It was widely believed that they were responsible for the Ballygawley bus bomb and that their deaths were revenge for that attack.

Margaret Thatcher was, in the words of Douglas Hurd, the British home secretary and former northern secretary, 'incandescent' with rage at the deaths of the eight young infantrymen. It was all he could do to restrain her from extraordinary repressive measures. In the end, he managed to confine her to banning Sinn Féin from the airwaves and introducing some new technical changes in search powers for security forces. After October 1988 Sinn Féin public representatives could be heard on British electronic media only during election campaigns. Although broadcasters quickly devised ingenious ways of lip-synching actors' voices to Sinn Féin spokespersons' interviews, the sanction, according to Sinn Féin, was a bad blow and had immediate effect. The Republican press centre claimed that in the four months after the ban, requests for interviews fell to a quarter of the number they had been before October. It seemed that, thanks to the IRA, the *cordon sanitaire* around Sinn Féin had been drawn tighter than it had been prior to the six months of talks with the SDLP.

The statements issued by the SDLP and Sinn Féin to mark the conclusion of their discussions seemed to indicate that nothing had changed, that the exercise had been a failure. John Hume restated the SDLP's position and Gerry Adams added a lengthy exposition to Sinn Féin's concluding statement in which he strongly criticised that position. He said the Sinn Féin delegation was 'perplexed that the SDLP continues to maintain that the British government is now a neutral party to the conflict in Ireland'. Adams said it was tantamount to conferring 'neutrality on the Turkish government whose military invasion has partitioned the island of Cyprus'. He also said the idea of unity by consent meant recognising and accepting 'the loyalist veto'.

Amid the tough talking, however, it was easy for someone like Hume to discern scope for development. A simple but fundamental point that few paid attention to at the time was that Sinn Féin wanted to cooperate with the SDLP and the Irish government. Most of the proposals in Sinn Féin's documents suggested joining together in some way to agree a strategy or to confront the British diplomatically. In other words, the idea that the IRA alone could fight the British to a standstill and that the British would then enter talks with Sinn Féin about withdrawal had disappeared. Sinn Féin knew they could not go it alone – an important step into the real world. Hume held out the prospect of a convention of all Irish parties with an electoral mandate. Of course, it was understood that violence would have ended first. There were other hopeful signs. Adams had moved on two points. He wrote:

> Our discussions elicited the shared political view that the Irish people as a whole have the right to national self-determination and that the Irish people should be defined as those people domiciled on the island of Ireland (and its offshore islands). The democratic position, and here the SDLP share our view, is that the search for agreement on a lasting, democratic and peaceful solution must involve Northern Protestants and every effort must be made to get their agreement and involvement in the constitutional, financial and political arrangements needed to replace partition and that the civil and religious liberties of Northern Protestants must be guaranteed and protected.

True, he referred to 'Northern Protestants', but Adams was perfectly well aware that Northern Protestants were overwhelmingly unionist. He certainly did not imagine that negotiating with the Protestant churches in the North would be a prerequisite to ending partition. A settlement could no longer simply mean dealing with the British: it must involve unionists.

The Sinn Féin/SDLP talks were crucial. The ice had been broken. Discussions began within the wider republican movement in 1988 on the issues raised in the talks and continued away from the glare of publicity. Mairtín Ó Muilleoir, a prominent and highly articulate Belfast Sinn Féin city councillor and a journalist with the *Andersonstown News*, caused some controversy in 1989 for saying publicly that a debate was going on within republicanism. Outsiders automatically assumed it was about violence. Others in the movement were becoming impatient with stupid mistakes which undermined Sinn Féin's position by highlighting the contradictions of a political party defending armed force.

On 7 July 1988 a booby-trap bomb at the Falls Baths had killed two local people, one a sixty-year-old woman out to buy milk. Gerry Adams expressed shock at the deaths but said he accepted the IRA explanation that the bomb, intended for a passing army patrol, had been triggered accidentally. One of his colleagues, however, councillor Sean Keenan, was angered by the incident and issued a statement saying there should never have been a bomb on the Falls Road. Keenan had played a prominent role in Belfast republican circles and was one of the passengers in Gerry Adams's car in 1984 when the UDA had attacked it, wounding Keenan in the face. In the weeks before the 1982 elections to Prior's assembly, he had been tipped as Gerry Adams's running-mate. But IRA figures in Belfast thought, correctly as it turned out, that he was too soft on the military side and insisted on having Alex Maskey nominated to run alongside Adams instead. Now that Keenan had spoken out against a military operation, reaction to his explicit criticism was swift. He remained as a Sinn Féin councillor in the Ballymurphy district, but his role as a public representative was taken over by Lily Fitzsimmons. Keenan never made another public statement. He was not nominated as a Sinn Féin candidate the following year and, despite his record in the movement, sank without trace after July 1988. His fate was a message to Gerry Adams as much as to Sinn Féin councillors in general. It was unacceptable to criticise the armed struggle.

What the Sinn Féin leaders did instead of saying anything critical of the IRA campaign was to begin to carefully modify Sinn Féin policy until the use of violence was left as a millstone for Sinn Féin, rather like abstentionism had been. Over a period of years from 1989, the notion of 'armed struggle' in the sense of a mobilised population was allowed to become an outdated and outmoded concept. Rioting and gun battles in built-up urban areas stopped as the tactical use of violence in the form of large bombs in urban centres came to the fore. The idea of the 'risen people' was never rejected but, rather, was quietly consigned to history along with a number of other republican watchwords.

Achieving the transformation in policy was like changing the direction of a fully loaded juggernaut travelling at sixty miles an hour with no brakes. It can only be done by gingerly nudging it off the main road onto a slip road and into a sand trap. It can remain there, fully loaded with its engine running, but it can never get under way again. The really dangerous task is nudging it. The slightest miscalculation will result in certain death and destruction.

In the late 1980s the IRA resembled a fully loaded juggernaut. Following the capture of the *Eksund*, the size of the IRA's known arsenal caused consternation in Ireland and Britain. The British government lent the Irish government sophisticated electronic equipment to help it conduct searches for the IRA's *matériel*. It was in the interests of both governments to find the stuff. Several members of the Dáil were convinced the IRA presented a real threat to the stability of Irish politics. The extreme left-wing language used in republican literature and Sinn Féin's espousal of revolutionary causes around the world were sources of grave concern. Intelligence services in both states began to take the IRA's contacts with ETA, the Basque terrorist organisation, the ANC in Africa, the PLO in Palestine and other Islamic groups seriously. After all, if Colonel Gadaffi could send 150 tonnes of armaments to Ireland unbeknownst to anyone, what else had been going on that remained secret?

Gerry Adams, Martin McGuinness and the other politically-minded leaders of republicanism were keenly aware of the damage such concerns in Irish government circles could do to the movement. Already, in the aftermath of the revelations about the Libyan supplies, an unprecedented search had taken place across the Republic. Over 50,000 premises had been searched at the end of 1987 and some bunkers crammed with weaponry had been unearthed. The public reaction did not augur well for Sinn Féin's electoral hopes in the Republic.

It was no coincidence, therefore, that in the 1988 *Towards a Strategy for Peace* presented to the SDLP, Sinn Féin had taken the opportunity to spell out that the IRA's actions 'are aimed at the six-county state and not at the twenty-six counties. *Towards a Strategy for Peace* repeated an extract from *An Phoblacht/Republican News* of December 1987 designed to reassure the Irish government. It quoted IRA General Army Order No. 8, to the effect that 'all IRA volunteers are under strict orders not to come into conflict with the armed forces of the twenty-six counties. They are not the enemy. There is no campaign or armed conspiracy against the institutions of the twenty-six-county state nor will there be.'

Gerry Adams and the Sinn Féin team talking to the SDLP were in no doubt that whatever they said was being passed to the Irish government. Indeed, they probably hoped it was. To safeguard their own political position the SDLP published all the papers exchanged between the two parties in case unionists, in particular, suspected there was some kind of secret deal in the offing. As well as the published material, the SDLP gave their own private assessment to the taoiseach, Charles Haughey. This assessment was that the men they were talking to were sincere in wanting some way out of the impasse that had solidified in the North. The Sinn Féin leaders knew that the republican movement could continue its traditional strategy almost indefinitely, but that it was going nowhere. They could not defeat the British nor could the British defeat them. The British would not negotiate as long as the campaign of violence continued, and the IRA would not cease its campaign of violence until the British signalled they were ready to negotiate.

Despite Sinn Féin's anxieties about the Irish government's reaction to the discovery of the size of the IRA's arsenal, the knowledge of its existence was in one respect an advantage to Gerry Adams and other Sinn Féin leaders. It was clear that with such an extensive array of weaponry at its disposal since 1986, the IRA was not operating at full capacity. Why not? If some people in the republican movement were in a position to restrain the wilder members, then everything should be done to encourage them and strengthen their hand. If, as appeared to be the case, those people were the current leaders of republicanism, then it was desirable to ensure they remained in that position. Hume kept talking to Adams secretly.

Adams and his supporters within the movement were not idle. Working to change Sinn Féin's policies so that the only remaining obstacle was support for violence meant undoing attitudes and assumptions which had built up when the organisation was emerging in the early 1970s. Since many of those attitudes and assumptions had produced policies which reflected far-left thinking from those years, by the late 1980s they were showing distinct signs of being past their 'sell-by date'. When the Soviet Union and its satellites in eastern Europe began to collapse, culminating in sudden disintegration in 1989, it provided another powerful lever for Adams and the group of Sinn Féin leaders around him to promote a reassessment of republicanism. This meant looking at how republicans perceived the Irish government, the British government and the unionists. The result was a complete realignment of republican thinking, at least at leadership level, which is where it counted.

Traditionally republicans had regarded Dublin, London and the unionists as enemies, all conspiring in one way or another to maintain partition and frustrate the goal of republicanism. The new republican leadership had never fully subscribed to that view of the world. They shared the general attitude of northern republicans to the Irish Republic, which was completely different from that of traditional, southern-based republicans. In an interview with the author, Tom Hartley, an influential thinker in the movement from the 1970s right up to the early 1990s, explained the different perspectives:

> Inside the movement there were these discussions [in the late 1980s]. 'Where is it going? Is it just going to be a constant, but slight haemorrhaging of our struggle? You have the Brits there with all the resources and then you have us, and is it going to be us being isolated but keeping the struggle up for another twenty years?' And I think we started to look at it this way, 'OK, where is it we want to go?' And I mean, it's not so much the Brits that were the problem, it was about the SDLP and Dublin. I mean, for southern republicans, irrespective of the decision we made about Leinster House, Dublin was still the arch-enemy. The SDLP were just, I have to say, next door to them.

For southern republicans, the 'Republic' was a semi-mystical entity, something they swore allegiance to as the Fenians had done in the nineteenth century. It existed in people's minds, not as a body politic. The actual Irish Republic, formally established in 1948, was an impostor, something that had emerged illegally from the 1921 Anglo-Irish Treaty imposed by Britain. For the young northerners who poured into the movement after 1970, however, though they wouldn't admit it because of republican dogma, that Irish Republic was something they would have been quite happy to join. Of course, it was imperfect and they railed against its inequalities, its backwardness, its deadening Catholicism and so on, but all that could be changed. For them the Republic existed as an independent Irish State. It was a reality, not a spiritual entity. It was run from Dublin and was an equal partner with Britain in the EU. They would have been delighted to have been part of it. They wanted the Irish government, which, unlike southern dogmatists, they recognised, to be on their side, to support them against the British. They felt betrayed because it did not. Their southern colleagues, on the other hand, would have been amazed if it had.

As for the SDLP, Sinn Féin wanted its support and believed the SDLP opposed Sinn Féin because it wanted to conspire with the British to concoct some internal northern arrangement that would exclude republicans. They wished the SDLP would get out of the way and thereby leave the British no option but to negotiate with republicans. The SDLP was a nuisance, a catspaw of the British. Sinn Féin's long-term aim was to supplant the SDLP as the voice of northern nationalism and to leave Dublin no alternative but to support Sinn Féin's position.

By 1989 Sinn Féin's leaders knew none of this was feasible. On the contrary, if Sinn Féin were going to end its isolation from the political mainstream, it was Sinn Féin that would have to modify some policies and jettison others. The main change was going to have to be in the way they regarded unionists. Both Dublin and the SDLP, which was effectively Dublin's voice in the North, believed in Parnell's dictum that there would never be peace in Ireland until the minority on the island, the unionists, was conciliated. For Dublin and the SDLP, accommodating unionists and not expelling the British by armed force was therefore the solution. Any settlement was going to have to win over and include unionists, something that had been anathema to northern republicans who saw the North as a colonial and imperial problem with the unionists as settlers and Britain as the imperial power. The closest analogy they found that matched was the former French colonies of Algeria and Tunisia in North Africa. In the 1970s, Tom Hartley had developed this analogy fully and had found political theorists to suit the republican position, namely Frantz Fanon and Albert Memmi.

Fanon, a psychiatrist, was born on the French Caribbean island of Martinique in 1925. He had grown up believing himself to be French and had volunteered for the Free French Army in 1944. It was only in his twenties, while studying medicine in France, that it was borne in on him that he was not French, but was first and foremost black, and that his cultural and political ideas were the product of colonialism. When he arrived to work in a hospital in Algeria in 1953 during the Arab rebellion against the French, he threw in his lot with the rebels, the FLN (National Liberation Front). He died of leukaemia in 1961 at the age of thirty-six.

Fanon published a series of books and articles on colonialism, most notably *The Wretched of the Earth* and *Black Skins, White Masks*. They were translated from the original French in the 1960s and became deeply influential in the USA where black militants, such as Stokeley Carmichael and Eldridge Cleaver, called Fanon their 'patron saint'.

What attracted republicans in Northern Ireland to his thesis was Fanon's description of French colonialism in Algeria: the way a native middle-class had been encouraged to believe they were French, the attitudes of the settler middle-class, the education system, which was indistinguishable from that in France and, above all, the way the lower-class native majority was suppressed and treated as second-class citizens. Finally, of course, what republicans seized upon was Fanon's justification of violence in an anti-imperialist armed struggle. Albert Memmi, from Tunisia, followed much the same lines as Fanon, though never developed any comparable political philosophy designed to deal with the whole issue of colonialism in Africa as Fanon did.

Fanon's ideas were a potent version of Marxism redesigned and revamped to address racism and imperialism in the context of the anti-imperialist armed struggles of 1950s and 1960s Africa. For Sinn Féin's Tom Hartley, reading Fanon in early 1970s Belfast in the heated atmosphere of internment with thousands of British troops on the streets, the descriptions of Algeria and the French military response, including internment and torture, the attitude of the *pieds noirs* (the descendants of the French settlers) and the role of the insurgents, the FLN, all seemed to slot perfectly into the conditions in the North. For the French, read the British; for the *pieds noirs*, read the unionists; for the FLN, read the IRA; for the Harkis, the native Algerian militia who would be discarded when the imperialists decamped, read the RUC and UDR. Fanon's Marxist analysis of the class system also seemed to fit. The native middle-class in Algeria were educated as if they were French, though they knew they were Arab; Catholics in the North were educated as though they were English, though they knew they were Irish. The *pieds noirs* thought they were French, but the French did not think so; unionists thought they were British, but the English did not think so. It all seemed to fit so simply.

Asked why he was attracted to Fanon and Memmi, Hartley said:

> Well, I suppose I had a broad sort of anti-imperialist feeling about the world which was then reflected in books like that. I didn't see myself as being involved in a struggle or a movement just in Ireland. Fanon and Memmi were really going below the surface of politics. What has always intrigued me about politics is to try to make sense of all the movement of individuals and political parties and how it all comes together. You could look out on a street or into society and you see a mess. The secret of politics is to bring that down maybe to one line, to make it easily understood, to turn that into a strategic direction, to put it into the language of political forces.

For Hartley that was what Fanon did. He explained the situation in the North of Ireland in the anti-imperialist, Marxist terms current in the 1960s and 1970s. It helped republicans to link their struggle into what was happening elsewhere in the world. It has to be said the British helped them in that because they often reacted as if the North were a colonial struggle. Hartley's interpretation was very influential among the young men swept into the IRA in the early 1970s. Danny Morrison says:

> I think the first time Tom Hartley introduced me to Frantz Fanon
> and Albert Memmi was 1974, and then I would have been sending
> those books into jail. There would have been a lot of the anti-
> colonial outlook, anti-imperialist outlook, going a wee bit eccen-
> trically left-wing. Certainly when I was editing *Republican News*
> that's the sort of stuff I'd have been driving into it.

From the early days of the Provisional IRA campaign in the 1970s
therefore, links were made and analogies drawn with anti-imperialist liberation struggles in Africa and the Middle East, especially the ANC and
PLO, thanks largely to the discovery of Frantz Fanon and the influence his
work had on Tom Hartley. No one outside the republican movement
shared that analysis. Certainly the Marxist aspect of it was repugnant to all
the other protagonists – Dublin, London, the SDLP and unionists –
though in truth no one in Sinn Féin fully subscribed to Marxism either.
That was left to the despised Stickies. Sinn Féin's young men mouthed
Marxist catch-phrases in the 1970s because they embodied anti-
imperialist rhetoric, but no one took them seriously. More objectionable
by far was the advocacy of armed struggle leading to the overthrow of the
state. Everyone knew Sinn Féin was deadly serious about that.

Superficially there were similarities between the North of Ireland
and other partitioned, former colonised areas. One such place was
Cyprus. John Hume admitted the similarity in his talks with Sinn Féin.
But when Gerry Adams retorted that Hume's claim that Britain was neutral on the North was like saying Turkey was neutral on Cyprus, Hume
responded:

> It is purely academic to argue that the Unionist people have no
> right to a veto on Irish unity or on the exercise of self-
> determination, or that British policy confers such a right on them.
> The harsh reality is that, whether or not they have the academic
> right to a veto on Irish unity, they have it as a matter of fact based on
> numbers, geography and history, and they have it in the exact same

way as Greek or Turkish Cypriots have a factual veto on the exercise of self-determination on the island of Cyprus.

In Hume's opinion, since Gerry Adams had admitted publicly that there could be no military victory in the North of Ireland, and the British had agreed, then the only effect of continuing violence was to increase divisions and postpone the inevitable conference where a settlement would be negotiated. Unionists would have to be there. How would Sinn Féin get there? It would be necessary to jettison the analysis that regarded Britain as a foreign power occupying part of Ireland for imperialist reasons and the unionists as dupes of the British who would magically 'throw in their lot with the rest of the Irish people' if and when the British left. The Fanon thesis had to be dropped first.

The painfully slow process of change in republican thinking was spearheaded by the leadership from 1989 on. The talks with the SDLP had been the critical breakthrough into the political arena. Winning votes was one thing, acquiring political legitimacy was something entirely different. The voluminous exchange of papers and unwritten, unrecorded conversations had been an eye-opener for the Sinn Féin team, and for Adams in particular. Jim Gibney, who was back in jail for a large part of the 1980s as a result of supergrass evidence against him, was released again in 1988, too late to be included in the talks. He became involved in policy-making again soon afterwards. He says of the talks:

> I think what happens – and I've talked to Gerry Adams about this – is that it's the SDLP talks in 1988 that had a role to play in changing the thinking. There's no doubt in my mind. I thought it at the time, and I'm more convinced of it now, that those talks opened up possibilities in Gerry Adams's mind because of the way in which they were greeted on the nationalist side – universally welcomed ... And the effort and energy that were put into those talks on our side were quite considerable. I was only out of jail, so I was looking at it from the outside in, and you could see there was a huge effort put

into those talks … It's what those talks begin to do between Gerry Adams and John Hume. They maintain contact. I do think that there's a relationship there that builds up between those two men. What's also important is that Hume's in a position to talk to the Brits, he's in a position to talk to Dublin, he's in a position to talk to the US. While he's doing none of that on Gerry Adams's behalf at all, nonetheless Gerry Adams has got access. At least he's getting feedback. So I think those talks begin a new phase in people's thinking.

After 1988 Sinn Féin was in the political loop. The party's leaders, not only Gerry Adams and Martin McGuinness but also others close to them, knew about the secret talks and Adams's continued contacts. They were also being provided with 'feedback' from Hume's ability to meet important Irish, British and American politicians and officials. Hume, however, was on a solo run. None of his senior colleagues in the SDLP, apart from Mark Durkan, whom he was grooming to succeed him as party leader, knew he was continuing to meet Adams.

Given the nature of the republican movement, it would have been an unthinkable risk for Adams, even if he had so wished, to engage in talks kept secret from other leading figures in the movement. At any rate, it could not have been done as the daily personal risk that Adams faced meant he had to have a driver and bodyguards. Besides, he was such a well-known figure that he could not go anywhere without being recognised. The major difference between Sinn Féin and the SDLP was quite stark. If knowledge of Hume's continuing meetings had leaked out there would have been a big row at the next party meeting. If Adams had tried something similar it could have ended in gunfire.

Those considerations required that a small group within the republican leadership be kept fully informed but, in any case, Adams wanted to bring people along with him. For a start, the IRA had to be kept on side lest any suspicion grew that the 'war' was being run down. Thus, to most people it looked as if the 'war' was actually being stepped up after 1987. The IRA had been able not only to extend its range of attacks into England on a regular basis but, in 1989, into mainland Europe, too. Allies of Adams controlled the IRA, North and South, from 1987. The chief of staff, a Tyrone man, supported Adams, as did Northern Command, his real power-base, where Martin McGuinness played a crucial part. Pat Doherty, born in Scotland but raised in east Donegal, is reported to have become OC Southern Command. He later became Sinn Féin's national organiser. Since Southern Command played a quartermaster role, supplying the 'war zone', this gave Doherty influence in the control of the big Libyan weapons dumps. Doherty, McGuinness and Adams have in one capacity or another commanded the support of the whole republican movement, both military and political wings, from 1987 until the present day.

One other important element, often overlooked, also supported the Adams line: the prisoners and, most importantly, the ex-prisoners. The republican movement had had long experience of imprisonment and its effects. In response to internment in 1971 the movement had quickly established an extensive, though not always competent, support network for prisoners and their families. As the years went on, however, and more and more men and women went to jail in Ireland and Britain, the prisoners became a crucially important constituency within republicanism. They had to be consulted and kept on side. They were the people who had made sacrifices for the movement second only to those who had died. Their importance and influence within the republican community could not be underestimated.

By the 1980s there were more men and women in the movement who had served or were serving time than there had ever been before. More people were serving longer sentences in England and Ireland than any republicans had served since the nineteenth century. By the late 1980s, dozens of men had been in jail since the early and mid-1970s, including Pat Doherty's brother, in jail since 1975 and serving a recommended minimum of thirty years. There were many others like him.

It was crystal clear to the prisoners that when Gerry Adams and others said there could not be a military victory, that the British could not be driven out, that there might be a 'long war', perhaps another twenty years, such language meant full sentences would have to be served if the campaign continued. The gates would not 'fly open', in the words of Ernest Blythe when speaking about the way the 1932 Fianna Fáil government released the IRA prisoners in the Free State. Because of the large number of recommended minimum sentences, people sentenced in the mid-1980s often faced release dates from 2010 onwards. The young age of many IRA prisoners meant that there was a high proportion of what were called 'SOSPs', people held, in the archaic language of the British royal prerogative, 'at the Secretary of State's pleasure', that is, they had no set release date and were in the worst possible psychological position of having indeterminate sentences.

Obviously it was in the interests of the prisoners that some political settlement was reached, though no one in the republican movement would ever admit openly to such a consideration. It has to be said that there was no falling off in volunteers because of long sentences. Nevertheless, by the 1980s the older men in the movement – ex-prisoners in their thirties, often playing important roles in Sinn Féin – did not want to see their children and their friends' children spend the best part of their lives in jail, as they had.

Equally important was the role of men of similar age in jail, some of legendary status among northern republicans, who fully supported the leadership of Gerry Adams and Martin McGuinness on the outside. Many men fell into this category, but the five most important were Gerry Kelly, Bobby Storey, Brendan 'Bik' McFarlane, Seanna Walsh and Padraig Wilson. For many republicans in Belfast, Storey was the Dan Breen of the

1970s, a man who had been involved in numerous armed confrontations with the RUC and British Army. Well over six feet tall, of enormous strength and power, Storey was entrusted with leading the biggest jail break in Europe since the Second World War when, on 25 September 1983, thirty-eight IRA prisoners escaped from the notorious H-blocks. Bik McFarlane from Ardoyne, who also played a major role in the escape, had been an OC in the prison during the hunger strike of 1981. He had been recaptured in Amsterdam in 1986 along with Gerry Kelly.

Kelly, jailed for bombing the Old Bailey in 1973, played a crucial part in the execution of the 1983 escape, helped by the terrifying reputation he had nurtured among prison warders. In 1998 he was to win a seat in the Stormont assembly after the Good Friday Agreement and become Sinn Féin spokesman on policing. Seanna Walsh and Padraig Wilson, men who had been in and out of jail since the 1970s, became prison OCs in their turn in the late 1980s and 1990s. Like the others mentioned here, they were serving long sentences as repeat offenders and had earned the respect of prisoners and the republican community outside jail. All these men endorsed what Adams, McGuinness, Doherty and others were doing and reassured the prisoners under their command about the direction the movement was taking.

The simple fact was that if the prisoners supported the leadership of the movement, then any dissenters on the outside did not have a leg to stand on. So it proved. Adams's men were always in charge in the prison. They were kept in communication with the leaders and were always able to explain political developments and the significance of Sinn Féin speeches to fellow inmates. So important was the role of prisoners that in the early 1990s the NIO permitted even 'Red Book'[3] prisoners, like McFarlane, repeated parole to allow them explain to IRA meetings on the outside why the peace process should be supported. All these men, since 2000 all ex-prisoners, continue to play this role today. From 1989 on, the support of IRA veterans, particularly those who moved into Sinn Féin, became of critical importance because the 'feedback' from meetings with John Hume, which Jim Gibney referred to, produced effects which required modernising republicanism.

A new northern secretary, Peter Brooke, a man with a detailed grasp of Irish history and whose ancestors hailed from the Cavan–Armagh border, began to make intriguing speeches. Brooke took office in July 1989. He appeared to be bumbling and diffident, hopeless in press conferences and quickly reminded people of the sobriquet 'Babbling Brooke' that his father, a former Tory home secretary, had earned. Despite his public image, however, Brooke proved to be one of the most thoughtful and innovative northern secretaries ever to take up the post. Within three months he had read himself into his brief and was ready to grasp opportunities to end what one northern journalist put to him was a 'Mexican stand-off' between republicans and the British government.

John Hume, Irish government officials and politicians had all impressed on Brooke the four items isolated by Hume in 1988: republicans' belief that Britain had an imperialist interest in Ireland, that Britain rejected the right of the Irish people to self-determination, that the British used the unionists as colonial dupes and that the only way to change all this was armed struggle. The question was how to persuade Sinn Féin that if they were wrong on the first three items, then there was no justification for pursuing the fourth as a means?

In November 1989, to the consternation of unionists and some of his fellow Conservatives, Brooke took the first step. In response to the journalist's question about a Mexican stand-off, he replied, in his convoluted way, that if 'terrorists were to decide that the moment had come to withdraw from their activities, then I think the government would need to be imaginative.' He then went further and referred to Cyprus and 'the move to independence' there. He said a British minister had used the word '"never" in a way which within two years there had been a retreat from that word.' He said he hoped a British government would be 'sufficiently flexible and if flexibility were required it could be used.' Obviously, Brooke was completely familiar with the documents the SDLP and Sinn Féin had exchanged in 1988 and, at the urging of John Hume, was using language taken from those documents.

Still, movement was glacial. A year later, in November 1990, speaking in his London constituency, Brooke made the single most important speech in launching the process that eventually brought Sinn Féin into public talks with the British government. At the end of the speech he said:

> The British government has no selfish strategic or economic interest in Northern Ireland: our role is to help, enable and encourage. Britain's purpose is not to occupy, oppress or exploit, but to ensure democratic debate and free democratic choice.

That phrase, 'no selfish strategic or economic interest', was to appear again and again in joint communiqués between London and Dublin and in documents passed between republicans, Dublin and London over the next four years. From this point on, the process of Sinn Féin's entry into negotiations accelerated dramatically. By 1993 it had become clear that the sort of statements Peter Brooke was making in 1989 and 1990 were the tip of a very large iceberg, nine-tenths of which was concealed below very murky water. Observers thought they were watching an elaborate *pas de deux* between Sinn Féin and the British, conducted through newspaper articles and press statements. In fact, an infinitely more complex performance was taking place that would give rise in later years to the repeated use of the word 'choreography'. Only the directors and producers had an overview of the performance and it was sometimes embarrassingly obvious that some of the individuals on stage knew nothing more than their own steps as they often collided with other performers.

At the outset of the performance, Margaret Thatcher was removed from the stage in a sudden political *coup de théâtre* in November 1990. Immediately, her departure freed up all kinds of blockages. Brooke was able to make his famous speech denying any strategic or economic interest. He also authorised the opening of so-called 'back channel' talks with the IRA through an MI6 officer and intermediaries the British government had used from time to time since the 1970s. It is not known when exactly in 1990 the 'back channel' was reopened, but it was probably around the time of Thatcher's abrupt departure in November. Confusion surrounds the date because when the fact of contacts with the IRA leaked out in November 1993, the British government had been firmly denying any such thing for almost a year. Prime minister John Major and others tried to cover their tracks by claiming the contacts only began in 1993, but Peter Brooke has subsequently gone on record as opening contact on the advice of John Deverell, head of MI5 in the North, in late 1990.

In parallel with these exchanges between republicans and the British government, links with the Irish government had also developed. Dr Martin Mansergh, the taoiseach's special advisor, and Dermot Ahern TD had met Gerry Adams, Pat Doherty and Mitchel McLoughlin in the Redemptorist monastery in Dundalk as early as May 1988. Contacts continued sporadically through the good offices of Fr Reid. As well as maintaining his exchanges with Gerry Adams, John Hume liaised continuously with senior officials at the Department of Foreign Affairs and with the taoiseach, Charles Haughey, keeping them up to date with republican thinking.

In the midst of this cat's cradle of overlapping and compartmentalised contacts, the one certainty is that the Sinn Féin leaders, Gerry Adams, Martin McGuinness and Pat Doherty, were the only people who knew about everything that was going on. No outsider knows for sure, but it is unlikely that the Irish government knew about the contacts between the

IRA and MI6, something Dublin always frowned upon. John Hume certainly had no idea that it was happening under his nose in his own city. For their part, the British would have had minimal knowledge of the web of contacts that Fr Reid, Sinn Féin and Irish government officials maintained: they were all wary of the telephone. Only the top Sinn Féin people, overlapping as top IRA men, held all the strings in their hands.

The Sinn Féin leaders had responded with alacrity to Peter Brooke's public overtures in November 1989. The version of *A Scenario for Peace* presented to the SDLP in 1988 was taken off the shelf and distributed to all political parties in Ireland and Britain. Gerry Adams, Martin McGuinness and Mitchel McLoughlin held a joint press conference to show how interested they were in Brooke's statement regarding independence and Cyprus and the possibility of dealing with republicans. But that was as far as it went. Sinn Féin was no closer to talks with the British than it had been since 1975. No ceasefire: no talks.

The refusal of the British government to contemplate talks with them had made Sinn Féin extremely agitated because Peter Brooke managed to get talks going among the other northern parties in spring 1991. There was deep concern in Sinn Féin that an internal settlement would be cobbled together that would set their isolation from the political process in concrete. To avoid alienating Sinn Féin and undermining Adams's project, NIO officials engaged the party at arm's length during the talks. It emerged only later that the NIO had supplied Sinn Féin with the position papers of all the parties to the talks, including, to the intense annoyance of Dublin, those the Irish government presented to the British. Despite the risk to his talks – the unionists would have stormed out if they had known – Brooke was correct in this policy because the papers showed Sinn Féin, and in turn allowed them reassure the IRA, that the position the SDLP and the Irish government had presented to them in private was the truth: there would be no internal settlement in the North.

It has to be emphasised what a high-risk exercise his indulgence towards Sinn Féin was for Peter Brooke. It was not just a matter of unionists crying foul and leaving. The IRA did nothing to make Sinn Féin's inclusion in talks any easier. It is true that it had called the first formal Christmas ceasefire in fifteen years in December 1990, but on 7 February 1991 it mortared 10 Downing Street during a meeting of the Gulf War Cabinet. The closest shell exploded just fifteen metres from the building where the British prime minister was chairing the meeting. The Cabinet committee ended up hiding under the table. That was only the most spectacular of many attacks in England in 1991, which place Brooke's continuing contacts with the IRA and Sinn Féin in perspective yet, at the same, time show how impossible it would have been for a British government in 1991 to enter negotiations with Sinn Féin. Publicly it was still a stand-off.

On the other hand, substantial progress was being made behind the scenes on the Irish side to try to bring republicans into the process. Central to this progress was the idea of a joint declaration by the Irish and British governments, which would lay out an agreed position not only on Northern Ireland but on the rights of the Irish people as a whole. It would be an attempt to restate, in modern terms, the relations between the two islands and the two sovereign governments, and at the same time to show the position held by Sinn Féin to be archaic and irrelevant in a modern world where Ireland and Britain were partners in the European Union, the Cold War was over and Marxism discredited.

The first attempt at such a declaration was a document called *A Strategy for Peace and Justice in Ireland*, pulled together by John Hume on 6 October 1991. Over the next two years it went through eleven drafts until it emerged, with most of its fundamentals unchanged, as the Downing Street Declaration of December 1993. Hume's first go at it tried to incorporate what he had learnt from talking to Gerry Adams, to Peter Brooke, to Charles Haughey and to senior Irish officials, like Seán Ó hUiginn, head of the Anglo-Irish division of the Department of Foreign Affairs, and Dermot Nally, former Irish Cabinet secretary and a long-time participant in dealings with Britain.

Essentially, Hume's draft was built around the points he had concentrated on from Sinn Féin's 1988 *A Scenario for Peace*: self-determination, the role of Britain and the position of unionists. He had reason therefore to believe his draft might be broadly acceptable to Sinn Féin. If the British did not agree to a joint declaration, he proposed a conference of Irish parties to persuade the British to accept Irish strategies and objectives on the problem. Implicitly that conference would include Sinn Féin but, of course, it was also assumed the IRA would have given up violence beforehand. By the end of October 1991 Irish officials had drawn up a revised version, endorsed by the taoiseach, which Hume could show to Gerry Adams.

While Hume and the Irish government had been working towards this document, Sinn Féin's leaders had been labouring since late 1990 to alter their own position on a number of critical points which they had learnt were unhelpful or non-negotiable. Being privy to the position papers of all the other parties to the 1991 Brooke talks was, of course, a great help. Now, receipt of the draft of the proposed joint British–Irish declaration agreed by Haughey spurred them towards completion. The result, published in February 1992, marked a revolution in republican thinking. The document was entitled *Towards a Lasting Peace in Ireland*. A second edition became the party's manifesto in the 1992 British general election.

Just as with *A Scenario for Peace,* hardly anyone paid any attention. The document was produced against the background of a devastating new bombing campaign in Belfast and in other provincial towns, and a few weeks after the murder of eight Protestant workmen in a landmine explosion at Teebane crossroads in Tyrone on 17 January as they returned from work on a British Army base. In the face of the upsurge in violence and widespread condemnation from all sides, including the taoiseach and the Catholic Church, the document seemed irrelevant.

Yet *Towards a Lasting Peace in Ireland* marked in black and white the huge sea change that had taken place in republican thinking. The manifesto edition, a condensed version of the February document, was important not only for what it said but for what it did not say. Gone was the colonial and imperialist analysis and, even more fundamental, gone was the traditional demand for a British withdrawal. Ruairí Ó Brádaigh, interviewed by the author, claims he had spotted the shift earlier, in 1991, in the Bodenstown address, the traditional occasion for announcing policy changes. Asked when he thought Adams and his supporters had decided to run down the armed struggle, he replied:

> Well, a benchmark, a public benchmark was the Bodenstown address in 1991 where, for the first time, they don't mention British withdrawal. So that was the outward sign of an inward shift in position. I remember meeting some of the Provos in the street and saying, 'How was it you didn't mention British withdrawal?' 'Ah, we can't be doing that every year.' Well, it's been said since Wolfe Tone died. But after Bodenstown in 1991 it has never been mentioned since by them. Of course, it was already an accomplished fact internally before they publicly dropped the reference.

In 1972 the IRA gave the British three years to leave; in 1987 Sinn Féin had extended it to the lifetime of one parliament, or five years. By 1992 not only was there no deadline (even in private documents which did still ask for British withdrawal) but Sinn Féin acknowledged there was a role for Britain to play in Ireland. The manifesto listed three key requirements for creating the conditions in which peace would flourish:

> 1. A British government which makes the ending of partition its political objective.

2. A Dublin government which has the same end.

3. Cooperation between the British and Irish governments to bring about in the shortest possible time the reunification of the country.

Then another major change in thinking:

Democracy and practicality demand that this [reunification] be done in consultation with the representatives of the Irish minority – the Northern Unionists – as well as with the representatives of the Northern Nationalists. In effect a process of national reconciliation.

Sinn Féin had moved a long way from resettlement grants. Instead of republicans negotiating a British withdrawal over the heads of everyone else, that paragraph envisaged a conference where both unionists and nationalists would negotiate with the two governments. By 1992, six years of the Anglo-Irish Agreement had inured Sinn Féin to the concept of London working with Dublin. *Towards a Lasting Peace in Ireland* said the search for peace is 'specifically the responsibility of the London and Dublin governments. They [note the plural] have the power to effect the necessary change.'

In an important speech at the time, Jim Gibney said:

We know and accept that the British government's departure must be preceded by a sustained period of peace and will arise out of negotiations involving the different shades of Irish nationalism and unionism.

Clearly, Peter Brooke's denial in November 1990 of any British strategic or economic interest in the North had enabled Hume and Irish officials to demolish some of the central pillars of Sinn Féin's argument. Yet, few outside the republican movement accepted there had been any change, largely because the main obstacle remained in place: the armed struggle. *Towards a Lasting Peace in Ireland* had reduced it to 'an option of last resort', a considerable demotion from its 'primary importance' in Adams's 1986 book, *The Politics of Irish Freedom*. But it was still there.

There was a prospect of movement though. The 1992 document did publicly ask the question Sinn Féin had put to both Irish and British politicians: 'There is an onus on those who proclaim that the armed struggle is counterproductive to advance a credible alternative. The development of such an alternative would be welcomed by Sinn Féin.' Sinn Féin was searching for 'an effective unarmed *constitutional* [author's italics] strategy'. Could the Irish and British governments provide one?

Although it is now known that such a search was taking place, and that by February 1992 Sinn Féin's leaders had dispatched Fr Reid to Dublin with their revision of the Haughey-approved draft declaration given to them in October 1991, all the evidence on the streets indicated republicans' unshakeable commitment to violence. Certainly there was no reason for foot-soldiers in the republican movement to believe the leadership of the movement was engaged in a fundamental rethink – perhaps the very reason the leaders got away with the explicit changes in *Towards a Lasting Peace in Ireland*.

Then in April 1992 the whole process received a series of blows. The British prime minister John Major had called a general election. Sinn Féin fielded thirteen candidates in the North. The party's share of the vote slipped to 10% and its total vote declined too. That would have been bad enough, but the party lost the jewel in its crown, Gerry Adams's West Belfast seat, by 589 votes. About 2,500 unionists in the Shankill area had voted tactically for the SDLP candidate in order to stop Adams. He was no longer a public representative. It was a bitter blow.

That same day, 10 April, the IRA struck. Against the odds John Major had just been returned as prime minister, winning an election many pundits had believed would prove to be Neil Kinnock's chance to be the first Labour prime minister since 1979. In the midst of

Conservative euphoria, an immense blast tore through the financial district of the City of London, destroying the Baltic Exchange and wrecking scores of other prestigious financial houses. The total cost of the damage came to over stg£750 million – amazingly, incredibly, more than all the compensation that had been paid out in the North of Ireland where there had been almost 10,000 bombs since 1969. The bomb also killed three people.

Did the IRA still believe they could bomb the British into talking to them? For a dozen reasons no European government could be seen to respond to such a bomb. Unionists pointed with satisfaction to their predictions that appeasement of the IRA, which was how they described Peter Brooke's policies, would produce nothing but more violence. How could Gerry Adams say, with any credibility, to John Hume and the Irish government that he was looking for peace?

When John Major announced his new Cabinet, the name of his northern secretary caused a sharp intake of breath among nationalists and the Irish government. Sir Patrick Mayhew QC, MP for Tunbridge Wells, had a long association with the British Army. Solicitor-general from 1983 to 1987 and attorney-general from 1987 to 1992, in both capacities he had taken decisions which had annoyed Irish governments, the main one being his refusal, on grounds of 'national security', to authorise the prosecution of eleven RUC men in connection with the shooting of six unarmed men in 1982. Dublin objected privately to his appointment, but Mayhew was the man who had offered John Major his first step on the ladder in 1981 and this was his reward: the prime minister was not to be moved.

Mayhew chose a partner for the North in the same mould as himself – Michael Mates. A career officer who had reached the rank of lieutenant-colonel, Mates had served in the North and was known for his very strong line against republicans. Now he was in charge of security in the North. There had hardly ever been such a visible swing to the right in the NIO than the arrival of these two perceived hardliners in the wake of Peter Brooke's administration. It seemed Sinn Féin would receive short shrift from Mayhew and Mates.

In fact, most of the dire predictions about the two 'military men' proved to be entirely wrong. Mayhew, at sixty-three the oldest man in Major's Cabinet, had never thought he would make the Cabinet. He owed his position completely to the prime minister and faithfully carried out Major's policies on Ireland, as did Mates. Sinn Féin was part of the political landscape and the attempts to help the party into the political process continued behind the scenes. Mayhew picked up exactly where Brooke had left off and, despite the devastation caused in the City of London, authorised the continuation of the secret contacts with the IRA.

As for Sinn Féin, all the groundwork had been laid. A number of the republican movement's sacred cows had been successfully and silently slaughtered, their demise unnoticed in the noise of the IRA campaign. How far the party had travelled can be measured by the distance between *A Scenario for Peace* in 1987 and *Towards a Lasting Peace in Ireland* in 1992. But the big question remained: how to end the IRA campaign?

11. NEGOTIATING THE ROADBLOCKS
The Pendulum Swings to Sinn Féin

The ultimate success of the long, protracted and, for many people, infinitely tedious business of what came to be called the 'peace process' is a testament to Gerry Adams's leadership of Sinn Féin. Many other individuals, various political parties in Ireland and Britain, and several governments – Irish, British, American and South African – all played important parts. In the last analysis, however, since the peace process meant bringing the republican movement intact into the political mainstream, the central figure responsible for achieving that goal was Gerry Adams.

The judgement of all concerned was that while there was, and still remains, a small coterie of people close to Adams – a kitchen cabinet in political parlance – only Gerry Adams could deliver the republican movement in one piece. Any other result would have been worse than useless. If the movement had split, as it had always done in the past, with those favouring exclusively political means leaving behind a powerful group clinging to militarism, the consequence would have been an immediate security crisis in the North of Ireland and in Britain. By the early 1990s the IRA had not been going at full tilt for years. In the event of a split, the militarists, suddenly bereft of a political rudder, could have set to work with everything at their disposal, namely over 100 tonnes of modern munitions, unprecedented expertise in explosives and twenty years' experience of guerrilla war.

Some of the militants did indeed split from the IRA in the 1990s, most notably the so-called Real IRA, but those who left the main movement did so as disaffected individuals, not in a substantial *bloc* as in earlier years. The republican movement as a whole has remained intact. Keeping by far the biggest part of it together required all the subtlety, political caution and personal authority Gerry Adams could command.

The process of weaning the republican movement from the armed struggle took much longer and involved many more twists and turns and setbacks than any of the protagonists could have imagined at the outset. It was carried through in the face of outside pressure, impatience, exasperation, setbacks and political mischief-making in both Ireland and Britain. In the end Sinn Féin had to upend a number of cherished beliefs. In the referendums after the 1998 Agreement, the party would campaign for a devolved assembly at Stormont in the North and the replacement of Articles 2 and 3 of *Bunreacht na hÉireann* (the Constitution of Ireland) in the South, both of which were proposals republicans had once fiercely and violently opposed.

Inevitably, Gerry Adams had to concede more than he had bargained for – he certainly never thought the IRA would have to dispose of weapons – but the extraordinarily rapid political progress of Sinn Féin has more than vindicated his policies and has enabled him to make departures from traditional republican positions that he had not envisaged, nor anyone would have believed possible, in the early 1990s.

As a result, the contrast in Sinn Féin's fortunes between the beginning and end of the decade could not be greater. In 1992 Gerry Adams was defeated in West Belfast and Sinn Féin's vote looked to be in decline in Westminster elections. In the nine years following, as the peace process accelerated, Sinn Féin increased its support in every Northern Ireland

An taoiseach Albert Reynolds welcomes Gerry Adams and John Hume at the Taoiseach's Office following the IRA ceasefire in 1994.

Gerry Adams and Martin McGuinness outside number 10 Downing Street.

An Taoiseach Bertie Ahern outside Sinn Féin's
office on the Falls Road with Gerry Adams.

Gerry Adams emerges from Sinn Féin's heavily fortified Falls Road office.

Jim Gibney, one of the republican
movement's most influential political
strategists, photographed
in February 2002.

Sinn Féin's newly refurbished office
on the Falls Road, February 2002.

Sinn Féin's leaders locked out of talks at Stormont in
1996 after the IRA ceasefire had ended.

Sinn Féin activists at Stormont demanding inclusion in the talks.

Martin McGuinness, on home ground
with members of the Bogside Residents'
Group, confronts a member of an RUC
Divisional Mobile Support unit.

Gerry Adams addresses a Sinn Féin rally in the Ulster Hall – a symbolic
location in the history of Ulster Unionism.

The launch of Sinn Féin's 1992 general election manifesto,
which contained republicans' new political thinking.

British prime minister John Major with northern secretary
Sir Patrick Mayhew at Stormont Castle.

Ulster Unionist leader and the North's
First Minister, David Trimble MP.

Dr Mo Mowlam, northern secretary at the time of the Good Friday Agreement,
seated with John Hume and Gerry Adams.

US president Bill Clinton takes tea with Gerry Adams and Martin McGuinness.

Sinn Féin's MPs in their new Westminster office, January 2002,
with the Irish tricolour on the right of the picture.

election. The icing on the cake was the appointment in 1999 of two Sinn Féin ministers to the most important spending departments in Northern Ireland: Education, run by Martin McGuinness, and Health, run by Bairbre de Brún. In 2001, in both local government and Westminster elections in Northern Ireland, remarkably, one in five people who voted, voted Sinn Féin. From having no Westminster seat in 1992, Sinn Féin entered the new century with four, and simultaneously achieved the party's long-held ambition of overtaking the SDLP, the main nationalist party in the North.

In the Republic, after more than a decade of fruitless forays into Dáil elections, at last in 1997 Sinn Féin won a seat in Cavan–Monaghan when Caoimhghín Ó Caoláin topped the poll there. The number of the party's councillors in the South grew throughout the 1990s to reach a total of sixty-three by the end of the decade and, helped by the high profile of Sinn Féin's leaders in the North, opinion polls showed Sinn Féin at its highest level of popular support in the Republic since the 1920s.

If no one thought the process of bringing Sinn Féin into even quasi-constitutional politics would take so long, it is also true that no one foresaw Sinn Féin's gains would be so large and so rapid. The speed of the party's advance in substituting recourse to the ballot box for reliance on the Armalite, and the immediate dividends the voters bestowed on Sinn Féin's public figures as a result, had the useful effect of balancing and compensating for the difficulties and internal strains the party had faced during the 1990s. In retrospect, it is easy to see how those political developments helped to sway the hard men or at least to undermine their arguments. For much of the process, however, it certainly did not seem to the leaders of the republican movement that many benefits were accruing to Sinn Féin or that any quick progress was being made.

On the contrary, for republicans everything seemed to slow down in mid-1992. Following the February election of Albert Reynolds as taoiseach in the Republic to replace Charles Haughey, a new secretary of state, Sir Patrick Mayhew, took office in the North in April. The new men needed time to find their bearings.

Behind the scenes, however, things were happening. It should be borne in mind that the Irish side of the 'peace process' had been underway for at least five years before it became public in 1993, and that until 1992 Sinn Féin had had the initiative. It was Sinn Féin that had asked for meetings with nationalist leaders North and South, and when the meetings began to happen in 1988, it was Sinn Féin that had proposed cooperation between parties in the North and the Irish government. Neither the SDLP nor the Irish government had rejected the suggestions outright, apart from the obvious objection that there could be no cooperation while violence continued. Essentially, what Sinn Féin had been discussing, though few realised it at the time, were the terms on which the party could be admitted onto the Irish political scene. As soon as he became aware of what had been going on, the new taoiseach, Albert Reynolds, continued the process, authorising his advisor, Dr Martin Mansergh, to meet Sinn Féin in secret.

Unknown to the Irish government even more secret talks had been going on since 1990 between the IRA and the British government through an elaborate arrangement called the 'back channel'. This arrangement had operated sporadically for years since the 1970s and involved 'contacts' in Derry, mainly the former priest, Denis Bradley, who had officiated at the wedding of Martin McGuinness. Bradley and two others relayed messages to and from senior IRA men to an MI6 man, Michael Oatley, who purported to present the British government's position. After 1991, there were also face-to-face meetings between the IRA and Oatley's successor and, later still, with a senior NIO official, Quentin Thomas. In the case of these talks, contrary to what British ministers would later maintain, it was the British government and not the IRA that took the initiative in 1990, and it was the British government that held the initiative throughout the exchanges.

Sinn Féin fielded separate teams for the two sets of talks, with Martin McGuinness being the only representative in both. Besides him and his advisor, fellow Derryman Aidan McAteer, son of the 1940s IRA chief of staff Hugh McAteer[1], the men involved as Sinn Féin representatives in face-to-face talks with various Irish officials and politicians were Gerry Adams, Mitchel McLoughlin, Pat Doherty, Tom Hartley and Jim Gibney. Danny Morrison, who had participated in the original talks with the SDLP, had gone back to jail in 1990 and remained there during the crucial period to 1994, after which he left the movement to take up writing full-time. Representing the IRA with McGuinness in talks first with MI6 and then with the NIO was Gerry Kelly, who had been released from jail in 1991. Kelly had been in prison or on the run since 1973.

Sinn Féin had different objectives in each of the talks. First, in dealing with the Irish government through the SDLP leader John Hume and separately through Dr Martin Mansergh, the party was pursuing a double strategy. Its short-term objective was to end the isolation of republicans by building an alliance with the Irish government and the SDLP. The long-term aim was to construct an agreed Irish strategy for a settlement and to present it to the British, a line of approach advocated publicly in December 1990 in an *Irish Times* article by Fr Alec Reid. Secondly, in the secret talks with the so-called British government representative, the objective was to secure cast-iron guarantees that the British would be prepared to negotiate on withdrawal from Ireland and that negotiations would begin *before* a ceasefire. Republicans were prepared to demonstrate that they were able to suspend military operations for a time, but would not declare an open-ended ceasefire prior to talks.

The IRA's demand for something concrete to enable it to call a ceasefire was of absolutely crucial importance to republicans because of the history of the previous ceasefire in 1975. Adams and McGuinness in particular, along with Kelly, the link man to the Army Council, were adamant that they would not repeat the mistake Ruairí Ó Brádaigh and Dáithí Ó Conaill had made, namely being lured into a ceasefire with no prior commitment by the British to substantive negotiations. The IRA believed that any ceasefire period would be dragged out while the British lied and prevaricated and the IRA atrophied – and the movement lost the bargaining power it believed its military campaign provided. Accordingly, the IRA had repeatedly said that there would be no ceasefire until the British announced their intention to withdraw from the North: the logistics and consequences of such a withdrawal would then be negotiated.

In the end, it was the Irish talks that produced the successful results, partly because Irish government officials had a greater understanding than their British counterparts of the issues involved for republicans, partly because the Irish had a clear strategy and policy aim. In addition, since republicans were not engaged in armed action against the Dublin government, it was not inconceivable for Irish officials to consider circumstances in which an Irish government could cooperate with Sinn Féin to achieve a settlement in Ireland – after military violence had ended. There was steady progress until summer 1992. By April 1992 the Dublin government had presented to Sinn Féin a fourth draft of a declaration on self-determination to be agreed jointly by the Irish and British governments. Then progress stalled: nothing seemed to happen except more revisions of the document.

Ultimately the secret talks with the British representative came to nothing and apparently collapsed in November 1993. 'Apparently', because only the British and the republicans know what secret contacts there have been since. During the whole of the period of the Troubles, from 1969 until the IRA ceasefire in 1997, there was scarcely a time when the British security services, MI5 or MI6 or both, did not have a channel

open to the IRA. Even during the early 1990s when the IRA was deto-
nating enormous bombs in London, mortaring Downing Street and
blowing up towns in the North of Ireland with renewed regularity, the
British representative kept talking to them, sometimes on a weekly basis.

The contents of the talks, which became public when the republican
movement released the documentation in November 1993 under acri-
monious and disputed circumstances, are interesting for a number of reasons. Surprisingly, until spring 1993 the British government was prepared
to talk to the IRA in more radical terms than the Irish government
considered possible in its drafting of the proposed joint declaration. In one
set of talks, Irish officials were trying to convince Sinn Féin that it was
pointless to present the British with a proposal for a joint governmental
declaration that included a time-scale for British withdrawal but did not
contain very strong references to the principle of consent. At the same
time, the British representative talking to the IRA was envisaging, as late
as March 1993, that in the event of a two-week ceasefire delegation meetings between the British and republicans would follow, and would even be
facilitated by flying republicans out to a location in Scotland or Scandina-
via for the purpose.

In the most controversial excerpts from the talks between the British
and the IRA, the British representative is minuted by republicans as telling Martin McGuinness and Gerry Kelly in March 1993:

> Any settlement not involving all the people, North and South,
> won't work. The final solution is union. The historical train –
> Europe – determines that. We are committed to Europe. Unionists
> will have to change. This island will be as one.

The representative repeated the request for a fortnight's suspension
of violence to allow talks to begin and told McGuinness and Kelly that if
such a suspension happened, then clearance for meetings between delega-
tions would follow immediately. He added that only the prime minister

John Major, the northern secretary Sir Patrick Mayhew, the foreign secretary Douglas Hurd and the Cabinet secretary Sir Robin Butler knew of all this. In the event, of course, nothing happened. The British did not respond to a Sinn Féin document of 10 May 1993 saying the IRA had agreed to the fortnight's suspension of operations as required. By the end of May the British representative told the IRA's contact that the offer of the delegate conference had been withdrawn.

The precise details of these talks are still unclear. The version provided by the republicans may be wrong or deliberately hyped up or, as most observers seem to have concluded, it may be that it was the British, not the republicans, who lied and misled the public about their contents. Even if the details are wrong, however, the fact remains that the British government had authorised such contacts while the prime minister was engaged in regular exchanges with the taoiseach about an entirely different policy approach, which Irish governments, Sinn Féin and the SDLP had been working on for years by spring 1993. John Hume had briefed the permanent secretary at the NIO, John Chilcot, in detail about the joint declaration approach in the summer of 1992.

Apart from the duplicity revealed, what also appeared to have been exposed when these contacts between the IRA and the British became public in November 1993 was the chaotic nature of policy-making about Ireland that prevailed at Cabinet level in London. After all, the Downing Street Declaration, the genesis of which had been in Ireland in 1991 and which was to involve thousands of hours' work by politicians and officials in Ireland and Britain, was agreed in December 1993. Yet until a few months earlier, the British prime minister and his northern secretary seemed prepared to contemplate a totally different scenario. Did the right hand not know what the left hand was doing? How could this state of affairs exist?

The answer, of course, is that it could not. The British had reactivated the back channel in 1990 on the advice of John Deverell, the MI5 boss in Northern Ireland, who had intelligence that changes were taking place in republican thinking. MI5 knew about the continuing meetings between John Hume and Gerry Adams. They also knew about the meetings in Dundalk with Dr Martin Mansergh and Dermot Ahern TD. Peter Brooke intimated in a 1995 interview that the purpose of originating the back-channel meetings was intelligence gathering. Was it possible that by 1993, with all the intelligence assets at their disposal, the British still had no take on the sea change that had taken place in republicanism? Had they not read Adams's *Towards a Lasting Peace in Ireland*? Did they not believe what Albert Reynolds was telling John Major, or what John Hume was telling John Chilcot? Did they not accept that Sinn Féin was prepared to endorse the sort of language that was being used in drafts of the joint declaration, which, by 1993, John Major was aware of?

Of course they did. In fact, it is known from accounts given by the Derry-based contacts that the British knew details of most of the meetings between John Hume and Gerry Adams and had a copy of the Hume–Adams document in early 1993. Why, therefore, would the British representatives speaking to the IRA continue to indulge republican ideas of British withdrawal, or even hold out the possibility of negotiations between the IRA and the British about that issue and others, including Irish unity? Where would the Irish government, Britain's partner in the 1985 Anglo-Irish Agreement, fit into all this, not to mention the unionists and the SDLP?

The answer is breathtakingly simple. The British were no more serious in 1992–93 than they had been in 1975. That is not to say that the British officials involved were operating in bad faith. On the contrary, they were carrying out the instructions of Conservative politicians – some of the speaking notes have become public – and felt very let down when the venture was abandoned. From the politicians' point of view the back-channel talks were always exploratory, never substantive. The ministers in the Cabinet committee who authorised the talks could never have had any intention of making any binding commitments at such meetings.

There are only three discernible objectives the British could have had. The first is that they were trying to ascertain the IRA's bottom-line in negotiations without actually negotiating. The second is that they were trying to find the IRA's price for a ceasefire and, when they believed they had discovered it in April 1993, immediately refused to pay. The third possibility is that they were trying to inveigle the IRA into a long ceasefire by holding out the possibility of talks about Irish unity, talks which would imply British withdrawal and therefore meet the IRA's criterion for a ceasefire.

The British failure to respond to the IRA ceasefire offer in May 1993 left republicans feeling very sore. After desultory attempts to renew negotiations, Sinn Féin sent a message to the British government in September that said:

> The positive response by the leadership of the IRA underlined the willingness on the republican side to facilitate movement towards a real peace process. The rejection of this substantial gesture by you has not only prevented further movement but has damaged the project and increased the difficulties involved. This, and your present attempts to deny this aspect of the contact between us, can only be regarded with the utmost scepticism and must raise serious questions about your motives in all of this.

The behaviour of John Major's government in those talks with the IRA was indeed profoundly damaging and, in some respects, mischievous. First, it has to be made clear why there was no chance whatsoever that any of the offers the British representatives dangled before the IRA in 1993 could have been serious or could have come to fruition. Quite simply, they would have been politically impossible.

In 1993 the Conservative Party in Britain began to tear itself apart on the issue of the European Union. John Major had won the 1992 general election with a much reduced but workable majority. However, he proved to be a pathetically weak leader with little personal authority in the party. When it came to EU issues, enough Conservative MPs defied him to deprive him of a working majority. In these circumstances, the nine Ulster Unionist MPs, led by Jim Molyneaux, became a vital *bloc* for Major as crucial voting on ratifying sections of the Maastricht Treaty loomed in 1993.

While Major did not enter into any formal agreement with the unionists, nevertheless an understanding emerged that, over the next four years, enabled them to extract from him important concessions at critical moments in the peace process in return for their continued support on Europe. Whatever Major's failings as a leader, at least he could count and, as a former Conservative Party whip, he knew from early 1993 that the survival of his government depended on judicious handling of Jim Molyneaux. This fact alone would have made it impossible for the offers the British representative made to the IRA to be serious. The relationship with the unionists, which had begun in summer 1993, dominated the rest of Major's administration and caused the temporary collapse of the peace process in 1996.

Leaving aside the power that the Ulster Unionists, along with a clique of right-wing Tories, had to veto anything arising out of secret talks with republicans, there was also the other side of the political coin, namely the SDLP and the Irish government. The reality is that neither the Irish government nor the Ulster Unionists would have stood for the British entering into substantive negotiations on a bilateral basis with republicans about relations between Britain and Ireland.

The official talks with republicans were damaging and mischievous because the British government knew all these political facts yet continued to raise republican expectations well into 1993. Republicans took the British overtures very seriously indeed, investing an enormous amount of time and effort in their detailed responses. In fact, they became quite excited about them in March, setting up a small working party chaired by Gerry Adams to deal with what they thought were serious proposals by the British government. Indeed, it is quite likely that what Sinn Féin believed to be a *bona fide* offer of negotiations by the British actually delayed and distorted the ongoing discussions with Irish officials through John Hume and Dr Martin Mansergh.

One other damaging aspect of the British approach was that it ignored the process that Gerry Adams was carefully nurturing to swing the pendulum in the republican movement slowly but imperceptibly from the IRA towards Sinn Féin. The British paid no attention to this important development, instead adopting the line John Hume had taken in 1985 when he refused to speak to Sinn Féin, assuming that Sinn Féin carried no clout and that the only people who mattered were those who could speak for the IRA. As explained in the previous chapter, John Hume and those in the Irish government privy to developments in republicanism had accepted since 1988 that the leaders of Sinn Féin wanted to break the cycle of violence and to establish the party as a political entity in its own right. By ignoring Sinn Féin's political credentials the British overtures undermined the whole process undertaken by the Irish, which was to bring republicans into the political arena through recognising Sinn Féin as the element to deal with and by trying to assist Adams, and others close to him, in their efforts to enhance Sinn Féin's position in the republican movement.

The blandishments of the British representatives in spring 1993 must also have engendered doubts in the republican leadership about whether the Irish approach was the correct one. Perhaps the IRA would succeed in bombing the British to the negotiating table? Perhaps they already had?

The mighty blast that had destroyed the Baltic Exchange in April 1992 had certainly sent reverberations through the British government because it made investors think twice about locating important financial offices in London when Frankfurt was the alternative choice. The City of London is worth billions of pounds annually in 'invisible earnings' to the British economy. Any loss of confidence among international financiers would be very expensive. The enormous compensation costs for bomb damage had sent a shiver through the insurance industry, a pillar of the financial services sector in the City.

Throughout 1993 the IRA kept up its attacks on England with bombs, hoax bombs and bomb warnings, which caused traffic chaos and closed London tube and mainline train stations. Inevitably there were 'mistakes', that is, civilian casualties, which drew down bitter condemnation, none more so than the infamous Warrington bombs, which killed two children, one aged three, and injured fifty-six people. Tens of thousands turned out to a peace rally in Dublin to express their detestation at what had happened. Little did those people know that the British kept talking, even meeting Gerry Kelly and Martin McGuinness on 23 March, three days after the Warrington bombs, while the wave of revulsion the bombs had provoked still rolled across Ireland and Britain.

So maybe the bombing was working? On 24 April 1993, the seventy-seventh anniversary of the 1916 Easter Rising, the IRA detonated a 2,000lb bomb at the NatWest Tower at Bishopsgate in the City of London, killing a *News of the World* photographer who had got inside the security ring. It was a vast explosion, which followed eighteen misleading telephone warnings. The blast destroyed many buildings, including the prestigious Hong Kong and Shanghai Bank, and caused a mind-boggling stg£300 million damage. Was this the sort of event that had induced the British to talk to the IRA? Senior IRA figures thought so. Many unionists agreed, and to this day still maintain that the fear of devastation of

London's financial district led Major's government to look for a settlement the IRA would accept.

What little evidence there is suggests the opposite was the case. The Bishopsgate bomb exploded on 24 April 1993. Thereafter the British failed to respond to the IRA's offer of a fortnight's ceasefire. Some time later the British passed this message to the IRA:

> Events on the ground are crucial, as we have consistently made clear. We cannot conceivably disregard them. We gave advice in good faith, taking what we were told at face value. It is difficult to reconcile that with recent events.

The 'recent events' were not only the London bomb but huge bombs in towns in the North of Ireland, including one on the day of the local government election results in May 1993 that inflicted extensive damage on the Opera House in Belfast and on the adjacent and repeatedly bombed Europa hotel. John Major later said the Opera House bomb was 'one too many'. Apparently, talking to the IRA was not having any effect. On top of that, the prospect of the talks being publicly disclosed in the midst of the tragedies visited on people in spring 1993 entailed horrendous political consequences for the British, particularly since the talks were going nowhere and, from the British perspective, achieving nothing.

In fact, the real action was elsewhere – in the elaborate network of meetings taking place in Ireland between Gerry Adams and John Hume on one side, and Sinn Féin, Dr Martin Mansergh and Fr Reid on the other. The Hume–Adams side became public in April 1993 when Adams was seen entering John Hume's house in Derry, a sighting that is hard to believe was accidental, although John Hume insists it was unintentional and unhelpful. A welter of criticism, even outrage in some quarters, followed. Ten days later, at the significant republican date of Easter, Hume and Adams decided to issue a joint statement about their contacts. As it turned out, their statement coincided with the devastating Bishopsgate bomb. Far from the criticism quietening, it grew into sustained attacks on Hume for having anything to do with Adams. The British administration, itself still in secret contact with the IRA, joined in.

While those concerned in the nexus of meetings with Sinn Féin, including the Irish government, maintain that they were unhappy at the revelation of the Hume–Adams meetings, there is reason to believe that going public suited the purposes of both Hume and Adams. The two men had reached agreement nine months earlier, in June 1992, on a fundamental set of points which became known as the 'Hume–Adams document'. Essentially, it was their draft for a joint Irish–British declaration. What was vitally important about it from Hume's perspective was that it had gone to Dublin with the support of Sinn Féin. By March 1993, however, Dublin officials had produced three more drafts of it, watering down its republican tone, particularly on the issue of self-determination, to try to make it more acceptable for presentation to the British. However, Major's administration remained unhappy with the whole concept of a joint declaration from the moment it was first suggested to them in 1992.

Suddenly, in April 1993, after Sinn Féin had received the third revision of the Hume–Adams document from Dublin, the IRA Army Council sent Dublin a message saying that it was sticking by the original Hume–Adams version of June 1992. Was this decision taken because the IRA was fed up with the nine-month delay and all the revisions? Or did they go back to the previous year's document because their secret contacts with the British in early 1993 had led them to believe that they could extract a lot more than the Irish officials were leading them to believe?

The Army Council message sent to Dublin, announcing the intention to revert to the original Hume–Adams document, said:

> While accepting the integrity of BAC's[2] seriousness about the project we are nevertheless unable to convince ourselves that the outline package proffered, of joint declarations/steps/timetable

and BAC's 'understanding' of a 15/40 years time-scale would produce the necessary dynamic.

The '15/40 years time-scale' in the message referred to progress
towards a united Ireland. The language used by the British representatives
in talks with the IRA had implied a great deal more speed and exactitude
than the vague fifteen to forty years that the Irish government was talking
about.[3] The issue of British withdrawal and its time-scale was still the
major obstacle for the IRA. They would not consider a ceasefire without
it. It was the only point that Gerry Adams and John Hume had not agreed
upon, either in June 1992 or by April 1993.

Going public about their meetings and the concepts they had agreed
between them did have a number of attractions for Hume and Adams. It
put pressure on the Irish government, which had been passing papers
back and forth since the previous summer. It showed how far republicans
had travelled and weakened the position of the militarists in the republican movement. Significantly, it also scotched any lingering hopes the
British administration in the North might still have entertained about
cobbling together a deal among the 'centre' parties – the Ulster Unionists
and the SDLP – and thereby excluding Sinn Féin. The down side of going
public was that, given the British government's dependence on the
unionists and the IRA's campaign of destruction in England, it was
impossible for the British to accept any document that had, in the phrase
the British used, 'Gerry Adams's fingerprints on it'. John Hume never
fully came to grips with this reality and it caused him growing frustration
throughout 1993. As far as Hume was concerned all the major players had
the Hume–Adams document, the basis for a ceasefire. Why would they
not act upon it?

Hume was too close to the process to see that while the document
might be the basis for an IRA ceasefire, if it were not acceptable to the
British there would be no ceasefire. As it stood it was unacceptable,

certainly to a British government dependent on unionist votes. Apart from the fact that Gerry Adams was involved in drafting it, there were many other objections to the content. The most serious objection was the matter of an agreed time-scale for British legislation to give effect to Irish self-determination. Paragraph 4 of Hume–Adams read:

> The British government accepts the principle that the Irish people have the right collectively to self-determination, and that the exercise of this right could take the form of agreed independent structures for the island as a whole. They affirm their readiness to introduce the measures to give legislative effect on their side to this right [within a specified period to be agreed] and allowing sufficient time for the building of consent and the beginning of a process of national reconciliation.

The expert Irish officials, Seán Ó hUiginn, Dermot Nally and Dr Martin Mansergh, could see the major snag immediately and tried to explain it to Sinn Féin and to John Hume. A time-scale for Irish unity could not exist in the same document as another clause guaranteeing the consent of the people of Northern Ireland to constitutional change because unionists would refuse to consent to Irish unity. Writing in a time-scale for unity cancelled out consent to unity. Likewise, the British could not be persuaders for Irish unity as Sinn Féin wanted because the British had to remain agnostic on what the outcome of Irish self-determination might be. The British had declared they had no strategic or other interest in Ireland: the outcome of self-determination was a matter for the Irish people alone.

Nevertheless, the joint statements which John Hume and Gerry Adams issued periodically from Easter 1993 showed the extent of movement in republicanism. Adams had now publicly accepted the proposition that John Hume had put to him in 1988. This was that the Irish people were divided on how to exercise self-determination and therefore that self-determination could come about only by agreement among the Irish people. In effect, that meant recognising the necessity for unionist consent. It was helpful not just to let the general public know that this was the case but, more importantly, to make the republican movement at large aware too. Another advantage was that the North's local government elections were due on 19 May 1993. During the campaign the British government's broadcasting ban would be lifted so Sinn Féin candidates would be able to present the position agreed with Hume to the media.

What did not become known publicly at that time was that the republican movement had, in the Hume–Adams document of June 1992, accepted a far more explicit version of the consent principle and had also accepted that 'it will be a fundamental guiding principle that all differences between the Irish people relating to the exercise in common of the right to self-determination will be resolved exclusively by peaceful means.' Both Hume and Adams believed their document was about as far along as they could bring the IRA militarists. Indeed, in the message the Army Council sent to the Irish government reiterating their adherence to Hume–Adams and rejecting further amendments, their jitters were apparent:

> We earnestly believe that the position put by us in the June draft [Hume–Adams] is the surest way of providing what is required. We remind you that in coming to the June position we've accepted the concepts which form no great part of our traditional political vocabulary.

That was surely one of the understatements of the whole process and one of the reasons John Hume became increasingly agitated during the rest of 1993. The main reason for his dismay, however, was that from Easter onwards he and Adams lost control of the whole process.

The Irish government agreed with the British that any document known to have been prepared with the cooperation of Gerry Adams and Sinn Féin was not a runner. The two governments therefore cut Hume and Adams out and now began to draw up their own document, which ultimately became the Downing Street Declaration of December 1993. Unionists and loyalist paramilitaries, too, had to have their 'fingerprints' on such a document because of the role republicans had played in earlier Irish drafts: so Irish officials and intermediaries contacted loyalists to ascertain their concerns. Dublin officials also had to accept watering-down by British redrafting, not least because it would be naive to believe that any government would simply sign up to another government's document. The big question at the end of it all was, would the IRA accept the finished product, very different in many respects from 'Hume–Adams', as the basis for a ceasefire? It took a long time and much exegesis of the Declaration for Sinn Féin's benefit by Dr Martin Mansergh, Seán Ó hUiginn, Fr Reid and others to persuade them.

The reason the Downing Street Declaration was successful in the end in bringing about an IRA ceasefire lay not just in the Declaration itself, though some of its phraseology is a diplomatic work of art, but in the thinking behind it. In comparison to the bull-in-a-china-shop approach by the British government in spring 1993, Dr Martin Mansergh and the officials from the Department of Foreign Affairs operated at an entirely different level of subtlety and intellectual sophistication. They engaged Sinn Féin leaders in debates about republicanism and Irish identity and sought to encourage them to take their place in Irish politics. They took Sinn Féin seriously. They treated its representatives with respect.

The Irish officials knew that if they could find the minimum position Sinn Féin could live with, then they could argue for more than that in talks with the British. They would, in fact, be able to tell the British what would not work. The prize was, that if the two governments agreed a declaration that defined the position of the governments of Ireland and Britain on the North of Ireland and on Irish self-determination, then Sinn Féin would be able to advise the IRA to call off the military campaign.

The reason Sinn Féin could do so was plain. If the Irish government agreed a joint position with the British, then no IRA campaign, nor indeed any other republican military campaign, could possibly succeed in overthrowing it. What would be the point of such a campaign? Armed resistance against a joint declaration that left self-determination in the hands of the Irish people and eschewed any role in it for Britain would completely isolate the IRA and conclusively ruin Sinn Féin's electoral and political ambitions. The plan was that, after a joint declaration, the next stage for Dublin would be to work urgently with London on agreed structures to give effect to the agreed position on self-determination. That was the thinking behind the policy the Irish government followed, and it was because of Irish officials' deep understanding of the republican position that the Irish peace initiative succeeded.

Though republicans were dismayed and disappointed with some of the phraseology in the Downing Street Declaration, the consequences of rejecting the Declaration were made clear to them. The job of persuasion was one for Gerry Adams and the northern leadership. Throughout the spring of 1994 there were meetings of republican activists at several venues across the North. Prisoners with maximum 'street cred', like Bik McFarlane, were released on parole by the NIO to tell activists that the prisoners supported 'the Irish peace initiative', which all republicans firmly believed they owned. Leading figures, like Pat Doherty, travelled Ireland explaining the policy to activists.

While this process was going on some of the most important and dramatically persuasive action was taking place 3,000 miles away. The policy of Gerry Adams and his senior Sinn Féin supporters was endorsed and encouraged with characteristic vigour and forcefulness by the most powerful man in the world, the American president, Bill Clinton. In what was a diplomatic revolution in early 1994, president Clinton took the advice of the Irish government against that of the British government when he granted Gerry Adams a visa to visit the USA. In a break with normal US practice, which astonished and dismayed the British government, the president overrode the traditionally pro-British State Department and directed his administration's policy through the National Security Council, hand-picking advisors like Nancy Soderberg who adopted a hands-on approach to Ireland.

Clinton's interest in the North of Ireland was the successful culmination of a major effort by Irish diplomats, led by the Irish ambassador to the USA Dermot Gallagher, millionaire Irish-American businessmen like Bill Flynn and Chuck Feeney, and Democratic politicians led by Senator Ted Kennedy, a powerful ally of Clinton as the chairman of the Senate Foreign Relations Committee. They had been working on Clinton since the early days of his presidential campaign in 1991. Now their work paid off. By contrast, members of John Major's government had interfered in the USA presidential campaign on the side of George Bush to the extent that Foreign Office records from the 1960s were trawled to see if they would yield any dirt on Clinton's own visa application to study at Oxford.

Clinton's personal intervention in the North caused profound shock and alarm to the British government and initially produced a typically childish and petulant response from John Major. For a fortnight after Adams got the visa, the prime minister refused to take phone calls from Clinton. Apart from concern at Clinton's personal involvement in what many Conservatives fondly maintained was a 'UK problem', the British were angry that Clinton followed the Irish government's line on Sinn Féin.

After the Downing Street Declaration of December 1993, Gerry Adams had asked for clarification of many points in the document. Major had refused point-blank, but Albert Reynolds had instructed his officials to provide all the clarification necessary. The thinking behind the Irish response was this: Sinn Féin had asked publicly and privately for evidence that entering the political system would achieve more than the Armalite/ballot box strategy. Irish governments did everything possible to smooth their path, to provide material to show the IRA how politics could make things happen. For their part the British tried to build a fence around republicans, seal them off and then offer them only one way out – the route the British had decided was appropriate. That policy never worked; indeed, it tended to produce a predictably violent reaction from the IRA.

The decision to give Adams a US visa was, for the reasons just explained, strongly supported by the Irish government but equally strongly opposed by the British who kept demanding a Yes or No to the Downing Street Declaration. It was the first in a long series of stand-offs between Major and Adams, which ended only with Major's comprehensive defeat in the 1997 general election.

When Gerry Adams arrived in New York in January 1994 the welcome he received confirmed all the worst fears of the British government and the Ulster Unionists. He was fêted at receptions everywhere. His speeches received thunderous applause. He appeared on the 'Larry King Show'. He was on coast-to-coast TV programmes. There was an absurd attempt by the British government to prevent satellite telecasts of Adams's US interviews appearing on British TV because it contravened the 1988 British broadcasting ban. In the meantime Albert Reynolds had, on the other hand, lifted the Irish media ban on Sinn Féin, which had been in operation for twenty years.

John Major and his government was furious. In vain did Irish and American officials try to explain to the British that Adams's visit would have a crucial effect in advancing an IRA ceasefire, that Adams being fêted in New York made a ceasefire more likely, that if he failed to deliver he would be dropped like a hot potato and there would never be another visa, that Adams and the republican movement were being inexorably sucked into the political system.

Not so well publicised was another reason for granting the visa. Adams and his entourage (some of whose visas had also caused outrage in the British security services) were mollifying republican supporters in the USA, many of whom were actually more militant than the IRA in Ireland. Their message to them was that there was no sell-out of republican principles. Adams was as anxious to avoid a split among republicans in the USA as he was to avoid a split in Ireland. The last thing he needed was sympathisers in the USA prepared to finance dissidents in Ireland, which, as Adams knew only too well, was exactly what had happened in 1970.

At home in Ireland discussions within the republican movement continued, but no decision was reached on the Downing Street Declaration. The bristling hostility between republicans and the British remained, with both sides adhering to their traditional methods. The IRA used violence to put pressure on the British to make political concessions; the British refused to respond publicly to IRA pressure and questioned the sincerity of Sinn Féin. IRA actions were hugely provocative, almost daring the British to walk away from the process.

The most astonishing and threatening IRA attack during this time caused no casualties but made a laughing stock of security at Britain's biggest airport, Heathrow. On 9 March 1994 the IRA fired five mortar rounds onto the runways: none exploded. Two days later four more hit the airport building. Two days after that four more mortar rounds were fired, one landing on the roof of Terminal Four. No explosions. After each attack there were intense follow-up searches, but they failed to uncover anything except the launch tubes. The IRA had doctored the mortars so that they would not detonate, leaving the question: what if they had? On the day of the final attack, 13 March, the IRA issued a statement criticising the 'negative attitude' of the British government and complimenting themselves that their own 'flexible attitude to the peace process' was 'positive and enduring'. John Major was infuriated. The Irish government and Bill Clinton were exasperated.

So it continued for another five months. It is now known that the decision to call a ceasefire had already been taken in principle. What took time was 'housekeeping'. First, Sinn Féin wanted to know for certain that, upon declaration of a ceasefire, negotiations on a settlement would begin quickly. It was told talks would take place 'within weeks'. It was concerned about prisoners in English jails and also about the extent of remission for those in jail in Northern Ireland. In June the British announced that forty prisoners would be transferred to the North. The big IRA weapons dumps in the Republic had also to be secured under the supervision of reliable quartermasters, that is, Adams's supporters. Sometimes it meant changes of personnel to bring in northerners. It all took time.

There was other business: scores to settle. There had been a huge upsurge in loyalist violence in the previous three years with the UDA and UVF outstripping republicans in killings for the first time. One of the worst periods had been just prior to the Downing Street Declaration when loyalists murdered a large number of Catholics (and some Protestants, too) in indiscriminate attacks with automatic weapons. They were retaliating for what became known as the 'Shankill bomb'. That attack had occurred in October 1993 when an IRA bomb, intended for the UDA leadership, exploded prematurely in a crowded fish shop, killing one of the bombers and nine Protestants. The targeted UDA leaders had left earlier.

Throughout the summer of 1994 the IRA killed a number of senior loyalists, including Ray Smallwood, the chairman of the UDA's political wing and the man who had been the driver for the gang that shot and wounded Bernadette McAliskey in 1981. Other loyalists suspected of random attacks on Catholics in Belfast were shot dead. The bloodshed went on into August. The IRA's last victim before the ceasefire was Martin Cahill, the Dublin criminal known as 'The General'. Cahill was killed instantly by four bullets fired by an IRA hitman who accosted him in Ranelagh, Dublin. Cahill was targetted because he had helped the UVF to carry out an attack on Widow Scallan's pub in central Dublin on 21 May, during which the doorman, an IRA man, was killed.

Just when some members of the Irish and British governments and northern politicians were beginning to think there would be no ceasefire, the announcement came:

> Recognising the potential of the current situation and in order to enhance the democratic process and underlining our definitive commitment to its success, the leadership of Óglaigh na hÉireann have decided that as of midnight, 31 August [1994], there will be a complete cessation of military operations.

It was an historic moment. Few people, even senior members of the security forces with access to intelligence sources, had believed there would be an unqualified ceasefire. The announcement was greeted with a wide range of responses: euphoria, relief, tears, deep suspicion, apprehension.

Albert Reynolds and his government, president Clinton and everyone who had helped build credibility for Sinn Féin were vindicated. Loyalists and unionists feared a secret deal with the British, and they had every reason to after the previous year's revelations regarding secret talks. What would the UDA and UVF do? What would the IRA do if loyalists continued killing Catholics? Only the IRA knew and it was not saying.

Since they obviously had advance information, Sinn Féin had been able to take advantage of the euphoria and open joy of the nationalist community. They organised 'impromptu' celebrations in west Belfast where the Falls Taxi Association led a flag-waving cavalcade along the Falls Road and through Andersonstown. There were similar demonstrations in Derry. The scenes of jubilation screened on TV reinforced unionist grassroots concern that a deal had been done behind their backs. Two days later, an opinion poll in the North's main pro-union newspaper, the *Belfast Telegraph*, showed 56% believed that the IRA ceasefire was the result of a secret deal. Unionist leaders did not know what the ceasefire meant for them, or how to respond – a bewilderment that lasted for months.

Why had the IRA done it? Why had Adams, McGuinness, Doherty and others in the leadership of Sinn Féin advised them to do so? After all, they were advising the IRA Army Council to do what Adams and McGuinness had said they would never again do after the experience of 1975, namely declare a ceasefire without guarantees of any kind from the British government. There may have been understandings, perhaps, but nothing in black and white. Why was it different this time?

The reasons had been presented to senior members of the republican movement in what was known as the TUAS document. Sinn Féin's leaders had drawn up the paper in early summer 1994 after soundings throughout the movement had been completed. TUAS stood for *Totally Unarmed Strategy*. The document explained that the 'main strategic objectives' of the republican movement was:

> To construct an Irish nationalist consensus with international support on the basis of the dynamic contained in the Irish peace initiative. This should aim for:
>
> a. The strongest possible political consensus between the Dublin government, Sinn Féin and the SDLP.
>
> b. A common position on practical measures moving us towards our goal.
>
> c. A common nationalist negotiation position.
>
> d. An international dimension in aid of the consensus (mostly USA and EU).

The document continued for over 1,000 words, outlining in great detail the movement's stance. It concluded:

> It is the first time in 25 years that all major Irish nationalist parties are rowing in roughly the same direction. These combined circumstances are unlikely to gel again in the foreseeable future. The leadership has now decided that there is enough agreement to proceed with the TUAS option.

One of the crucial arguments in the case that Adams put to the Army Council was that the personal intervention of the president of the United States had lent unprecedented power and strength to the peace process. Clinton had overridden British opposition, particularly on the matter of Adams's visa. He had demonstrated his willingness to do so again just days before the ceasefire when he rejected British objections to a visa for Joe Cahill, a veteran IRA man whose record ran back to the 1940s when he had been sentenced to hang for murder. But Clinton worked unremittingly behind the scenes as well, pressurising the British government, giving an 'international dimension' to the process. Those points outlined in the TUAS paper formed the basis on which the IRA Army Council decided to call a cessation of military operations. Only senior members of the movement were privy to the TUAS strategy and the document. Republican activists had been told that the ceasefire was conditional. If the British did not respond, it was back to war.

The IRA had taken their own decision on the cessation. They did not have to meet any conditions set by anyone, British or Irish, outside the movement. No time limit was placed on the duration of the cessation. Rather it was based on the 'combined circumstances' presented in the TUAS document. If any of those circumstances ceased to obtain, the IRA could end the cessation. It was over to Adams to deliver the political dividends which he had claimed were made possible by the prevailing circumstances. The IRA would watch and wait, intact and fully armed, with its members still training, gathering intelligence and planning operations.

Sadly, over the next two and a half years the pattern that had emerged in late 1993 repeated itself. On every substantive issue a stand-off developed between the British government and Sinn Féin. John Major's immediate response to the ceasefire announcement was to demand to know if the ceasefire were permanent. The British would not talk to Sinn Féin until the IRA declared their ceasefire permanent.

Faced with this rigid stance by the British government, the 'combined circumstances' listed in the TUAS document came to the aid of Sinn Féin. In contrast to Britain's lukewarm response and refusal to meet Sinn Féin, Albert Reynolds met Gerry Adams on 6 September and afterwards they joined with John Hume outside the taoiseach's office where the three men posed for the photographers, exchanging historic handshakes. They issued a joint statement that said:

> We are at the beginning of a new era in which we are totally and absolutely committed to democratic and peaceful methods of resolving our political problems. We reiterate that our objective is an equitable and lasting agreement that can command the allegiance of all.

The British demurred. They devised a series of hoops for Sinn Féin to jump through and, despite pressure from Dublin and the USA, refused to meet Sinn Féin at anything other than official level. By October both unionists and the British government had raised the issue that was to dominate the peace process for the next eight years: the disposal, or 'decommissioning', of IRA armaments. It became clear that the British government would not accept Sinn Féin into talks until movement towards decommissioning had begun.

The reaction to this precondition was consternation amongst nationalists and the Irish government. There is no doubt that the matter of the IRA's arsenal had been raised in discussions in 1992 and 1993, but the idea that handing over weapons would be a precondition for talks had never been considered. Some senior Irish officials considered British politicians illiterate when it came to republicanism, but even after lengthy tutorials in the complexities of republican thinking and how dangerous the demand for weapons surrender was, the British remained unmoved. The Irish government and northern nationalists of all shades were of one mind – that decommissioning was a political ploy to avoid substantive talks which included Sinn Féin.

Albert Reynolds's government and president Clinton's government did all in their power to bring Sinn Féin into the political arena. In Dublin, Reynolds established a Forum for Peace and Reconciliation to which representatives of all parties in Ireland were invited, allowing Sinn Féin to take its place alongside other elected politicians. Gerry Adams could, and did, go back to America. He met senior officials of Clinton's government. American politicians made speeches supporting Adams and Sinn Féin. Clinton devised all kinds of conferences on economic aid and investment programmes. Nothing made any difference. The British government would not move towards all-party talks. The unionists stated they would not attend if such talks were convened.

Then in December 1994 one of the props which supported the IRA ceasefire was knocked away. After a lengthy political crisis in the Republic, John Bruton was elected taoiseach, leading a coalition of Labour and Democratic Left. The latter party was led by Proinsias de Rossa, a former republican internee and a member of the Official Republican movement in the 1970s. Because of this political background, de Rossa was viewed with deep suspicion by Sinn Féin. The party's main concern, however, was the new taoiseach, whose record showed that he was almost as negative about the republican movement as many British politicians.

Bruton had no take at all on northern political realities. He remains the only taoiseach in history ever to be criticised in an editorial of the biggest-selling morning newspaper in the North, the nationalist *Irish News*. The criticism was for his mishandling of the peace process, which began within a week of his taking office. Following a meeting with John Major in London, Bruton stated that 'substantive progress' on decommissioning was required, thereby adopting the British position.

One of the requirements of TUAS was an Irish government that would contribute to the aim of producing a 'common nationalist negotiating position'. The whole basis of the peace process was a common front to pressurise the British; since 1993 unionists had been calling it the 'pan--nationalist front'. Clinton's influence was an unlooked-for and indispensable bonus, but an essential ingredient was a proactive Irish government. Bruton failed to provide that ingredient. Dick Spring, the Labour Party leader and tánaiste, had been an irritant to Sinn Féin when in government with Albert Reynolds. Now he swung against Bruton to become the champion of the peace process, earning himself the description by the unionist MP John Taylor of being 'the most detested man in Ulster'. Spring's efforts were in vain. Bruton's instincts were all wrong. He always seemed to make the wrong choice at the wrong time. The whole of 1995 was frittered away without all-party talks.

What was particularly frustrating for Sinn Féin was that, after the 1993 Downing Street Declaration, Irish officials had rapidly taken the process on to the next phase, which was the plan to devise institutions to give expression to the self-determination described in the Declaration. By the summer of 1994 a blueprint for such institutions had been sketched out by Irish and British officials. It was shown to Sinn Féin to help them move the IRA to a ceasefire. Sinn Féin's leaders were quite encouraged by the plans, which contained all-Ireland bodies with executive powers. Yet when the completed plans were published in February 1995 by John Bruton and John Major as the Frameworks Document, Sinn Féin had still not met any British minister and was no closer to talks than it had been when the IRA had declared its ceasefire five months earlier.

The thinking behind the Frameworks Document was absolutely fundamental to removing the basis for a republican military campaign, and that thinking was one of the reasons why all-party talks on the document were so important to Sinn Féin. The core hardline republican position on political institutions was that the last expression of Irish self-determination had been the 1921 election to the Second Dáil, which had been frustrated by the British when they imposed partition in the Treaty of December 1921.[4] The idea of the Frameworks Document was that the all-party agreement on new Northern Ireland and all-Ireland institutions would be put to the Irish people in referendums North and South. Those referendums would be a new expression of the self-determination of the Irish people, superseding the 1921 elections (which had also been conducted in two jurisdictions, Northern Ireland having been established in 1920). The traditional republican position of rejecting both the Stormont and Dublin administrations as illegitimate would then be untenable since the Irish people as a whole would have voted for new institutions and new links between them.

The whole process – Declaration, Frameworks Document, referendums – that had been devised by Irish officials was being held up at a crucial stage by the absence of any negotiations. The British government was blocking it by refusing to talk to Sinn Féin at ministerial level about anything but decommissioning of IRA weapons. There the matter stood throughout 1995. Tensions rose within the republican movement. Was it 1975 all over again? It seemed so.

As well as refusing to convene talks, the British had not moved on the question of prisoners, a key issue for republicans. Yet in July 1995, in a breathtaking display of arrogance and political opportunism to help John Major in a leadership crisis within the Conservative Party, Sir Patrick Mayhew announced the release of Lee Clegg, a paratrooper convicted of murdering a joyrider in west Belfast. Intense rioting erupted in nationalist areas. The following week, in what was to become an annual agony until 2001, a confrontation developed in Portadown as Orangemen attempted to march along the Catholic Garvaghy Road. The violence spread. Loyalists blocked roads across the North and blockaded Larne harbour, halting commercial traffic and preventing many people from going on their summer holidays. Catholics' homes in flashpoint areas were attacked.

As the first anniversary of the IRA ceasefire approached, very serious strains built up within the IRA. Adams desperately needed action from the British on the main front: a date for talks. But by the end of the summer John Bruton seemed, on the contrary, as if he were going to agree with the British government to establish a body to supervise decommissioning *before* talks, another delaying tactic. Sinn Féin sent out frantic signals that this would be the last straw. On 4 September, after a two-hour meeting with Sir Patrick Mayhew, Adams said:

> What they [the British] are actually saying is that before there can be all-party talks there has to be a beginning of the IRA surrendering its weapons. We can't deliver that. What we can deliver is republicans to the table, as others should deliver their particular constituencies, to work out our future and deal with all the issues, including demilitarisation, and disarmament.

After more rumblings in the IRA, Adams and Hume together asked to meet Bruton. He refused. The basis for the ceasefire in TUAS therefore no longer obtained. It is now known that from this time, October 1995, Adams had lost the support of the Army Council. Work had begun in south Armagh on converting a vehicle to transport a huge bomb to London. All the measures which the Irish government took, along with steps taken by Bill Clinton, to maintain a semblance of movement in the peace process for the next five months turned out to be irrelevant. Clinton's hugely successful visit to Ireland, the establishment of Senator George Mitchell's Commission on Decommissioning, which was almost forced down the throat of the British Cabinet, various high-profile meetings with Sinn Féin – none of it mattered. In the utmost secrecy the IRA had decided to renew its campaign. The only question was when.

The answer was 9 February 1996. A 1,000lb bomb exploded near Canary Wharf, the prestigious skyscraper in the heart of London's Dockland. It killed two newsagents and caused over stg£85 million worth of damage to the City, London's financial district. In its statement announcing the end of its cessation, the IRA demanded 'an inclusive negotiated settlement'. All the years of their campaign since 1970 had still not taught the IRA that the method guaranteed *not* to get them into a negotiated settlement was an event like the Canary Wharf bombing.

At the time, many observers believed that the bomb was a response to the announcement of elections to a Belfast Forum, which John Major had made when he dismissed Senator Mitchell's recommendation that decommissioning should take place alongside all-party talks. David Trimble, who was elected Ulster Unionist leader in September 1995 after the seventy-five-year-old Jim Molyneaux resigned, had wanted an election. Nationalists saw it as another delaying tactic and also as a means for Trimble to secure an environment where unionists would be in the majority and could control proceedings.

Subsequently, it was revealed that the bomb had been manufactured long before Senator Mitchell's report or Major's announcement of elections and that there had been a dummy-run three weeks before the real bomb exploded. Later in February, Gerry Adams and John Hume met with the Army Council to request another ceasefire. Afterwards, Adams made public the reasons the Council had given for its actions: it believed the British 'were waging war by other means and were seeking to fracture Irish republicanism and to split the IRA.' There was also the question of prisoners. The Army Council also criticised John Bruton. Their view, according to Adams, was that:

> John Bruton responded more to the British agenda and made no significant attempt to advance an Irish agenda in Ireland, in Britain or internationally. He seemed more content to manage the situation than to build upon it. Mr. Bruton's call for the IRA to make a gesture on arms last March [1995], his refusal to meet John Hume and myself in October, his support for the Unionist election proposal and his public rejection of any nationalist consensus approach undermined the second element on which the cessation was based. Once this basis was removed, through the breaking of the consensus and the reneging on negotiations by the British, the collapse of the peace process became inevitable.[5]

In other words, the IRA had decided that the 'combined circumstances' for TUAS, the basis for the ceasefire, no longer existed. It was to be nearly eighteen months before all the elements of TUAS were back in place again. Whatever the reasons for the IRA's return to a military campaign, the result was that Sinn Féin had no chance of being involved in the talks scheduled to begin on 10 June 1996. Efforts by John Hume to have them included if there were a new ceasefire were rebuffed by John Major in the autumn. Major responded that even if the IRA restored the 1994 ceasefire, there would have to be a lengthy period of quarantine before Sinn Féin could be admitted to talks. Since there had to be a British general election by summer 1997, that meant there was no time for a 'quarantine' (which Sinn Féin would have rejected anyway), and hence there could be no inclusive talks.

Sinn Féin did, however, take part in the election to the David Trimble-inspired Belfast Forum in May 1996 in order to get a mandate for abstaining from it. What they learnt from the election campaign was that most nationalists agreed that John Major was to blame for the collapse of the ceasefire, but also that most nationalists wanted the ceasefire restored. The election to the Forum began a trend that has continued in northern elections ever since: Sinn Féin's vote soared because voters wanted to encourage them to pursue peace. The party received its highest percentage share of the vote to date – 15.5%. The result was repeated in the British general election on 1 May 1997 when the party polled 126,921 votes, 16.1% of the vote, the most since 1955. Martin McGuinness was elected MP for Mid-Ulster, becoming Sinn Féin's second MP after Adams. In the North's local government elections on 21 May 1997, Sinn Féin recorded 16.9% of the vote and increased its number of councillors markedly from fifty-one to seventy-four. For the first time there was a distinct swing away from the SDLP to Sinn Féin. In the 1993 district elections the party split was 75:25, SDLP to Sinn Féin. In 1997 it was 55:45, SDLP to Sinn Féin.

The most decisive changes in 1997 had taken place in Britain and in the Republic. Under the leadership of Tony Blair, the British Labour Party had trounced the Conservatives in the general election. Blair became prime minister with an unprecedented majority of 179, the greatest victory in the Labour Party's history and the greatest Conservative defeat since 1906. Gone was the unionists' stranglehold on progress. It was instantly apparent that Labour was going to be in government for the next ten years. Even if he lost 100 seats at the next election, Blair would still have a majority of seventy-nine. He could push through any measures he wanted. David Trimble could not stop him.

In the Republic, John Bruton's government was also rejected, though by nothing like as decisive a vote as that which had toppled John Major's administration. The Fianna Fáil leader, Bertie Ahern, squeaked in, heading a coalition with the Progressive Democrats and relying on the votes of three, later four independents. For both Blair and Ahern the priority was to get the peace process up and running again, code for getting Sinn Féin into the tent with the other parties.

The first aim for both new premiers was to have the IRA ceasefire restored. The way to do this, Sinn Féin spokesmen kept saying, was to announce all-party talks. Blair hit the ground running. He announced exploratory talks with Sinn Féin. Dr Marjorie 'Mo' Mowlam, the new northern secretary, also wasted no time. An astonishing contrast to the stiff, condescending Mayhew, Mowlam's earthy *bonhomie* shocked and surprised many unionists and made them feel uncomfortable. They perceived that she favoured nationalists. One prominent unionist attacked the 'huggy-wuggy, lovey-dovey secretary of state' for 'embracing the enemy'. Very quickly, David Trimble began to go over her head to appeal to Tony Blair.

Mowlam's main merit was that she was prepared to talk to anyone on equal terms as human beings. She treated Sinn Féin people the same as anyone else, something Sir Patrick Mayhew and his Conservative colleagues had simply been unable to do. She made it plain, publicly, that Sinn Féin would be invited to talks within six weeks of the 1994 ceasefire being restored: no preconditions. Her directness worked magic. There were some dreadful incidents of IRA violence, particularly the murder of two policemen in Lurgan on 16 June who were both shot in the back of the head as they walked on patrol. But Sinn Féin knew from private contacts that the new British government wanted to accelerate the process and, unlike Major, would not be constrained by unionist threats about the Westminster parliamentary arithmetic. All the elements of TUAS, and more, had fallen back into place. Now a British government as well as the Irish government wanted a settlement. After waiting to see how the annual Drumcree stand-off panned out, the IRA called a ceasefire on 20 July.

Republicans had learnt a lot during the period since the Canary Wharf bomb. Elections showed that nationalists wanted peace and were prepared to vote for Sinn Féin to encourage the republican movement to opt for peace. The IRA had also learnt that there was no longer the necessary level of support for military violence in the nationalist community. People had simply been ringing the police and telling them when they saw bombing teams leaving a primed device at its target. The IRA had to issue an unprecedented statement warning people in nationalist areas of the consequences of informing on IRA operations. It was clear that the IRA was unable to sustain a campaign with popular support across nationalist areas of the North.

The reaction to the Lurgan murders came as a shock to republicans. An editorial in the *Andersonstown News*, a paper usually sympathetic to the republican position, alarmed Sinn Féin and expressed the feelings of nationalists:

> It is no longer good enough for the leaders of Sinn Féin to stick to the tired old mantra of refusing to indulge in the politics of condemnation. The IRA is fast becoming not a symptom of the problem as they have liked to portray themselves over the past 28 years, but part of the problem itself. What happened in Lurgan was wrong, brutal and counterproductive and demands to be condemned.

Such an editorial comment on the shooting of two policemen would have been unthinkable three years before. On top of the reinstatement of the TUAS conditions, it was this change of attitude in the nationalist community between 1994 and 1997 that helped Sinn Féin to persuade the IRA to call its ceasefire a month later.

The new British government leaders were as good as their word. By 10 September Sinn Féin had their talks team ensconced at Stormont. Gerry Adams had shaken hands with Tony Blair inside the building and again shortly afterwards at 10 Downing Street. It was the first occasion since 1921 that a British prime minister had greeted a leader of Sinn Féin. Adams had led Sinn Féin to one of the party's major objectives: talks involving both Irish and British governments and the major parties in the North (minus Ian Paisley's DUP) on the single issue of the merit of Sinn Féin's electoral mandate.

There were still some snags for Sinn Féin to unravel. The negotiations covered three sets of relationships: between the communities in the North (Strand One); between North and South (Strand Two); and between Ireland and Britain (Strand Three). Sinn Féin was going to have to make concessions that would be unpalatable to republicans. The question of weapons was also still lurking in the background. Would Sinn Féin be able to take vital decisions without going back to the IRA for approval at every juncture? Did the IRA literally still call the shots? The other participants in the talks wanted to know the answer. Gerry Adams and Sinn Féin's chief negotiator, Martin McGuinness, also wanted to be sure they could make a deal. They could not allow the IRA to cut the feet from under them as they had done at Canary Wharf in 1996.

In autumn 1995, under pressure about getting into talks and circumventing the decommissioning roadblock that John Major had erected, Gerry Adams had taken his eye off the military wing. The IRA Army Council is a fluid body with voting and non-voting members. Membership changes often. The decision to end the ceasefire in autumn 1995 was taken by the closest margin, one or two votes, accounts differ. Adams and McGuinness and Doherty had slipped up. In autumn 1997 they had to be sure there would not be a second slip. If there were, Sinn Féin's project would be finished. The Sinn Féin leaders also needed to change the IRA's constitution so that the Army Council, which their supporters once again controlled, could take final decisions on concessions to be made at the talks without having to go to a General Army Convention.

Adams knew that some of the concessions which would be necessary went to the heart of traditional republican theology. Even getting into the talks had meant signing up to what were called the 'Mitchell Principles', which required parties in the talks to agree to use 'exclusively peaceful means' and committed them to 'the total disarmament of all paramilitary organisations'. Sinn Féin had signed up. Murmurings of discontent appeared in *An Phoblacht*. It was all very well signing up because that did not require any concrete action by the IRA, but did the Sinn Féin negotiators intend to disavow the use of violence to achieve the movement's traditional goal? They did, but they couldn't admit it because central to republican belief is the right of Irish people to use arms to remove the British presence in Ireland. But what else did it mean when Gerry Adams and Martin McGuinness repeatedly said that they wanted 'to remove the gun from Irish politics'?

To change the IRA's constitution would require a General Army Convention. It convened in Donegal in October 1997. Adams, McGuinness, Doherty and their advisors had spent a long time preparing the ground. Masters of procedure and with a careful eye on the make-up of the 100-strong Convention, the Sinn Féin leaders outmanoeuvred their opponents, one of whom, Bernadette Sands-McKevitt, is alleged to have made an emotional attack on Martin McGuinness that antagonised many present. The outcome was a victory for the leadership. Following their defeat, those in the IRA who opposed the Mitchell Principles and the inevitable changes to Articles 2 and 3 of the Irish constitution left to form the Real IRA.

The crucial point is, that as a result of that IRA convention, the pendulum within the republican movement had swung decisively towards Sinn Féin. Under Adams's leadership there would be no return to military violence to pursue political aims. IRA operations might continue, and indeed have continued, but directed against what Sinn Féin calls 'antisocial elements', for example, drug dealers, and occasionally in retaliation for loyalist attacks. Indeed, Sinn Féin was briefly excluded from the talks in February 1998 for such retaliation. But both Irish and British governments had adopted an ambivalent attitude to such actions, not classing them as 'military operations' in the terms of the original 1994 ceasefire. Actually, the NIO privately refers to punishment shootings and beatings as 'housekeeping'.

The conclusive evidence of Sinn Féin control over the movement was the beginning of the decommissioning of IRA weapons in September 2001, a move that few people ever thought would happen and many in the republican movement had strenuously opposed. From the time the demand for decommissioning was first made, graffiti in republican areas read: 'Not a bullet, not an ounce.' During the negotiations leading to the Good Friday Agreement, Martin McGuinness, as chief Sinn Féin negotiator, had been able to convince the Irish and British governments that it would be impossible to ask the IRA to surrender weapons before an agreement, and that any movement on weapons could happen only in the context of the implementation of such an agreement. Clearly, if there were an agreement that republicans found satisfactory and that was endorsed in referendums, then there would be no need for weapons. McGuinness did admit though, that 'the weapons have to be banjaxed'.

The wording of the section on decommissioning in the Agreement could have been written by Sinn Féin:

> All participants accordingly reaffirm their commitment to the total disarmament of all paramilitary organisations. They also confirm their intention to continue to work constructively and in good faith with the Independent Commission [on decommissioning], and to use any influence they may have to achieve the decommissioning of all paramilitary arms within two years, following endorsement in referendums North and South, of the agreement and in the context of the implementation of the overall settlement.

Republicans stuck rigidly to the letter of this paragraph, but they eventually lost out in the propaganda war on the issue. The general public, nationalist and unionist, North and South, accepted the unionist position that there was no need to hold on to weapons once the agreement was in place. Even though unionists were refusing to implement the agreement until decommissioning began, opinion polls showed the people just wanted the IRA to start disposing of *matériel*. This issue brought the agreement to the brink of collapse at various times in 2000 and 2001 as David Trimble, under pressure from dissidents in his own party, refused to continue in office with Sinn Féin unless the IRA delivered on weapons.

The IRA and Sinn Féin regarded the agreement's phrase – 'implementation of the overall settlement'– as meaning more than simply the establishment and operation of political institutions like the new northern assembly and proposed all-Ireland bodies. These were essential components. But equally important to the IRA were the paragraphs in the agreement on demilitarisation and the provisions for reforming the police force and the criminal justice system in the North. Sinn Féin continued to negotiate with the British, sometimes with IRA Army Council members to hand, about demilitarisation and the other matters, using decommissioning as a *quid pro quo*. Only on 6 May 2000, after detailed negotiations with Sinn Féin involving the taoiseach Bertie Ahern and the British premier Tony Blair, did an IRA statement concede the principle of disposing of weapons. As a first step they allowed inspection of selected arms dumps.

It would be another year before the IRA and Sinn Féin were content that the British had honoured most of their part of the bargain that had been struck in May 2000. Following more talks in August 2001, a package was produced with a list of British military installations in the North to be demolished. On its side, in May 2000 the IRA abandoned the principle of never disposing of weapons. Once that principle was gone, it was then only a question of timing. The logic was that in the context of the full implementation of the agreement, with Sinn Féin ministers in office, there would be no need for a military wing of the republican movement. The IRA would wither on the vine. Indeed, it is the logic of the whole process and would be the ultimate triumph for the project Gerry Adams initiated when he became leader of the republican movement in 1985.

The IRA militarists' own limitless capacity to demonstrate publicly their lack of political *nous* hastened the first act of disposing of weapons. The IRA had already been responsible for embarrassing gaffes during the course of the peace process, for example, when some members were discovered buying weapons in Florida in 1999. Then, in August 2001, fuzzy images appeared on television in Ireland and Britain of two prominent IRA members and a Sinn Féin activist under armed guard after emerging from the jungles of Colombia where they had spent time with a guerrilla organisation called FARC, which raised its money from taxing cocaine growers. FARC is an organisation that is high on the list of the US government's least favourite people – Marxists involved with drugs. The leaders of Sinn Féin ran for cover.

The dust from the IRA's Colombian escapade had not settled before the immense catastrophe of 11 September 2001 struck New York, Washington and Pennsylvania. As the US government turned ferociously on all manifestations of terrorism, the IRA found it prudent and politic to announce that a quantity of armaments had been 'put beyond use' under the supervision of General John de Chastelain, the chairman of the Independent Commission on Decommissioning, which was established under the terms of the Good Friday Agreement. Other acts of decommissioning will follow over the years as the British deliver their side of the package agreed in May 2000 and August 2001.

Decommissioning is a requirement of the Agreement, but it is also the inescapable logic of the thinking behind the Agreement, embodied in the amendments to *Bunreacht na hÉireann*. Gone are the old Articles 2 and 3 with their geographical definition of 'the national territory' and claims to that 'national territory'. Instead is substituted: 'the entitlement and birthright of every person born in the island of Ireland … to be part of the Irish nation.' In other words, the old nineteenth-century concept that the self-determination of the Irish people can be expressed only through the ownership of territory has been replaced with the concept of the right of the Irish people, guaranteed by the constitution and by an international agreement, to express their identity in diverse ways.

These new concepts are designed to undermine the arguments for having an armed body to fight for Irish self-determination. Since the Irish and British governments and the people of Ireland, North and South, have voted in referendums to support that principle, how could there be any reason for a body like the IRA to exist? The British government has committed itself to legislate for any form of unity the Irish people vote for. What, therefore, is the point of anyone engaging in a struggle to drive the British government out? As a result of the new rights-based thinking adopted in the Good Friday Agreement, the *raison d'être* the IRA claimed for its existence has gone. It is the outworking of the dialogue begun in 1988 between the SDLP and Sinn Féin, and Dr Martin Mansergh and Sinn Féin.

There is another reason why it is necessary to 'put weapons beyond use'. During the whole peace process and in the negotiations leading up to the Agreement, Gerry Adams and the other leaders of Sinn Féin never lost sight of their all-Ireland objectives. At the very first meeting with British officials at Stormont in 1994, Sean McManus, a senior Sinn Féin man from Sligo who had been one of the movement's link-men with Libya in the early 1980s, was present. On other occasions Lucilita Breathnach from Dublin was in the front rank. Another Dubliner, Bairbre de Brún, is one of Sinn Féin's ministers in the northern administration. Martin Ferris from Kerry also occasionally appears for the cameras at

Stormont. It is Sinn Féin's way of emphasising that the party is the only party on the island that organises nationally.

Since the 1980s Sinn Féin has built up a formidable organisation in the Republic, but until the peace process gathered momentum in the mid-1990s the party was unable to capitalise on its work at grassroots level in the South. It languished at around 2% in the polls. For many in the Republic it remained a 'Brits out' party. Now, however, the lifting of the broadcast ban, the huge publicity boost the peace process gave Sinn Féin's leaders at home and in the USA, the frequent appearances of Sinn Féin leaders for photo-calls at Leinster House and the Good Friday Agreement itself have all acted to relaunch the party in the South.

There is no doubt that, ultimately, Sinn Féin looks to the day when a Sinn Féin minister from the North sits across the table from a Sinn Féin minister representing the Irish government on one of the all-Ireland bodies established by the Agreement. Asked about Sinn Féin's long-term hopes, Jim Gibney said:

> I would hope that in ten to fifteen years time we would have a size-able number of TDs, in double figures. I don't think that's a pipe dream.

Leaving aside the electoral challenge that goal presents, in order to reach a position where there is a Sinn Féin minister in the Irish government, the IRA will have to fade away. Fine Gael has set its face against coalition with Sinn Féin and Fianna Fáil has made it clear that Sinn Féin will have to sort out its relationship with the IRA (as Fianna Fáil itself did in the 1930s) before there can be talk of a coalition. There can be only one army in Ireland. That is why Gerry Adams said in January 2002:

> We accept entirely and absolutely the role of the Garda Síochána and the Defence Forces in this State.

That statement would once have been unthinkable for a republican leader, but Sinn Féin could hardly end up in the absurd position of accepting the new Police Service of Northern Ireland, which the party is moving towards, yet not accept the Gardaí. It is Gerry Adams's way of proceeding. Only rarely, and when assured of complete success, has he ever chosen confrontation within the republican movement. Instead, as with abstention, then with political violence, then with decommissioning, all the props are slowly and stealthily removed from the offending policy until it stands isolated as a bar to the progress of republicanism. So it will be with the IRA, too. The IRA has emerged as a problem to Sinn Féin's political advance in the Republic. Under Adams's leadership, Sinn Féin will never confront the IRA. It will take a long time, maybe Gibney's ten years, before the IRA fades away, but 2007 was the date set in January 2002 for final decommissioning of IRA weapons. Why did the British government select that date as feasible? Did someone in the republican movement intimate that the IRA will have faded away by then? Will there be a Sinn Féin minister in Leinster House by then? On the other hand, the date also implies that the British assume there will still be a coherently organised IRA in 2007, able to organise the disposal of its weapons.

When they began to search for a way out of the 'long war' in the late 1980s, Sinn Féin's leaders demanded that the political establishment in Ireland demonstrate that there was a political alternative. The political alternative devised by Irish governments and their officials delivers electoral dividends to Sinn Féin in direct proportion to the distance the party moves away from a military campaign. The conclusion is obvious. As a political party still associated with a dormant military organisation, Sinn Féin now exercises greater political influence than it has done at any time since 1921. It took five years from the IRA's first ceasefire in 1994 to reach ministerial office in the North. It took seven years from 1994, with 10% of the vote in the North and no MPs, to become the largest nationalist party in the North with four MPs and just over 20% of the vote. Sinn Féin's rapid political advance and the new nationalist thinking that underpins it have not only made the IRA redundant but have turned it into a political liability. The message from the electorate is that the only way to continue the advance is to become a completely constitutional party. That in itself shows how far the republican movement has come, because until 1981 the republican movement never paid any attention to any message the electorate sent.

In 1992 Gerry Adams wrote in the foreword of *Towards a Lasting Peace in Ireland* that he intended to make 'electoralism a central part' of Sinn Féin's strategy. He knew that meant that Sinn Féin would have to become the dominant partner in the republican movement. Gerry Adams has managed to transform Sinn Féin from the IRA's adjunct into a modern political party whose links with the IRA are a handicap. The process has not yet been completed, but the reversal of roles within the republican movement has been accomplished without the splits and internecine squabbles which have always prevented such a development in the past.

What would have been unimaginable a decade ago is now reality. The leadership of the IRA has accepted that there is no longer a need for political violence and have begun to put their weaponry beyond use on the advice of the political leaders of the republican movement. Bringing the republican movement with him into politics largely intact has been Gerry Adams's achievement, a feat that eluded all previous republican leaders who attempted it.

CONCLUSION

'Hello. Sinn Féin, Westminster.' This was the form of greeting used by Gerry Adams, Sinn Féin's leader, to answer his telephone on 21 January 2002. He was speaking from one of the new offices in the Palace of Westminster that Sinn Féin's four MPs took possession of after a meeting that same afternoon with the British prime minister Tony Blair. Along with the offices came over stg£100,000 in allowances for each MP. Although Adams has insisted that Sinn Féin MPs will 'never, ever' sit in the House of Commons, republican dissidents have accused him of relinquishing all republican convictions and have demanded that he stop using the name 'Sinn Féin' for his party.

Few paid any attention to the dissidents' criticism. As always, Conservative and Unionist MPs came to rescue Sinn Féin from critics on its own side of the fence. The splenetic response of these Conservatives and unionists to the arrival of Sinn Féin in Westminster – a party associated with people who had once been complicit in bombing London and who had supported the murder of MPs like Ian Gow – made the headlines, not the comments of unknown republicans fighting old battles. The rage of the Conservatives and the way in which the media ignored the frustration of dissidents served only to vindicate Gerry Adams's policies. The disregard of the dissidents' views was a reminder of the days when Sinn Féin's views counted for nothing.

Not nowadays. Gerry Adams coolly gave notice that gaining office space within the precincts of Westminster without taking the Oath of Allegiance to the Queen was just another step in the republican movement's onward march. Changed times indeed. Until a few years ago the republican movement confined its public activities to marching to Bodenstown and windswept republican plots in obscure Irish cemeteries while Sinn Féin was static, irrelevant and beached on the margins of Irish politics.

Until the mid-1980s that had been the scenario. For most of the twentieth century Sinn Féin remained a small, obscure, though potentially dangerous sect outside the mainstream of Irish politics. Politically the party was no threat to any government after 1923 because of its abstentionist policy. As a political organisation it virtually ceased to exist and was largely ignored by governments and voters alike. It was only its continuing association with the IRA that merited its members receiving the attentions of the Irish Special Branch in the South and of the RUC Special Branch in the North. After 1981 that state of affairs slowly began to change. Sinn Féin organised as a modern political party in both parts of Ireland, fought elections and began to take any seats it won. The established political parties, North and South, are still coming to terms with the consequences of this change in strategy by the republican movement. It has proven to have had a more profound effect on Irish politics than the most sustained IRA campaign of the last century, which lasted from 1970 to 1997.

Since it was founded in 1905, Sinn Féin has gone through at least five reincarnations. Some would say seven, arguing that the splits in 1986 and 1997 about abstentionism and the decision to occupy seats and take office at Stormont were each such radical departures from traditional republican doctrine as to constitute a new Sinn Féin. The crucial difference, however, between the splits in 1986 and 1997 and those of previous years is that, in the most recent instances, the leadership remained the same and the movement stayed largely intact.

The outcome of the two most recent splits is significant for other reasons. Before 1986 no rebirth of Sinn Féin had been marked by a reconstruction of the party as an electoral organisation. Since 1921 all attempts to do so failed because the majority in the republican movement always steadfastly refused to compromise on what was the goal of the Sinn Féin party established in 1917, namely an Irish Republic free of British influence. That Irish Republic would encompass the whole island. Diehard republicans refused to recognise any institution that offered less. They also refused to compromise on the methods used in the years 1918-21, which meant supporting military action by the IRA to achieve their goal. Any attempt by people in Sinn Féin to move from those tenets always resulted in an intransigent section declaring itself to be the true heir of the Sinn Féin party that won the 1918 general election, and proceeding to carry on using the means employed in the years 1918-21.

The aim of this book has been to chart the roller-coaster fortunes of Sinn Féin since its beginnings in 1905 and the phoenix-like reincarnations it has experienced after the occasions when it seemed to fizzle out into obscurity. During an extraordinary four years, from 1917 to 1921, Sinn Féin had become the National Movement, the expression of the political will of the Irish nation demonstrated repeatedly in elections in those years. For the following six decades, however, Sinn Féin attracted only minority support in the country, and often the size of that minority support was vanishingly small. For the vast majority of people in Ireland, the fact of independence from Britain was more important than the form of government adopted after independence. The more pragmatic members of Sinn Féin followed this line in 1917 and thereafter, but until the mid-1980s they had habitually constituted only a small minority within the party.

In the intervening years, the great majority of people who joined Sinn Féin found such pragmatism unacceptable. They had joined the movement because of its core beliefs, that is, republicanism and an Irish Ireland purged of all English influence. Sinn Féin, like Fenianism before it, has always offered an atavistic, enthusiastic, direct and simplistic vision of Irish politics, more connected with concepts like the nation's destiny than with the here and now. Those sentiments seemed to be the main preoccupation for most people who either stayed with Sinn Féin after 1921 or came into the republican movement after that date.

Only during those years of turmoil following the 1916 Rising did Sinn Féin's vision chime with the views of the Irish electorate. Only for that period of time did it seem appropriate and feasible to make the demand for independence the here and now of Irish politics. Once the majority of the country had achieved independence, people reverted to the usual priorities of politics. Those who re-established Sinn Féin in the Free State in 1923, and their successors down to the 1970s, tried in vain to recapture the heady emotions and the overwhelming support of the years of the War of Independence. They failed abysmally. Indeed, in their hearts they never believed that they could succeed. Despite their grandiloquent rhetoric they saw their task as keeping the flame of 'true republicanism' burning. They looked backwards. The days of glory were always behind them.

The first result of this stance was that for many decades Sinn Féin members lived in a political cloud-cuckoo-land, refusing to recognise the everyday political realities of life and thereby cutting themselves off from mainstream politics North and South, and from any hope of influencing the majority of the Irish people. The imagery and legacy of the years 1917-21 dominated Sinn Féin thinking until very recently. The second result was that the methodology of the years of Sinn Féin's greatest triumphs continued to obsess the movement, so that for many in Sinn Féin the means they believed had been successful in 1917–21, namely military violence, became more sacred than the end, namely self-determination for the Irish people in the shape of an all-Ireland republic.

While few supported the means, there nevertheless remained substantial sympathy in Ireland for the end. Being a member of Sinn Féin in the South meant being ostracised and periodically hounded by the Special Branch. Being a member in the North was positively dangerous. In both jurisdictions membership of Sinn Féin spelt doom for an individual's career. Therefore, few people were prepared to make the commitment that joining Sinn Féin entailed. Yet, North and South there were many 'sneaking regarders' – people who had too much to lose to risk joining Sinn Féin or publicly supporting the movement, but who agreed with the aims and also sometimes the methods of republicans.

In an assessment for British military intelligence in 1978, famous because it was leaked to the IRA, Brigadier (later General Sir James) Glover concluded that:

> Peace will only reign when there is a political solution and the military situation has been contained. The IRA will never be totally defeated. The cause of republicanism will remain as long as the island of Ireland is divided.

In the South that cause manifested itself after 1926 in a substantial core republican vote. Papers released from the Public Record Office in Dublin in January 2002 reveal that in August 1971 the chief of staff of the Irish Army, Major-General Thomas L O'Carroll, estimated that there were 1,900 'active republicans' in the South with 'about 20,000 to 40,000 active supporters.' On occasion, support for republicans could rise as high as 200,000. In the North the core vote was about 80,000, rising to 150,000 if the circumstances were right. That was the problem. The vote surged only in times of economic distress or high nationalist emotion, such as the 1981 hunger strikes, then evaporated. For most of the period after 1921 Sinn Féin was unable to translate 'sneaking regard' into tangible political strength, or to find a way to harness and retain aberrant electoral support that appeared to be nothing more than a surge of sentiment.

Most of the handicaps Sinn Féin faced after partition were of its own making. It was abstentionist, so it did not figure in the electoral calculations of any of the big parties or the voters. Its Dublin-based leadership, until the 1960s of the same vintage as many Irish government ministers, fought the wrong battle. They devoted their energies to opposing the Free State and their former colleagues who were running it rather than to opposing either unionism or the British. For most of the time after 1946 Sinn Féin was simply the political mouthpiece of the IRA and as such subject to repression, North and South. It held to impossible aims: it proposed to right a wrong – partition – which, as time passed, had happened before most people were born. Sinn Féin clung to the fantasy that in order to right that wrong it could persuade people in the South to reject the State to which 99% of the population freely gave allegiance.

It was only when young northern republicans took control of Sinn Féin in the mid-1980s that these handicaps were jettisoned one by one. The story of Sinn Féin from that time on is the account of the party's journey back into the mainstream of Irish politics. The northerners surged on the tidal-wave of emotion generated by the 1981 hunger strikes and managed to hold onto the votes cast that year because they campaigned in subsequent elections on issues that mattered to the everyday lives of people in the areas they represented. They exported the same tactics to southern cities.

They knew that to connect with the electorate Sinn Féin had to modernise its thinking. The republican movement would have to change tack to take the tide at the flood. To succeed, Sinn Féin would have to accept the political reality of the time its supporters were living in. The northern leaders therefore acknowledged that the Republic is a modern, sovereign, independent State that has the allegiance of its population, and that rather than provoking conflict between Ireland and Britain, the real issue for modern Ireland is the relationships between the two communities in the North and between Dublin and the unionist minority on the island. It was appropriate therefore that Sinn Féin be led by people from that part of the island where the problem is located. The change of tactics did not mean changing the long-term objectives of the republican movement, but it did require a radical shift in the way Sinn Féin expressed those objectives.

During a long, slow process, Sinn Féin's leaders quietly shelved the pretence that the republican movement was the embodiment of the national will as it had been in 1918, came down off their self-proclaimed moral high-ground and accepted that Sinn Féin is one of many political parties competing for votes. Of course, Sinn Féin remains closely associated with the IRA and therefore is still not an ordinary political party. But the fact that Sinn Féin leaders are willing to cooperate in administering the North, or to sit in the Dáil and play no role in government, demonstrates that the party no longer sees itself occupying the absurd position it used to claim, that is, of being the true government of Ireland, albeit government-in-waiting, and of having the right to wage war on behalf of the Irish people.

In its journey into mainstream Irish political life, Sinn Féin has not only modernised its ideas, it has modernised its party structures. It has been organising assiduously at grassroots level, North and South, for twenty years. The party's leaders have discovered that in elections in the South, while they can retain their core objectives (an all-Ireland Republic and enhanced Irish cultural awareness), they gain maximum electoral support by playing down those long-term core objectives and by concentrating on what affects people today.

That stance requires Sinn Féin to have different sets of manifestos for each jurisdiction. The platform in the Republic sets out to show people that Sinn Féin is not just a 'Brits out' party, mouthing watchwords from eighty years ago, but is relevant to people in Cavan or Cork. Sinn Féin's election addresses and leaflets in the Republic strongly emphasise the local issues of each constituency and deal with housing, drugs, crime, employment, the environment and government corruption. Those are the real campaign messages, which the party's activists have been working on at community level for years. The election manifesto contains the policies on the long-term objectives, a united Ireland, Europe, etc., but only other politicians read election manifestos. This modernised, multi-faceted approach by Sinn Féin brought the party to an average of 5% in opinion polls in the South in 2001, and to an all-time high of 8% in 2002, reflected in the general election in May when Sinn Féin won five seats.

In the North the party has also displayed a shrewd knowledge of the concerns of nationalists. Leaflets concentrate on local issues, like education, jobs, housing, the environment, but are larded with policies on policing, human rights, fair employment, justice, equality – all matters close to the heart of nationalist voters. Although Sinn Féin came late onto the electoral scene in the North, its literature reads as if the party invented those issues.

Sinn Féin's new, sanitised vocabulary has outraged both the SDLP and unionists in the North, although for different reasons. SDLP members gasp in amazement as Sinn Féin uses language the SDLP patented twenty years earlier and calmly promotes SDLP policies as its own. When Sinn Féin accepted the Good Friday Agreement in 1998, which is a pale reflection of the 1973 Sunningdale Agreement that the IRA vowed to destroy, Seamus Mallon MP, the SDLP's deputy leader, memorably described the Good Friday Agreement as 'Sunningdale for slow-learners'. But since the majority of the nationalist population is under twenty-five years of age, Mallon's reference to Sunningdale was as obscure to them as mention of the Dungannon convention of 1778 would have been.

For their part, Ulster Unionists are outraged at the repackaging of former IRA leaders as elected politicians. Unionists have reacted with dismay and bewilderment at the speed of change since the early 1990s and are unable to respond to the language of rights, equality and justice that seems to be the property of nationalists. Sinn Féin's rapid electoral advance has alarmed unionists and has divided them in a way that the IRA campaign of military violence did not. They regard Sinn Féin's conversion to electoralism with deep suspicion and many believe the demand for equality and justice is simply another way of waging the same war. Unionists have found it impossible to deal with the complex consequences of Sinn Féin's success at the ballot box compared to the simple response the Armalite provoked. Unionists' outrage has helped silence critics of Sinn Féin's policy within the republican movement. After all, the argument goes, if unionists are ranting about it then it must be good for nationalists.

The exact mirror opposite of that argument comes from unionists: if it is good for nationalists it must be bad for unionists. Not trusting the language of rights and equality, unionists have found themselves falling into the trap of opposing reforms which would benefit their own community and stridently criticising bodies like the North's Human Rights Commission. The more extreme unionists, unable to find a vocabulary to cope with the new constitutionalism of Sinn Féin, have become convinced that measures to establish equality and parity of esteem for nationalists automatically work to the detriment of unionists. The confusion and divisions produced among unionists are compounded by the enthusiasm for the changes among nationalists, best demonstrated by the legions of young workers available to Sinn Féin – a feature common to both North and South.

The fact that Sinn Féin's supporters tend to be young and predominantly male is a phenomenon that has been a constant since Arthur Griffith established his party in 1905. By the late 1990s, polls in the Republic showed Sinn Féin to be the first choice of 8% of men but only of 3.5% of women. While the party had the support of only 2% of those over sixty-five, 11% of eighteen- to twenty-four-year-olds supported Sinn Féin. In some universities in the Republic, Sinn Féin had become the largest political club by 2001. Figures for the North, though showing much larger percentages in favour of Sinn Féin, demonstrate the same trends. While young people may be less likely to vote than their elders, nevertheless the youth of Sinn Féin's party workers today, North and South, is reminiscent of the young people tramping the roads in 1918 spreading the word. None of the established parties, North or South, seems able to turn out the numbers of enthusiastic young volunteers that Sinn Féin can field.

Sinn Féin has access to another formidable group of workers that no rival party has at its disposal: former republican prisoners. Over 1,000 ex-prisoners live in Dublin alone, though Sinn Féin claims the total is closer to 1,600. Most of them are unemployed, or, if they have jobs, work in community groups associated with Sinn Féin and are available on a voluntary basis for election work. The same circumstances apply, though on a much larger scale, in Belfast, Derry and other northern nationalist towns. One of the many advantages of this veritable army of workers is that the northern contingent can be bussed south for election work and vice versa.

Traditionally the only other party in Ireland that knows its voters as well as Sinn Féin has been Fianna Fáil. What will be of compelling interest to political observers will be the constituencies where the two parties go up against each other for the same votes in the years ahead. Since the early 1990s Sinn Féin has been targetting, and in 2002 winning Fianna Fáil constituencies: Cavan–Monaghan, Kerry North and Inner City Dublin.

One of their targets is the north Dublin constituency of Taoiseach Bertie Ahern who has always ensured that there is no other strong Fianna Fáil candidate canvassing there. That was reckoning without a Sinn Féin candidate. Has he thereby left an opening for Sinn Féin in the future?

With Sinn Féin topping the poll in 2002 in Cavan–Monaghan and in Kerry North and winning seats in Dublin, how will Fianna Fáil respond to this challenge? So far the party seems to be as baffled as the Ulster Unionists about how to answer the challenge. All of Fianna Fáil's electoral tactics were designed in the absence of a modern, targetted Sinn Féin attack. Like the SDLP before 1981, Fianna Fáil never had to compete for votes on its own ground. Fianna Fáil is aware that, apart from the contest with Seán MacBride's Clann na Poblachta in the 1940s, it is in the same position as was the SDLP. Fianna Fáil party historians will also be acutely aware that the threat MacBride presented – attacking the party's republican flank – gave Fianna Fáil a nasty shock.

There is some evidence that Sinn Féin's appearance on their doorstep has spooked individuals in Fianna Fáil. The party's official title is Fianna Fáil, The Republican Party. With Sinn Féin targeting the young, male, working-class vote, will Fianna Fáil make the mistake of trying to 'out-republican' Sinn Féin? There are signs already that such a tactic may be attractive to Fianna Fáil, for example, the official state reburial in 2001 of ten IRA men executed by the British during the War of Independence. There are some even more blatant examples. Take this extract from a leaflet distributed in the Dublin Southwest constituency in January 2002:

> The republican movement is the movement which will establish an all-Ireland democracy and republic within five to fifteen years. It is the aim of all right-thinking republicans to establish a united Ireland.

To a casual reader this would seem to be a Sinn Féin leaflet, albeit an unusually crude and specific one. It is, in fact, a Fianna Fáil flyer trying to reclaim some ground from Sinn Féin. Such an approach is likely to boomerang. First, it should be obvious to anyone that it is impossible to 'out-republican' Sinn Féin. If republicanism became an issue in an election, voters would vote for the real republican party. Secondly, it would be paradoxical for Fianna Fáil to vie with Sinn Féin for a traditional republican vote because, apart from the fact that Sinn Féin is the undisputed owner of that vote, Sinn Féin has discovered that its candidates make greater electoral strides by leaving aside their republican credentials and emphasising everyday social and economic issues. Fianna Fáil is not alone in this type of reaction to the Sinn Féin challenge. Even Fine Gael's former leader, Michael Noonan, took his party's nationalist identity papers down from the shelf in 2002 and dusted them off, assuming, mistakenly, like Fianna Fáil that Sinn Féin intended to parade its republicanism before the electorate.

In contrast to such expediency, Sinn Féin's experience in the North has taught its leaders to take the long view. It took Sinn Féin twenty years to double its vote in the North and to supplant the SDLP as the largest nationalist party. Sinn Féin's leaders are aware that it may take another fifteen or twenty years to achieve its targets in the Republic. The party has only just begun its journey into mainstream Irish politics, North and South. Although the IRA is slowly fading into the background, as it must, it 'hasn't gone away', as Gerry Adams said. Until it does, Sinn Féin remains vulnerable to accusations that its community activism is backed by IRA muscle. While vigilantism may not have lost Sinn Féin any votes in deprived areas of Dublin, the party's strategists know they still have to convince the majority of voters in the Republic that the hand knocking at the door will carry only a ballot box, and that the Armalite is permanently abandoned. In the North there has been ambivalence towards intimidation and strong-arm tactics in districts where there has been no normal policing for a generation. In the Republic, where the Gardaí are universally accepted, there is a world of difference. Any suggestion that northern practices could be imported will scare off voters.

Sinn Féin's planners in the South know they must broaden the base of their support and that to do so means moving towards the centre, a process that will take time. If the party's performance in the North is anything to go by, the route will be planned, not surprisingly, like a military campaign, with each election as a staging-post. The leaders of the latest manifestation of Sinn Féin describe the Good Friday Agreement as a 'transitional phase'. Only time will tell if they are right. What is certain is that they are planning far ahead to ensure that the day will come when modernised republicanism is an electoral force to be reckoned with in both parts of the island. They realised over a decade ago that only as an electoral force, North and South, will Sinn Féin be able to advance its political aims.

Sinn Féin's place in history is still being written. The party's lifespan is already longer than that of any other political party on the island. It has flourished and faded in a bewildering series of reversals of fortune as the military and political wings of the republican movement jockeyed for authority. Given the history of republicanism and the events from 1916 to 1921, the single biggest problem since 1921 has been how to convince men and women, most of them imbued with noble aspirations, that a willingness to sacrifice their lives was not the only way to win freedom for their country. Only under its present leaders and only after a lengthy process of preparation has Sinn Féin come into the ascendant and set the republican movement firmly on the political highway.

A final judgement of Sinn Féin's place in Irish history must therefore await the verdict of a future generation. Looking back to its beginnings, it was Arthur Griffith's Sinn Féin that created the vision of Ireland which Irishmen and women aspired to throughout the twentieth century. It was Sinn Féin that became the national movement that gave Ireland 'the freedom to achieve freedom'. It was Sinn Féin, as a tiny, dedicated minority on the island after 1926, that kept alive a vision of an Ireland locked in a time warp, a vision that it believed had been dimmed in other parties by pragmatism, by the responsibilities of office, by corruption and by the passage of time. In pursuit of that vision from the past, Sinn Féin supported the IRA in cycles of futile military actions which culminated in the bloody campaign from 1970 to 1997. The biggest success for modern Sinn Féin has perhaps been in overcoming the weakness inherent in the republican movement's dual make-up and entering into the contemporary political world of Ireland. By doing so it has helped create the conditions in which Ireland can achieve the end that Irish leaders have sought down through the centuries.

FOOTNOTES

Chapter 1: 'Sinn Féin must be the Motto',

The Founding Years, 1900–07

1. Usually the IPP returned just over seventy MPs. Another eight to ten MPs sat for various splinter groups, such as the All-for-Ireland League. But if the issue of Home Rule came up for a vote, they would all support it.

2. Mary Butler came from landed gentry in County Clare. Although she played little part in Sinn Féin, she was a devoted follower of Griffith and wrote a novel called *The Ring of the Day*, in which the hero, Eoin O'Gara, was based on him. She and her sister contributed to the purchase of a house when Griffith married in 1910. Remarkably, Butler was a cousin of Edward Carson, the leader of the Ulster Unionist Party and Sinn Féin's most powerful opponent. Butler died in 1921.

3. In 1907 Pandit Nehru, the future prime minister of independent India, visited Dublin and wrote home that 'Sinn Féin's policy is not to beg for favours but to wrest them. They do not want to fight England by arms but to ignore her, boycott her and quietly assume the administration of Irish affairs.'

Chapter 2: Electoral Ups and Downs,

Facing the Voters, 1908–17

1. George Russell (1867–1935), poet and artist, known by his pen-name Æ (short for Æon).

2. On 17 August 1916, Irish time was harmonised with that of Britain. Until then Irish clocks were set twenty-five minutes behind GMT.

Chapter 3: A Different Tune,

Northern Nationalism

1. Thomas Sexton (1848–1932) was a Dublin-based financier and newspaper-owner. He was born in Waterford and there began his career as a journalist. He was defeated by a unionist candidate in 1892.

2. A reference to the *Ne Temere* decree (1908), which required the non-Catholic partner in a mixed marriage to sign a pre-nuptial agreement to bring up any children as Catholics. There were instances when the Catholic parent abducted children who were being reared as Protestants. There was a genuine fear in parts of Ireland where Protestants were a tiny minority that the Protestant community could die out in two generations.

Chapter 4: A Nation Organised,

Sinn Féin takes Power, 1918–21

1. Teachta Dála, or member of Dáil Éireann – the name Sinn Féin gave to the assembly they established after the 1918 election.

Chapter 6: Protecting the Flame,

The Lean Years, 1926–62

1. Tom Doyle, an IRA man of long standing and a former civil servant in the Department of Defence, had devised the famous raid on the magazine fort in the Phoenix Park in December 1939 when the IRA's Dublin brigade made off with virtually the entire stock of the Irish Army's ammunition, just over one million rounds, in a dozen lorries. Doyle remained firmly convinced of the merits of armed force.

Chapter 7: Veering to the Left,

Flirting with Marxism, 1962–70

1. It was called 'Provisional' because the leaders intended to convene another convention in 1970 to settle the issue in the movement. Even though they issued a statement in September 1970 to say that the provisional period was over, the title stuck.

Chapter 8: The Years of Agitprop,

Sinn Féin backs the War, 1970–81

1. This is a reference to the huts erected at the end of each street off the Falls Road where those guarding the streets' barricades sheltered from the elements. Interview with Patricia Davidson, 21 August 2000.

2. Liam McParland was adjutant of B company, 2nd battalion of the IRA's Belfast brigade. He was killed in November 1969 in a car accident on the M1 on his way back from County Leitrim. With him in the car was Gerry Adams, who was suspended from the republican movement when details of the accident emerged. It is believed McParland was bringing weapons to Belfast.

3. Interview with Jim Gibney 17 September 2001.

4. So named because they had not the means to buy silk or woollen stockings and therefore wore trousers instead of knee breeches or *culottes*.

Chapter 9: Armalite and Ballot Box,

Becoming an Electoral Force, 1981–86

1. Psephology is the statistical study of elections.

Chapter 10: 'Towards a Strategy for Peace',

Sinn Féin No Longer Alone

1. A reference to the campaign of the late 1940s led by the Irish government and involving northern nationalists. (*See* chapter 6, p.183.)

2. This phrase is a reference to ongoing attempts by the RUC to prevent paramilitary displays at republican funerals, which had resulted in unseemly stand-offs and scuffles, and IRA attempts in retaliation to disrupt funerals of RUC men with hoax bomb warnings.

3. 'Red Book' prisoners were those men listed in a red book that was carried around by prison-warders wherever they went in the prison, and was passed from warder to warder. They were continuously observed and every three weeks moved to a different H-block.

Chapter 11: Negotiating the Roadblocks,

The Pendulum Swings to Sinn Féin

1. Aidan McAteer is now special advisor to Martin McGuinness, Minister of Education.

2. BAC stands for Baile Átha Cliath, Irish for Dublin and the Army Council's shorthand term for the Irish government.

3. When Adams asked for some idea of the Irish government's time-scale for Irish unity, he was told 'a generation'. He pressed Albert Reynolds for a definition of 'a generation' and Reynolds's response was 'somewhere between fifteen and forty years'.

4. This republican view overlooks the fact that under the Government of Ireland Act 1920 partition had already been established and a Northern Ireland government was operating.

5. In fact, Bruton objected to the proposed elections and said holding an election 'would pour petrol on the flames'. For a full account, see E Malley/D McKittrick *The Fight for Peace* (Heinemann: 1996).

SINN FÉIN PRESIDENTS

Edward Martyn	1905–08
John Sweetman	1908
Arthur Griffith	1908–17
Eamon de Valera	1917–22 and 1923–26
JJ ('Sceilg') O'Kelly	1926–31
Brian O'Higgins	1931–33
Fr Michael O'Flanagan	1933–35
Cathal Ó Murchadha	1935–37
Mrs Margaret Buckley	1937–50
Pádraig MacLógáin	1950–53
Tomás Ó Dubhghaill	1953–54
Pádraig MacLógáin	1954–62
Tomás MacGiolla	1962–70
Ruairí Ó Brádaigh	1970–83
Gerry Adams	1983–present

A Note on Sources

Part of the challenge in writing a book on Sinn Féin designed to be accessible to a general readership is to manage the immense quantity of material available about the republican movement in such a way that, while the sources have a presence which enhances the book, they do not intrude on the text.

The approach adopted was that used by Professor Norman Davies of the University of London in his monumental *Europe: a History* (UK: Oxford UP, 1997). In his preface he wrote:

> 'Since most aspects of the subject have been thoroughly worked over by previous historians, primary research was rarely required. The book's originality, such as it is, lies only in the selection, rearrangement and presentation of the contents. The academic apparatus has been kept to a minimum. There are no notes relating to facts and statements that can be found in any of the established works of reference.'

Established works indispensable for dealing with the emergence of Sinn Féin as a national movement in the years after 1916 are: Michael Laffan's *The Resurrection of Ireland: the Sinn Féin party 1916–1923* (UK: Cambridge UP, 1999), David Fitzpatrick's *Politics and Irish Life, 1913–21: provincial experience of war and revolution* (Ireland: Cork UP, 1998) and his *The Two Irelands, 1912–1939* (UK: Oxford UP, 1998). One of Fitzpatrick's essays, 'The geography of Irish nationalism', in CE Philpin (ed.) *Nationalism and popular protest in Ireland* (UK: Cambridge UP, 1987), is particularly useful for the details of the local strength of Sinn Féin support around the west and southwest of Ireland.

Tom Garvin *Nationalist Revolutionaries in Ireland 1858–1928* (UK: Oxford UP, 1987), Joe Lee *Ireland 1912–1985: Politics and Society* (UK: Cambridge UP, 1989) and Robert Kee *The Green Flag: a history of Irish nationalism, volume 3 Ourselves Alone* (London: Penguin, 1972), all provide valuable overviews which place Sinn Féin's sudden predominance in the years after 1916 in a wider context. For the north of Ireland the most comprehensive and detailed work dealing with the period before the Second World War from a nationalist perspective is Eamon Phoenix's *Northern nationalism: nationalist politics, partition and the Catholic minority in Northern Ireland, 1890–1940* (Belfast: Ulster Historical Foundation, 1994).

At many points after 1919 Sinn Féin overlaps with the IRA. For details of the personnel and policies of the IRA, Tim Pat Coogan's *The IRA* (4th edn., London: HarperCollins, 1995) is the most readable. In *The Secret Army: the IRA* (3rd edn., Dublin: Poolbeg Press, 1997), J Bowyer Bell provides a useful foil for Coogan who sometimes gets carried away with enthusiasm for his study.

There is a vast amount of primary evidence about Sinn Féin: newspapers (including the party's own publications), diaries, government records, memoirs of participants in the republican movement. The most significant of these have been pulled together in books of documents and commentary, the most convenient of which is *Ireland 1905–25 Volume Two: the Documents* (Newtownards: Colourpoint, 1998) edited by Professor Tony Hepburn. A *sine qua non* for any study of original material on modern Sinn Féin is the famous Political Collection of the Linenhall Library in Belfast, which stores a wealth of newspapers, periodicals, election manifestos and other ephemera as well as personal memoirs, unpublished interviews and some material presented by individuals involved in the conflict after 1969 whose permission is required for use.

For the chapters dealing with the period after 1945 the author relied heavily on newspapers and interviews and conversations with surviving participants who are or who had been members of the republican movement in its various forms over the last fifty years. Ruairí Ó Brádaigh, former IRA chief of staff at the end of the 1950s campaign, later a member of the Provisional IRA's army council and president of Sinn Féin until 1983, provided a lengthy and helpful interview. Danny Morrison, also a former member of the Provisional IRA's army council and later the most effective director of publicity Sinn Féin ever had, gave many insights into the thinking of the modern republican movement in a long interview. Morrison, like former general secretary of Sinn Féin Tom Hartley, who also gave a long interview, was a member of a small group of west Belfast republicans close to Gerry Adams as he manoeuvred his way to the leadership of Sinn Féin and the republican movement.

Another member of this group, though from east Belfast, was Jim Gibney. He played a crucial role as an ideas man in the mid-1970s and is credited with the idea of nominating Bobby Sands as a candidate in the Fermanagh–South Tyrone by-election to Westminster in 1981, which launched Sinn Féin onto the electoral scene in Northern Ireland the following year. One man prominent in the republican movement from the 1940s, and who had served more time in prison than anyone until the 1970s, was Jimmy Drumm. Unfortunately, his failing health meant it was only possible to have a conversation with him and not the sort of interview his role would have warranted. He died in 2001.

Aside from people in the inner councils of Sinn Féin the most important interviews came from Patricia Davidson, who was a prominent member of Sinn Féin in west Belfast in the 1970s. She was able to provide valuable insights into the role of women in Sinn Féin and how the party functioned at street level in the violent and chaotic years when it was being established after the civil disturbances of 1969–70. Other people in the republican movement who gave interviews, particularly those who had been members of the former Official Sinn Féin, preferred to do so in confidence.

The writings of Gerry Adams, President of Sinn Féin since 1983, especially his autobiography, *Before The Dawn* (London: Heinemann, 1996), and *The Politics of Irish Freedom* (Ireland: Brandon Press, 1986) on close reading reveal much of the strategy of the man who has dominated the republican movement for the last twenty years and has transformed its fortunes.

Turning to the most recent period, the author of this book was an elected official for the whole of the 1980s and into the early 1990s, and as such witnessed many of the events which led to the greater politicisation of the republican movement and its successful entry into electoral politics in Ireland, north and south. As a member of the executive of the Social Democratic and Labour Party (SDLP) for many years, the author had access to documents and discussions which dealt with relations between Sinn Féin and the SDLP at crucial periods when the peace process was beginning in the late 1980s. These experiences and inside knowledge of events helped place the contents of interviews with prominent Sinn Féin figures in perspective.

Working with others for seven years from 1992 to produce *Lost Lives: the story of the men, women and children who died as a result of the Northern Ireland troubles* (Edinburgh: Mainstream Publishing, 1999), gave the author extensive research experience into newspaper and inquest reports from 1966 to the present. Much of the research proved valuable in tracking the development of republican thinking from the days of extreme violence in 1972 to modern Sinn Féin's first TD taking his seat in the Dáil at the end of the 1990s.

The best and most detailed books on the Irish peace process are those of David McKittrick, the distinguished correspondent of the *Independent* newspaper, and his co-author, Eamon Mallie: *The Fight for Peace: the secret story behind the Irish peace process* (London: Heinemann, 1996) and *Endgame in Ireland* (London: Hodder & Stoughton, 2002).

Newspapers such as the Belfast-based nationalist *Irish News*, Ireland's premier newspaper of record *The Irish Times*, the unionist *Belfast Newsletter* and *Belfast Telegraph*, the Dublin-based *Irish Independent* and English newspapers like *The Guardian* and the *Independent* all carried regular 'think pieces' on the travails of the north throughout the thirty-five years of the most recent conflict. These newspapers were essential reading for this book.

Finally, local weekly newspapers which burgeoned during the Troubles, like the *Andersonstown News* which is printed and published in west Belfast, offered their columns to republicans to explain their thinking, an offer that was readily accepted by people like Danny Morrison who now writes a column for the paper. The republican movement's own weekly newspaper *An Phoblacht/Republican News* is sold throughout Ireland. Strictly polemical, it presents Sinn Féin's political position and provided an indispensable source for recording the changes in Sinn Féin over the past generation.

While the sources, both primary and secondary, listed here are by no means a comprehensive catalogue of those consulted while writing this book, nevertheless they indicate the most important and rewarding places to look for anyone wishing to engage in further reading on the subject of Sinn Féin.

INDEX